THE STYLISH LIFE

SAILING

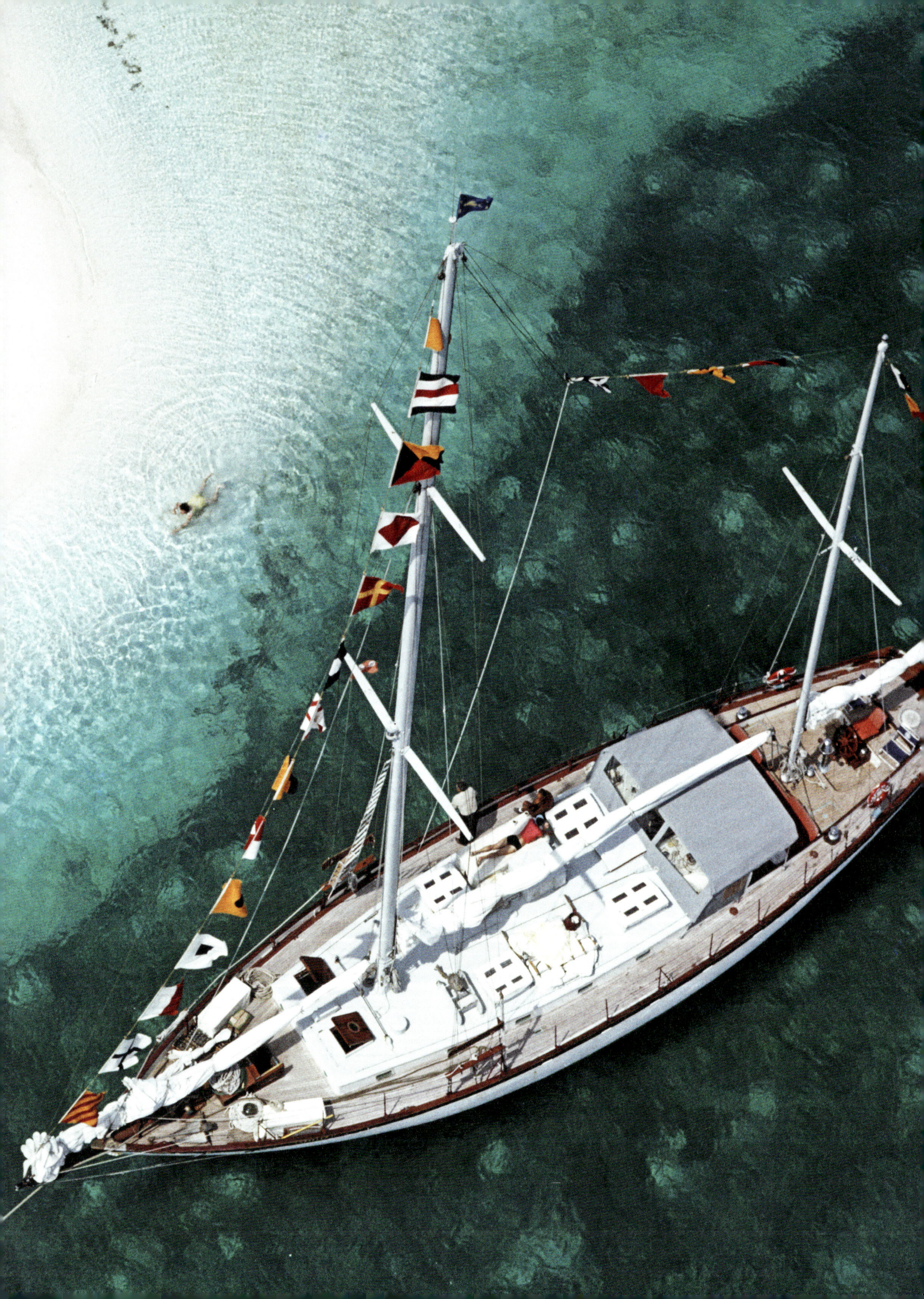

TEXTS BY GARY JOBSON

THE STYLISH LIFE

SAILING

teNeues

CONTENTS

INTRODUCTION 7

DESTINATIONS AND EVENTS 27

YACHTS 73

PEOPLE 111

FASHION 139

FILM 151

IMPRINT 176

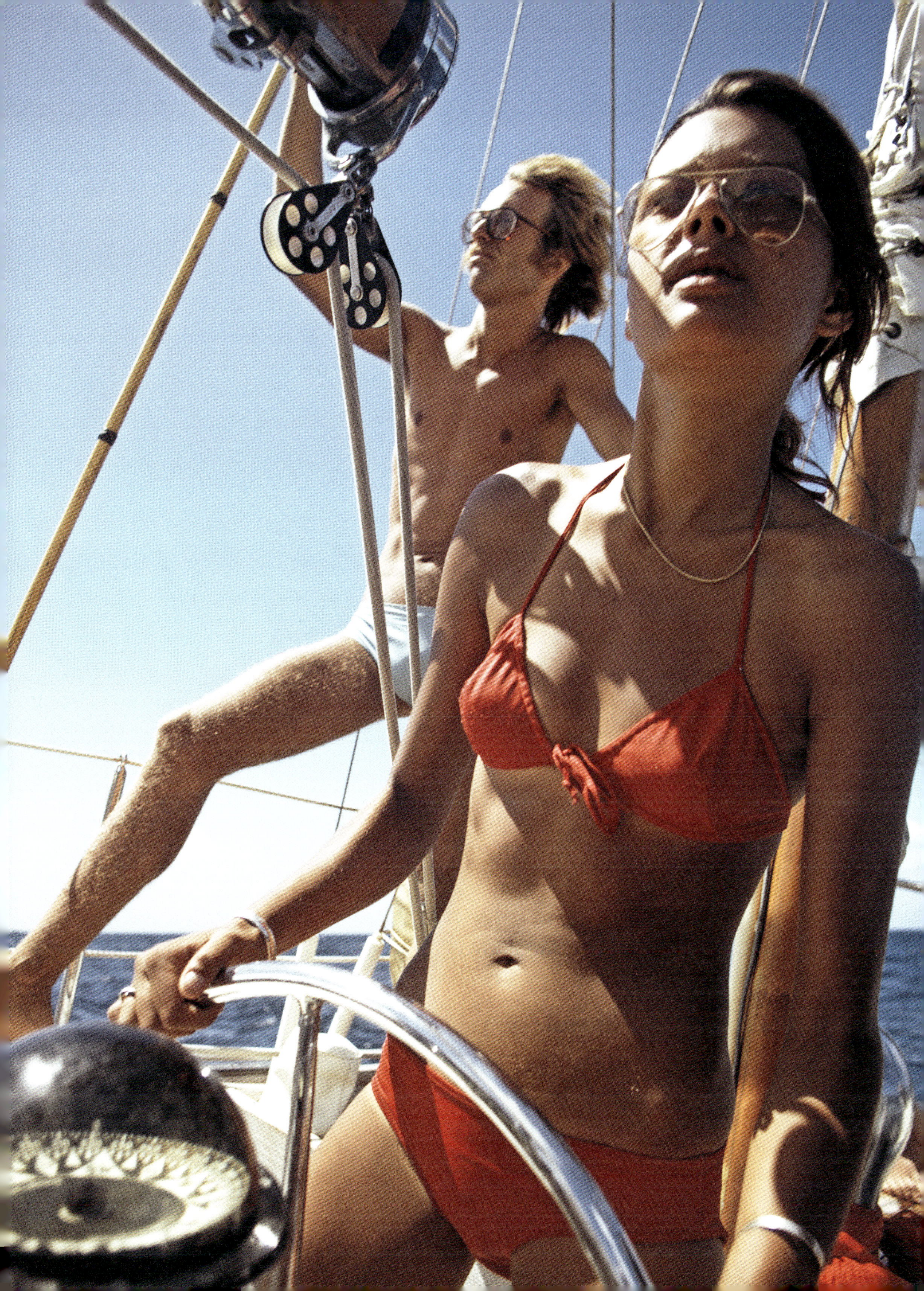

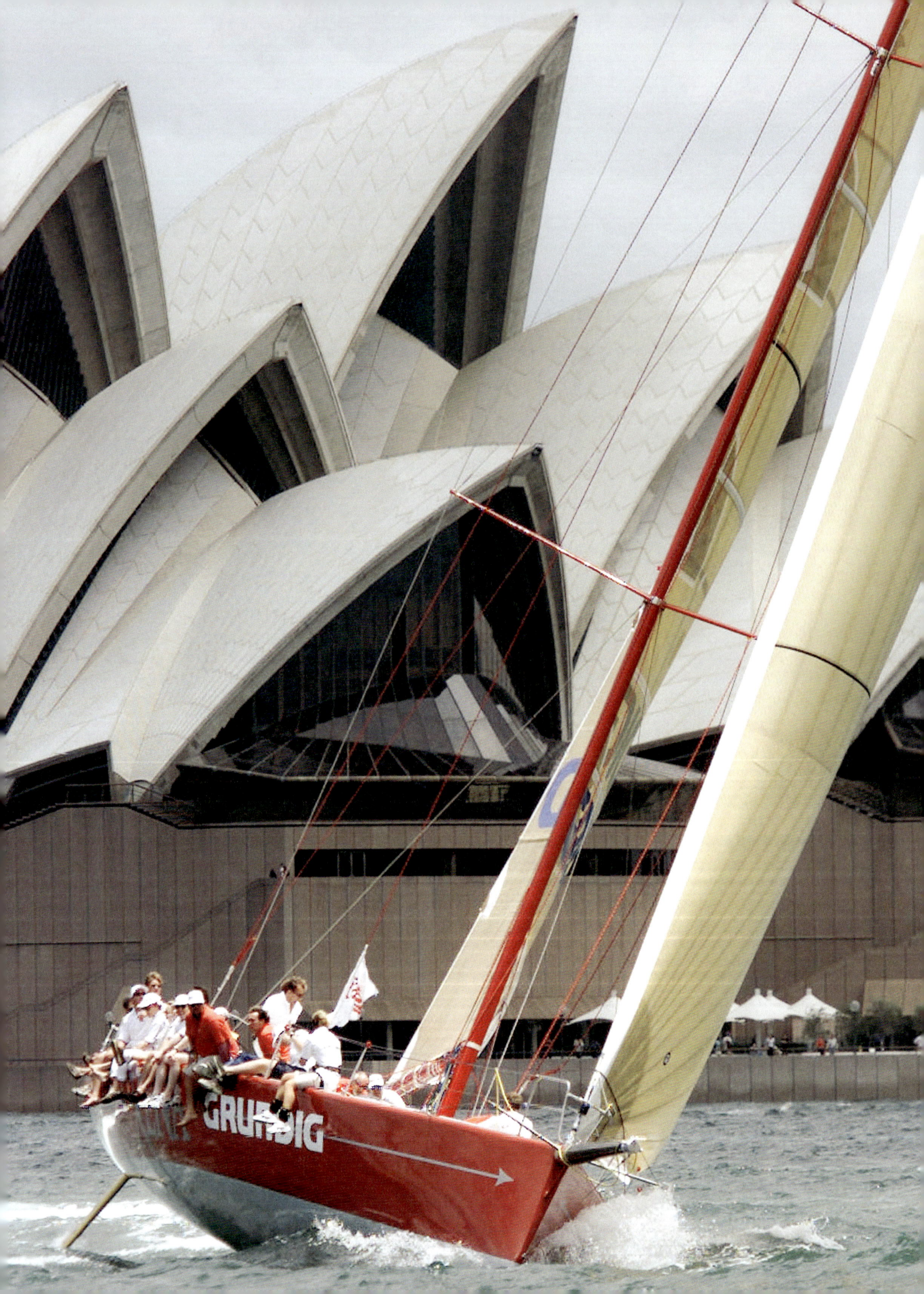
GRUNDIG

INTRODUCTION

BY GARY JOBSON

Though it's been millennia since humans began to use sailing vessels for travel, warfare, exploration and commerce, the modern sport of sailing is a relatively recent development. The first recorded races took place in the late 1700s, and the America's Cup (considered "the oldest continuously held sporting event in the world") began in 1851. But for as long as yachting has existed as a sporting pursuit, the quest to design, build and race the fastest vessel has been a compelling challenge for shipwrights, boat designers, captains of industry, scientists and clever sailors seeking fame and glory. The uncertainty of the outcome makes the game not only fun to watch but fascinating to play: most people who race sailboats are very successful in life, accustomed to winning at every endeavor they attempt, but in sailing success is never guaranteed. High-level competition is just one part of the equation, with the true yachting faithful building their lives, careers and families around the waterfront. Sailing is a sport you can engage with over your entire life and that connects generations, with well-entrenched traditions—such as good manners, sportsmanship and camaraderie—that you might learn from your grandparents and

Page 2: *68-foot charter ketch "Traveller II" at anchor in the lee of Stocking Island, across the harbor from George Town, Exuma, c. 1960.*

Page 5: *A sailing holiday in Saint Barthélemy, c. 1973.*

Opposite: *Sydney, Australia: 60-foot yacht "Xena" rounds the mark in front of the Sydney Opera House on the way to 4th place in the Canon Big Boat Challenge, a lead-up to the Sydney to Hobart event on Boxing Day. "Xena" was one of the favorites but finished well behind "Shockwave," an 80-foot vessel owned by New Zealand businessman Neville Crichton, which won the race by the large margin of four minutes. Generating considerable buzz in the sailing world with its size and state of the art technology, "Shockwave" became outright favorite for line honors in the Sydney to Hobart race.*

teach to your grandchildren in turn. That sense of integrity and continuity is essential. If you study the images in this book, you'll see that yacht design, fashion, and architecture have changed over time, that the intensity of competition has become more acute, and that advanced technology had led to ever-faster racing vessels. Yet running beneath all this change and evolution is a set of constant traditions, values and goals: the aim is to win, always, but to do so in a way deserving of respect. The style of the yachting life is one expression of that longstanding sporting culture.

TIME ON THE WATER

The sea is a great equalizer, with the vagaries of the weather leveling the playing field in unpredictable ways. Winning requires being able to sail a boat consistently well and to read the weather to take advantage of favorable winds, but at the same time there is often an element of luck involved in one crew getting into the lead over another. No sailor should get too excited when leading or too depressed when behind. Fortunes can change rapidly on the water. Or sometimes they change over longer periods—but just as dramatically. In 1980 Dennis Conner and his crew had won the America's Cup for the United States. But in 1983 the Australian team introduced an innovative new design whose wing keel had been kept a closely-guarded secret. Though Conner sailed brilliantly against the faster and more agile boat, and came agonizingly close to victory, when the tense contest came to a close the Australians had ended the US's 132-year winning-streak. Despite being vilified by the press, however, and suffering depressing as a result of the loss, Connor was not out. Forty months after the devastating defeat, on the patriotically-named "Stars & Stripes" Conner and his crew defeated the Australians in four straight races to reclaim the America's Cup. With the races broadcast on live television to viewers all around the world, Conner and his crew became international heroes and were honored by President Ronald Reagan at the White House.

Another yachting tale of perseverance in the face of adversity is that of Ted Turner. He's mostly known for founding the first 24-hour cable news channel, for which he was named *Time Magazine*'s Man of the Year in 1991 following the channel's coverage of the Gulf War. But before that he was also a yachtsman, and that part of his story wasn't always smooth sailing. By 1974 he'd won a respectable number of long-distance offshore yacht races for the US, but in the trials for that year's America's Cup his vessel, named "Mariner," was seriously off-pace, and Turner shouldered the blame for the failure. Undeterred, however, he determined to mount a comeback. He acquired "Courageous," a vessel that had won previously, recruited an ambitious young crew, and by compiling an impressive list of victories persuaded the New York Yacht Club's America's Cup Committee to select him to defend the trophy in 1977. Neither did he let them down, beating the Australian team handily in four straight races. Inspired by Ted Turner's success, Silicon Valley entrepreneur Larry Ellison decided to make his own bid for the America's Cup. His first two efforts came up short in 2003 and 2007, but he kept at it, and in 2010 challenged with a giant three-hulled trimaran boasting a 235-foot wing sail (named "BMW Oracle," somewhat oddly, for the team's sponsor). The Swiss defender, "Alinghi," was no match for Ellison's big boat, and he'd achieved his goal at last. The 2013 event, however, got off to a rockier start. Nine races in the New Zealand team had raced ahead to an 8-1 lead, needing only one more win to take the trophy. To win, the US team would have to produce a comeback of historic proportions—which, miraculously, they did. Along with his manager, four-time America's Cup winner and Olympic gold medalist Russell Coutts, Ellison took charge, introducing aerodynamic changes to the boat, swapping in new crews to the rotation, and beginning to turn the tide. Eventually the American boat won eight successive races to defend the cup, a victory that to this day is one of the greatest comeback stories in all of sports.

THE SAILING LIFESTYLE: AN HISTORICAL NARRATIVE

Formal sailboat racing was rare in the early 1800s. Although it's easy to imagine that when two sailing vessels came into close proximity sometimes an impromptu race would develop, the quest to build faster boats was pragmatic rather than sporting. For example, faster harbor pilots would reach arriving ships earlier, securing the fee for guiding them into port; profits from cargo vessels increased with the speed of their deliveries; passenger lines thrived when their ships sailed to schedule; and shippers were willing to pay handsome sums to get their wares to overseas markets in a timely manner.

But in the early 1800s wealthy yacht owners began to organize coastal races. Soon naval architects and sailors were searching for ways to build faster yachts, and regattas became popular events thanks to prominent coverage in newspapers, with passenger vessels carrying paying customers to watch the spectacle. Before long skippers were the sporting heroes of the era, and placing (often illegal) bets had become a regular pastime for spectators. The owner's families, friends and associates watched from grand private yachts as the yachts maneuvered for advantage. As one might expect, there were occasional collisions, groundings and spirited arguments on the right-of-way rules—arguments that surely stretched long into the night at local pubs.

CONCLUSION

There have been huge changes in sailing over the course of my lifetime. When I was young sailboats were made of wood, the sails mostly cotton. Today fiberglass and carbon fiber has replaced wood, and high-tech synthetic sails allow boats to move through the water with much greater speed. We have breathable foul weather gear, gyro-stabilized binoculars, strong rigs and hulls that can last decades, and foiling yachts that can sail four times the speed of the wind. The days of sailing by the seat of your pants are long gone, too, with modern computers and electronics making navigation easier and sailing safer. The downside is that younger sailors rely on artificial intelligence and advanced computers to make decisions, and don't develop the skills and instincts of previous generations. But there's no stopping progress, and no doubt that massive progress has been made in sailing technology.

It's hard—impossible—to know what the future will bring. Jules Verne imagined circumnavigating the globe in 80 days—will we one day see a sailing vessel do it in 40? Quite possibly. Will a boat be developed capable of sailing at 100 knots? I wouldn't bet against it. Other advances will no doubt be made that we can't even envision today. But equally I believe some things will never change. The values and heritage that define sailing culture are so much a part of the yachting life, so deeply ingrained in sailors' hearts and minds, that they are unlikely ever to disappear. Going along with yachting values and heritage is an unmistakable sense of style, at once traditional, chic and practical. And finally there's the sensation of being on the water, your trusty vessel beneath your feet, the wind in your hair, the calls of your companions in your ears. It's a magical feeling, and ultimately what the sailing life is all about.

Opposite: *A model wears a Mighty-Mac plastic-coated zippered boating jacket on the cover of* GQ *in the summer of 1962.*

Following pages: *French singer Julien Clerc on vacation in Saint-Tropez, 1972.*

Pages 14/15: *Three models pose on a Hotel Bora Bora sailing catamaran wearing swim trunks by Pierre Cardin and briefs by Jockey International (GQ, Summer 1975).*

GQ

GENTLEMEN'S QUARTERLY

SALTY SPORTSWE

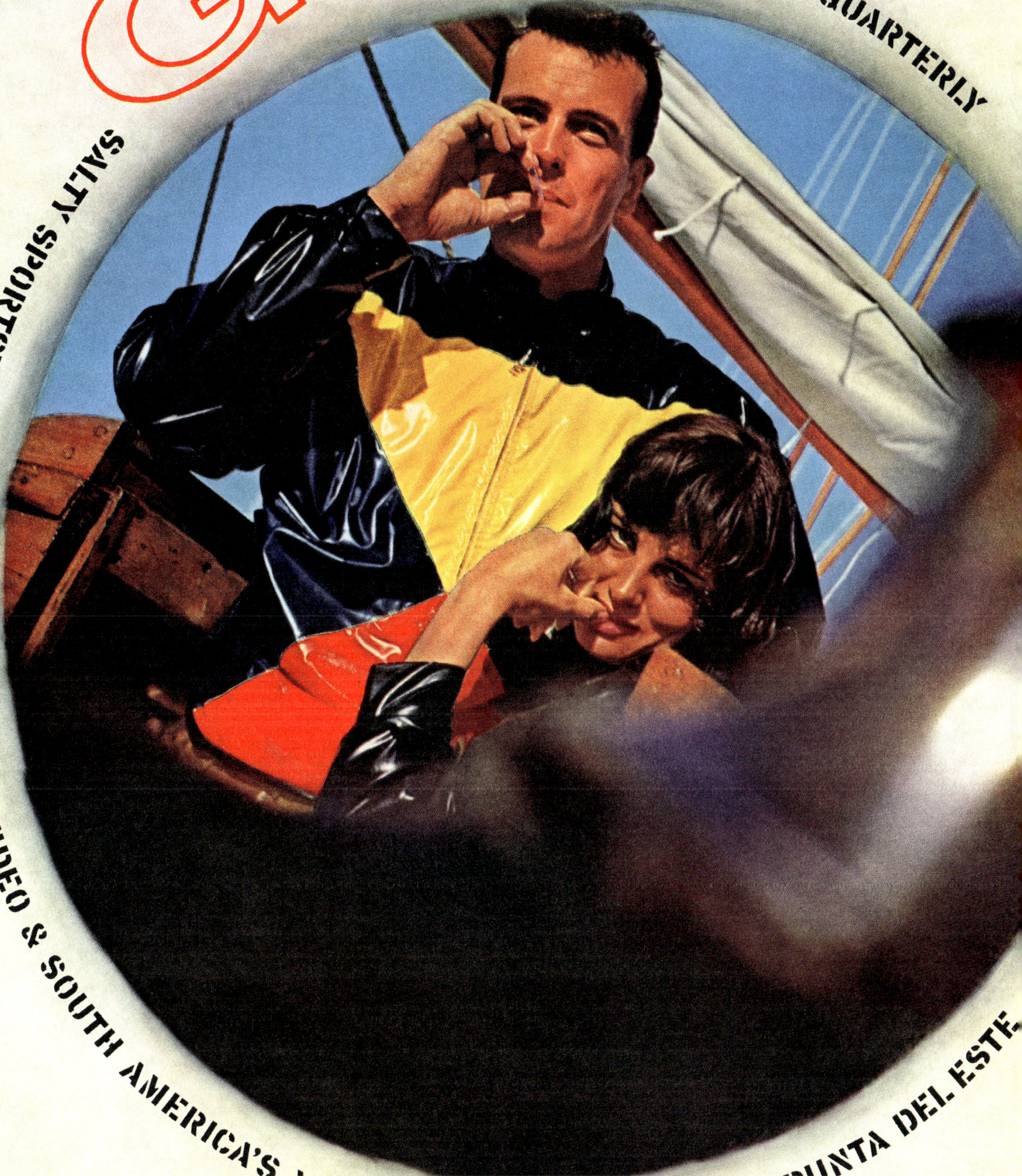

TEVIDEO & SOUTH AMERICA'S MOST FASHIONABLE RESORT, PUNTA DEL ESTE

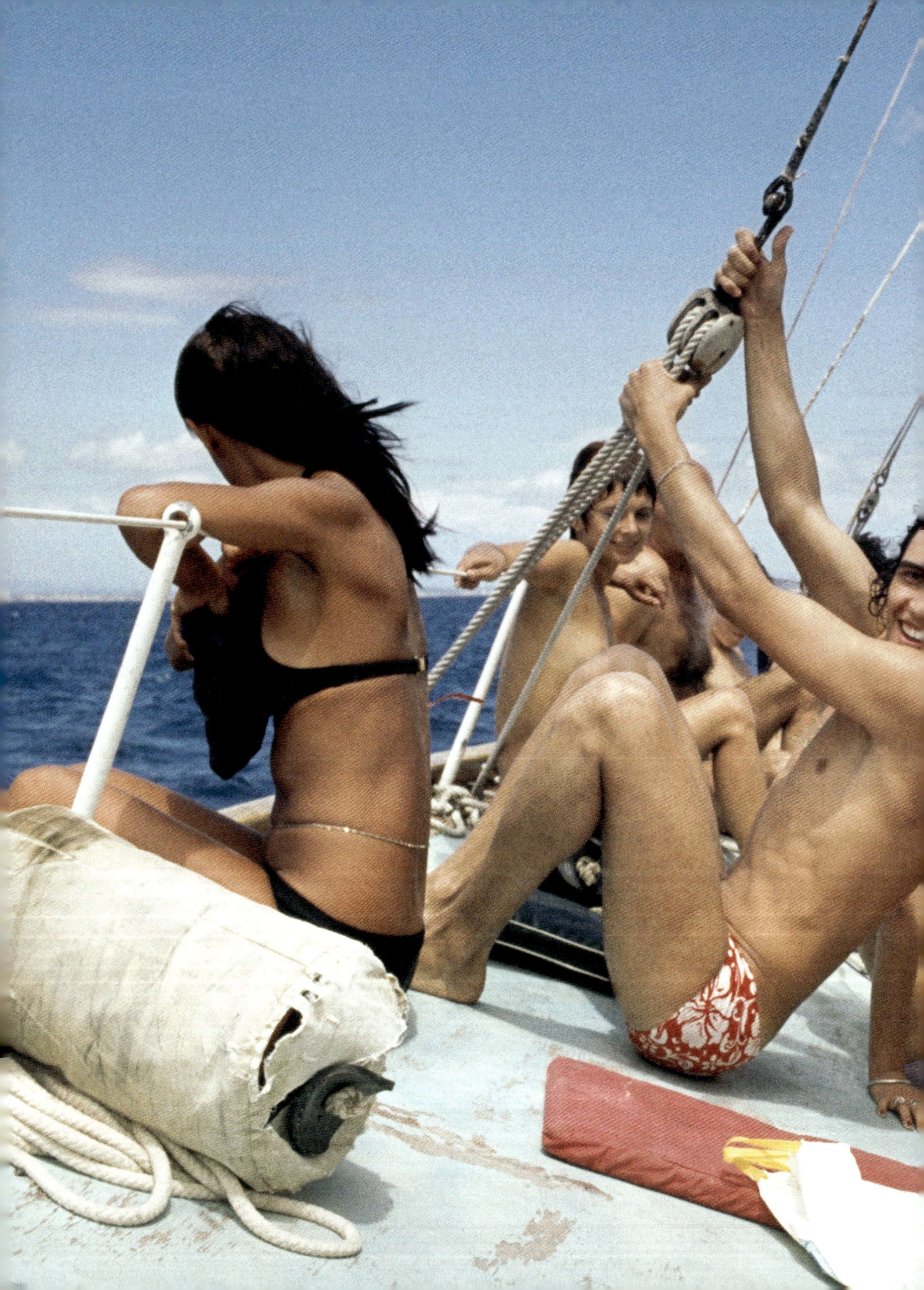

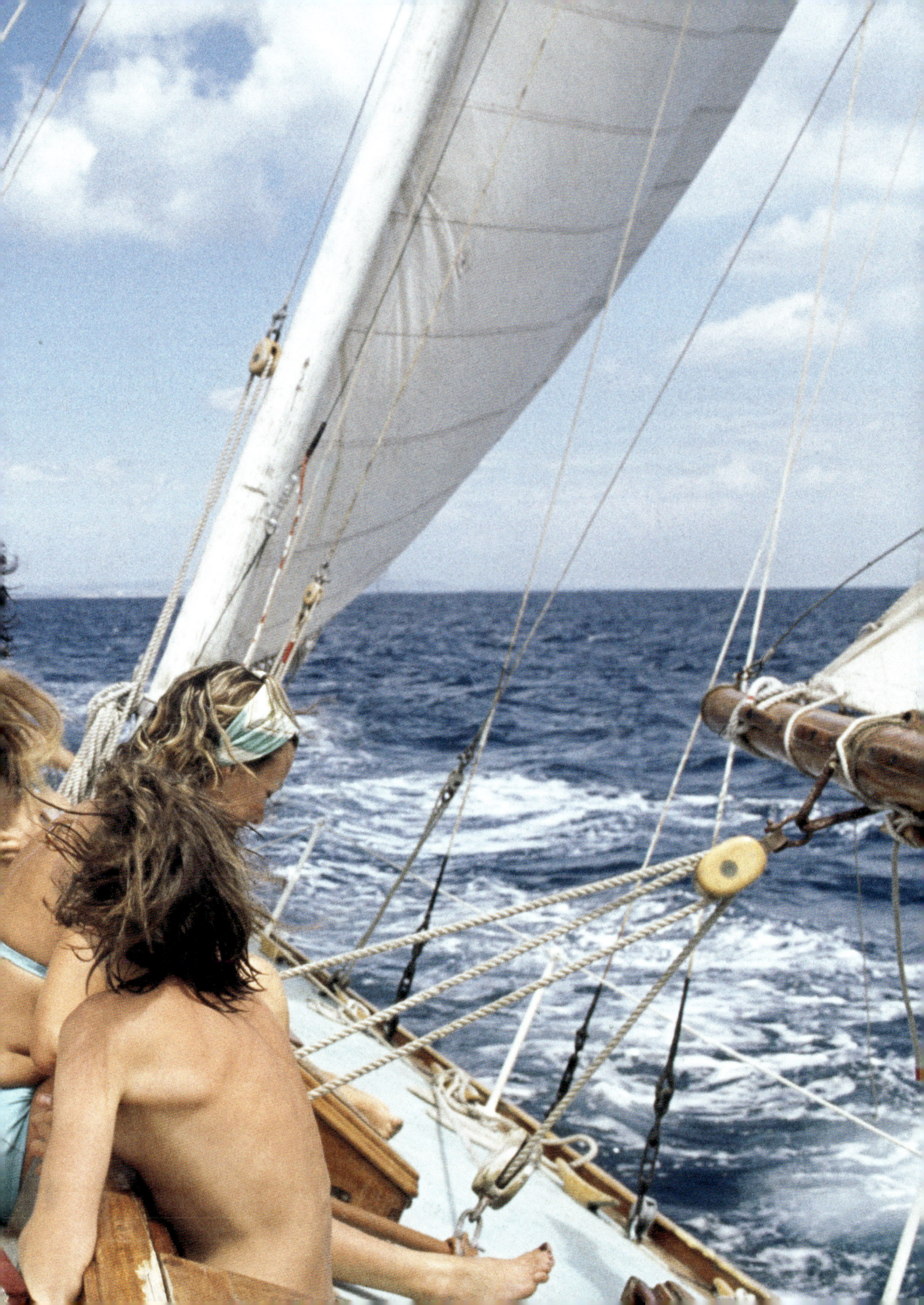

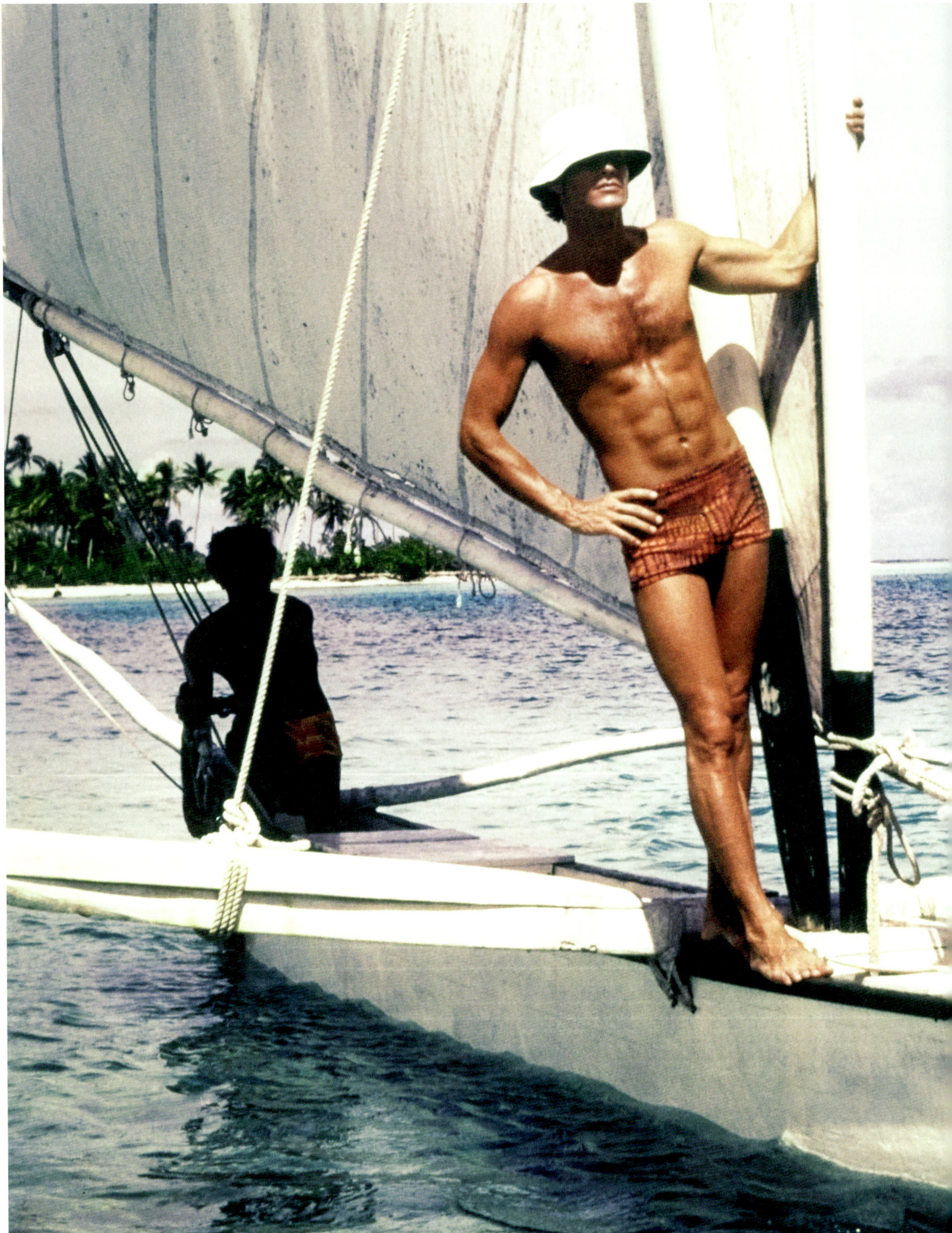

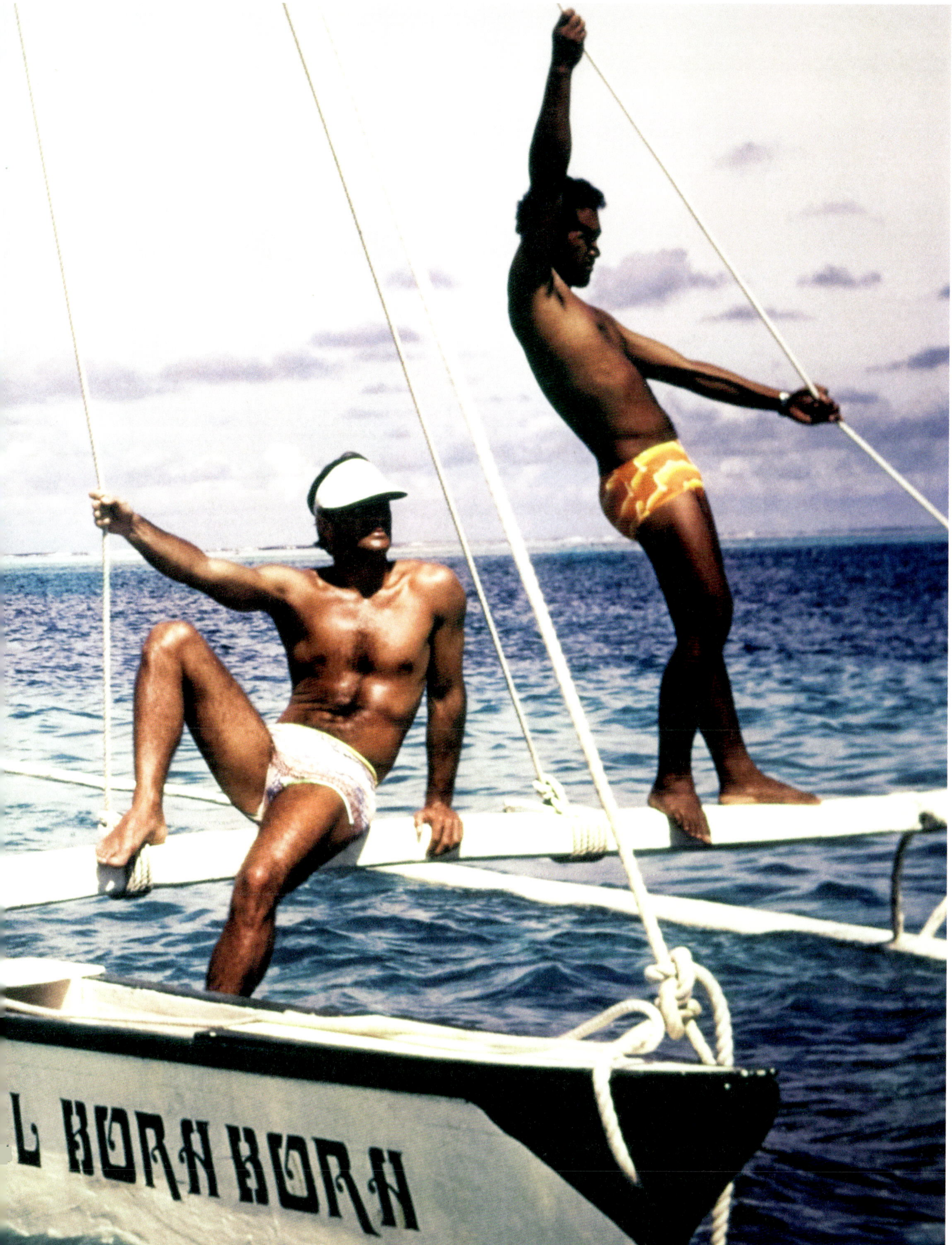
L BORA BORA

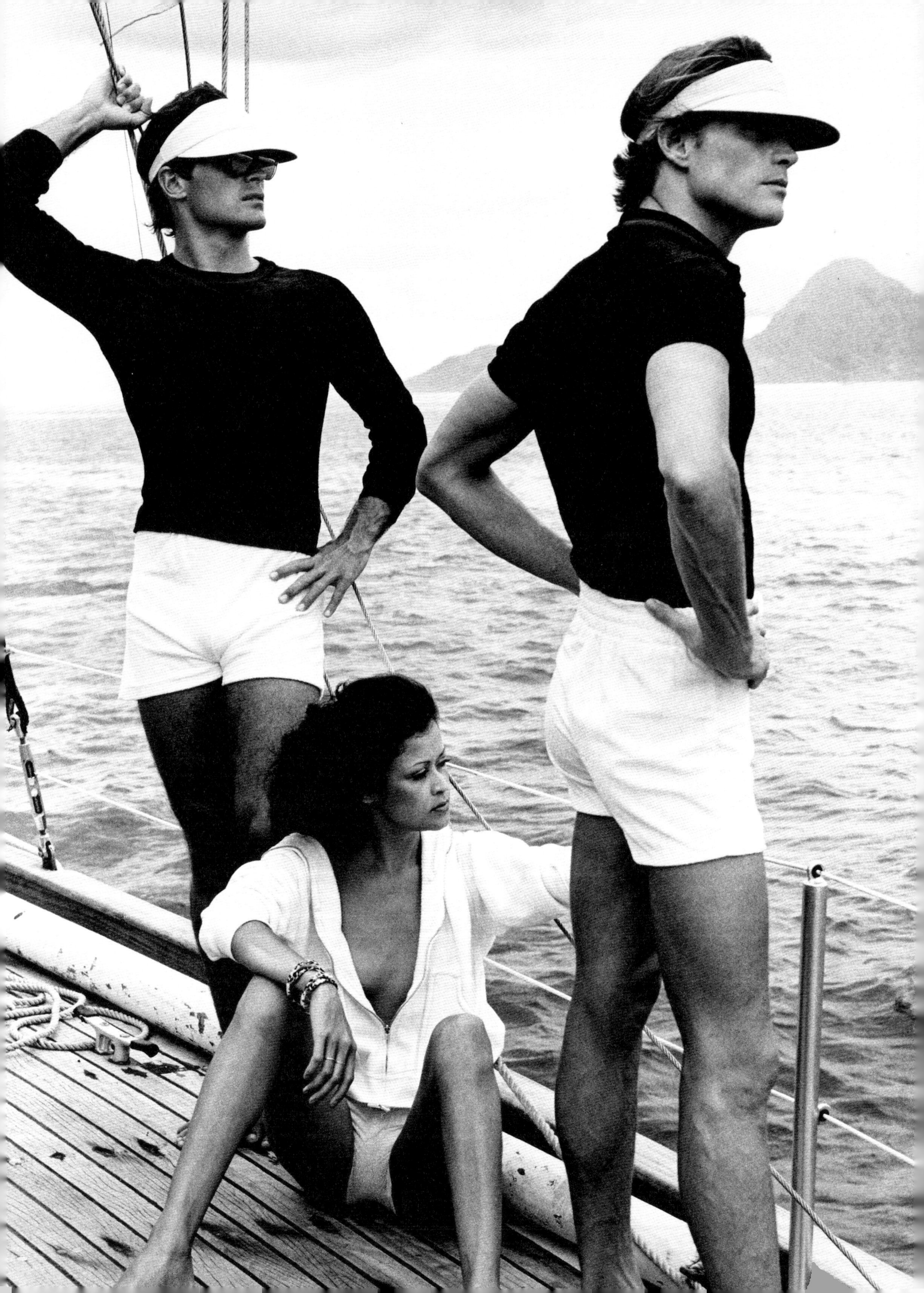

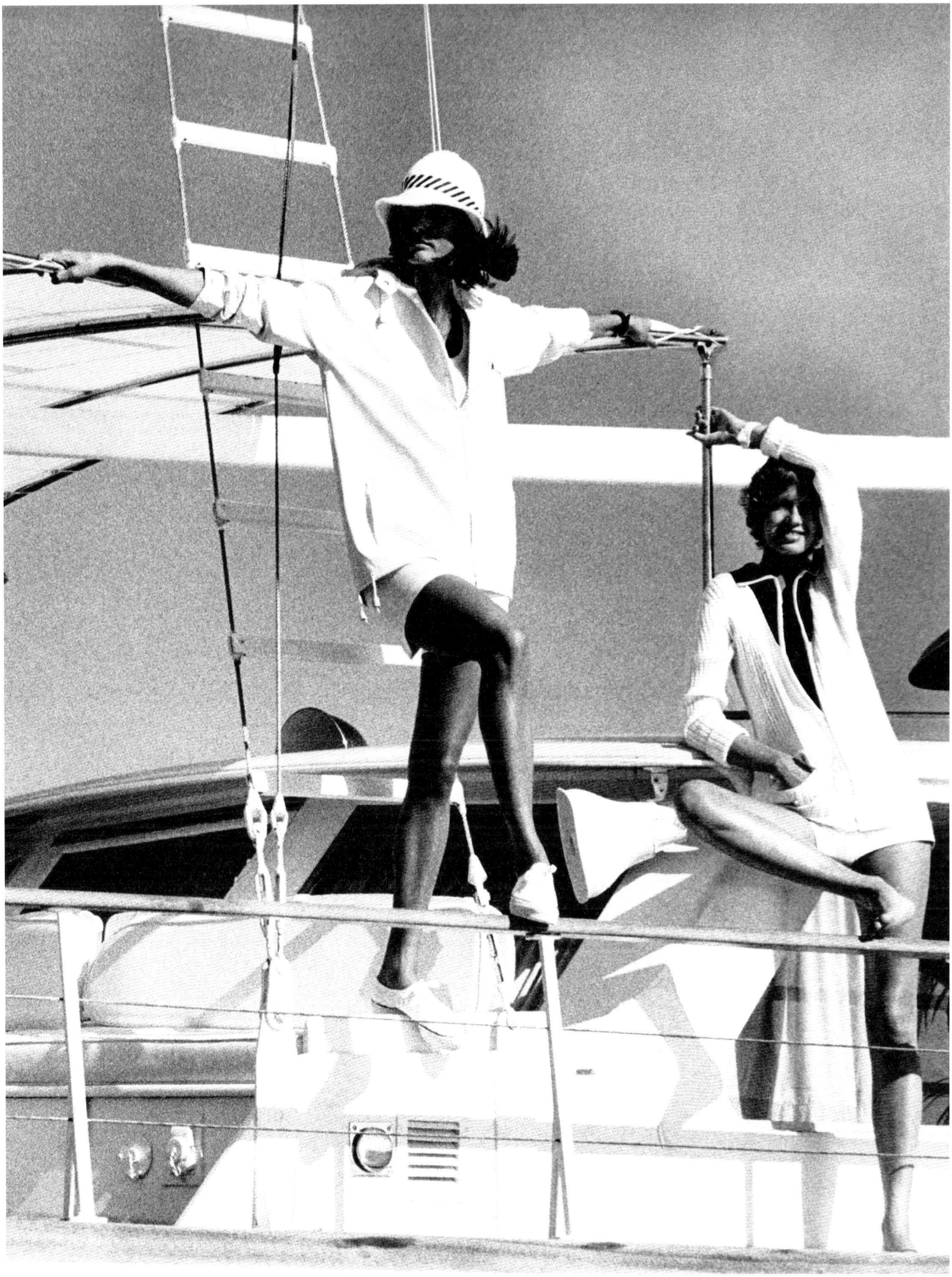

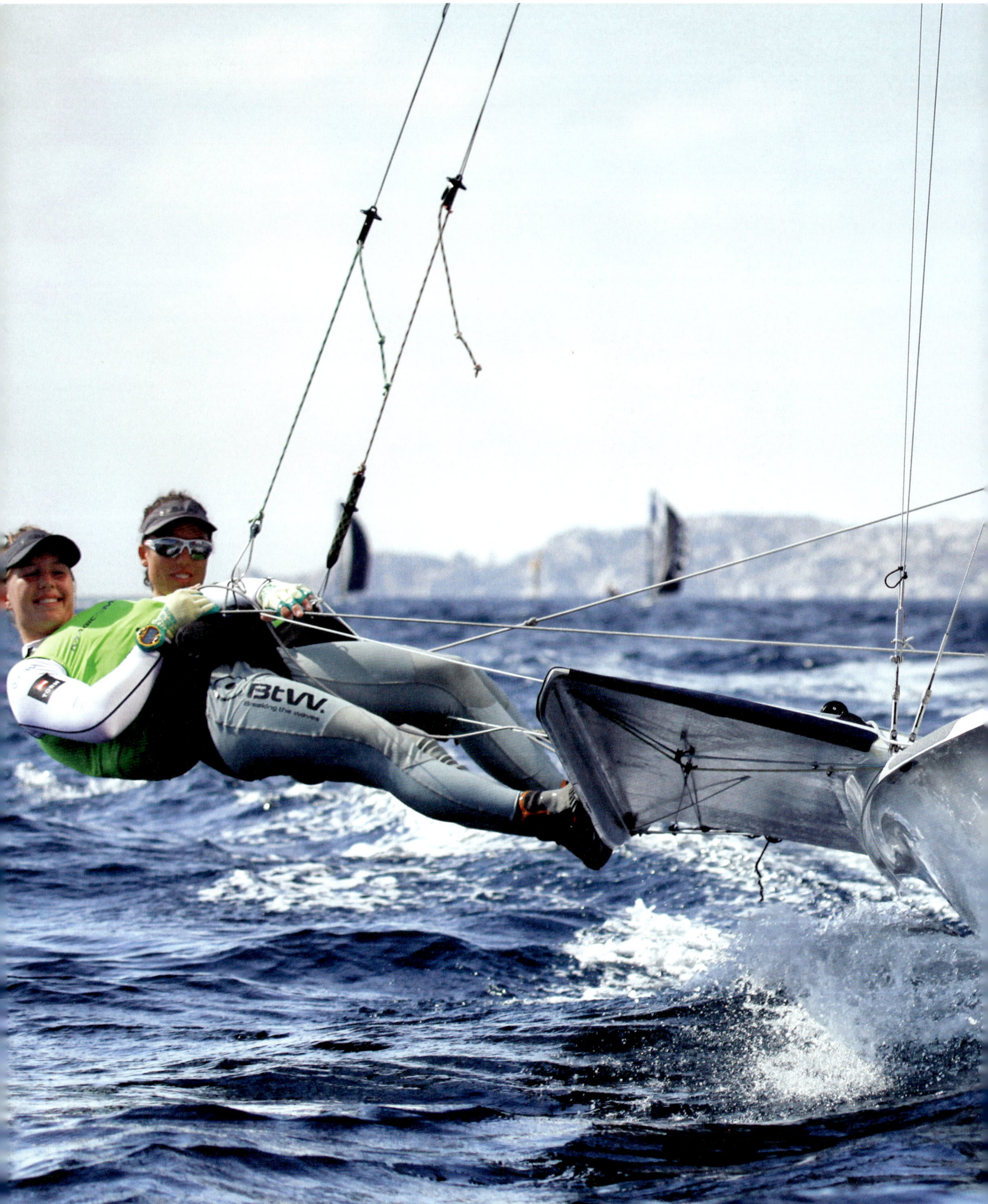
BtW.
Breaking the waves

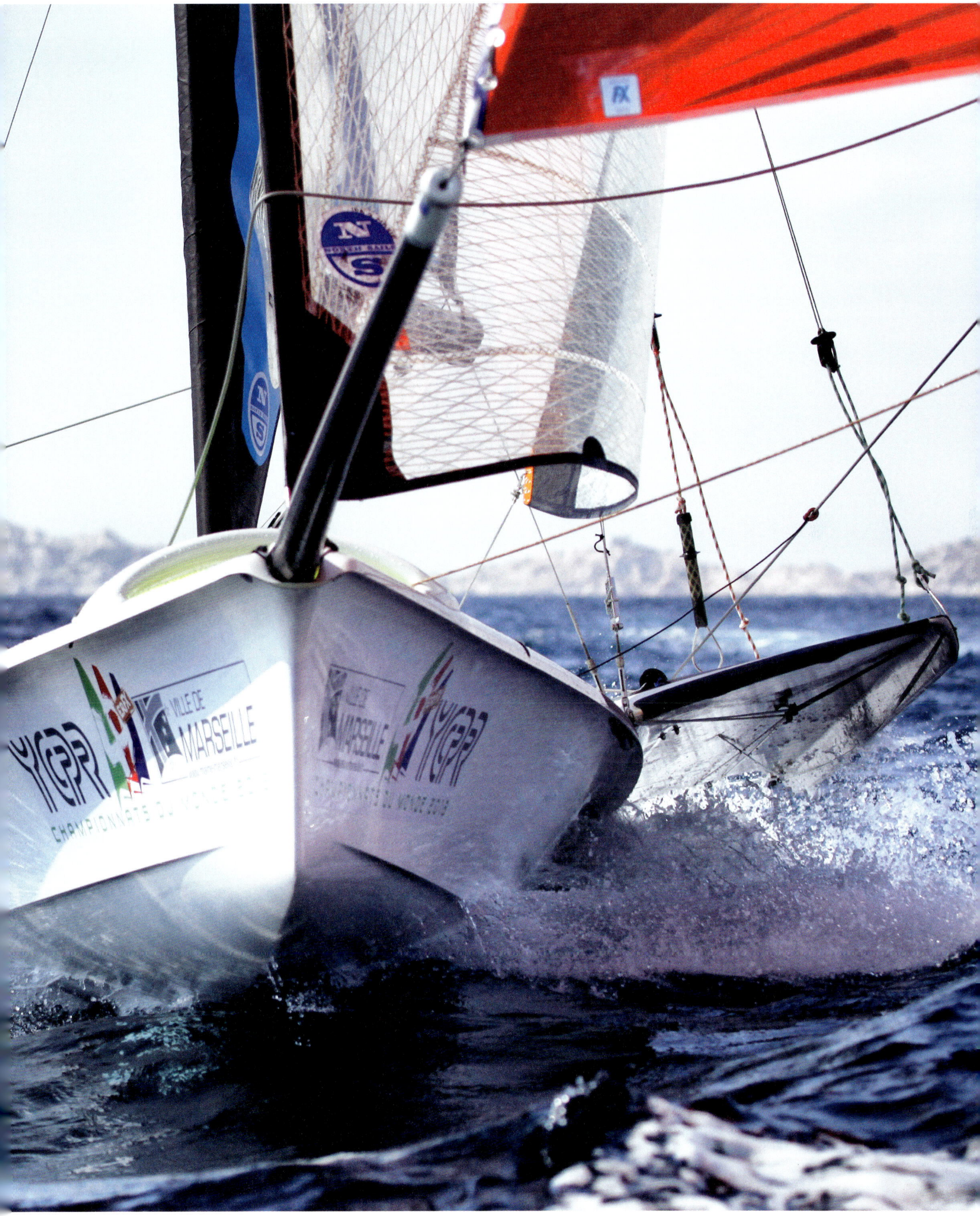
FX
VILLE DE
MARSEILLE
YCPR
CHAMPIONNATS DU MONDE 2019

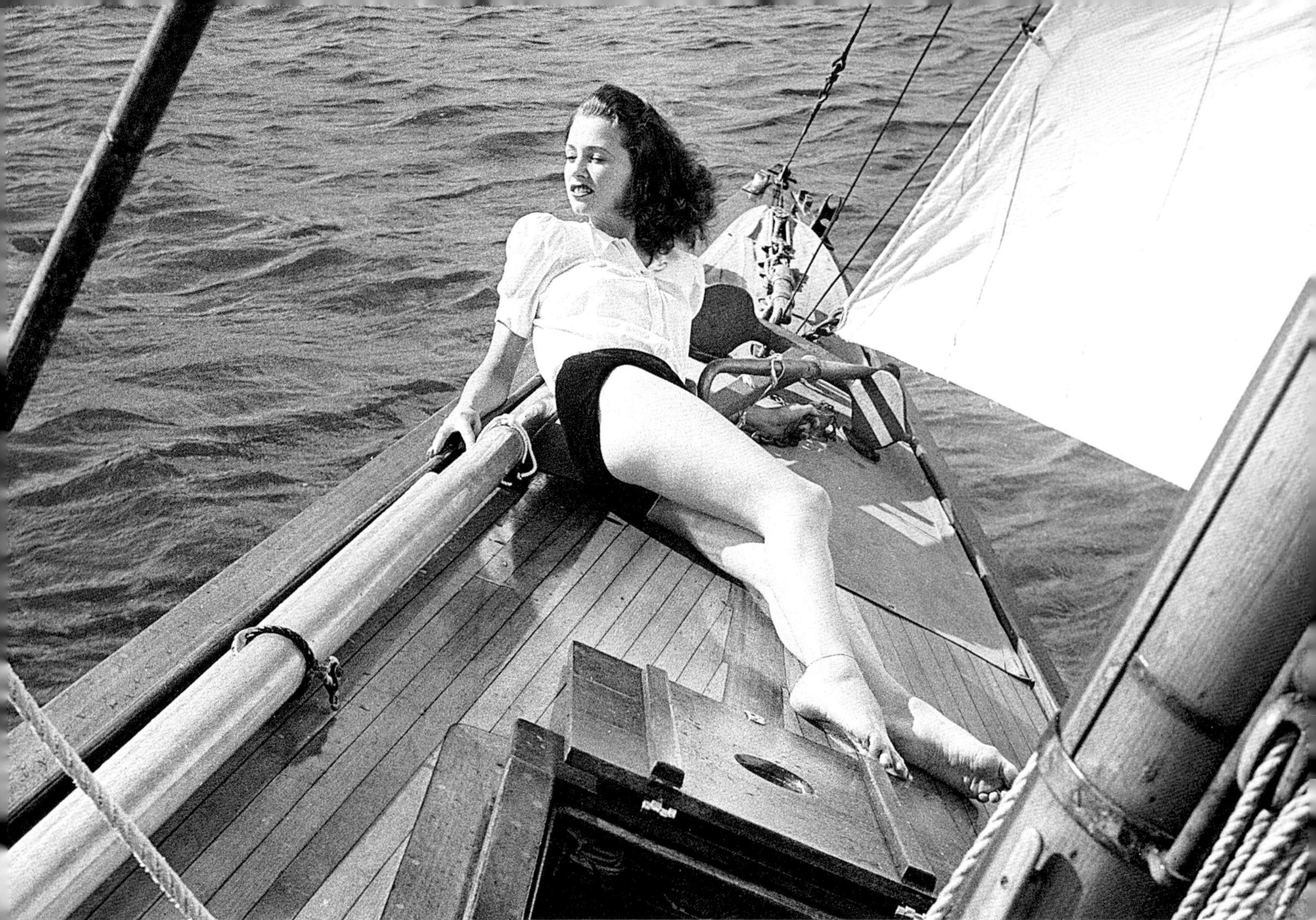
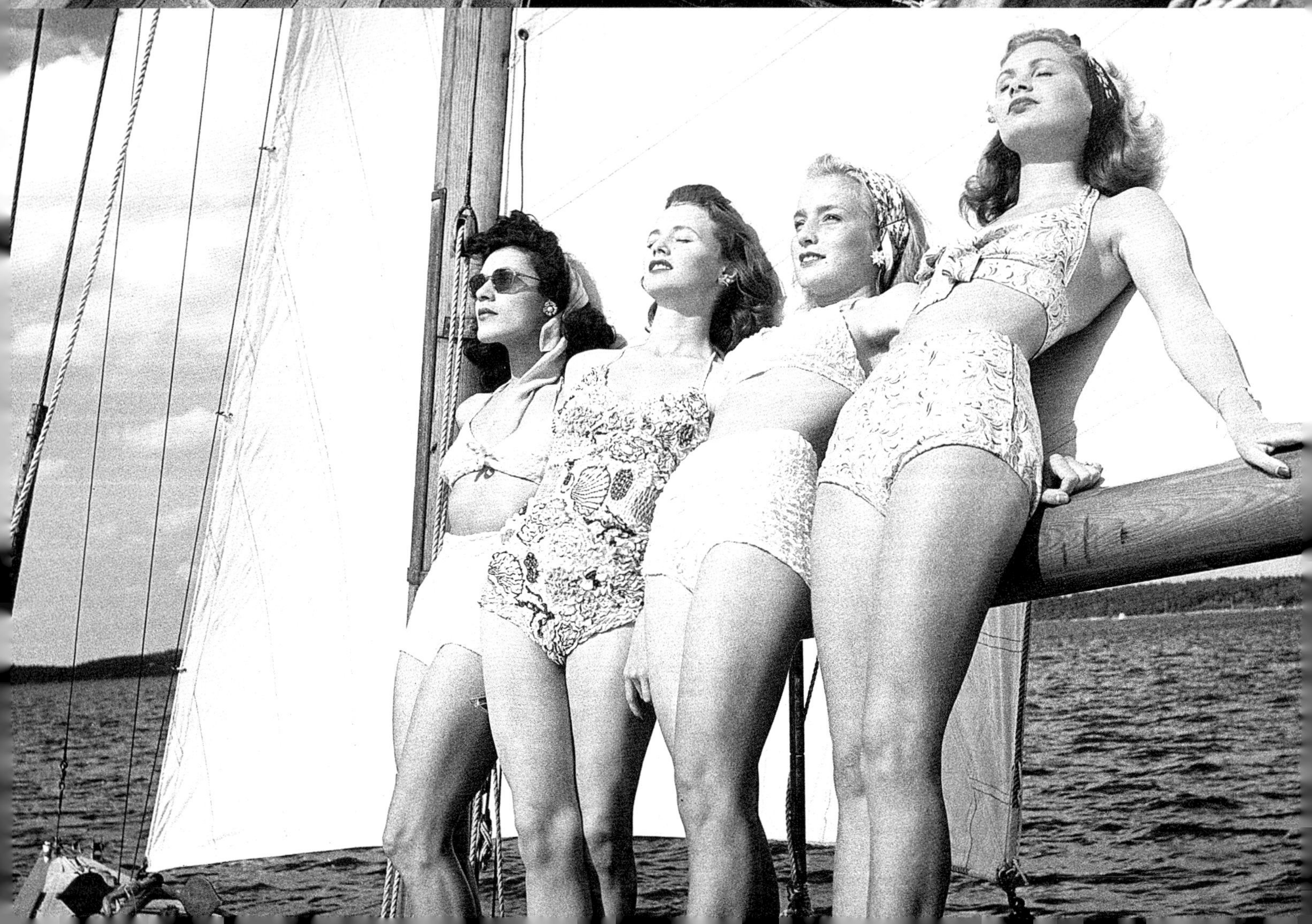

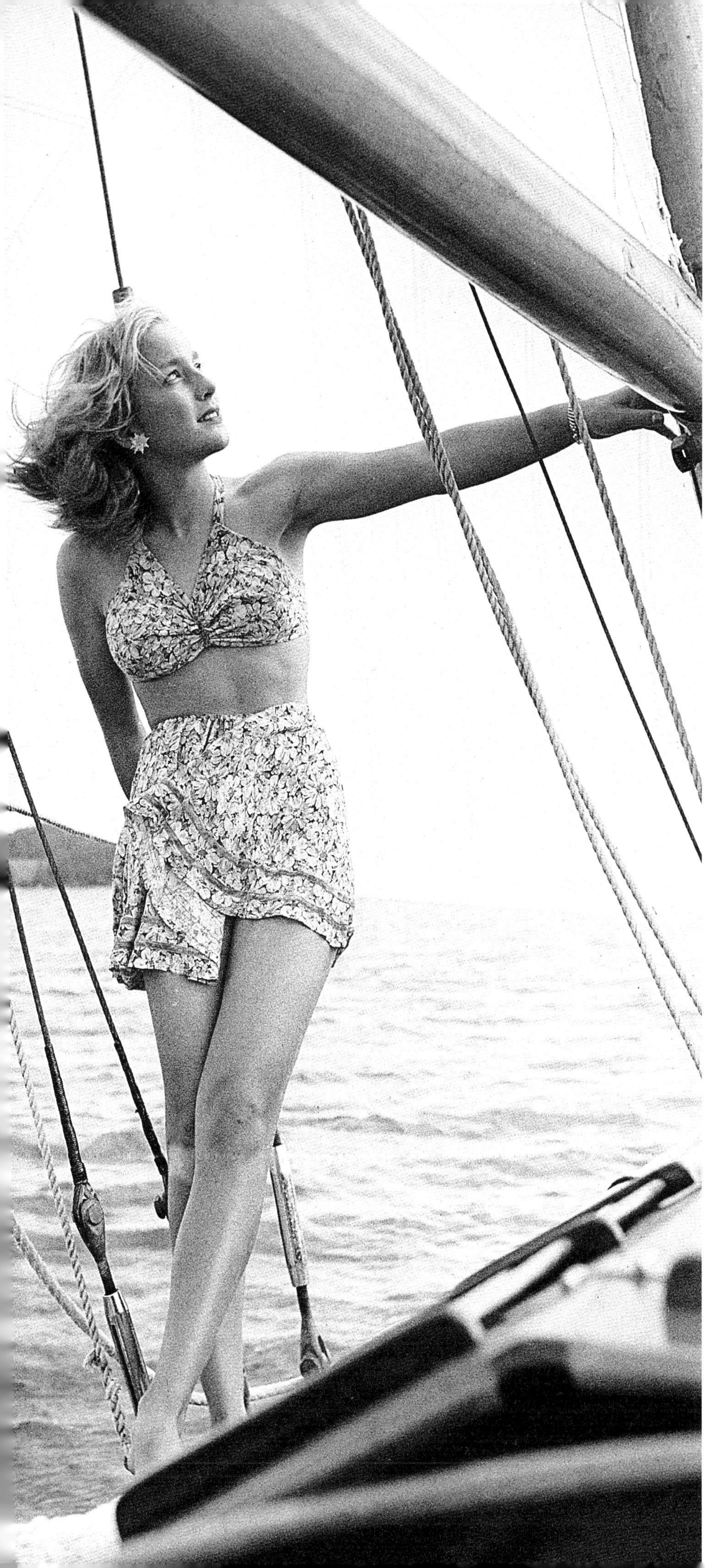

Page 16: *A group of models on a sailing boat, wearing nylon Waverly Mills shirts with Stuart Nelson and Bert Pulitzer shorts and visors from the Racquet Shop* (GQ, *Summer 1975).*

Page 17: *Two models on a boat in the Bahamas, wearing (left to right) a white zip-front sailing parka, shorts and knit tank top by White Stag, and a two-color wool boating sweater by Gucci with white shorts.*

Previous pages: *The 2013 Seiko 49er and 49erFX World Championships, held in Marseille, featured 150 skiffs from 28 nations.*

Oppsite, top: *Sweden, 1946: a young woman on the deck of a stylish sailboat with the wind in its sails. She is wearing typical 1940s yachting attire.*

Opposite, bottom: *Sweden, 1946: four young women leaning against the sails of a 1940s sailboat, enjoying the sun and wind and wearing the high-waisted swimsuits and bikinis typical of the era.*

This page: *Sweden, 1946: a young woman on the deck of a 1940s sailboat in a two-piece swimsuit.*

Page 22: *American stage actress Adelaide Neilson on an 1889 collectible tobacco card from the Yacht Colors of the World series (N91), distributed by Duke's Cigarettes. Each card features a celebrity dressed in the colors of a famous American yacht club. Neilson wears a blue sailor or pirate's cap and a uniform with a red undershirt; the anchor pendant on her necklace represents the Union New Jersey Yacht Club.*

Page 23: *Color illustration of a woman in yachting attire with the sea and a sailboat in the background* (Vogue, *1907).*

Pages 24/25: *Two British girls on a hitch-hiking trip to St Tropez, waiting for a lift by a signpost on the N98* (Picture Post, *1954).*

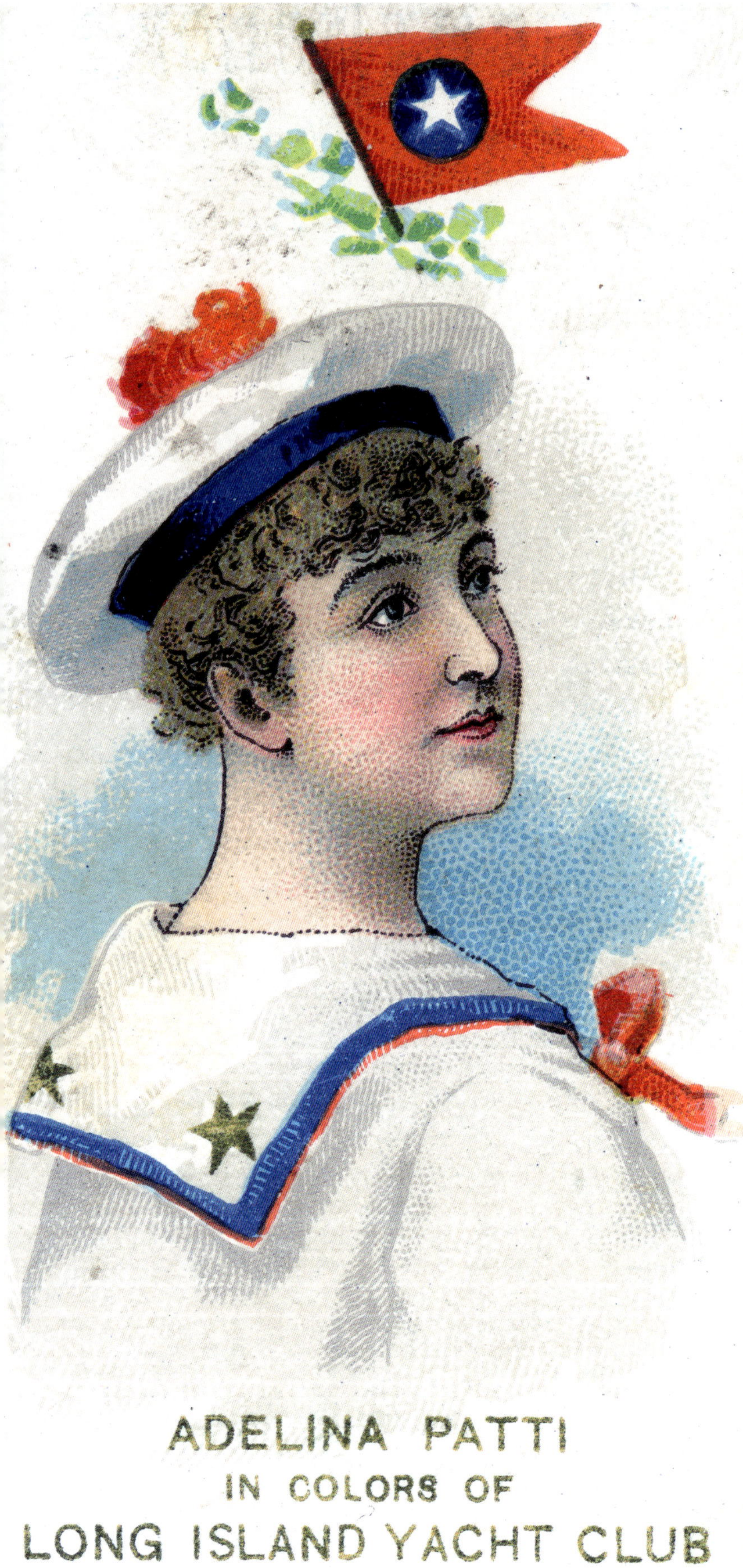
ADELINA PATTI
IN COLORS OF
LONG ISLAND YACHT CLUB

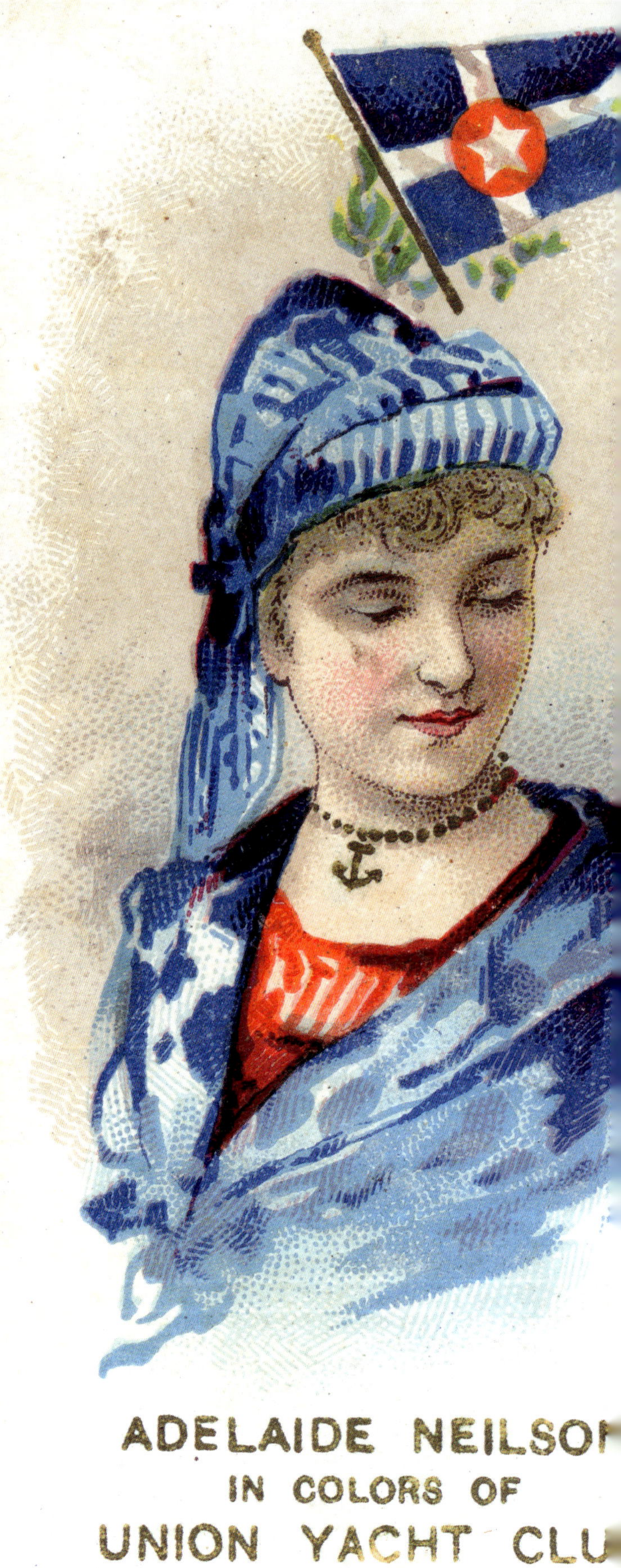
ADELAIDE NEILSO
IN COLORS OF
UNION YACHT CLU

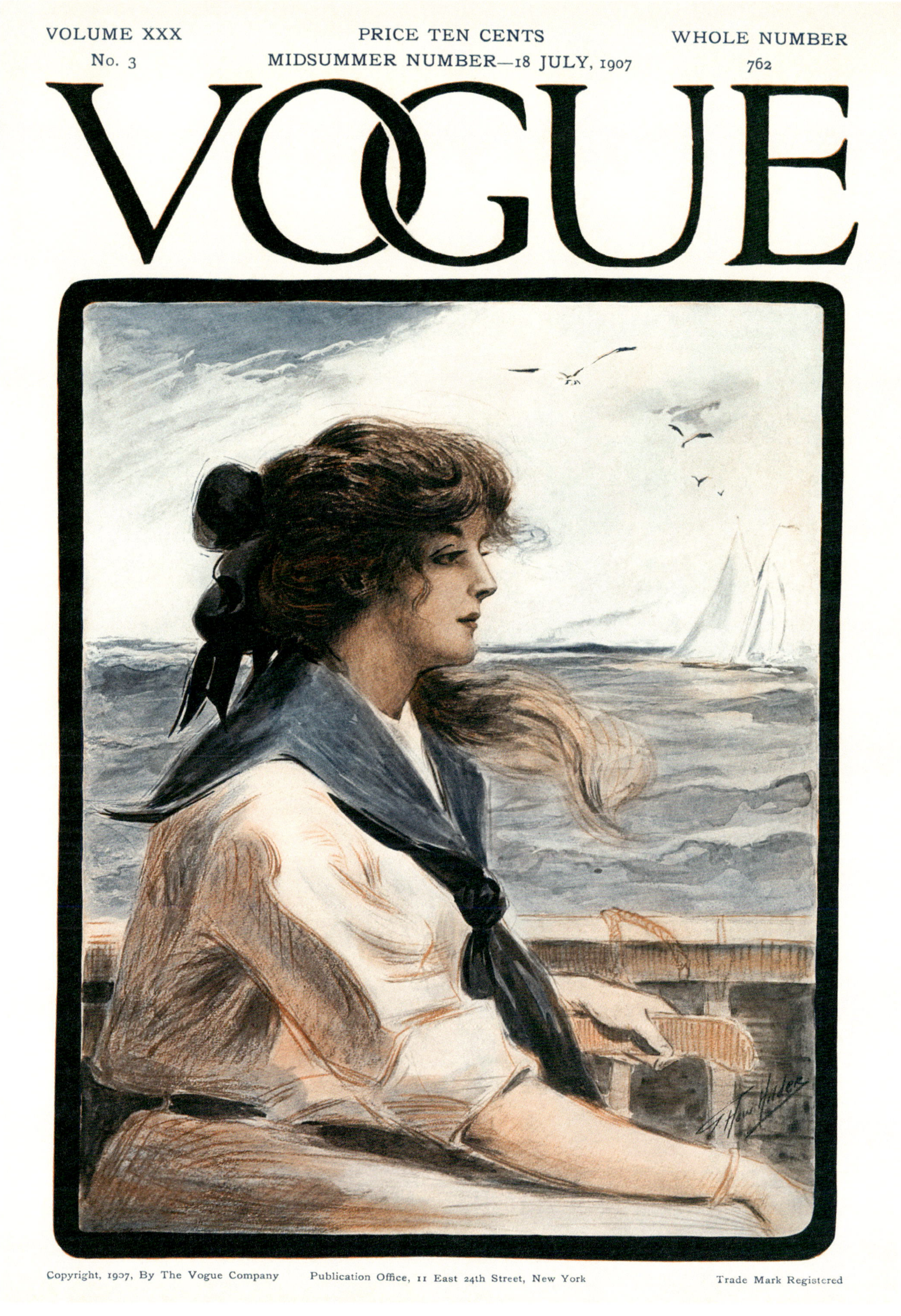
VOLUME XXX
No. 3
PRICE TEN CENTS
MIDSUMMER NUMBER—18 JULY, 1907
WHOLE NUMBER
762

VOGUE

Copyright, 1907, By The Vogue Company
Publication Office, 11 East 24th Street, New York
Trade Mark Registered

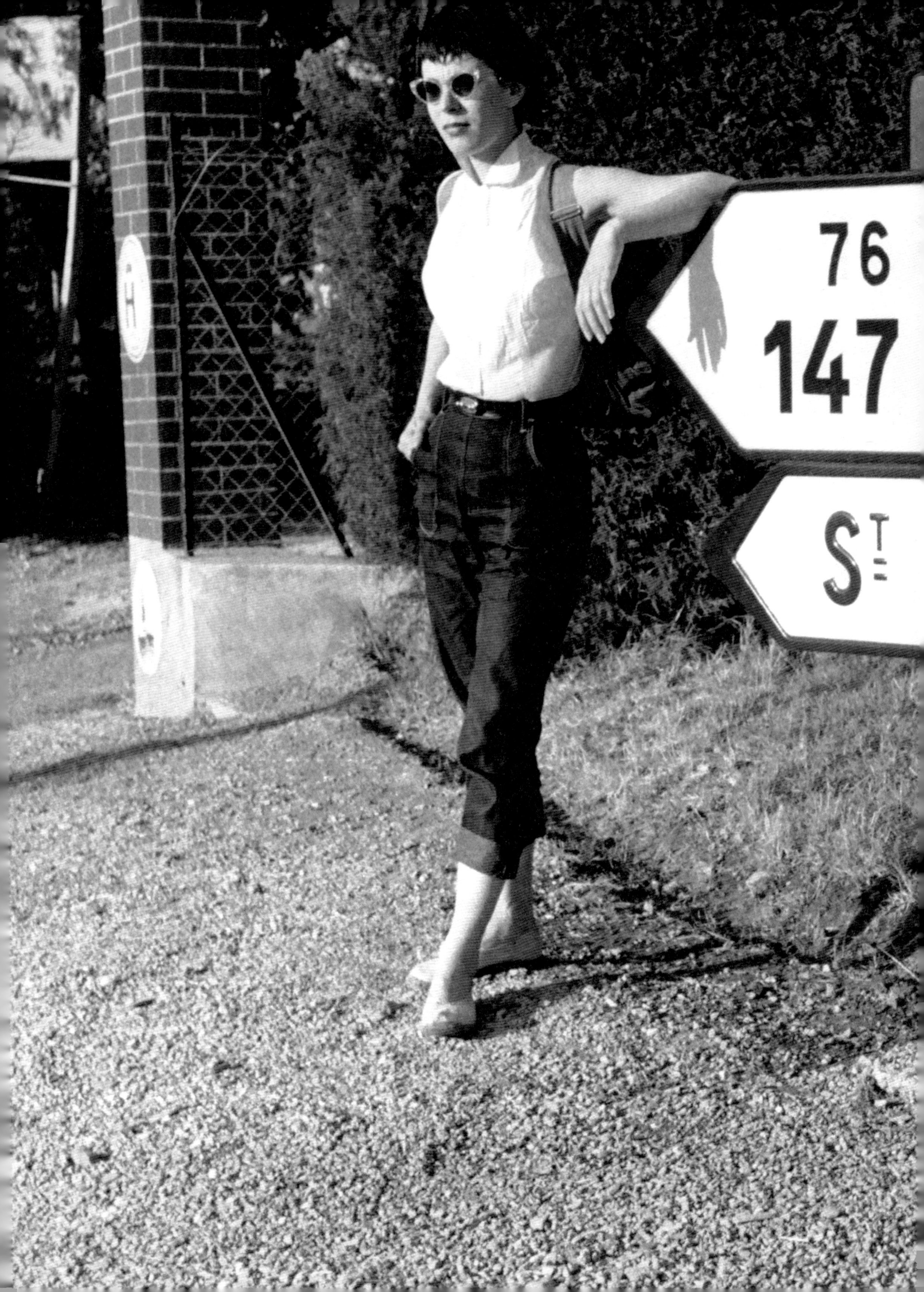
76
147
St

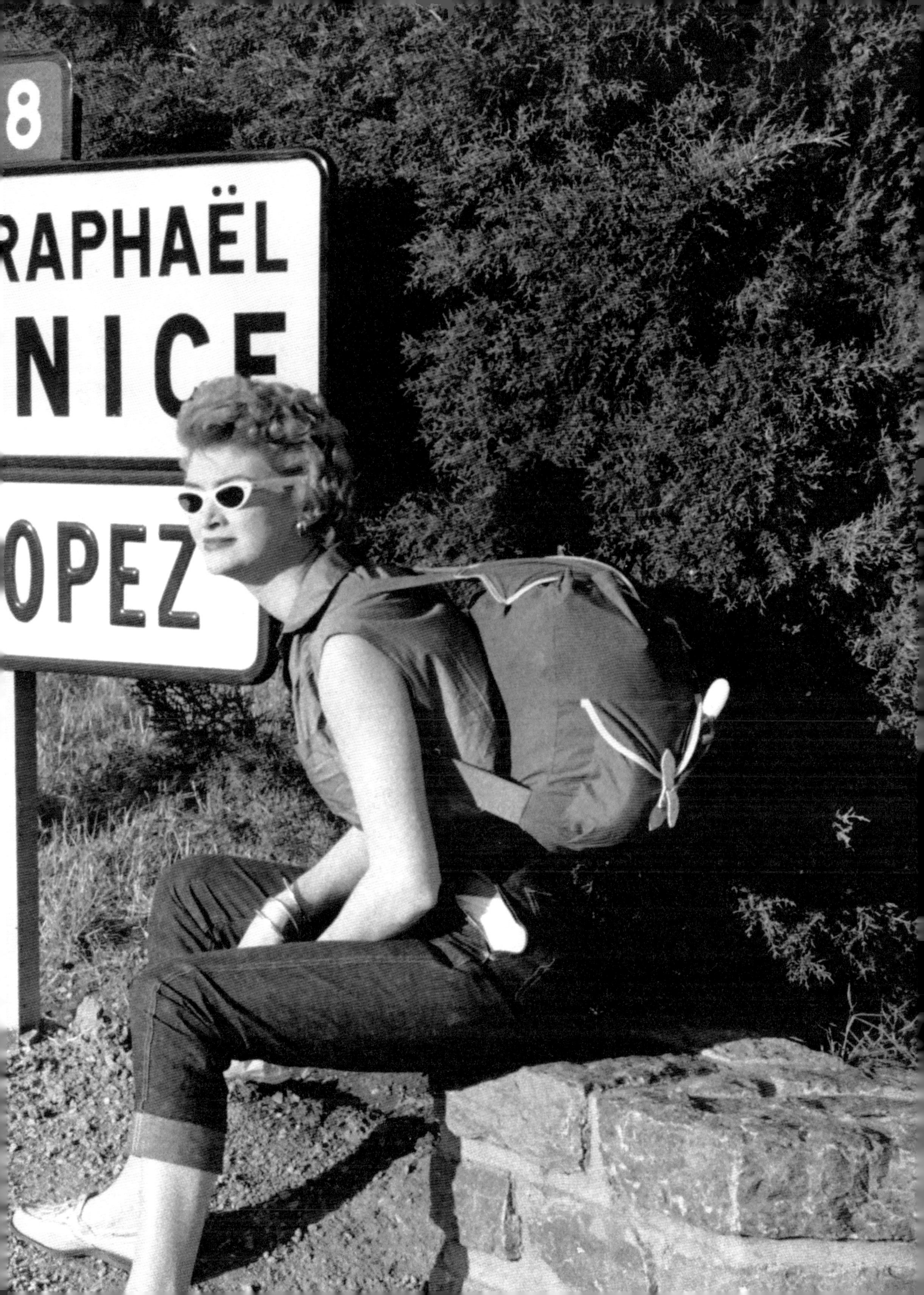
8
RAPHAËL
NICE
OPEZ

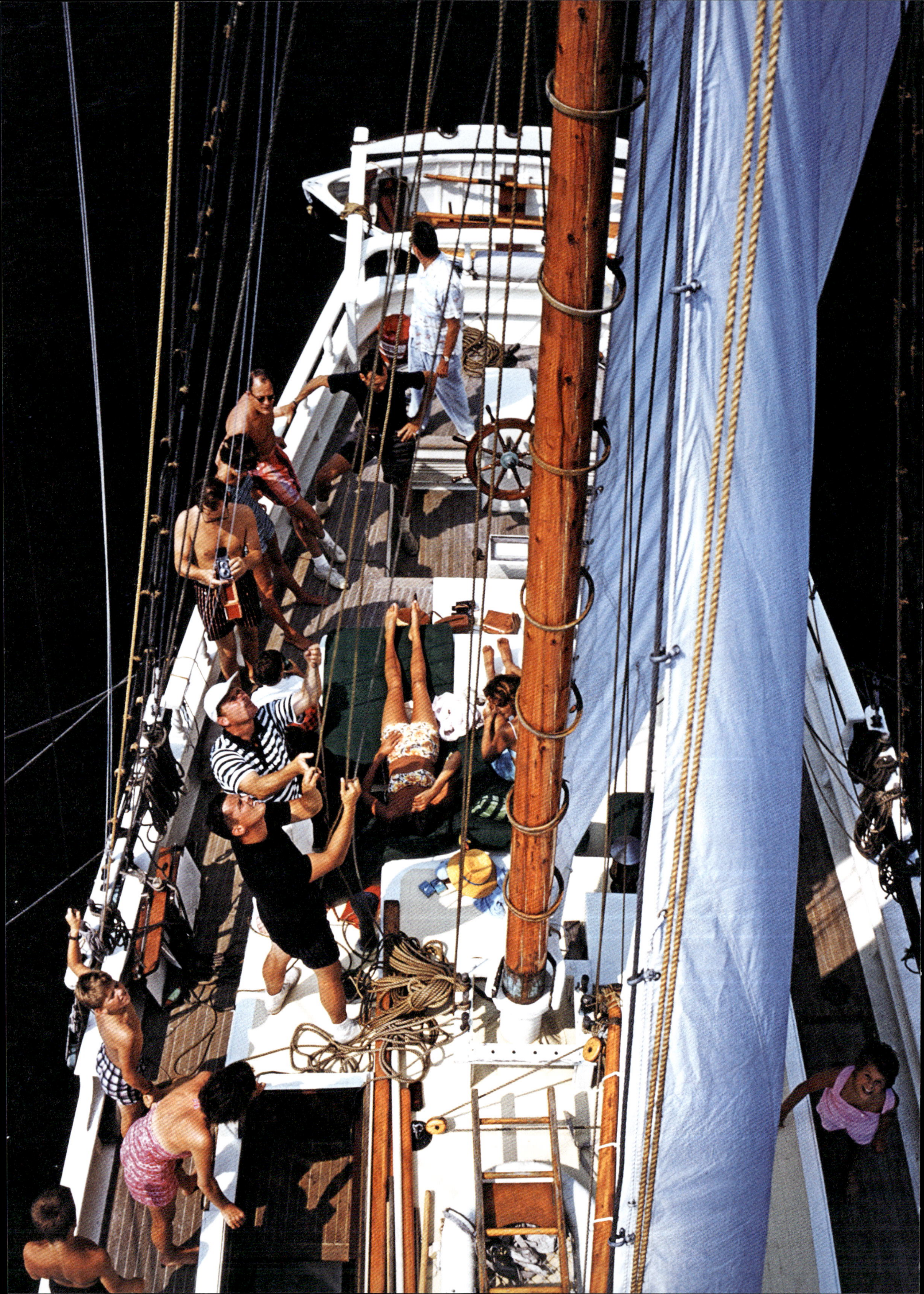

DESTINATIONS AND EVENTS

WHERE SAILORS MEET THE WORLD

Two of sailing's great benefits are the people you get to know and the places you get to visit. Every port has a distinct personality, combining topography, culture, restaurants, language, mode of travel (especially on the water), yacht clubs, marinas and sartorial style into something unique. Every sailor knows the feeling of excited anticipation that rises as a new port comes into view, and it's great fun to walk the docks or motor around the mooring field to get a close look at the array of visiting yachts.

Aeolian Islands, Italy: This group of seven volcanic islands north of Sicily, sparsely populated itself, receives over 600,000 visitors each year. Homer wrote about the area in the relating story of how Aeolus, the son of Hippotes, captured the winds in a bag to ensure Odysseus and his crew safe passage. But on the verge of arriving home some of the men opened the bag, thinking it contained treasure, and the unleashed winds blew them back to where they had come from.

Aguilla, West Indies: Aguilla is a British Overseas Territory in the northern Caribbean, known for pristine beaches and steady easterly breezes. The half-Dutch, half-French island of Saint Martin is a few miles to the south. Sailboat racing is the national sport here, and large crowds come out on holidays to watch.

Opposite: *Henry B. Cabot Jr. (in black) with his host Barclay (Buzzy) H Warburton III (in striped shirt) aboard the brigantine "Black Pearl." They are sailing off the North Shore region of Massachusetts around Manchester and Marblehead harbors, c. 1959.*

Annapolis, USA: Annapolis is known as "America's Sailing Capital" which is a play on words since the city of Annapolis is the capital of the State of Maryland. The historic town of 38,000 residents is located on the Chesapeake Bay. Over 3,000 boats are moored in marinas and waterfront homes. In the summer months about 200 boats race on Wednesday evenings providing spirited viewing for thousands of spectators along the shoreline, at the town's three yacht clubs, and waterfront restaurants. Annapolis is home to the United States Naval Academy founded in 1845 and St. John's College founded in 1696. Washington, D.C. is only 30 miles away, but politics are not the priority. People would rather go sailing. An annual in-the-water boat show is the biggest in the USA attracting many thousands of visitors every October.

Antigua, West Indies: Antigua enjoys some of the finest sailing waters in the world, with a steady easterly wind that's both a challenge and a delight for sailors. English Harbor on the southeast corner of the island attracts thousands of yachts throughout the winter season, and two of the most popular sailing events in the world are Antigua Race Week and Antigua Classic Race Week.

Auckland, New Zealand: Known as the City of Sails, Auckland is a yachting town through and through that proudly hosted the America's Cup races in 2000, 2003 and 2021. New Zealand is a small country with a small population of around 5.8 million people, but its sailors have excelled at every level of the sport.

Bahamas: The Bahamas comprise over 3,000 islands about 60 miles east of Florida and extending about 500 miles to the southeast. The country is a popular destination for cruising sailors, although the waters are notoriously shallow and careful navigation is a must. Small vessels known as Bahamian Work Boats race with up to 20 or more crew sitting on boards to provide stability; the races are especially fun to watch as vessels often capsize in strong winds. Hurricanes have wreaked havoc in the Bahamas over the years, and tourism is the most important economic driver.

Bermuda: At least four different offshore races finish at the eastern tip of the small island nation of Bermuda, a former British colony that features several vibrant by yacht clubs and hosted the America's Cup in 2017. Bermuda's own annual race week attracts crews from around the world, and the island hosts an annual Gold Cup match race that reliably draws a fleet of International One Designs from around the world. Many America's Cup sailors compete in the Gold Cup to sharpen their skills.

Boston Harbor: Boston is an old-world seaport, at least by the standards of the United States, and a large number of uninhabited islands dot the bay leading to the inner harbor. Most of the racing here takes place north or south of the city, and on the Charles River running through the centre, known for the shiftiness of its breezes as they flow around the numerous skyscrapers. Boston is a sporting town, and many of its storied universities—including Harvard University, Massachusetts Institute of Technology, Boston College, and Boston University—boast varsity sailing teams specializing in dinghy racing.

Capri, Italy: Capri is a scenic island to the west of the Gulf of Naples, a major luxury tourist destination with a spectacular landscape that's inspired noted artists including John Singer Sargent. The TP 52 Super Series took place off Capri in 2025, and the America's Cup is scheduled to be held here in the summer of 2027.

Corsica, France: Corsica sits just seven miles north of Sardinia, the two islands separated by the Straits of Bonifacio. Several annual long-distance races send yachts through the straits, where competitors must often battle the strong winds that funnel between the islands. The current is also strong, weaving through shallow waters and making navigation a challenge. The port of Bastia on the northeast corner of Corsica is filled with sailing and power yachts flying the national flags of almost every country in Europe.

Cowes, England: Cowes Race Week is a huge regatta, with different parts of race week handled by various local yacht clubs. The bi-annual Admiral's Cup was also revived recently and attracts some of the most skilled racers in the world. Cowes has held a special place in the heart of generations of sailors: the Royal Yacht Squadron is a centuries-old castle with majestic appeal, a walk down historic High Street is a step back in time, and the town is home to dozens of excellent inns and pubs.

Down East, Maine: The prevailing southwesterly thermal winds bring a cool breeze to the northern coast of Maine in the summer months, where the term "down east" refers to sailing downwind toward the border with Canada. The rocky coastline and surrounding waters have a huge lobster population, and hundreds of lobster workers haul their nets from dawn to dusk. The small towns along the scenic coastline are a throwback to the 1930s.

Fremantle, Australia: The fishing town of Fremantle established itself as an important sailing destination when it hosted the Louis Vuitton Challenger Series and the America's Cup in 1986 and 1987. During the summer months (November–March) an afternoon sea breeze known as the "Fremantle Doctor" brings cool winds to the hot coast. Fremantle is a popular stop for round-the-world racers, and its crystal-clear waters also make it a mecca for sailors, fishermen and people who simply enjoy the beach.

Key West, Florida: Key West, a vibrant town filled with music, tourists and sailors, sits at the southernmost point of the continental United States. For the North American yachting community, an annual race week here in January is a welcome relief from the cold of the northern states and Canada.

Marbella, Spain: Marbella is a city in southern Spain near the Strait of Gibraltar. About 60 years ago I was serving on a U.S. naval vessel in the region, and as we steamed passed Gibraltar our ship received a signal from the British naval station on the hill, asking, "What ship?" One of our officers replied, "What rock?" We all had a good laugh, but our captain was not amused.

Nantucket, Massachusetts: Nantucket, about 30 miles south of Cape Cod, is a pristine island that attracts thousands of visitors during the summer months and is a second home to some of the world's wealthiest people. The harbor is filled with mega-yachts, classic sailing vessels and small sailboats of all kinds, and each summer the island hosts Nantucket Race Week, an event for people of all ages that since 1973 has culminated in the Opera House Cup. Many spectators watch from their own vessels or the island's white sand beaches.

Newport, Rhode Island: Newport was an important port for the U.S. navy in the country's early days, and in the late 1800s and early 1900s was known for its opulence. Giant mansions were built along Bellview Avenue and Ocean Drive, whose owners referred to them as "cottages," and the first New York Yacht Club Annual Cruise took place in Newport in 1885. The America's Cup races were held in Newport from 1930 to 1983, and it's still considered one of the best sailing towns in the world.

Porto Cervo, Italy: Prince Karim Aga Khan IV essentially created Porto Cervo in the 1960s, turning a sparsely populated corner of northeastern Sardinia into an exclusive resort. The Costa Smeralda Yacht Club hosts many important regattas every year, and this is a special place to see and be seen.

Punta del Este, Uruguay: Punta del Este is a popular tourist destination and vacation spot for people from the surrounding region, a coastal city about an hour's drive from Uruguay's largest city, Montevideo. Several yacht clubs support strong junior sailing programs, and sailors from Punta del Este have represented the country at the Olympic Games.

Saint Barthélemy: St. Barts is a beautiful Caribbean island with French colonial heritage, known today for attracting mega-yachts from around the world. It is plush, unique and very expensive, and an invitation to race in the annual Bucket Regatta here is considered one of the highlights of a yachting life.

Saint Tropez, France: Late summer sailing off St. Tropez is some of the best in Europe, and the parade of classic yachts always moored stern-to-stern along the city's seawall is a remarkable sight. There is also an endless array of immaculate bars and restaurants in which to relax after a day's sailing.

Sydney, Australia: Regular races take place in Sydney Harbor, with the famous opera house and bridge providing a spectacular backdrop, and the Olympic Games were sailed here in 2000 as the world ushered in the new millennium. Australian sailors have a reputation for competitive grit and determination, and enthusiastic local spectators are always to be found placing bets on the races. An annual highlight is the start of the Sydney to Hobart Ocean Race on Boxing Day.

Tuscany, Italy: Tuscany, a region on the northwest coast of Italy, has been been one of the world's great cultural centers since the Middle Ages. The capital city, Florence, remains a major tourist draw, and the Tuscan Archipelago offers exceptional sailing as well. Punta Ala has been the home port for several Italian America's Cup challenges by Prada CEO Patricio Bertelli.

Virgin Islands: The British Virgin Islands and the United States Virgin Islands offer some of the best cruising areas in the world, with a steady easterly breeze that keeps boats moving year around. An additional draw for many sailors is the rustic pubs to be found on many of the islands, each with its own unique personality, and the musical culture that permeates life here is remarkable.

Following pages: *Sunbathers on the deck of the yacht "Traveller II" off the coast of Exuma in the Bahamas, April 1967.*

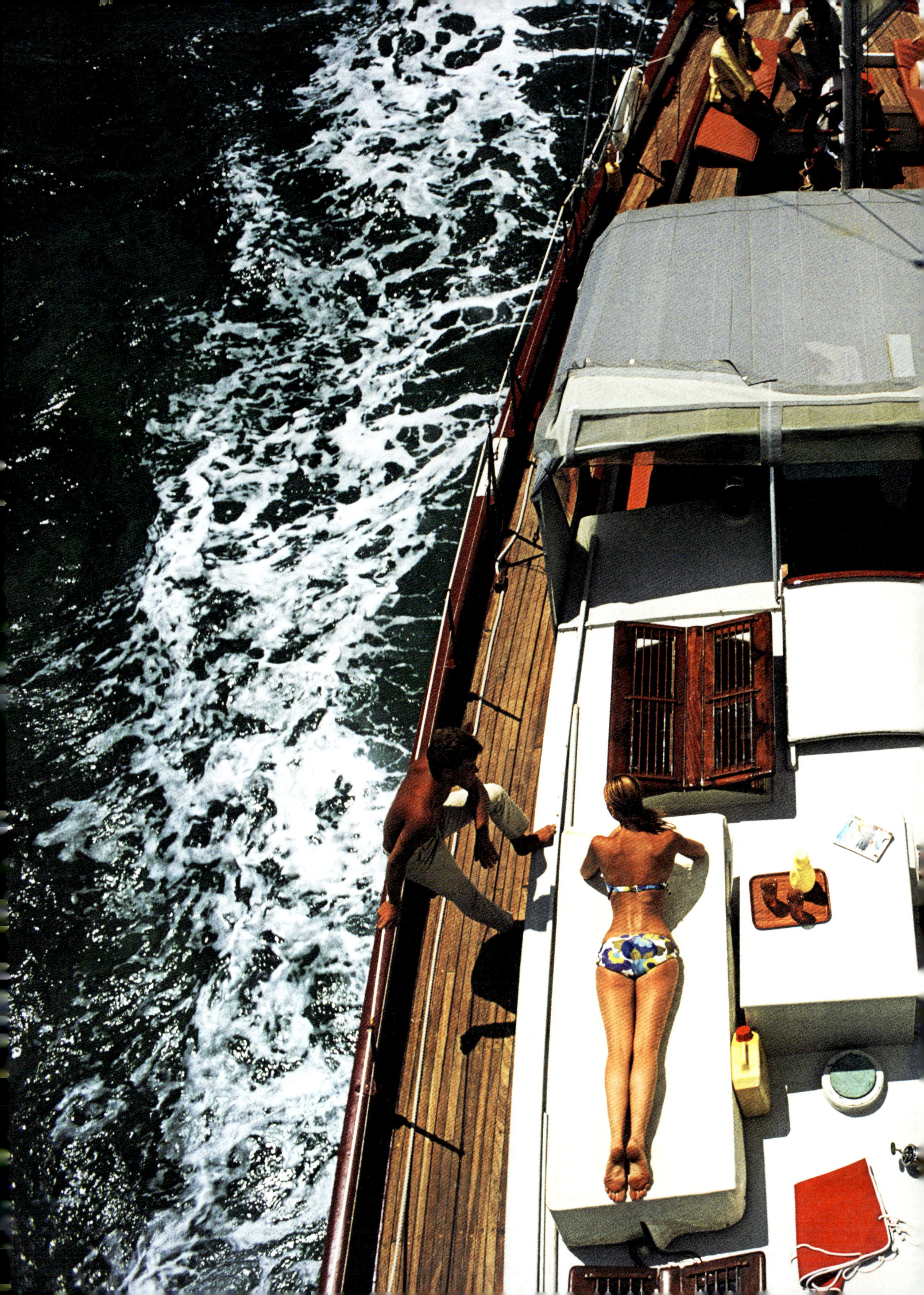

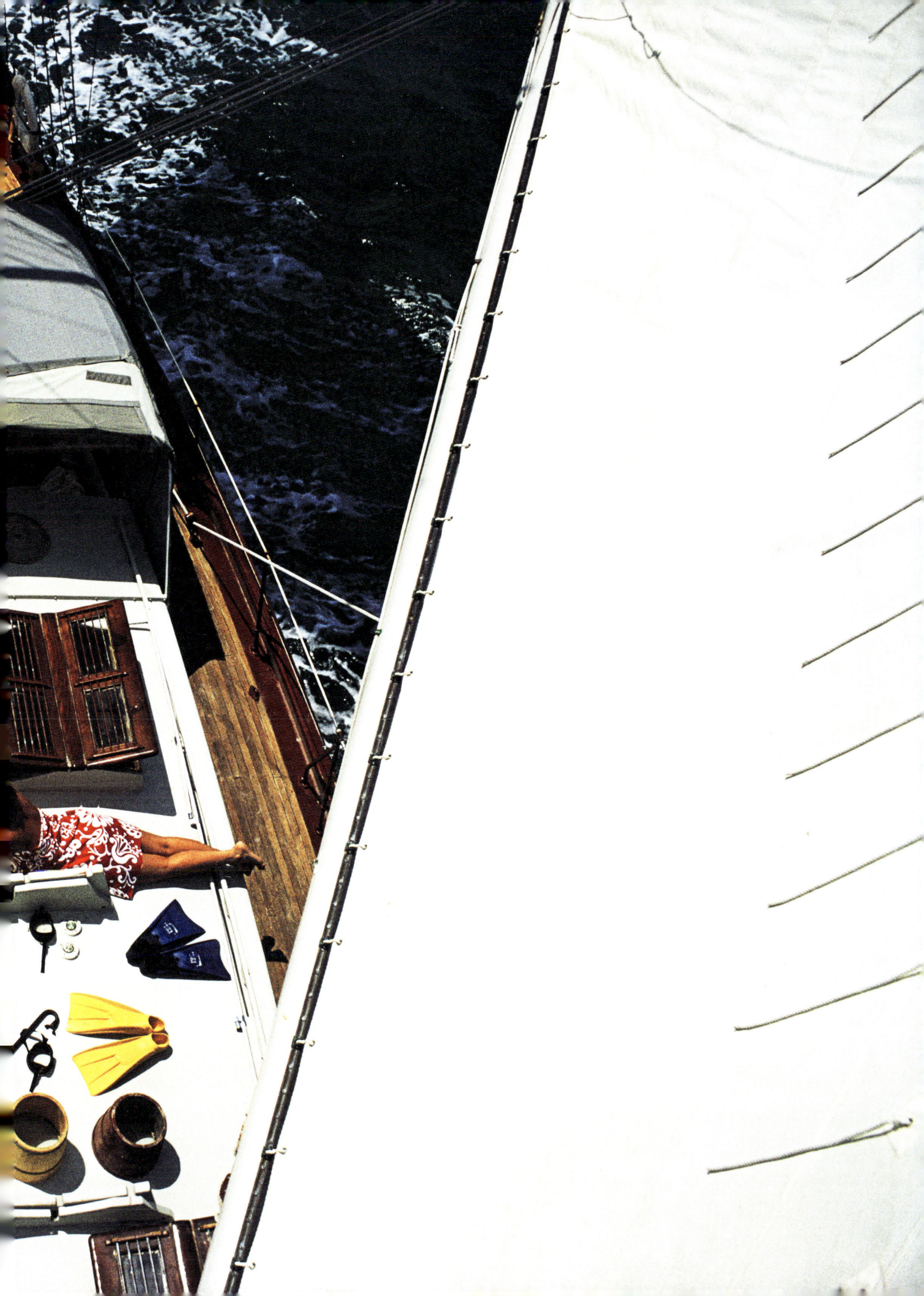

SPECIAL REGATTAS

America's Cup: Legendary editor Herbert Stone wrote eloquently in the 1930s: "The America's Cup is a synonym for things big and brave and famous." To that list I would add one more word: spectacular. For me, no sight is more beautiful than two America's Cup yachts racing bow-to-bow, sailing for glory and into our affections.

The America's Cup story began in 1851, with a race around the Isle of Wight off the south coast of England. The US schooner "America" defeated 18 British vessels to claim a gaudy ewer that the crew renamed "America's Cup" in honor of their yacht. Since then, the race has taken place 37 times, with the United States winning on 29 occasions. Being a member of a winning crew is a treasured feather in any sailor's cap, and victory earns the champion a lifetime of respect across the world.

The yachts taking part have changed dramatically over the years as advances in technology have allowed teams to increase their speeds dramatically. "America" sailed the 53-mile course around the Isle of Wight in 10 hours for a five-knot average. In 2024 foiling monohulls averaged well over 40 knots in the Cup races off Barcelona, Spain. But having studied every America's Cup race since 1851, I can say for certain that one thing hasn't changed: participants' sheer determination to win!

Offshore Races: It is a great accomplishment to complete a long-distance race. Sailors strive to be the first boat across the finish line, but victory is ultimately judged on "corrected time," which is based on a formula used to handicap yachts of different sizes and sailing characteristics. There is no perfect handicap rating rule, although with the advent of supercomputers the day might arrive when the sport will feature accurate and fair ratings on which everyone can agree. In the meantime, heated discussions and arguments regarding handicap fairness will doubtless continue.

Often the strength of the wind determines which vessel will prevail, with some offshore races plagued by frustratingly calm winds and others battered by horrific storms. But that's a tale as old as time: sailors have always journeyed into the unknown, and the greatest are those prepared for every weather condition and able to thrive on the challenge.

The Fastnet Race: The Fastnet Race has been sailed every two years going back to 1925, and is so popular that the nearly 500 places are taken only a few minutes after booking begins. The race takes the fleet from the Solent (the passage between the south coast of England and the Isle of Wight), across the Irish Sea and around Fastnet Lighthouse Rock, about 8 miles off the coast of Ireland. Historically the race finished in Plymouth, England, but more recently has concluded in Cherbourg, France.

In 1979 a violent storm battered the fleet, and only 87 of the 303 yachts that started the race reached the finish line. Sadly, 15 lives were lost, and 23 yachts either sank or were abandoned. (Media mogul Ted Turner won the grueling race aboard the 61-foot "Tenacious," designed by Sparkman & Stephens.) To this day the 1979 Fastnet Race is known as "the roughest ocean race on record." But the calamity inspired a renewed focus on safety, and stringent new regulations that have made the sport safer.

Newport to Bermuda Race: The first Bermuda Race began in New York in 1906, an event created by editor Thomas Fleming Day to prove that small yachts could race in the ocean. Tom Day won on the 38-foot "Tamerlane," but a notable feature of the race (for the time) was that the crew of a 28-foot vessel named "Gauntlet" included a woman, 20-year-old Thora Lund Robinson. The modern-day racecourse is 635 miles in length, and the current record is held by Jason Carroll, who made passage on his 70-foot trimaran in 33 hours and 9 seconds. Whether they win or lose, however, arriving at the island paradise of Bermuda is a reward every sailor cherishes.

Sydney to Hobart Race: The Cruising Yacht Club established this 630-mile ocean race in 1945, immediately after the end of World War II. The event starts on Boxing Day in Sydney Harbor, where many thousands of spectators line the shore as the fleet races out. The atmosphere is festive—but things don't always go smoothly. Competitors are often challenged by "southern buster" winds that blow in hard from Antarctica, and in 1998 a particularly powerful storm wreaked havoc: only 44 of the 115 yachts that left Sydney managed to reach Hobart, a total of five yachts sank, and six lives were lost. But Sydney Fisher, who raced in both the 1998 Hobart Race and the 1979 Fastnet, made it clear even this tragedy could have been worse. When asked how the two calamitous races compared, his answer was succinct: "The Fastnet was a tougher clap."

The Olympic Games: Sailing has been part of the Olympic Games since they restarted in 1896, though there have been some exceptions: in the first games strong Meltemi winds in the Aegean forced the organizers to cancel the final day of racing, and in 1904 the Games were held in landlocked St. Louis, Missouri, where the organizing committee was unable to find a suitable lake. But otherwise sailing has thrived at the Games, with sailors training for years beforehand to reach their peak at precisely the time of the event. At the 2024 Paris Olympics a historic sailing landmark was reached: the competitors comprised 165 men and 165 women, meaning that gender equity was achieved for the first time.

THE SAILING LIFESTYLE

Sailing adventures can range from a single-day sail to a three-year voyage around the world, and I myself have organized expeditions to some of the world's most remote regions. My list includes cruises down the Antarctic Peninsula, a navigation of the Beagle Channel, a rounding of Cape Horn, an exploration of the Svalbard Island group, a trip to Sable Island off the coast of Nova Scotia (known as the Graveyard of the Atlantic), a Transatlantic crossing on a tall ship, and the filming of five round the world races. In addition, I've cruised throughout the Caribbean, the coast of Maine, the Bay of Fundy, the well-named Desolation Sound in British Columbia, and throughout Scandinavia and the Philippines. Such trips require an extraordinary amount of preparation, but the opportunity to see remote areas, meet Indigenous peoples, and gain an understanding of different cultures provide ample incentives.

Opposite: *Spinnaker flying on the Costa Smeralda, Sardinia, August 1973.*

Following pages: *Princess Laudomia Hercolani and Prince Andrea Hercolani relaxing on deck on a cruise around the Aeolian Islands, 1954.*

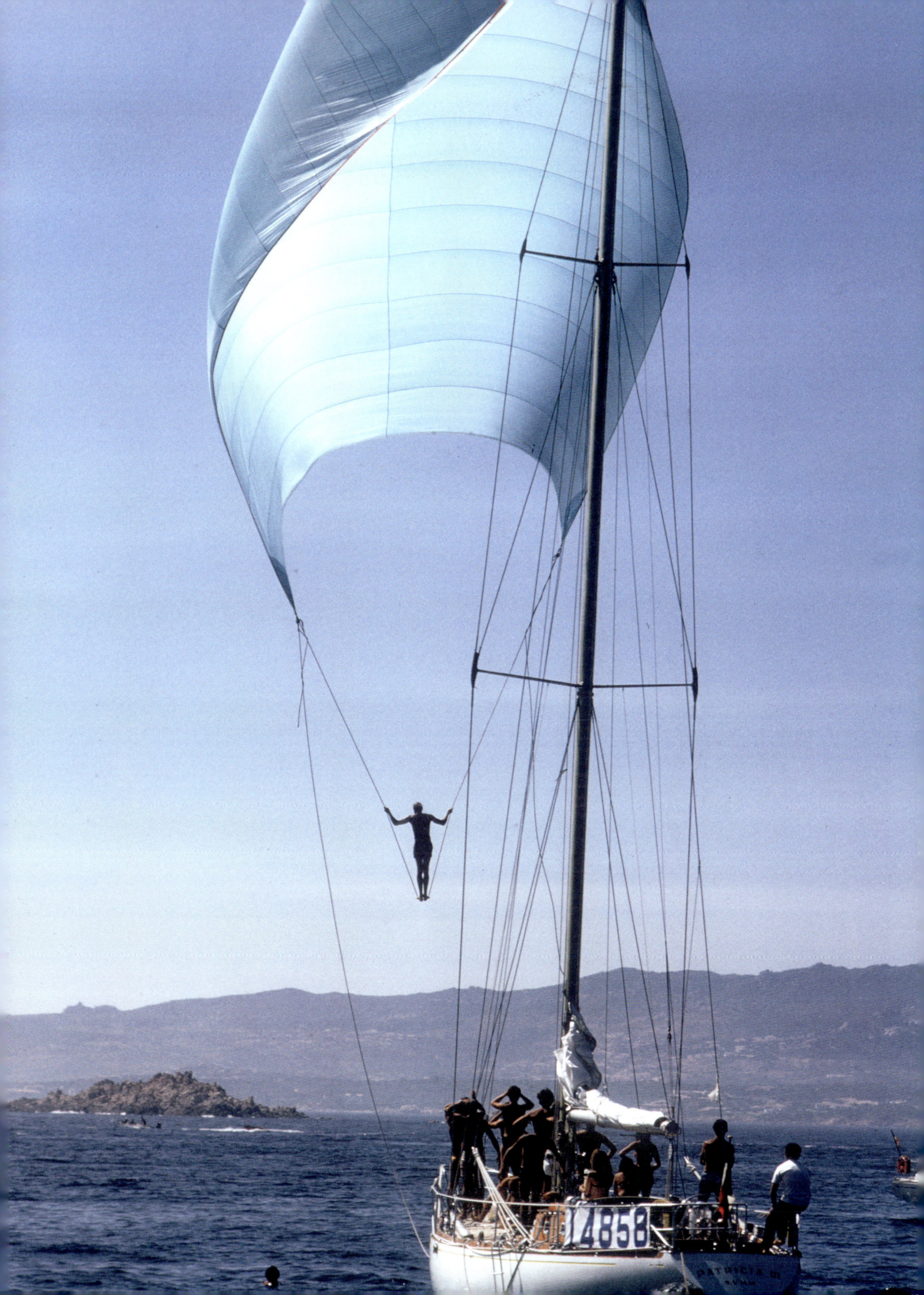
14858

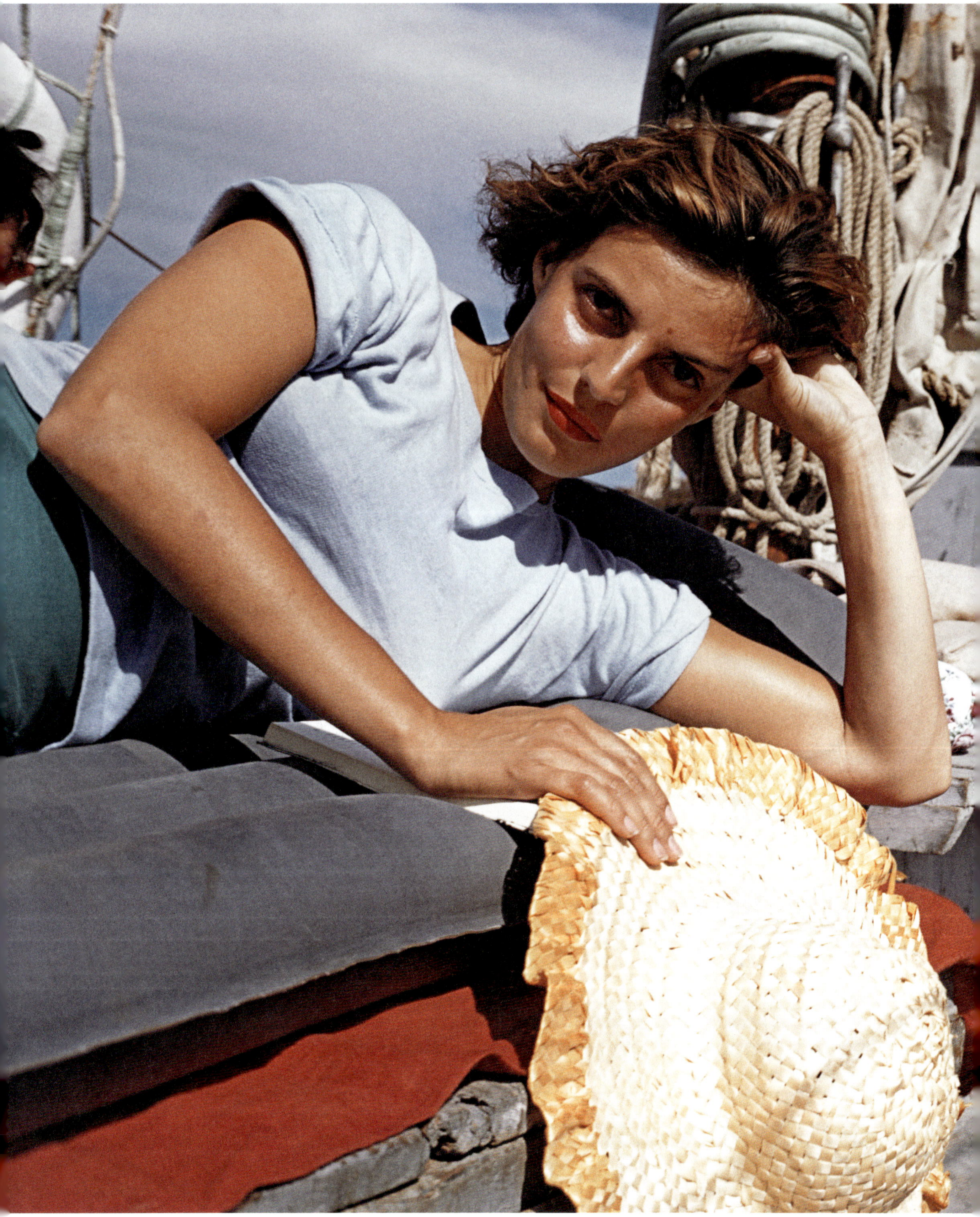

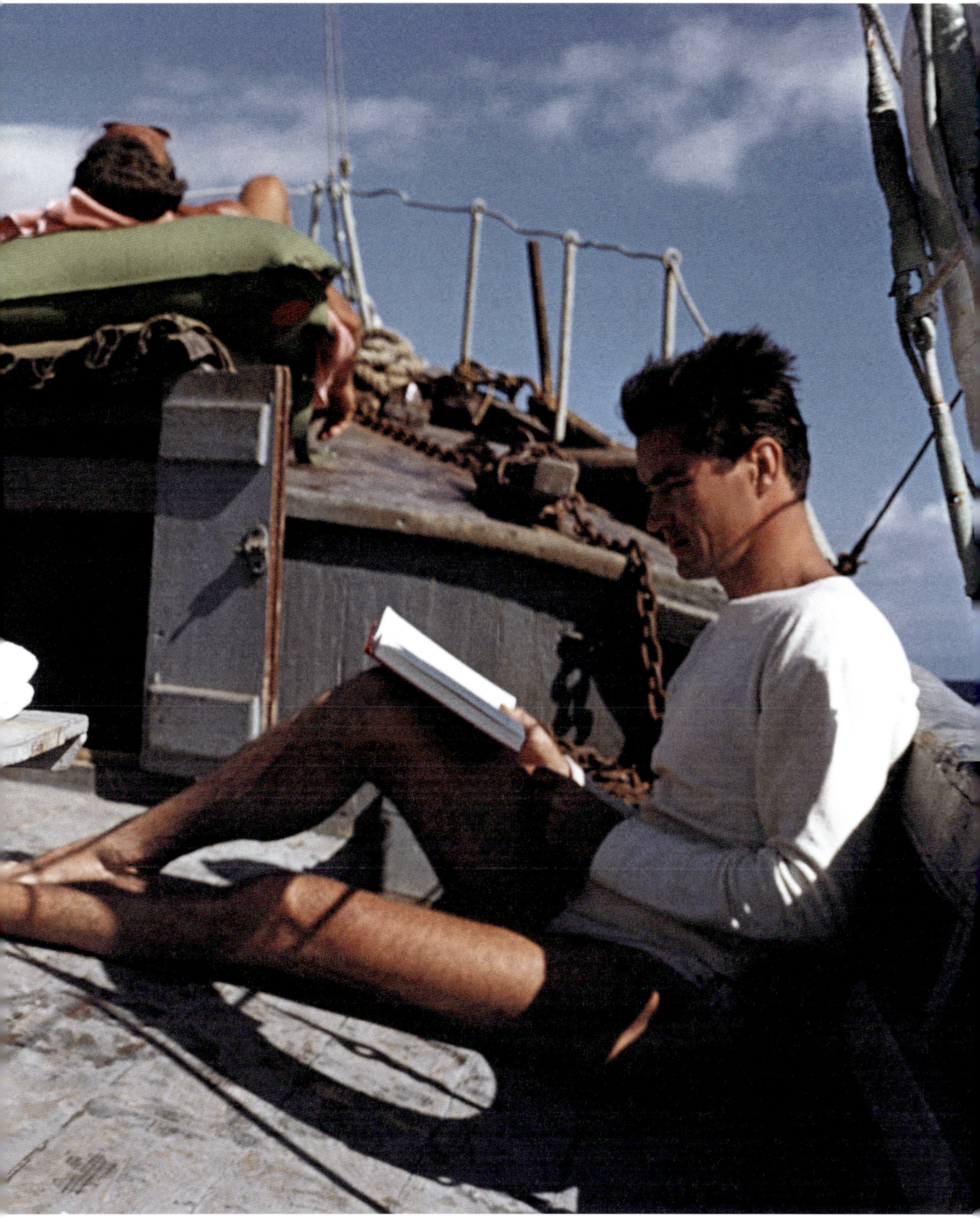

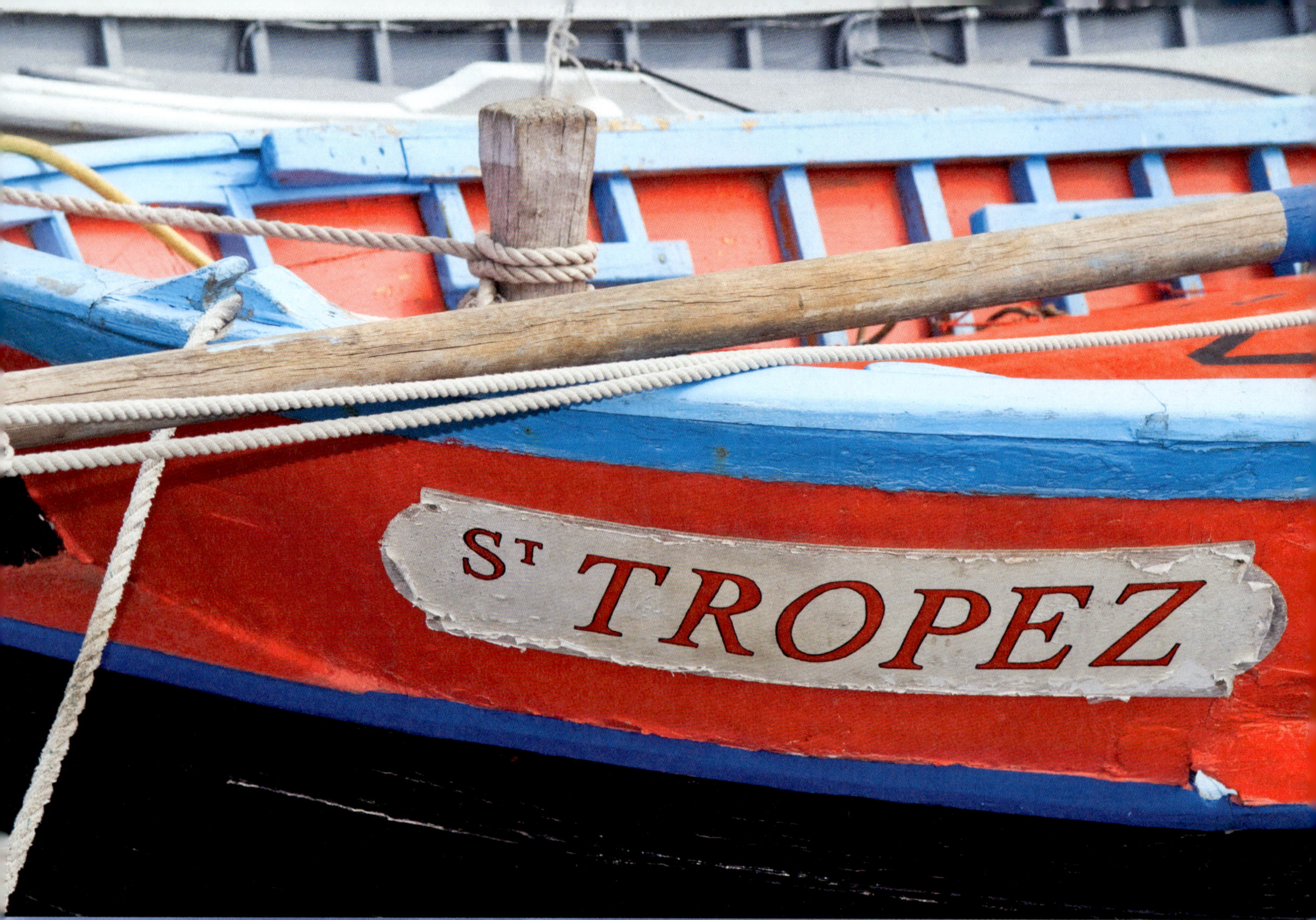
ST TROPEZ

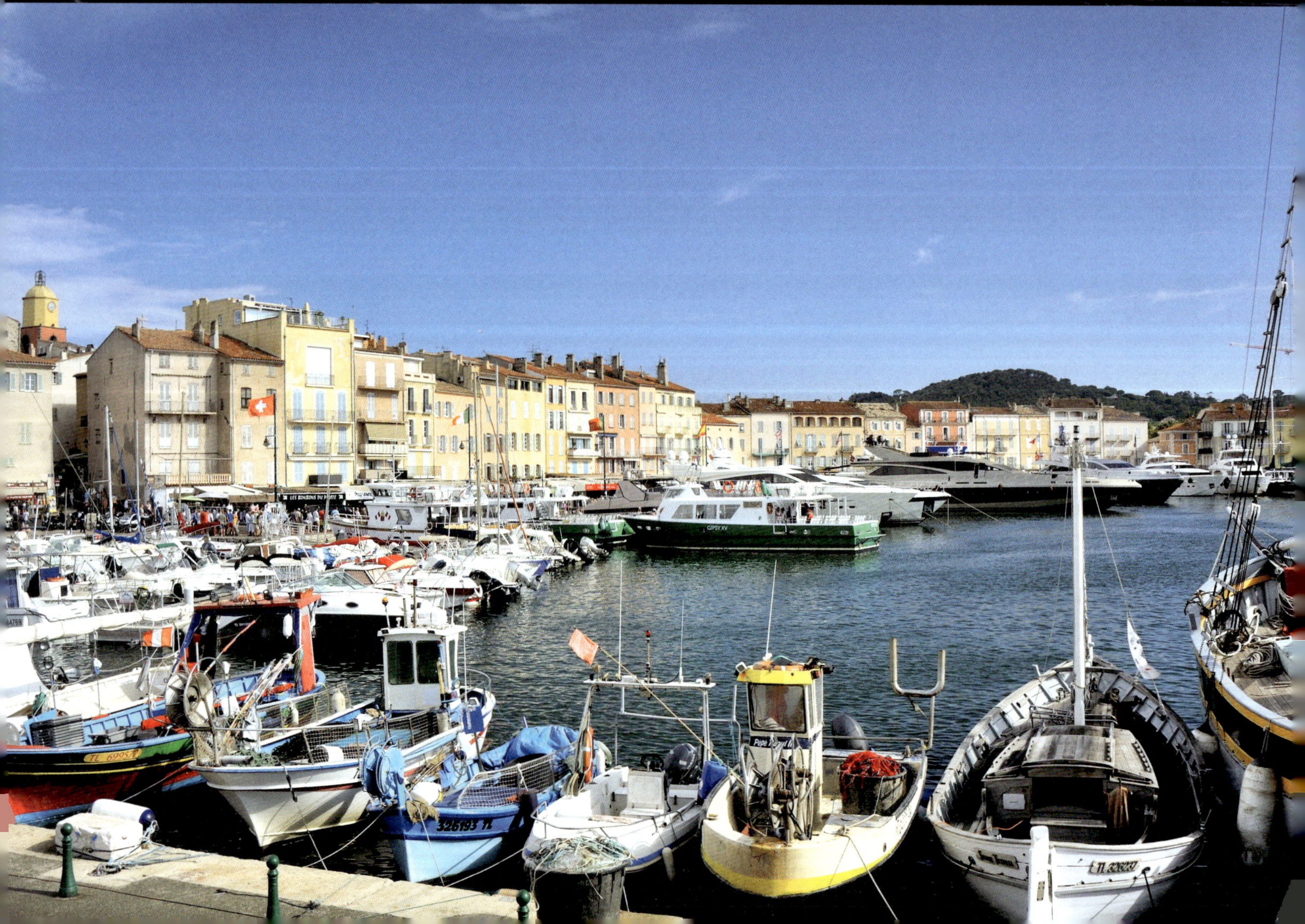

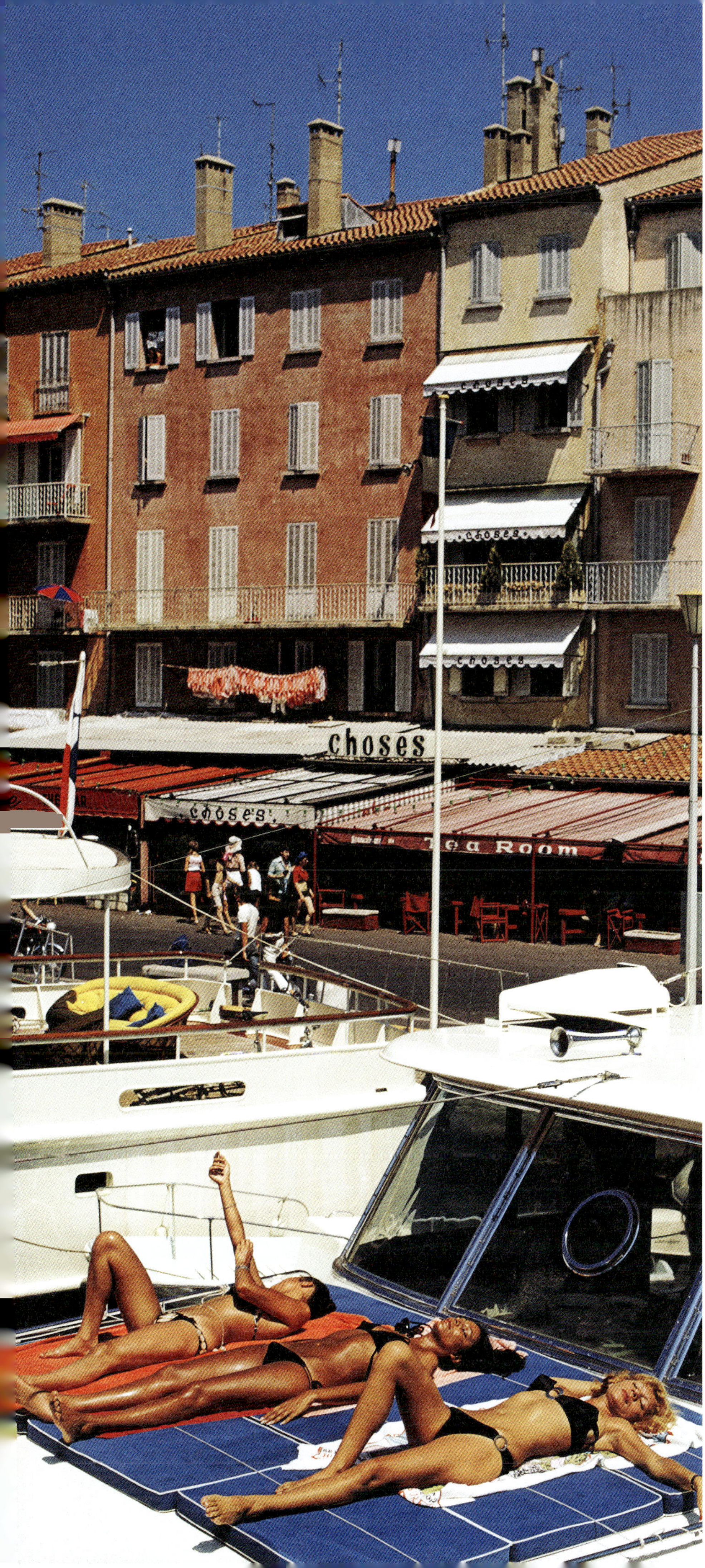

Opposite, top: *A colorful wooden sailboat in the harbor at Saint-Tropez.*

Opposite, bottom: *The harbor of Saint-Tropez.*

This page: *Holidaymakers lounging on the deck of their luxury yacht in Saint-Tropez, August 1971.*

Following pages: *Baroness Giovanna Borghese in Porto Ercole harbour, Tuscany, August 1969.*

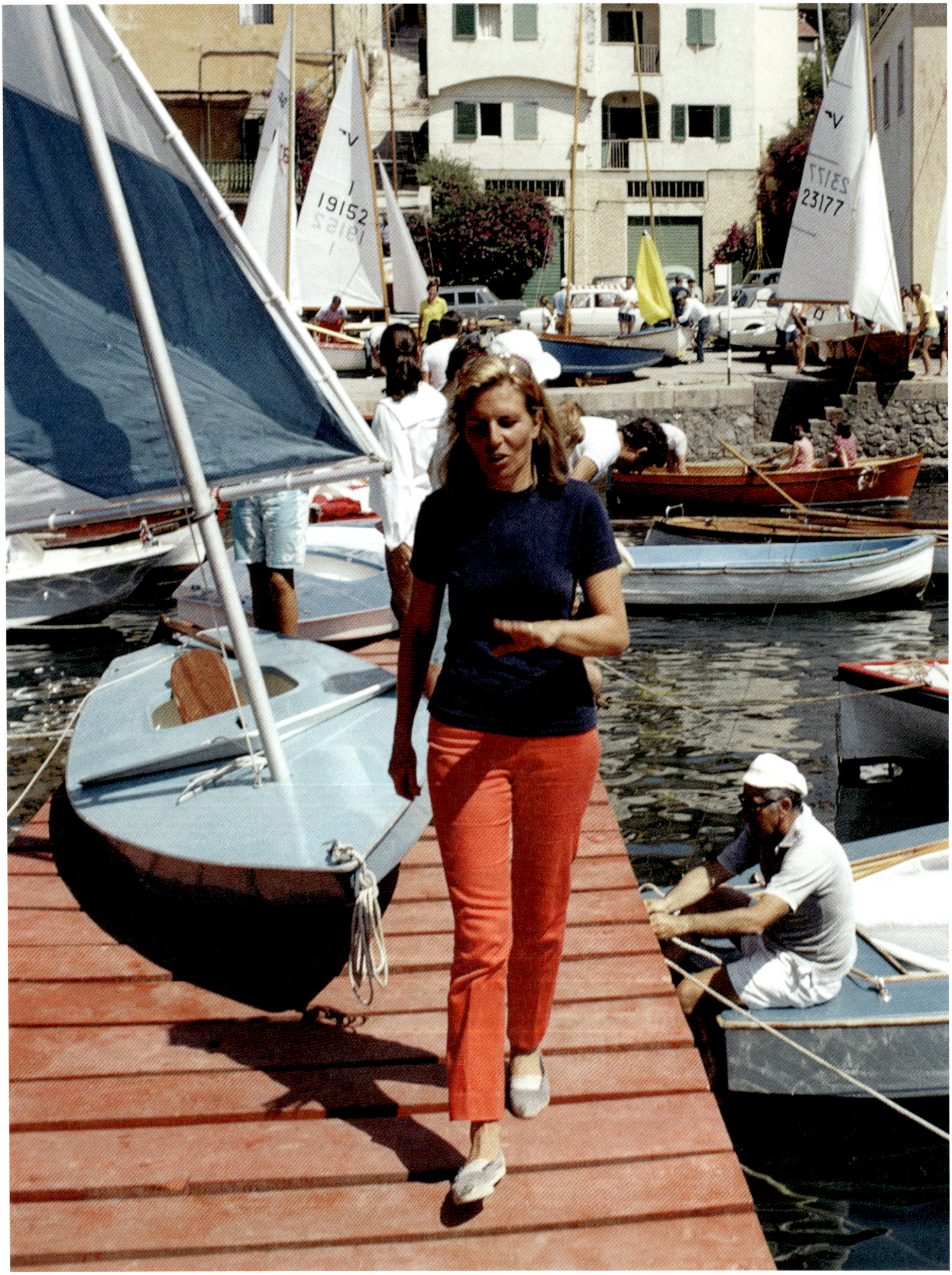
19152
23177

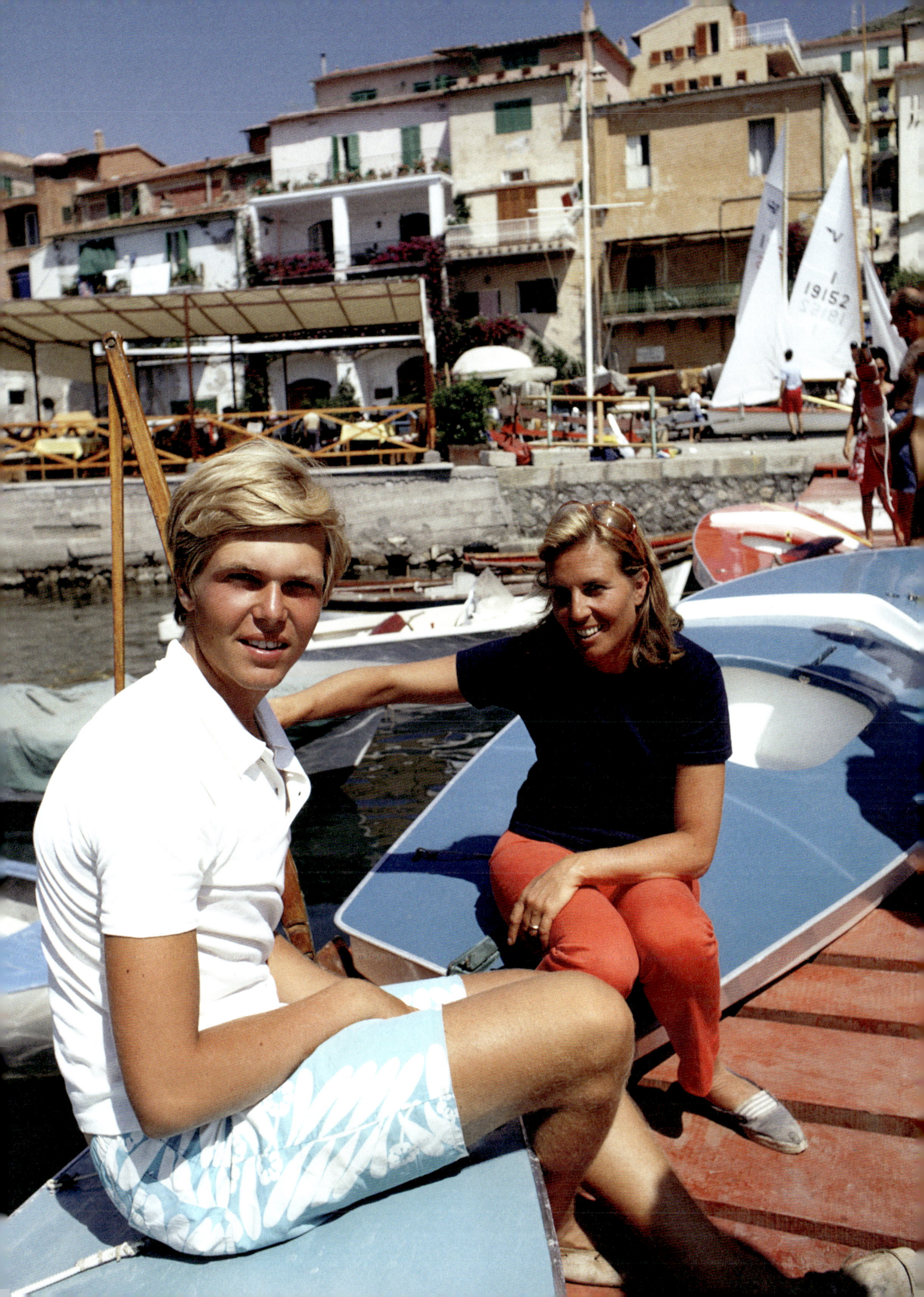
19152

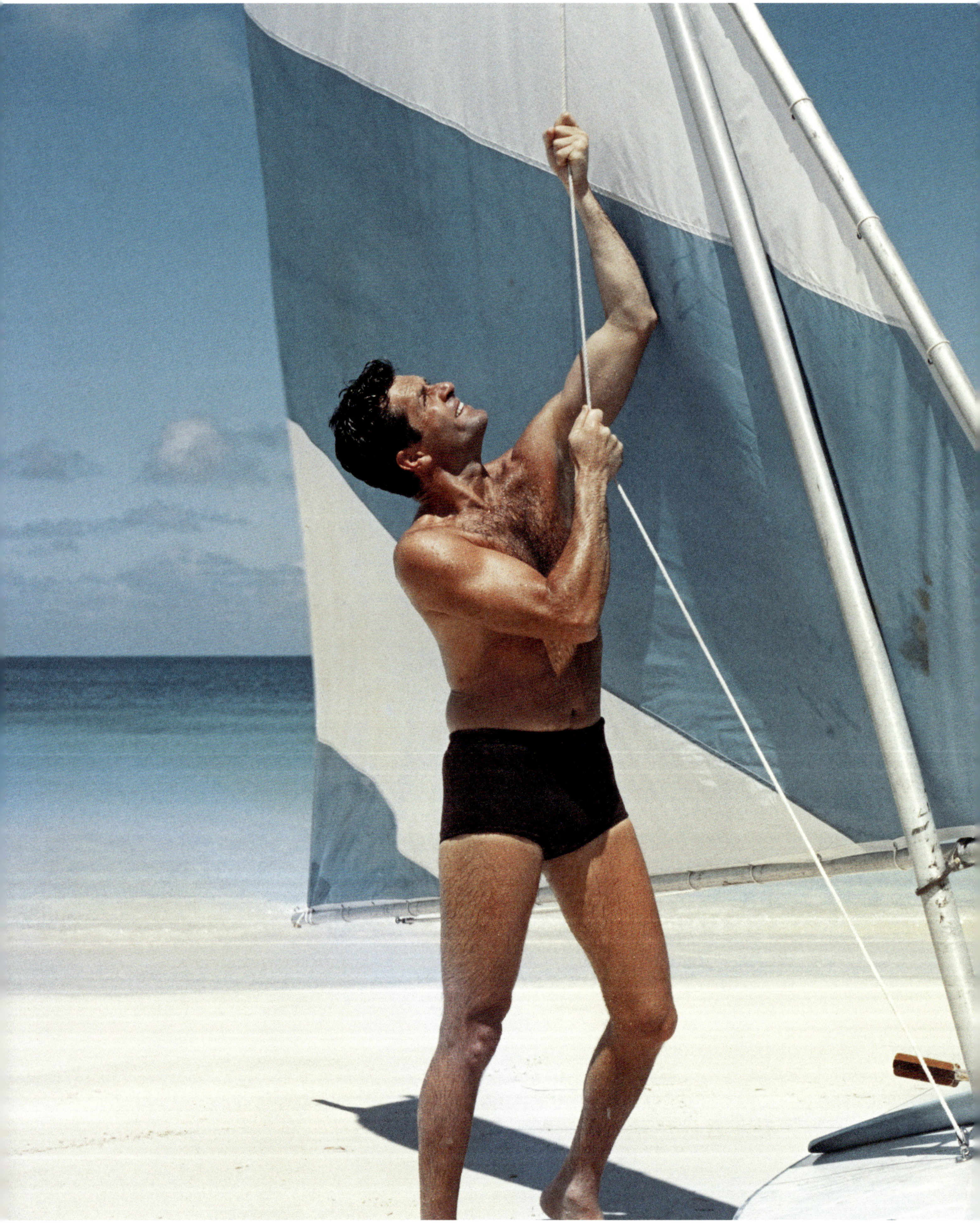

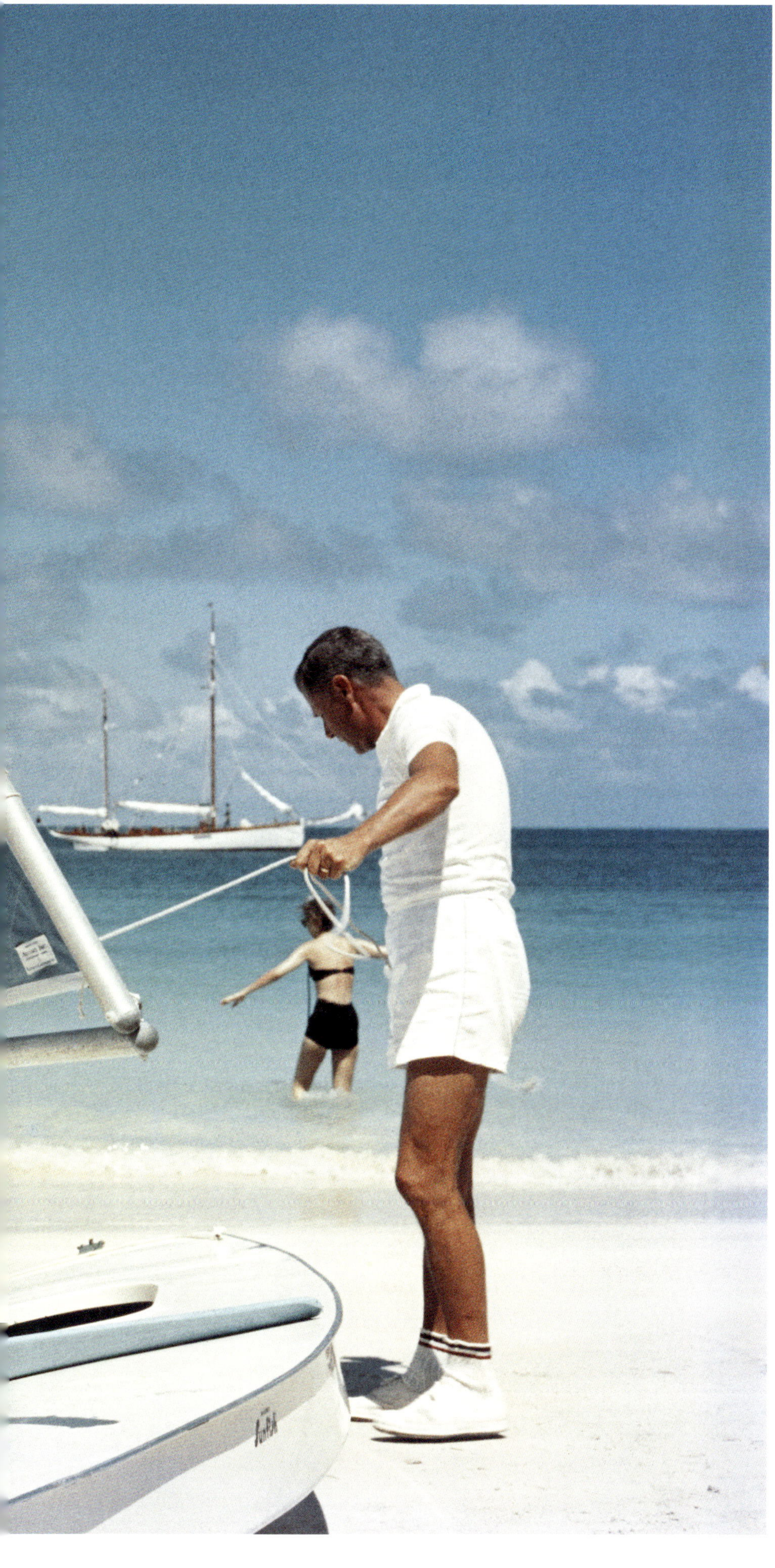

These pages: *American actor Hugh O'Brian (left) hoists the sail on a dinghy in Antigua in the West Indies, 1960.*

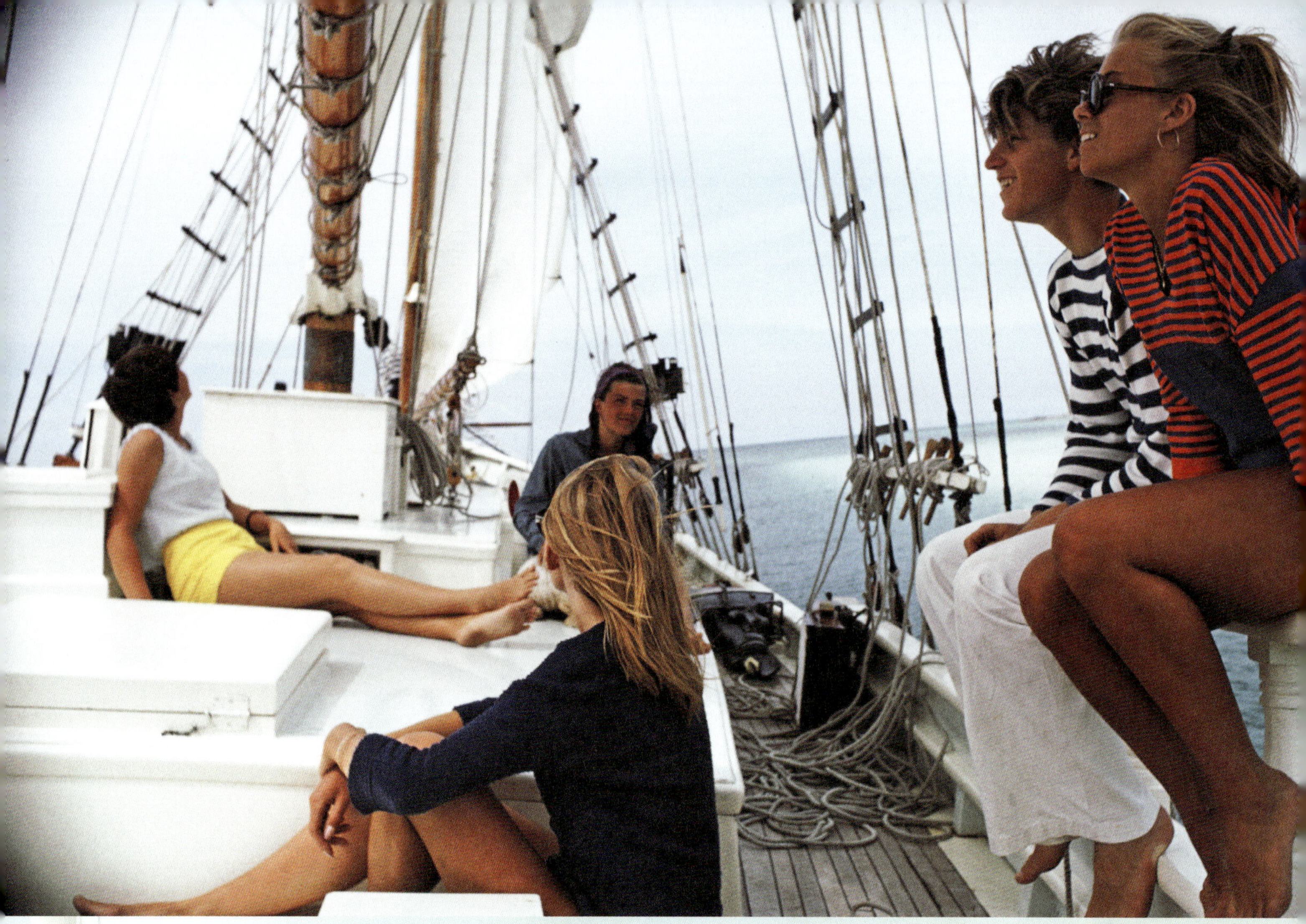

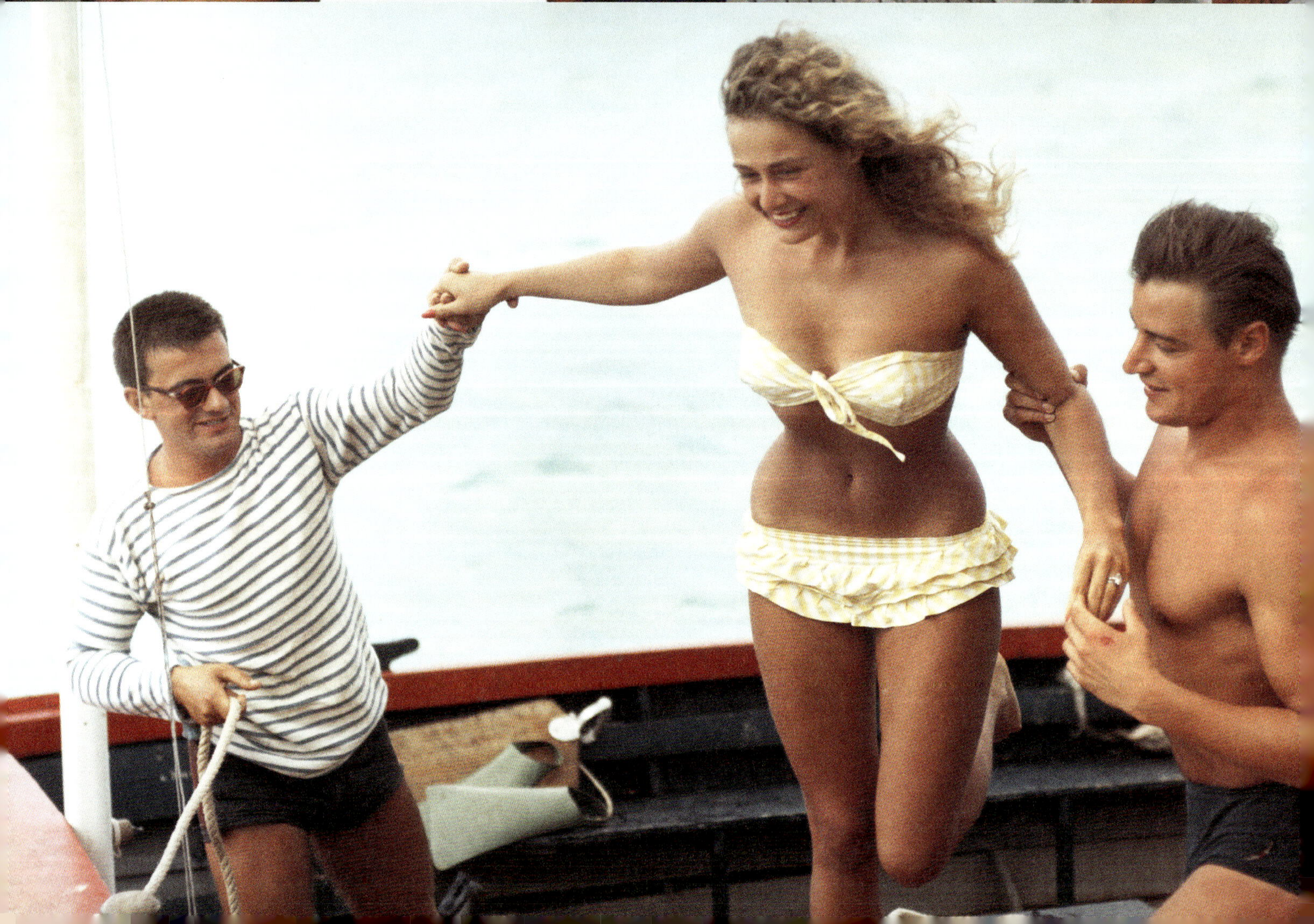

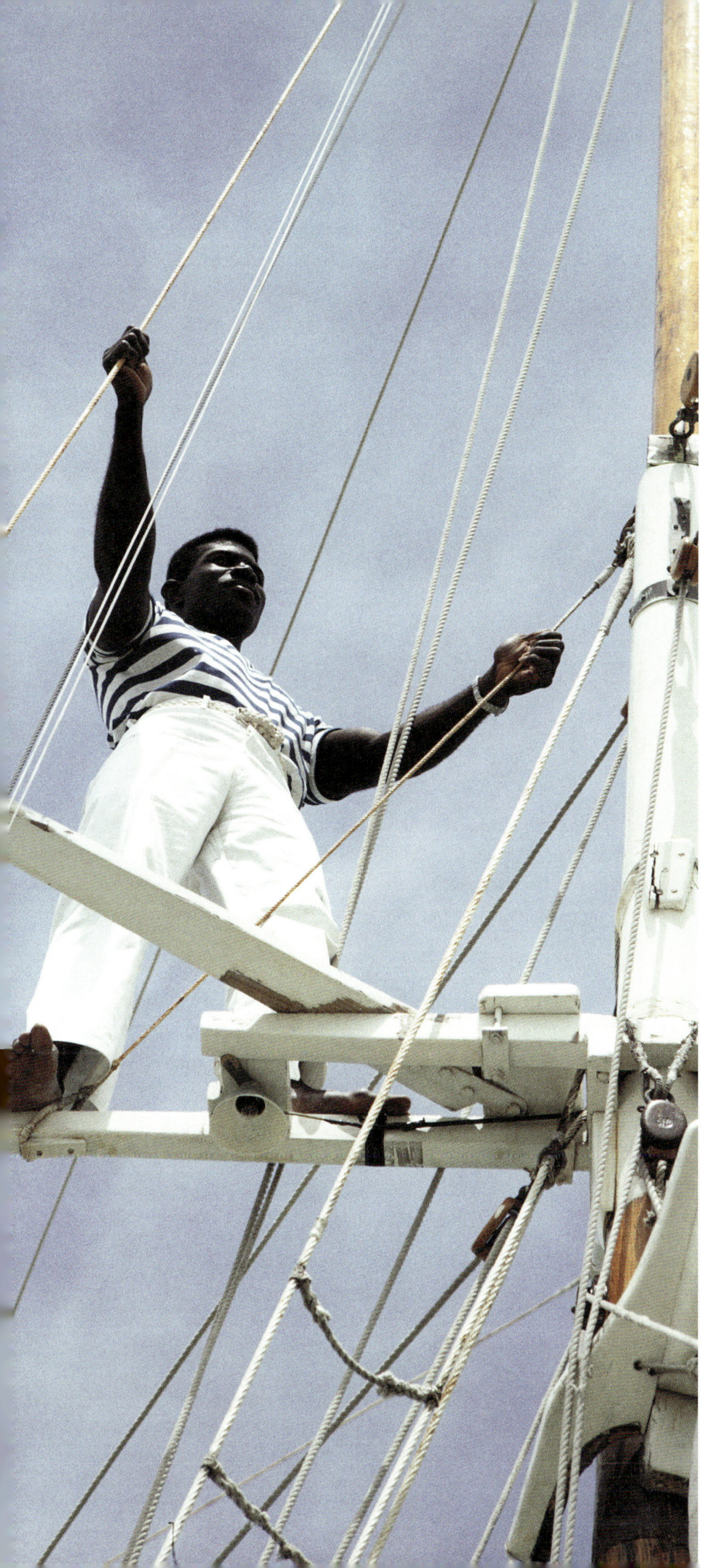

Opposite, top: *A group of friends enjoy a day sailing in Lyford Cay in the Bahamas, April 1966.*

Opposite, bottom: *Two men assist a woman disembarking from a fishing boat on Andros Island in the Bahamas, 1957.*

This page: *A crewmember tends to the rigging on a yacht in Lyford Cay in the Bahamas, April 1966.*

Page 48: *A high-angle view of a formation of sailing boats in the Bahamas, 1964.*

Page 49: *Yachts in a marina in Freeport in the Bahamas, April 1969. The Soling Class was selected for Olympic competition beginning in 1972.*

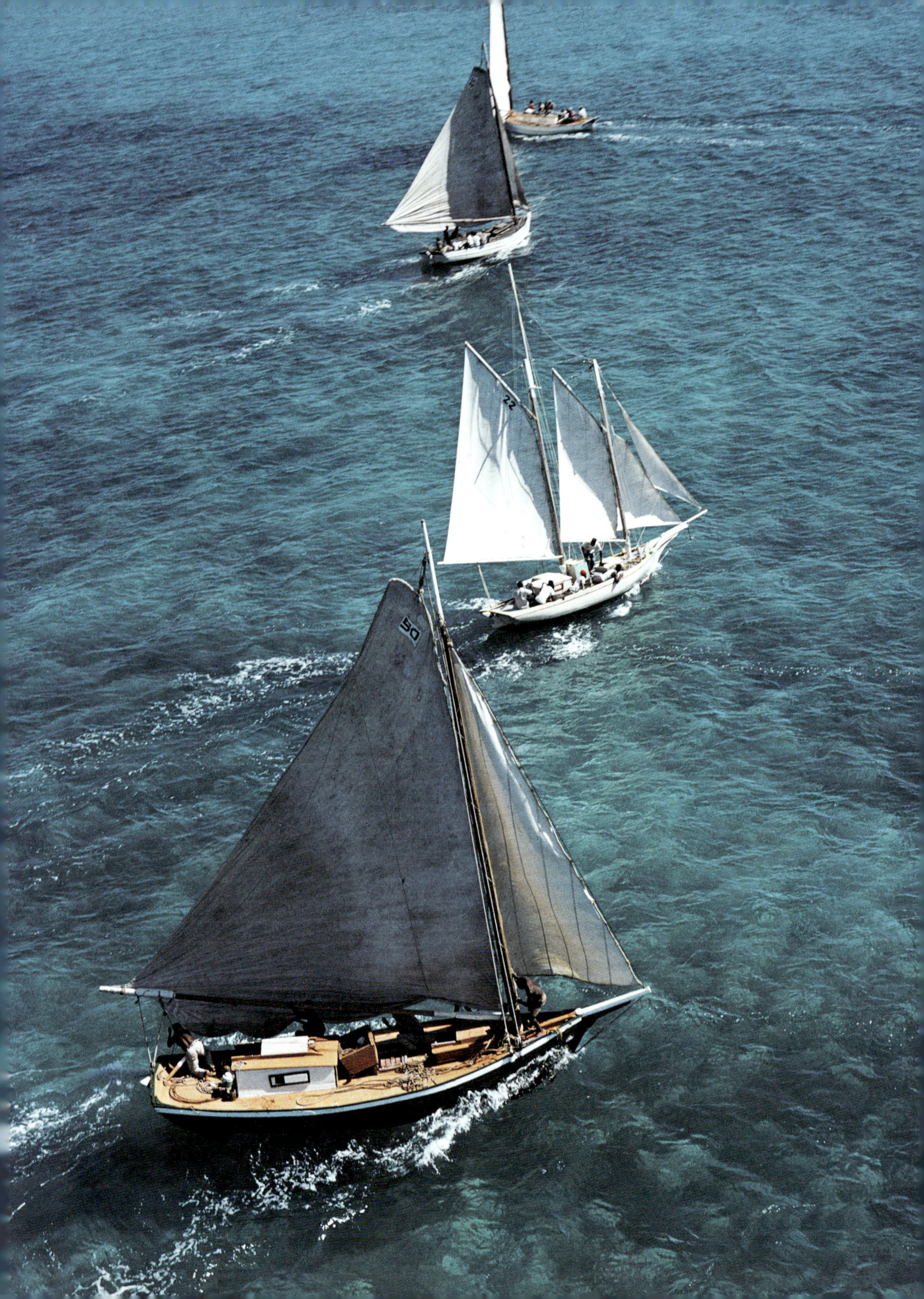
22
50

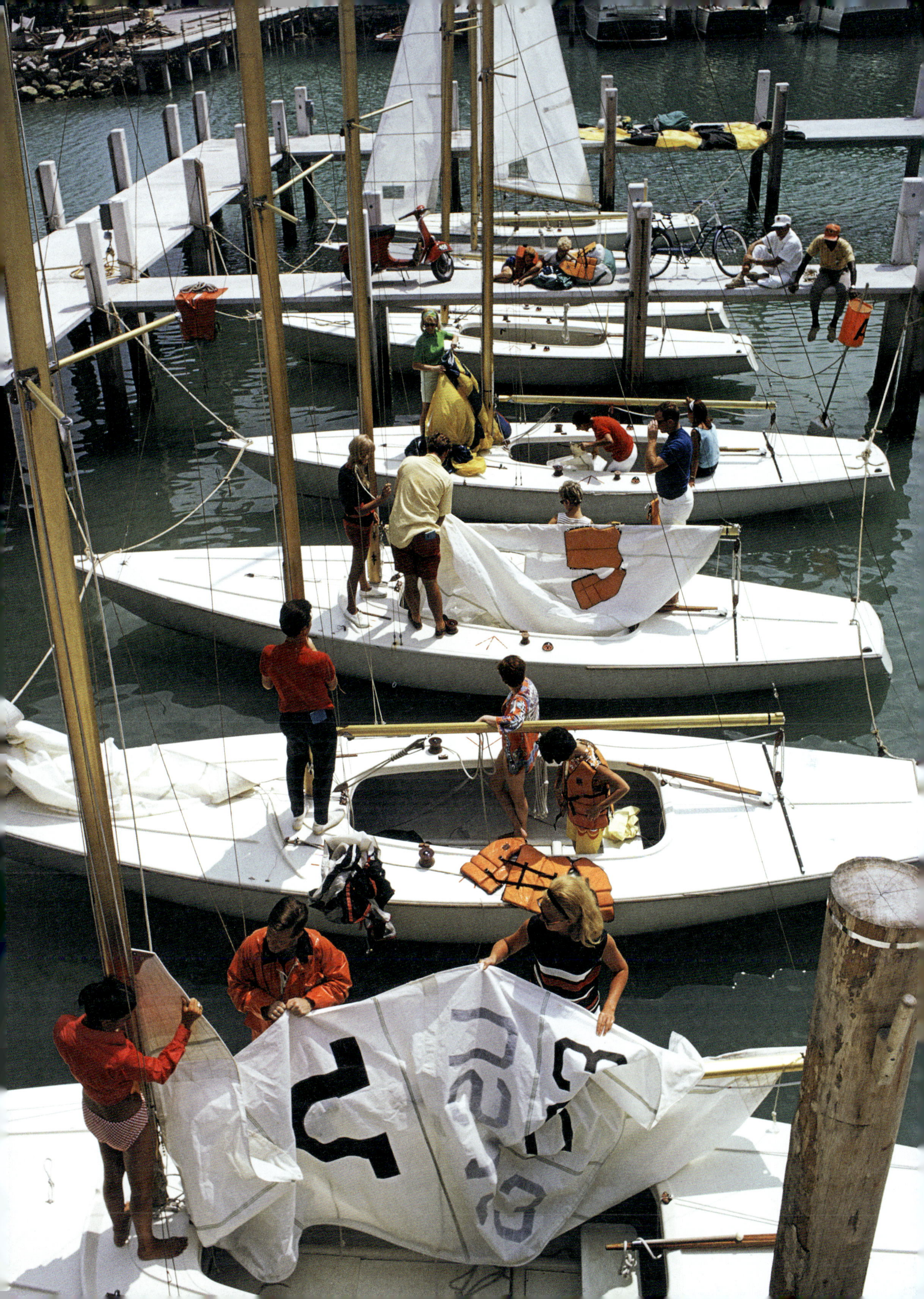

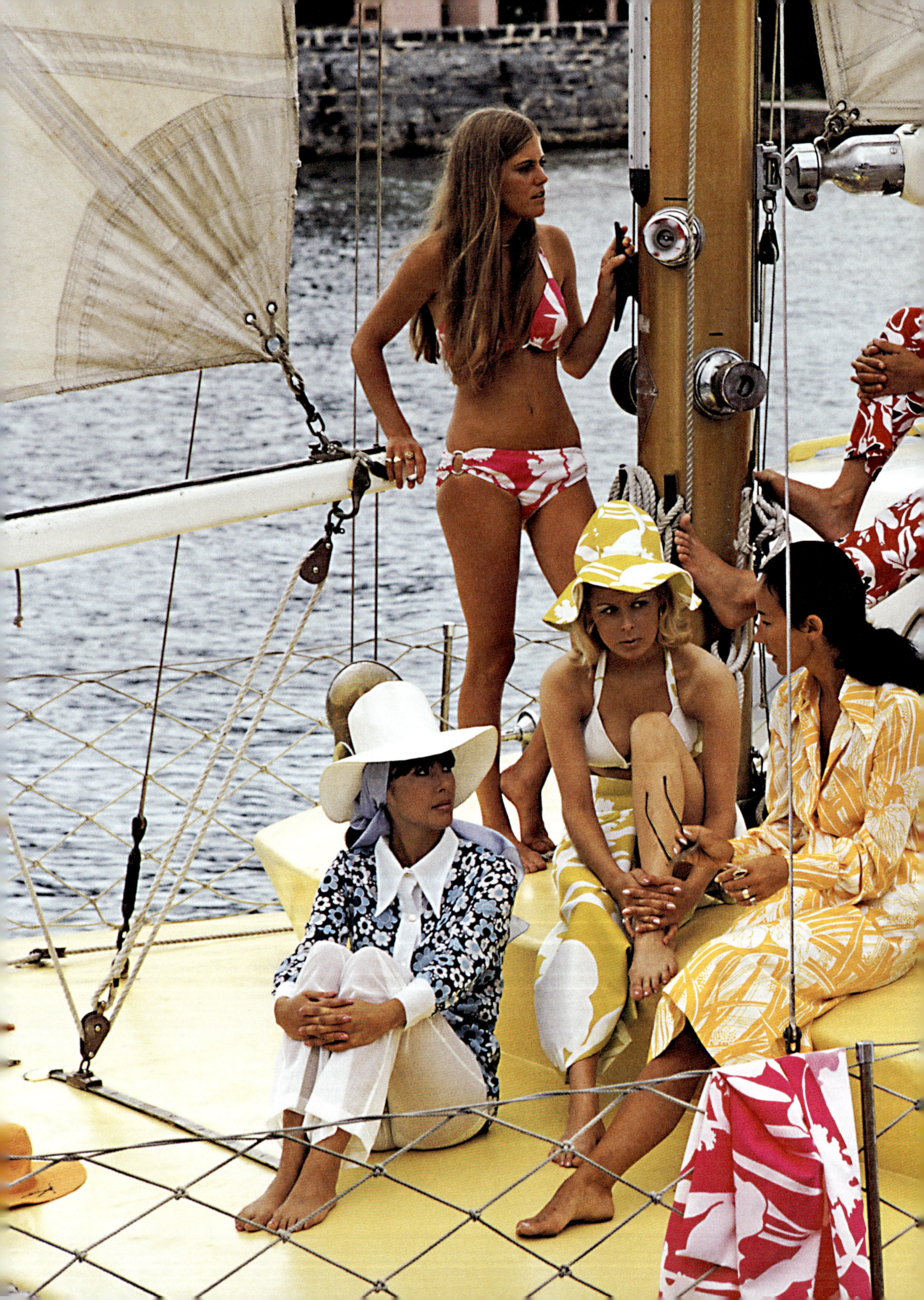

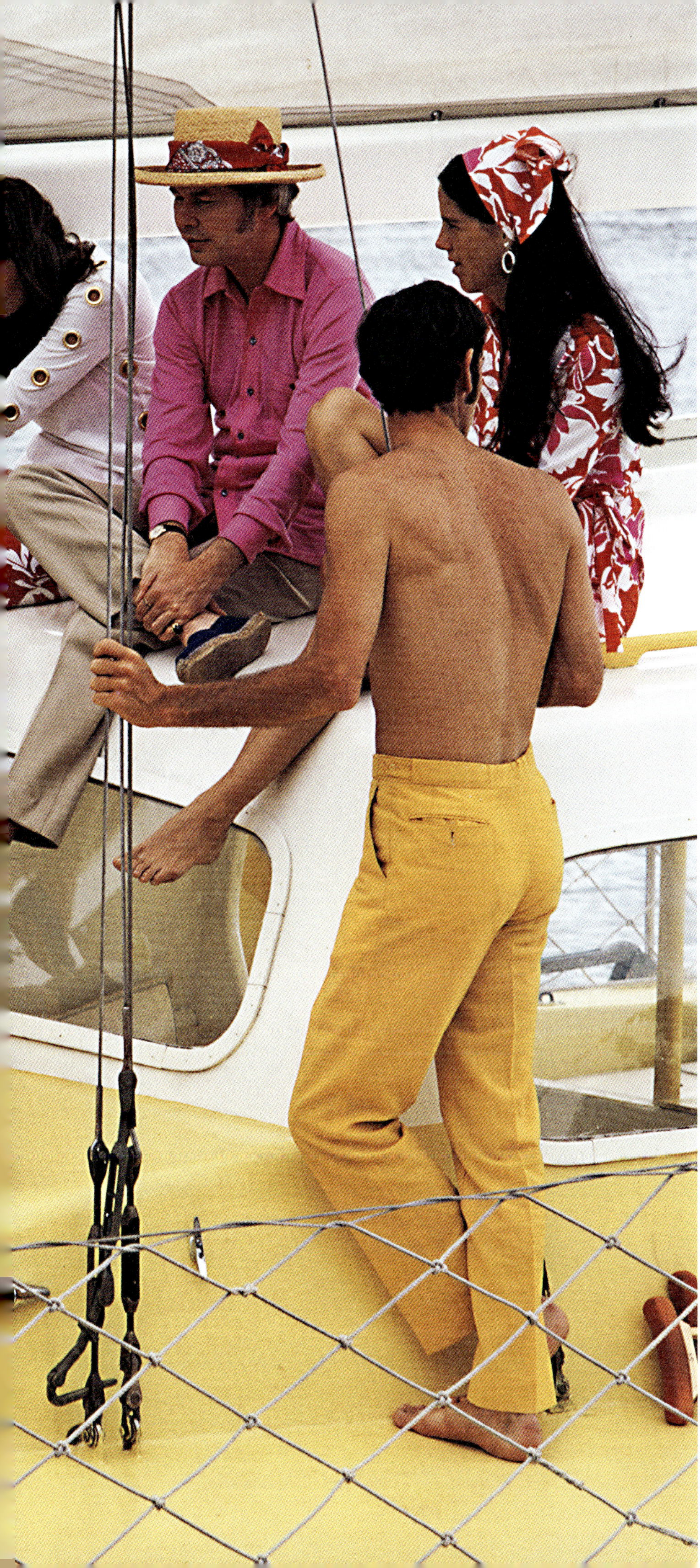

These pages: *A group on a yacht in Bermuda, June 1970.*

Page 52, top: *Lili Livi on Lake Como, Italy, 1955.*

Page 52, bottom: *The Castello di Paraggi near Portofino, Italy, August 1977.*

Page 53: *Tom Callinan holidays with family and friends on a yacht off the Amalfi coast, Italy, August 1984.*

Page 54: *Texas oil heiress Mrs. Blaffer Hudson at the wheel of Walter Gubelmann's yacht "Windago" in Newport, Rhode Island, 1965.*

Page 55: *Drena Van Alen aboard Walter Gubelmanns yacht "Windago" in Newport, Rhode Island, 1965.*

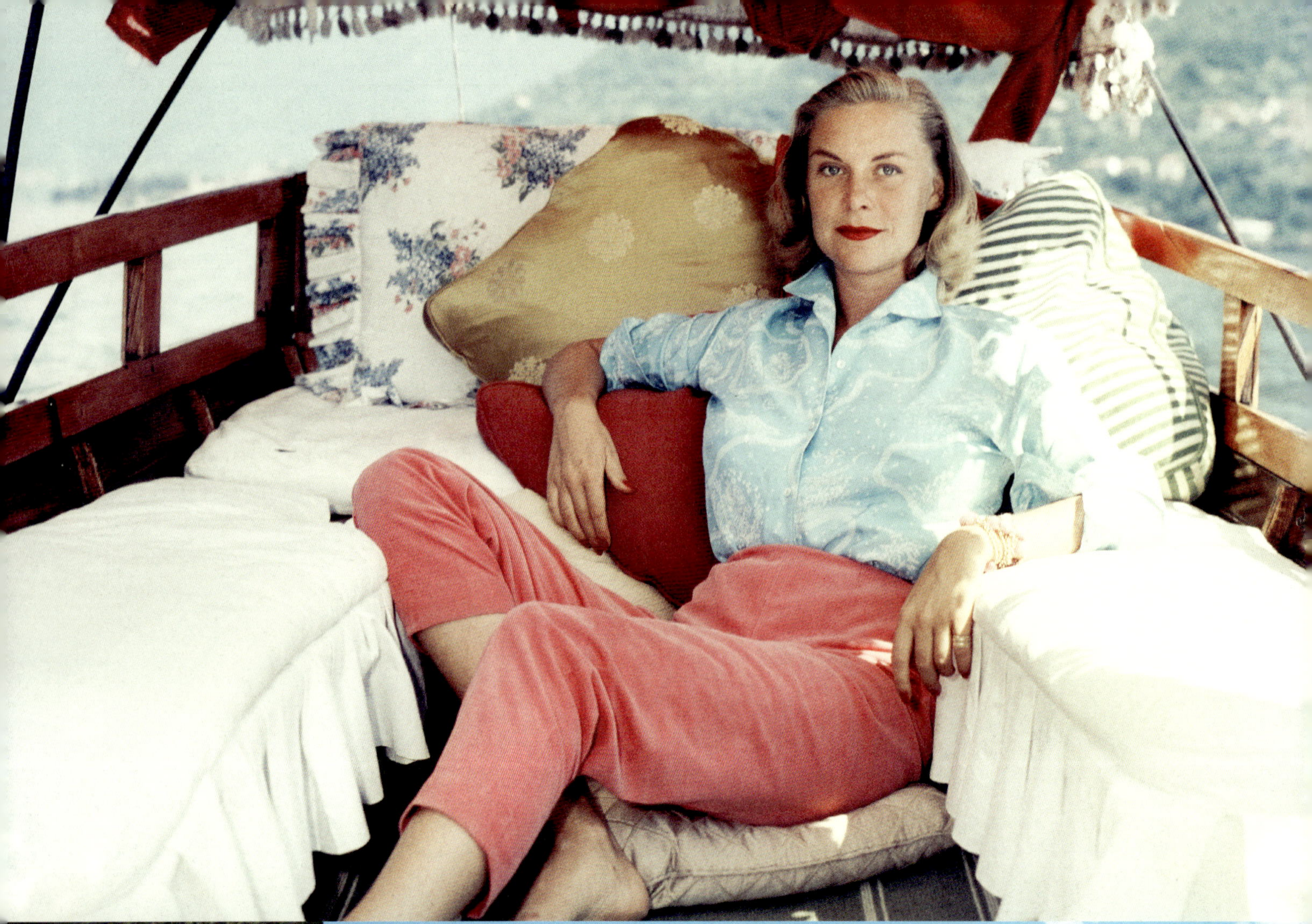

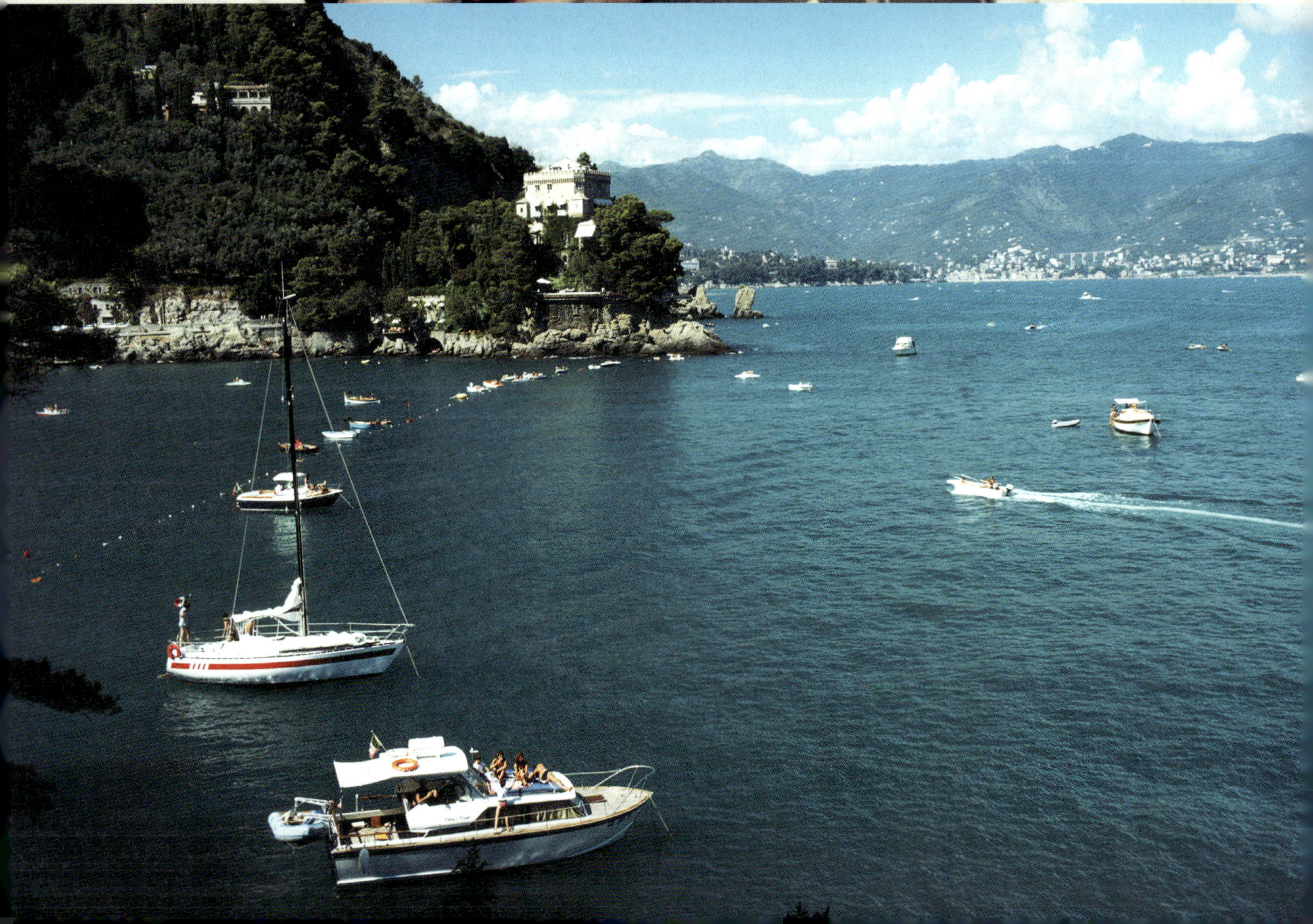

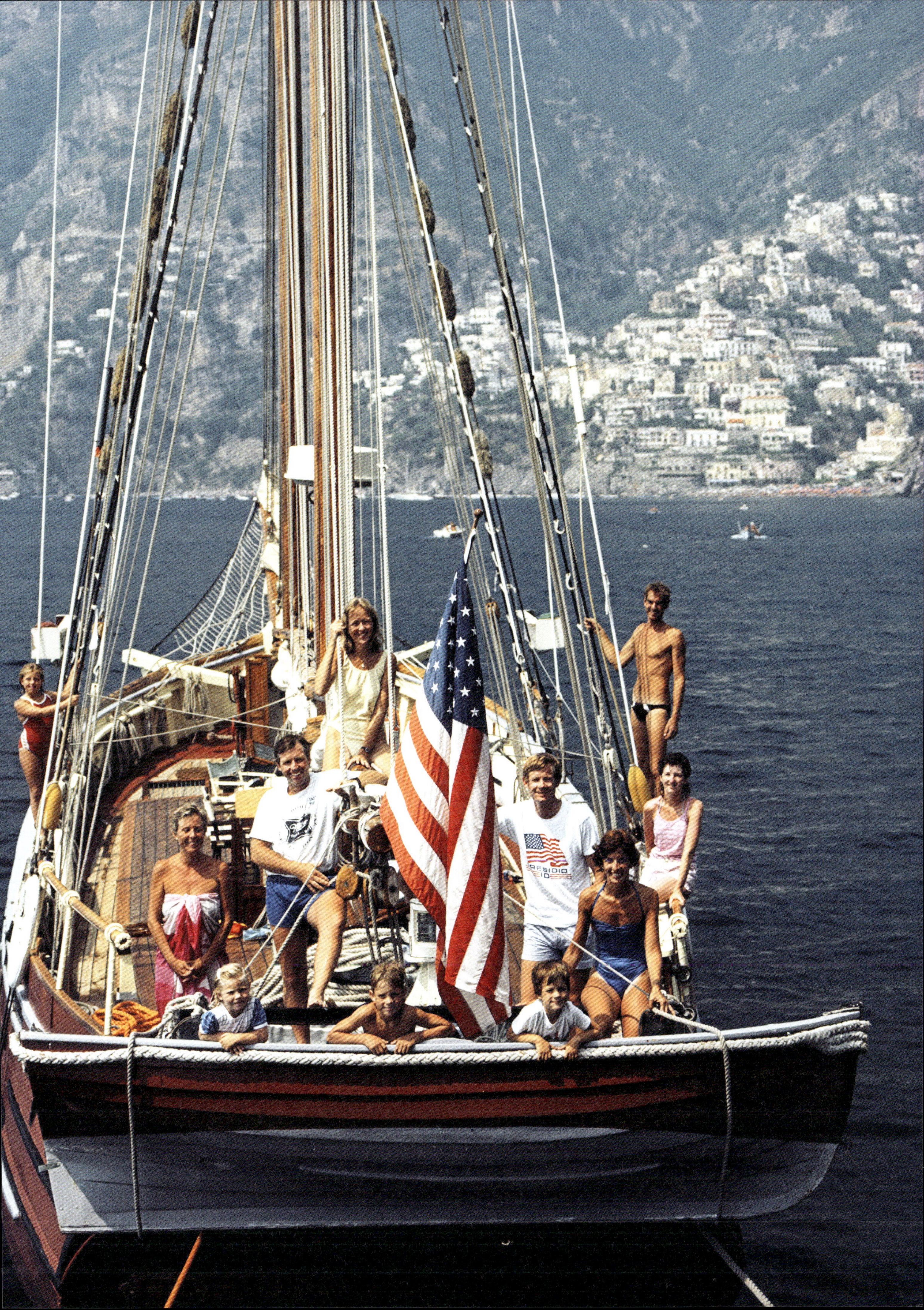

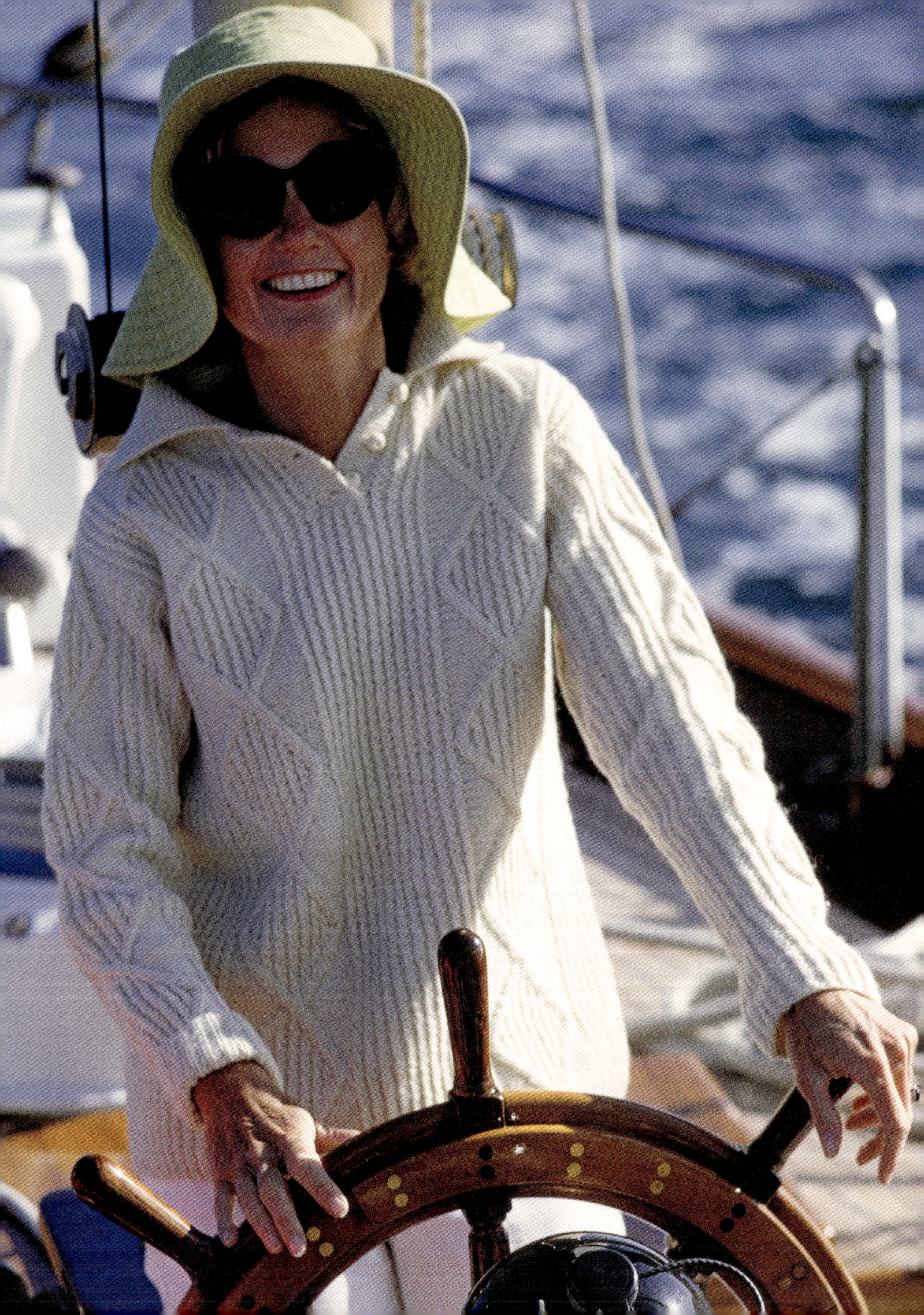

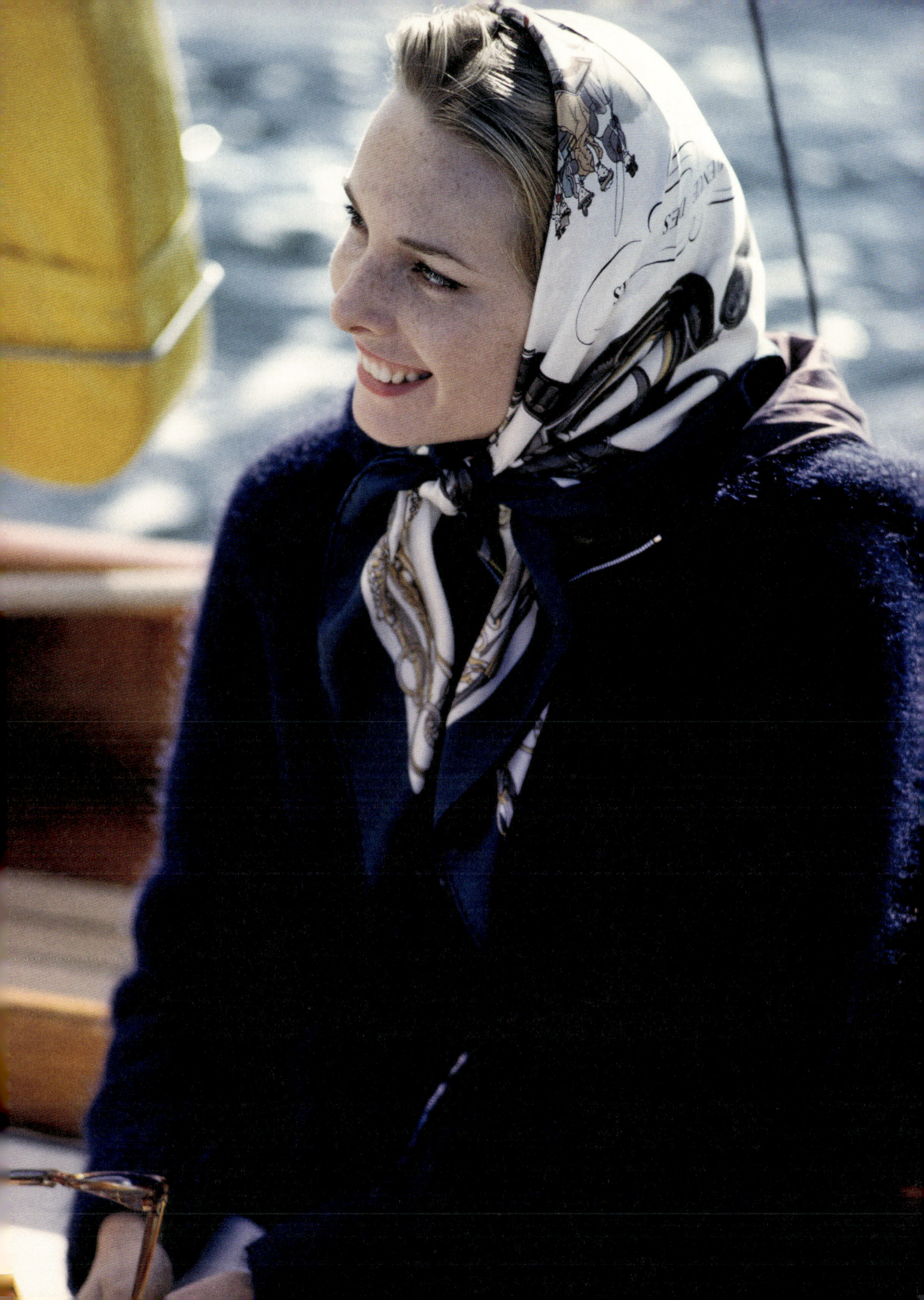

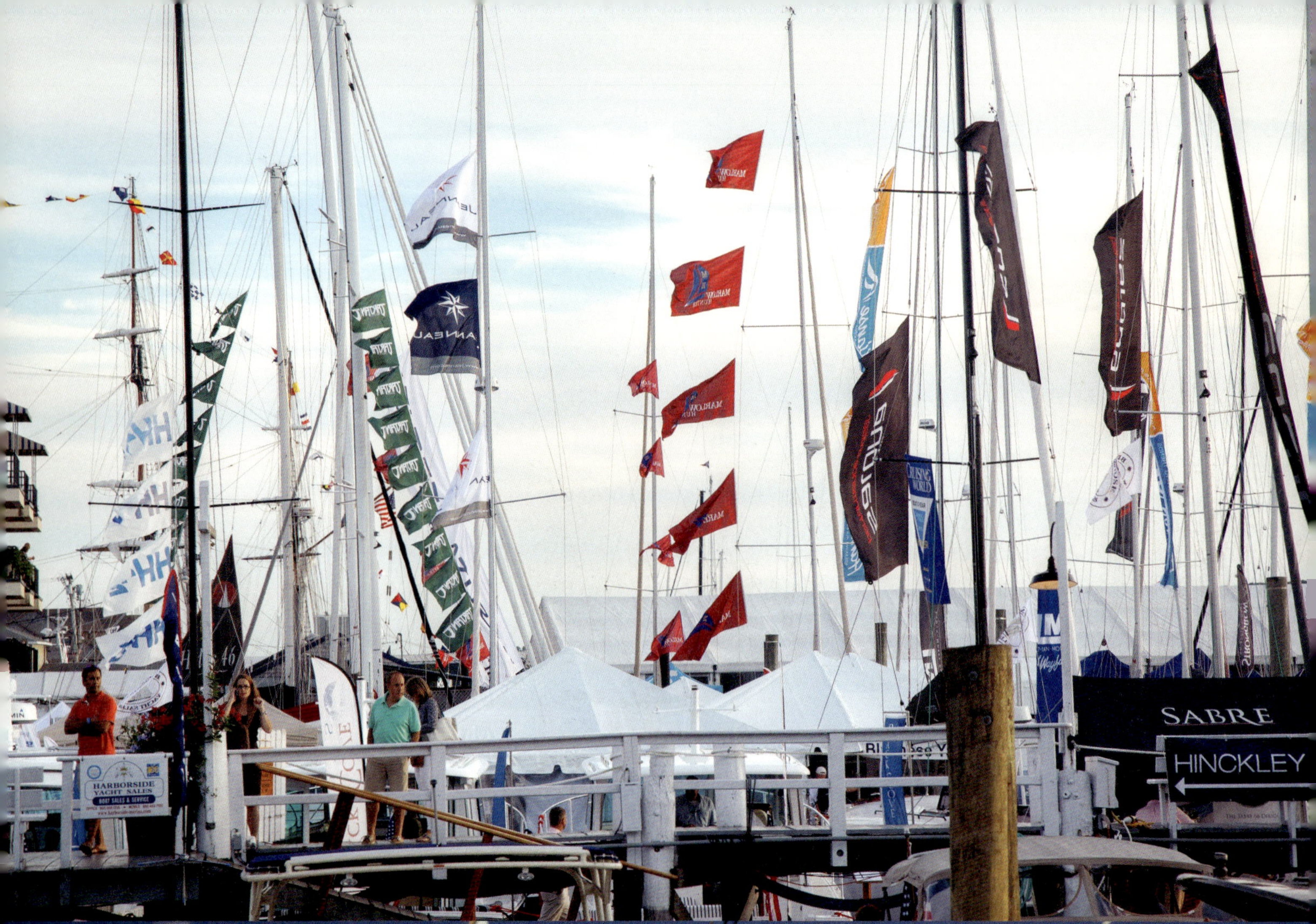
HARBORSIDE
YACHT SALES
SABRE
HINCKLEY

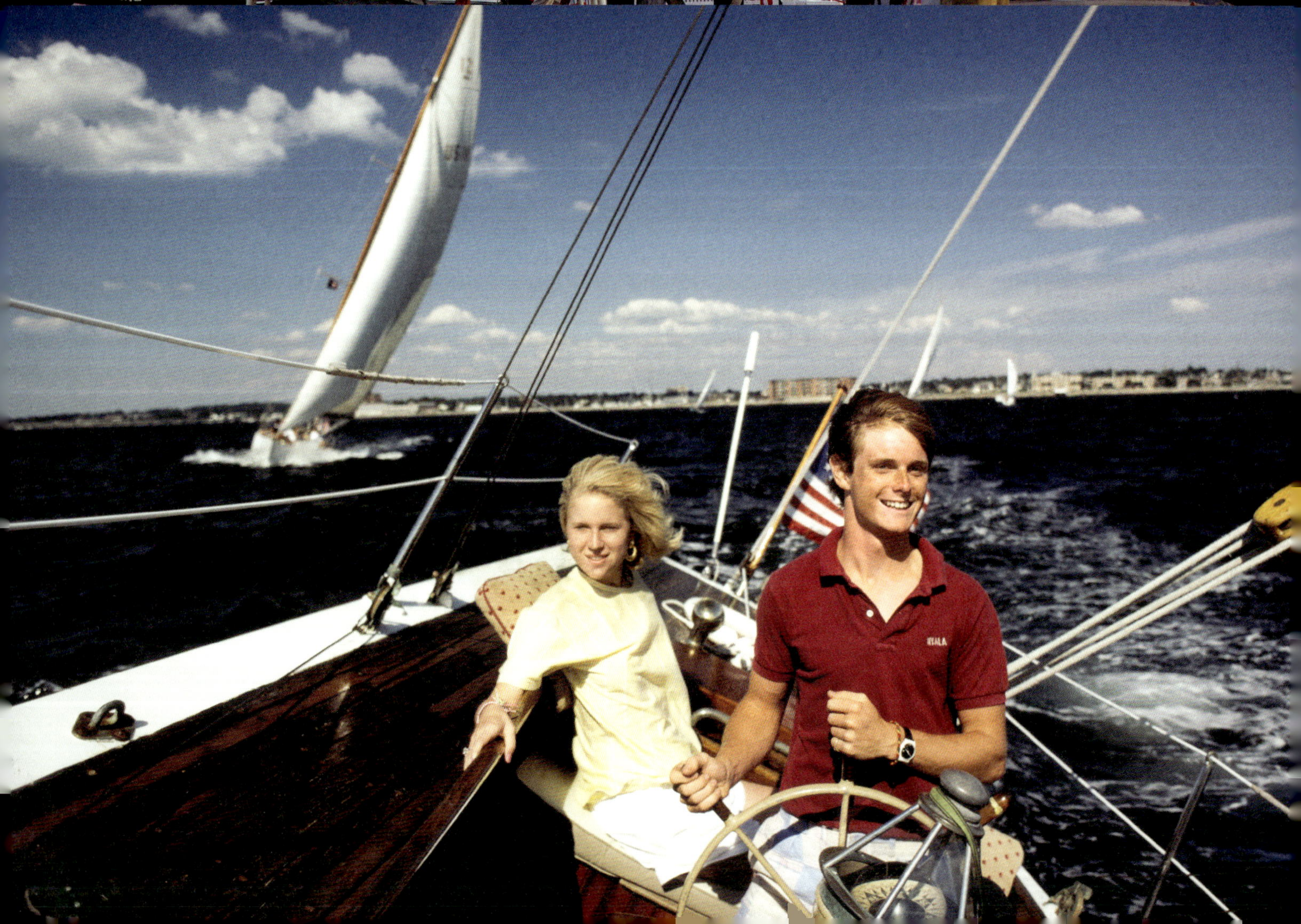

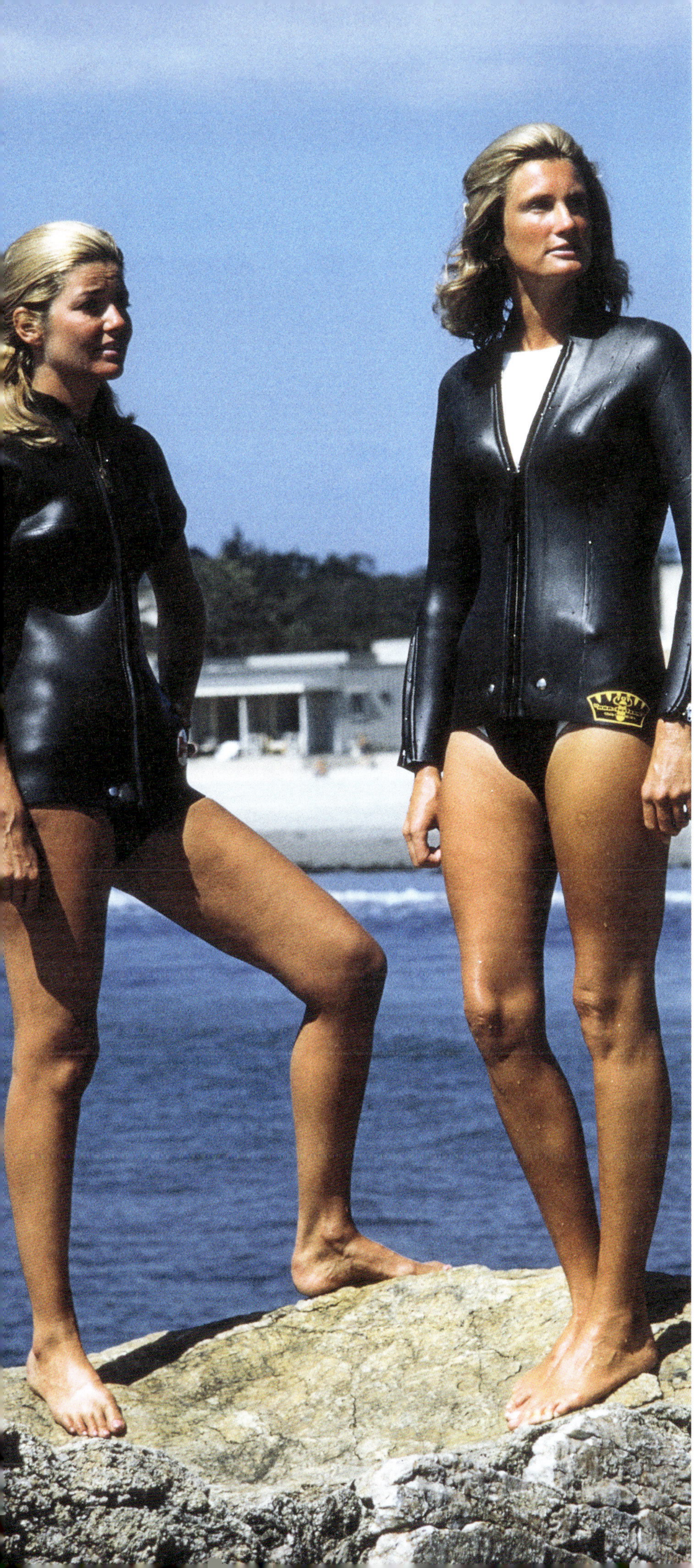

Opposite, top: *Newport, Rhode Island.*

Opposite, bottom: *Catherine and David Crabtree aboard their 12-metre sailboat "Nyala" in Newport, Rhode Island, 1987.*

This page: *Mrs. Peter Vought and Mrs. Howard Cushing at Bailey's Beach, Newport, Rhode Island, USA, September 1965.*

Following pages: *The New York Yacht Club Landing at Newport, Rhode Island, c. 1912.*

Page 60, top: *Holidaymakers on the deck of a yacht in Saint-Tropez, August 1971.*

Page 60, bottom: *Yachts in Saint-Tropez harbor, August 1971.*

Page 61: *A couple in an MG sports car in Saint-Tropez, c. 1965.*

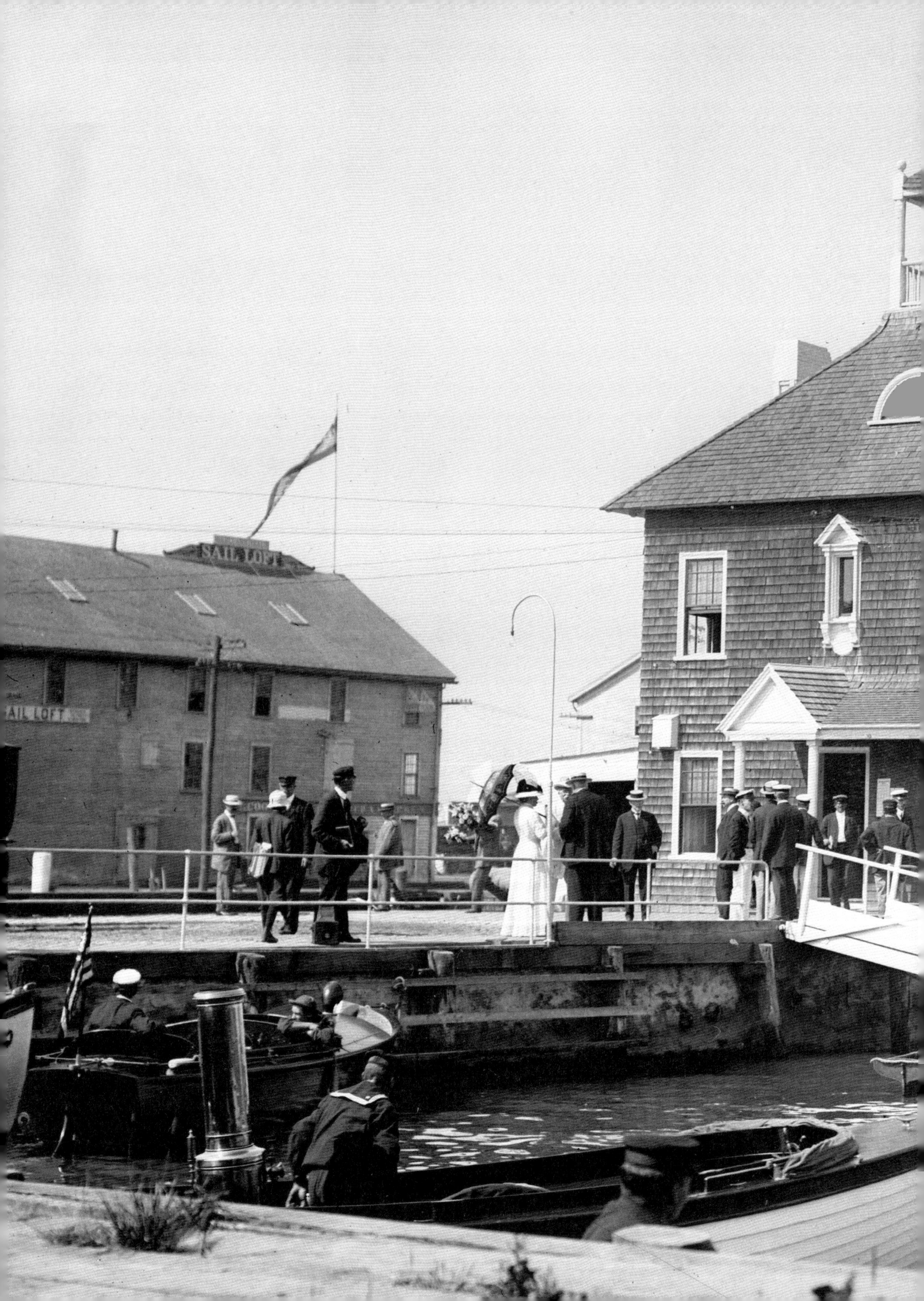
SAIL LOFT
SAIL LOFT

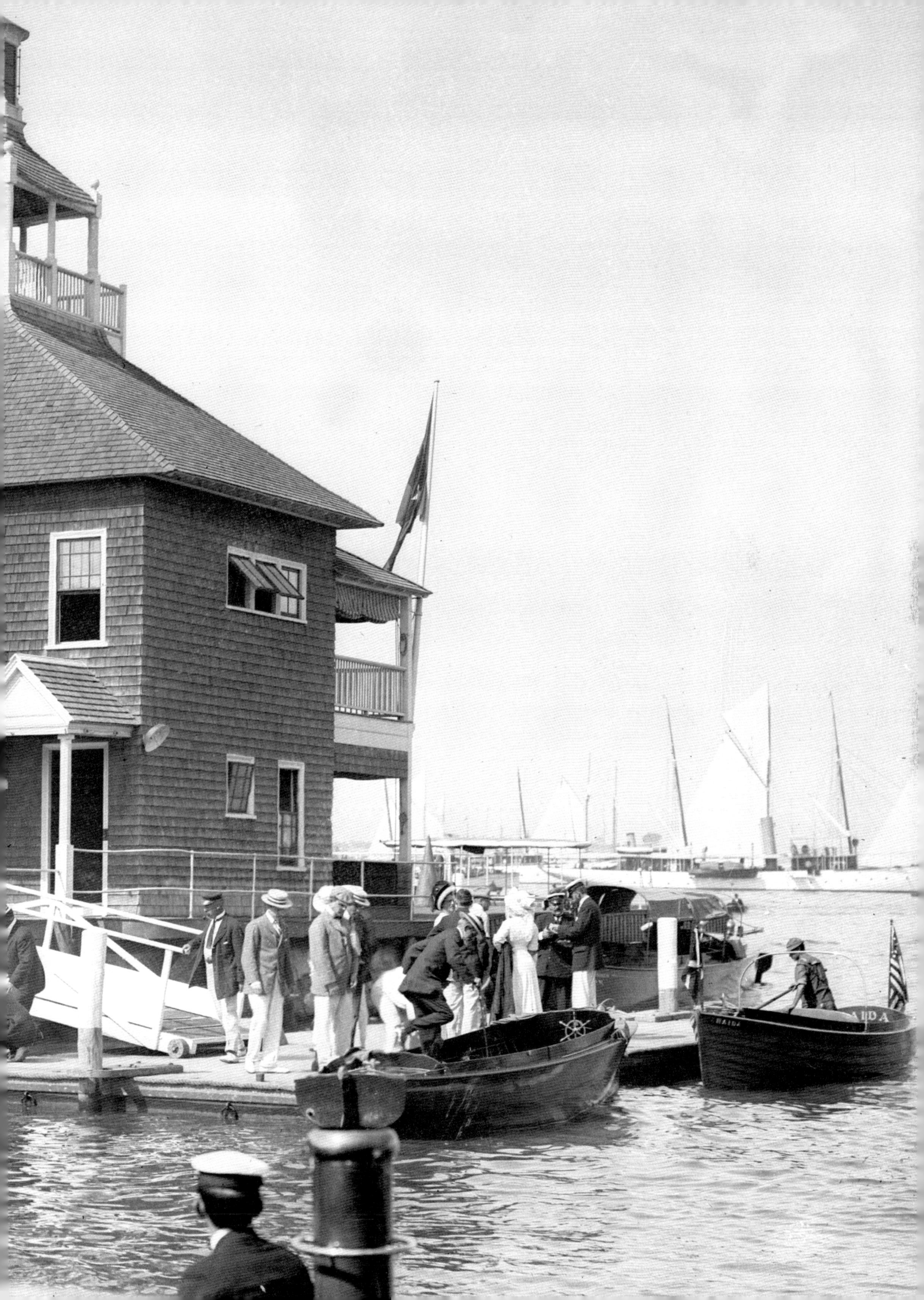

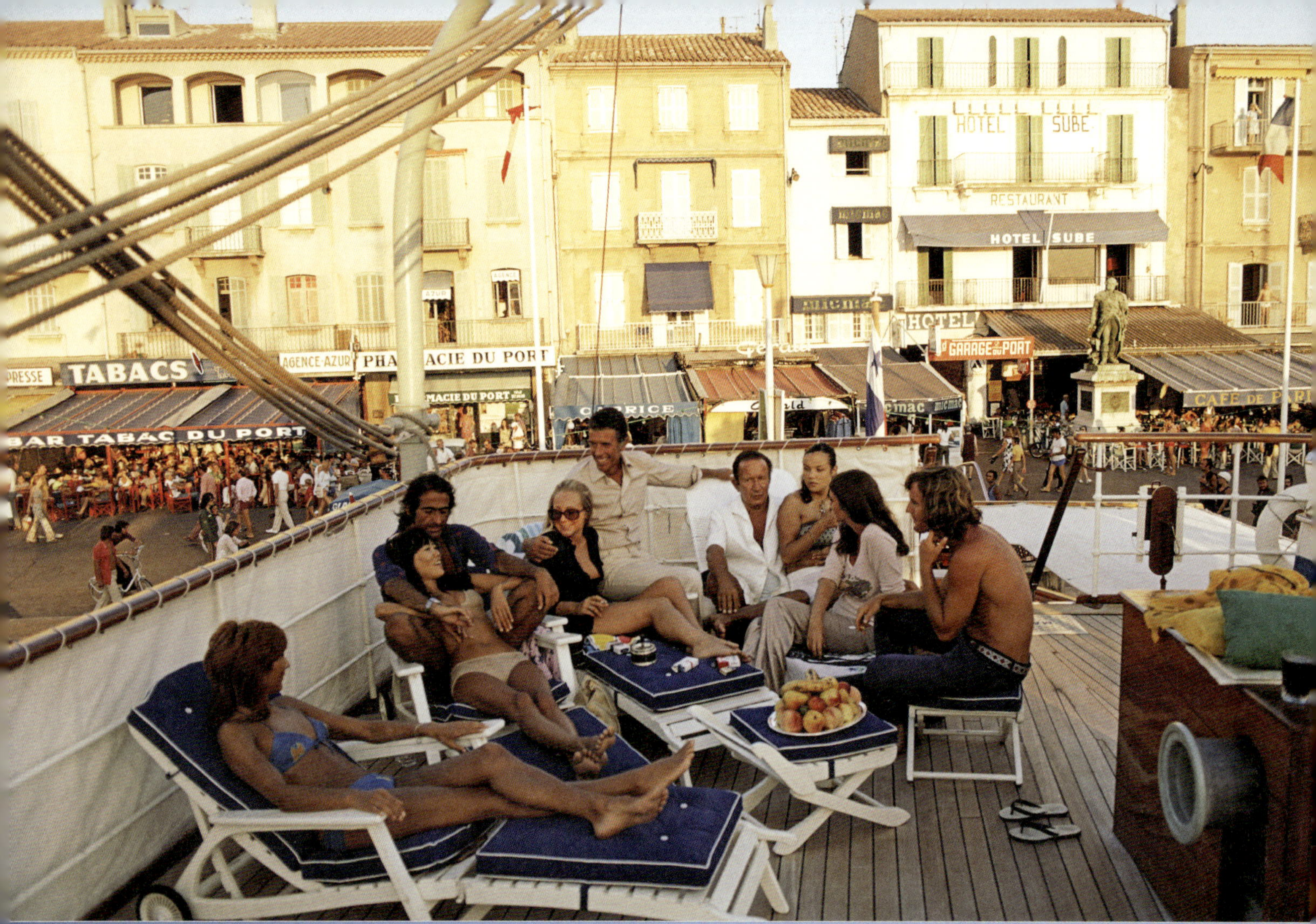
HOTEL SUBE
RESTAURANT
HOTEL SUBE
TABACS
AGENCE AZUR
BAR TABAC DU PORT
GARAGE du PORT

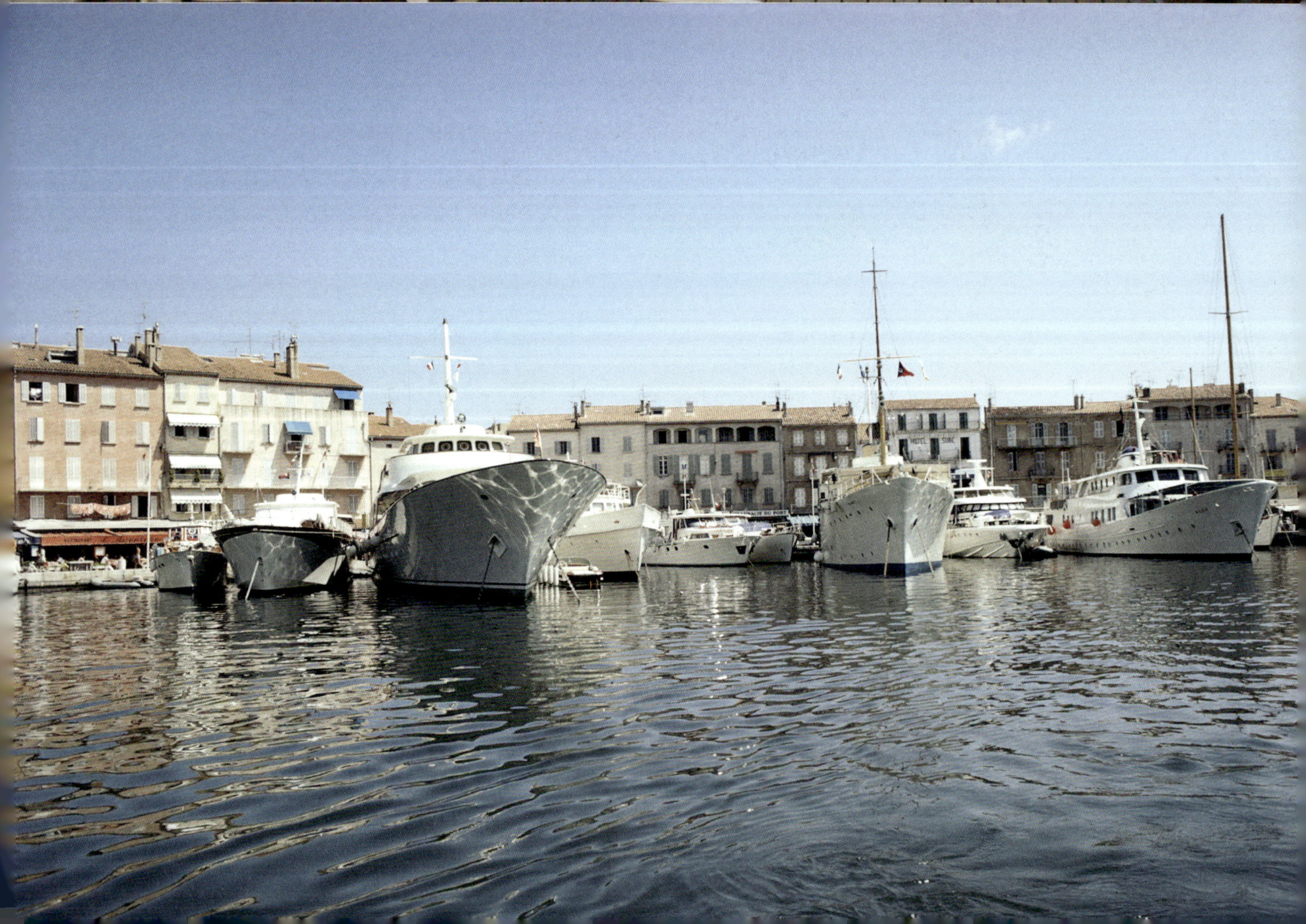

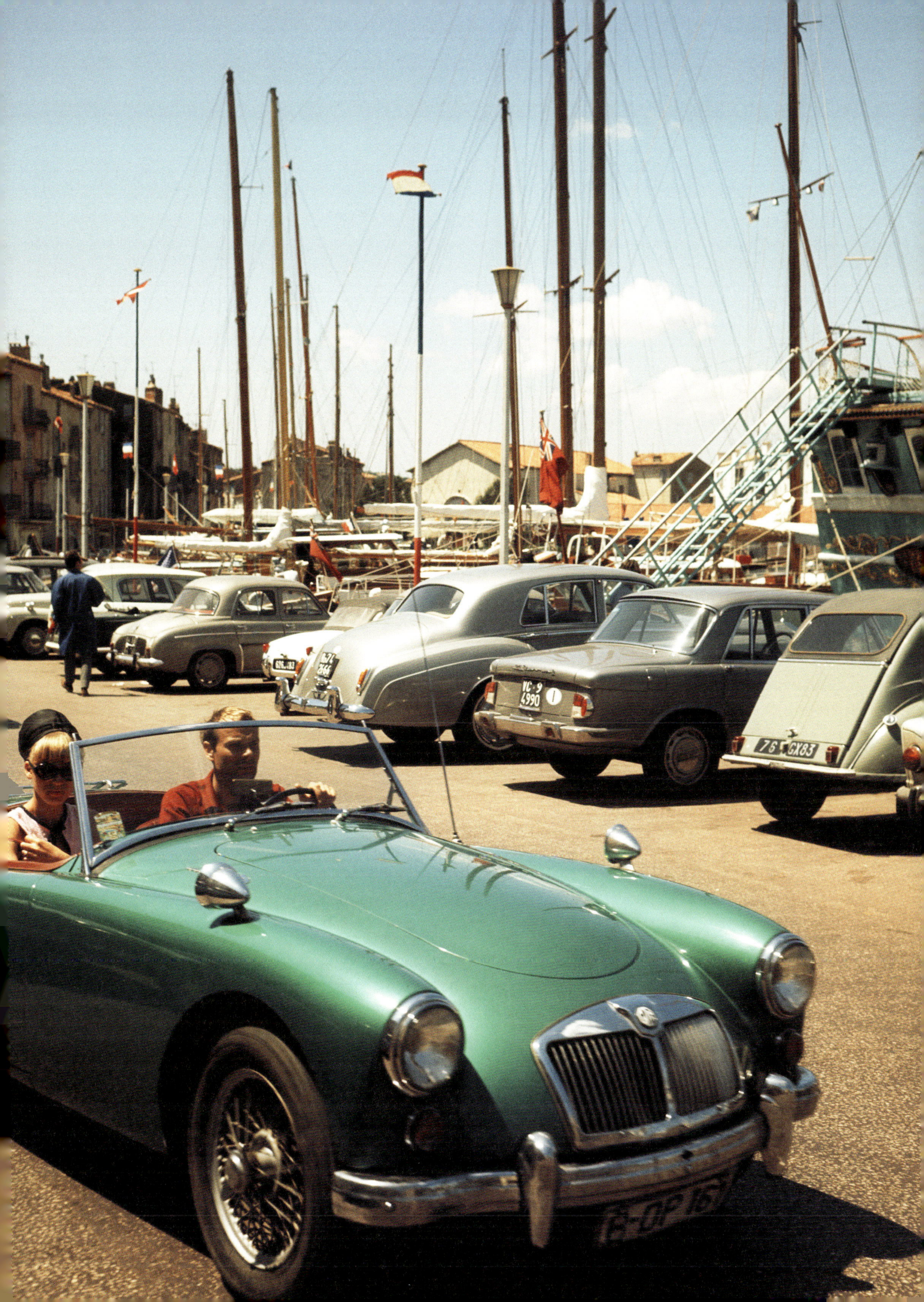

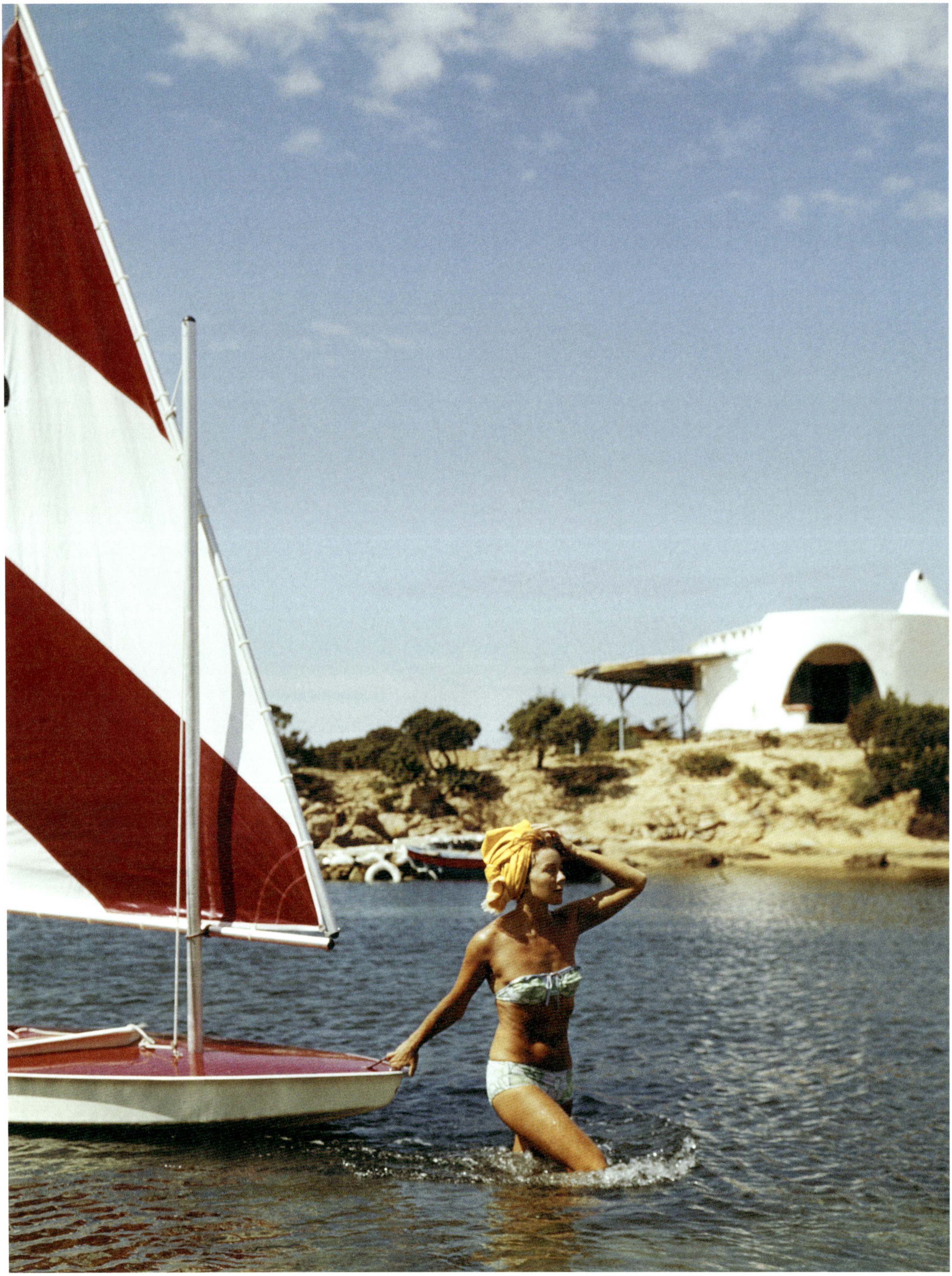

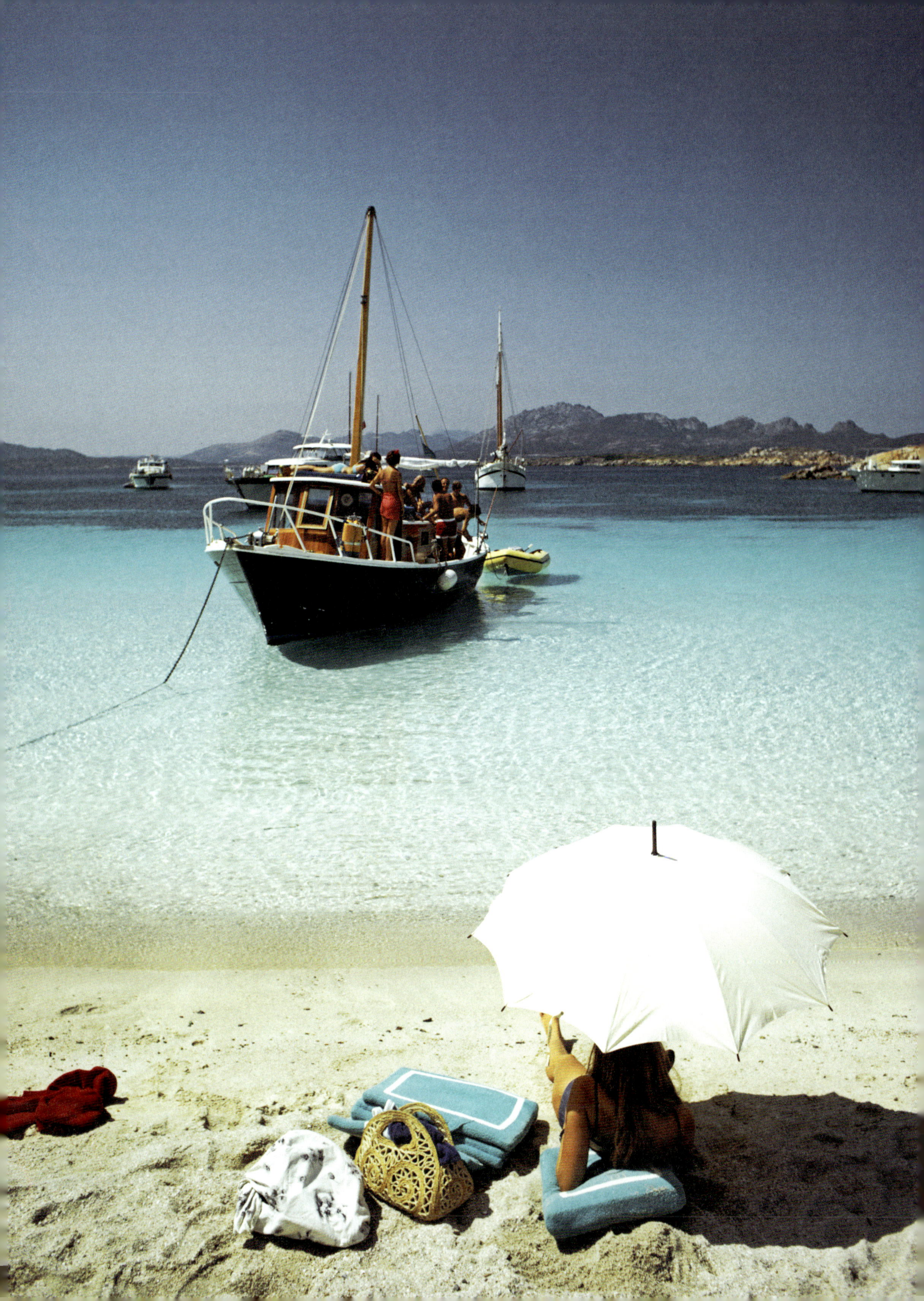

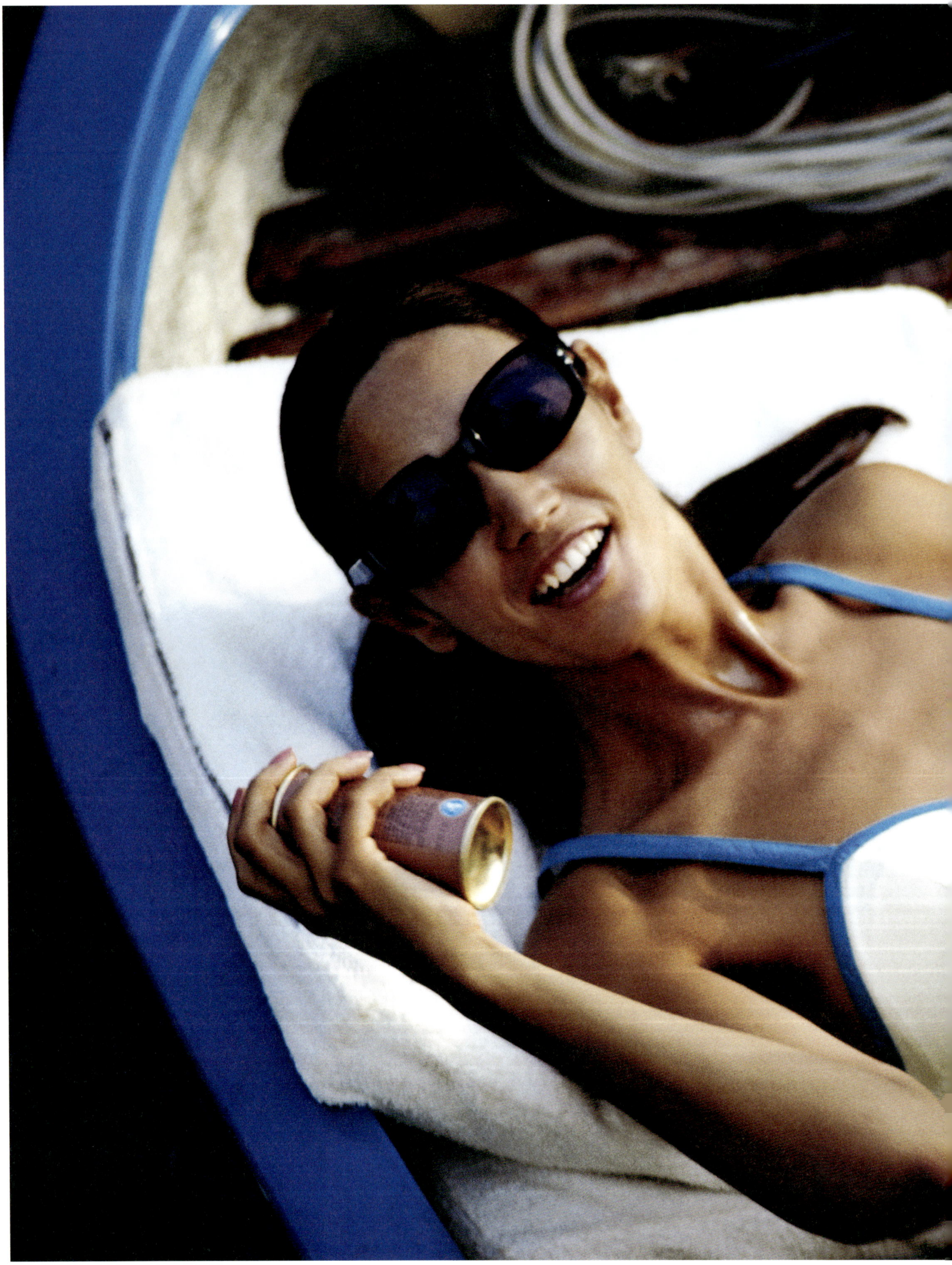

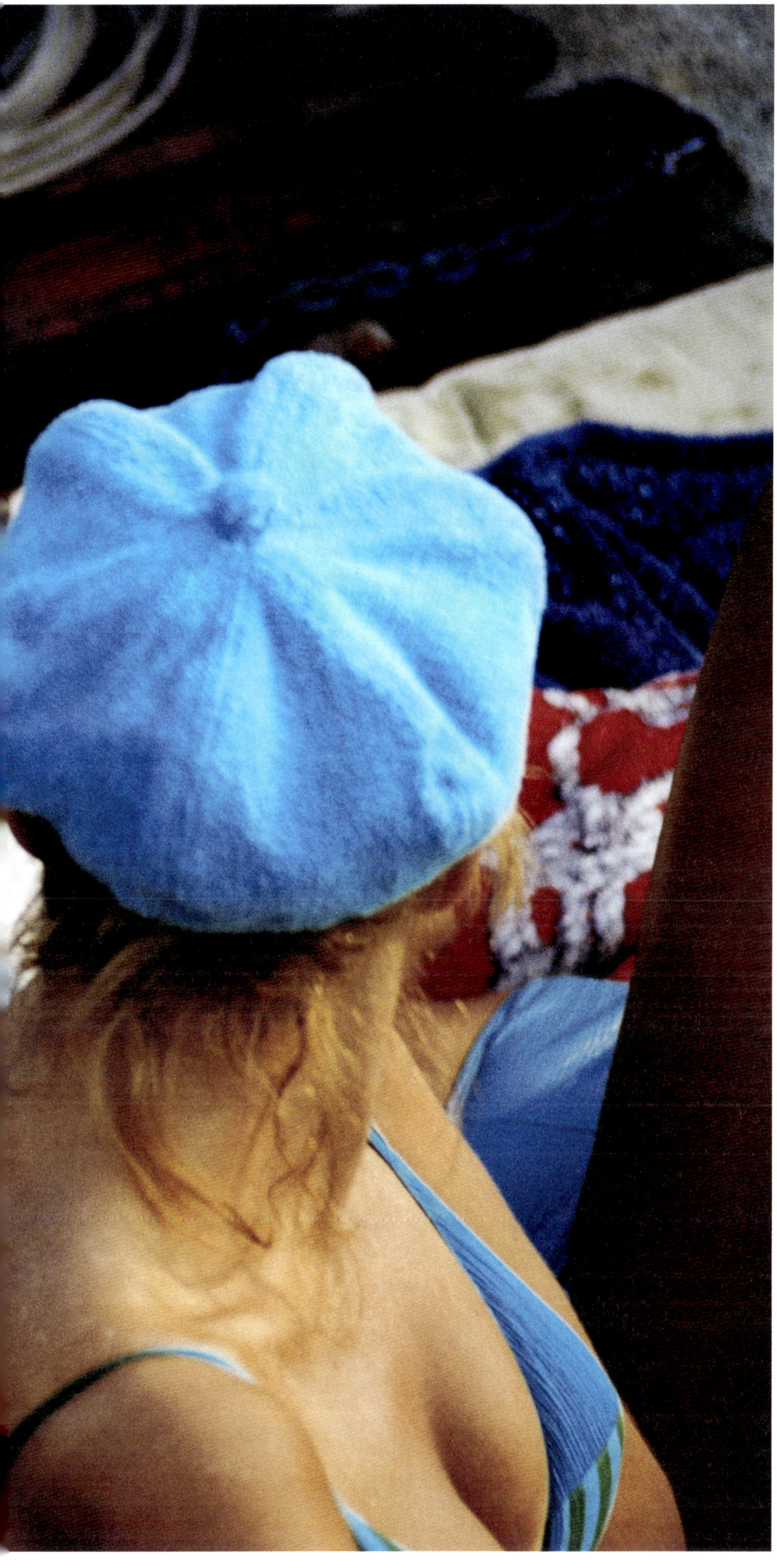

Page 62: *French model Bettina Graziani wading in the shallow waters of Costa Smeralda in Sardinia, pulling a small yacht behind her, 1964.*

Page 63: *A woman shelters under a parasol on a Costa Smeralda beach, Sardinia, 1967.*

These pages: *Two women sunbathing on a boat at Porto Ercole, Tuscany, August 1967.*

Page 66: *Holidaymakers on a boat trip off Porto Ercole, Tuscany, September 1986.*

Page 67: *A woman sunbathing by the sea in Porto Ercole, Tuscany, August 1969.*

Page 68, top: *Boats off Porto Ercole, Tuscany, September 1986.*

Page 68, bottom: *Yachts moored to a pontoon in Porto Ercole, Tuscany, 1980.*

Page 69: *A family jaunt in a motorboat in Porto Ercole, Tuscany, c. 1975.*

Pages 70/71: *Yachts off the privately-owned Peter Island in the British Virgin Islands, March 1973.*

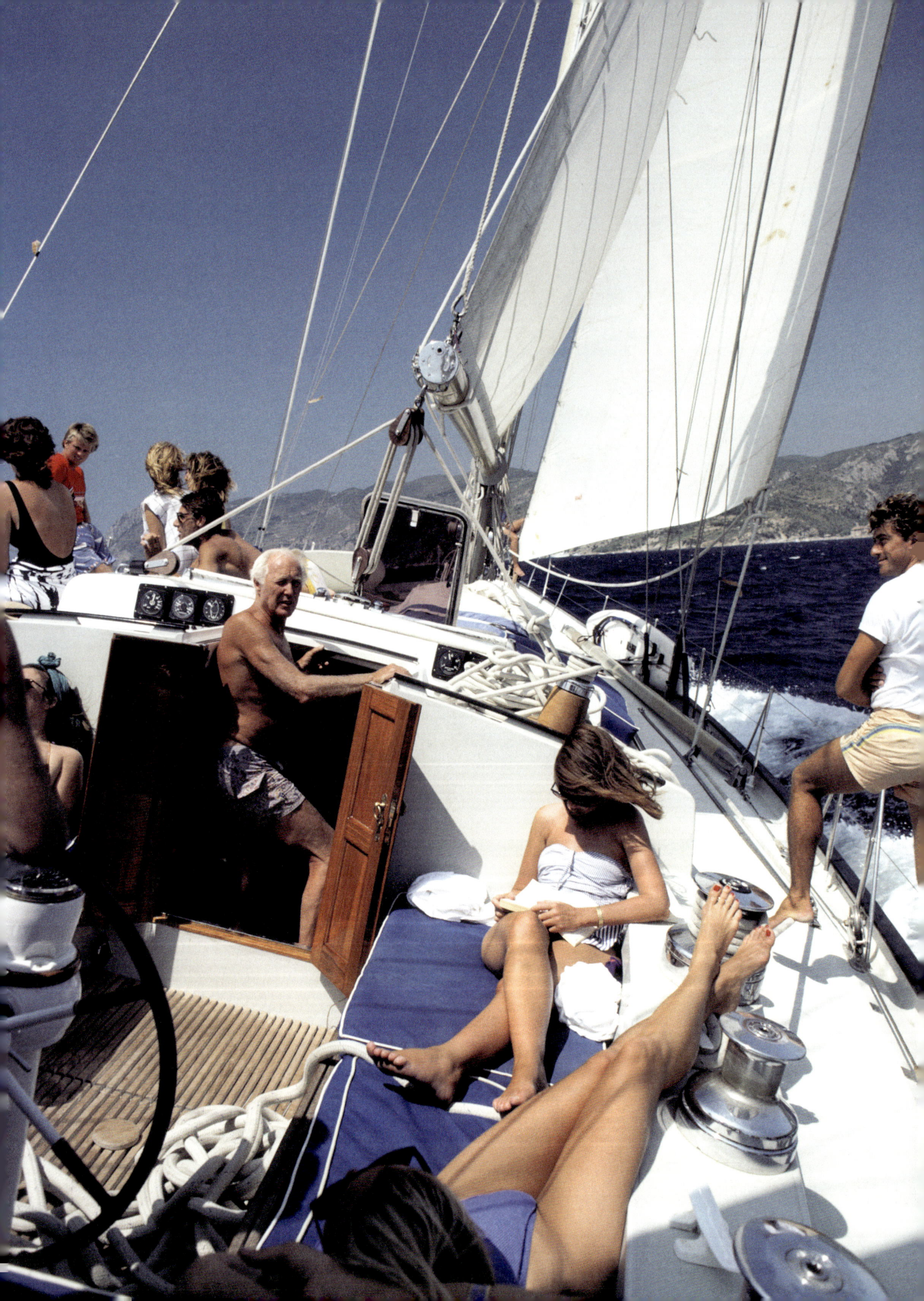

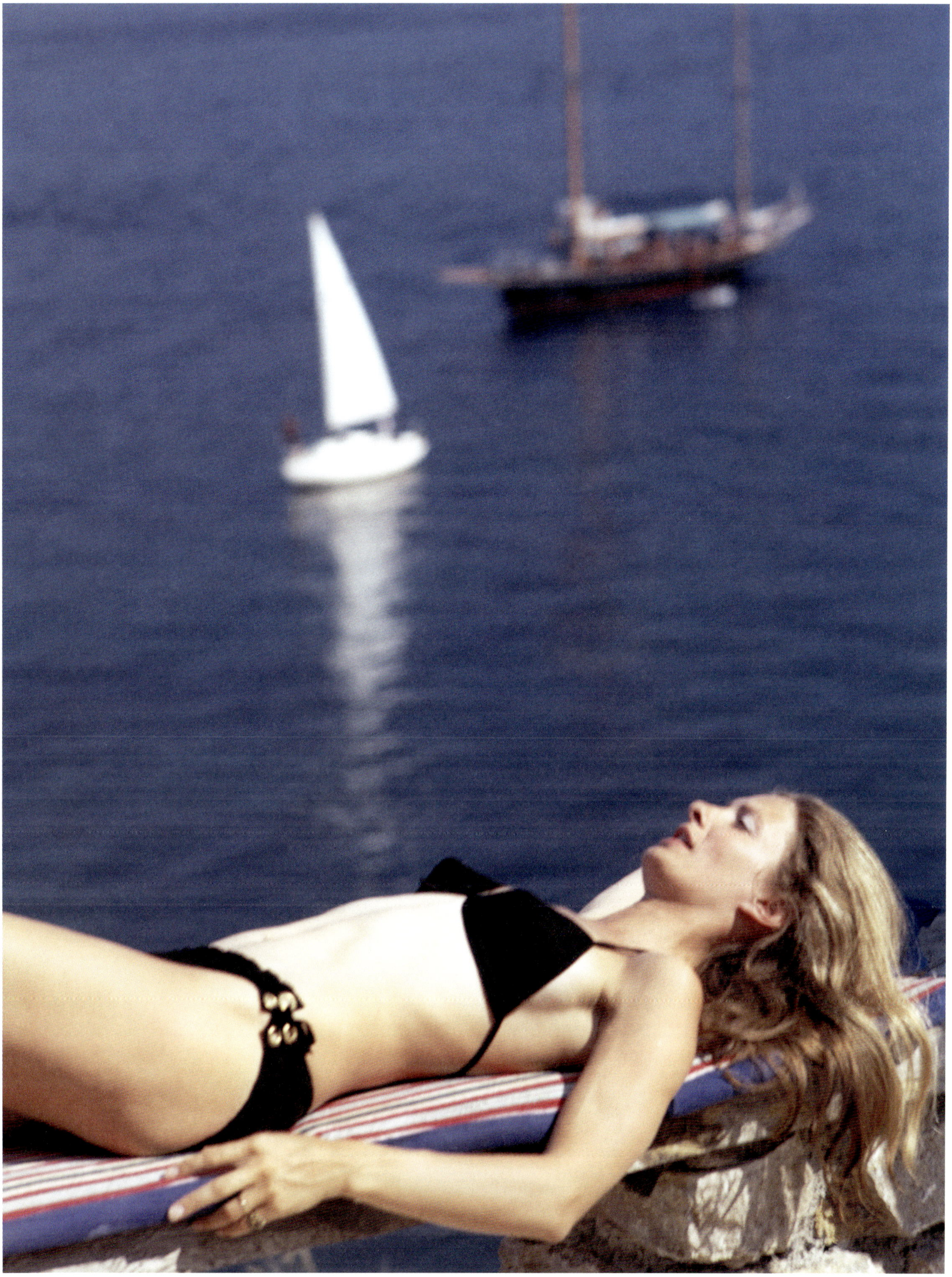

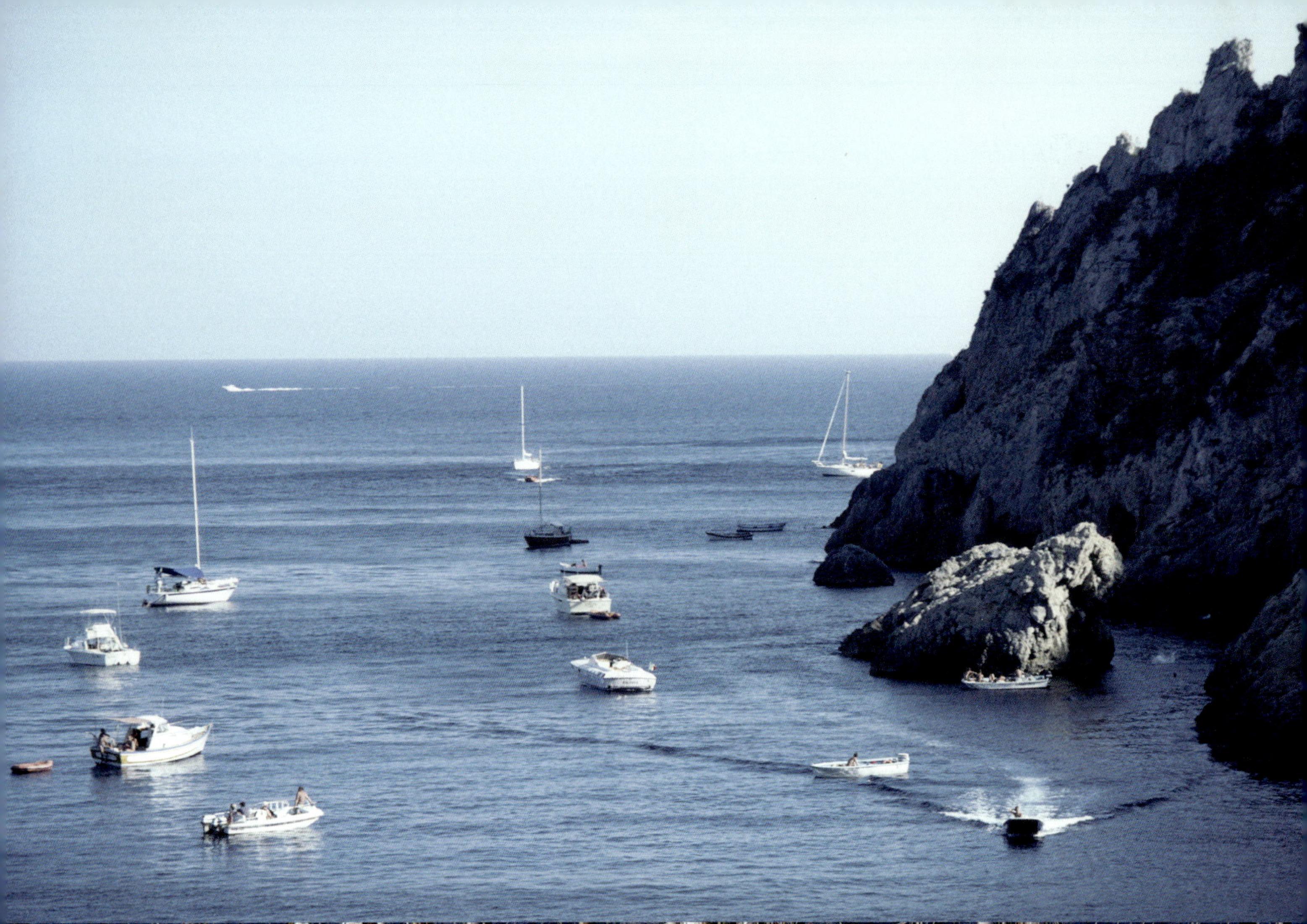

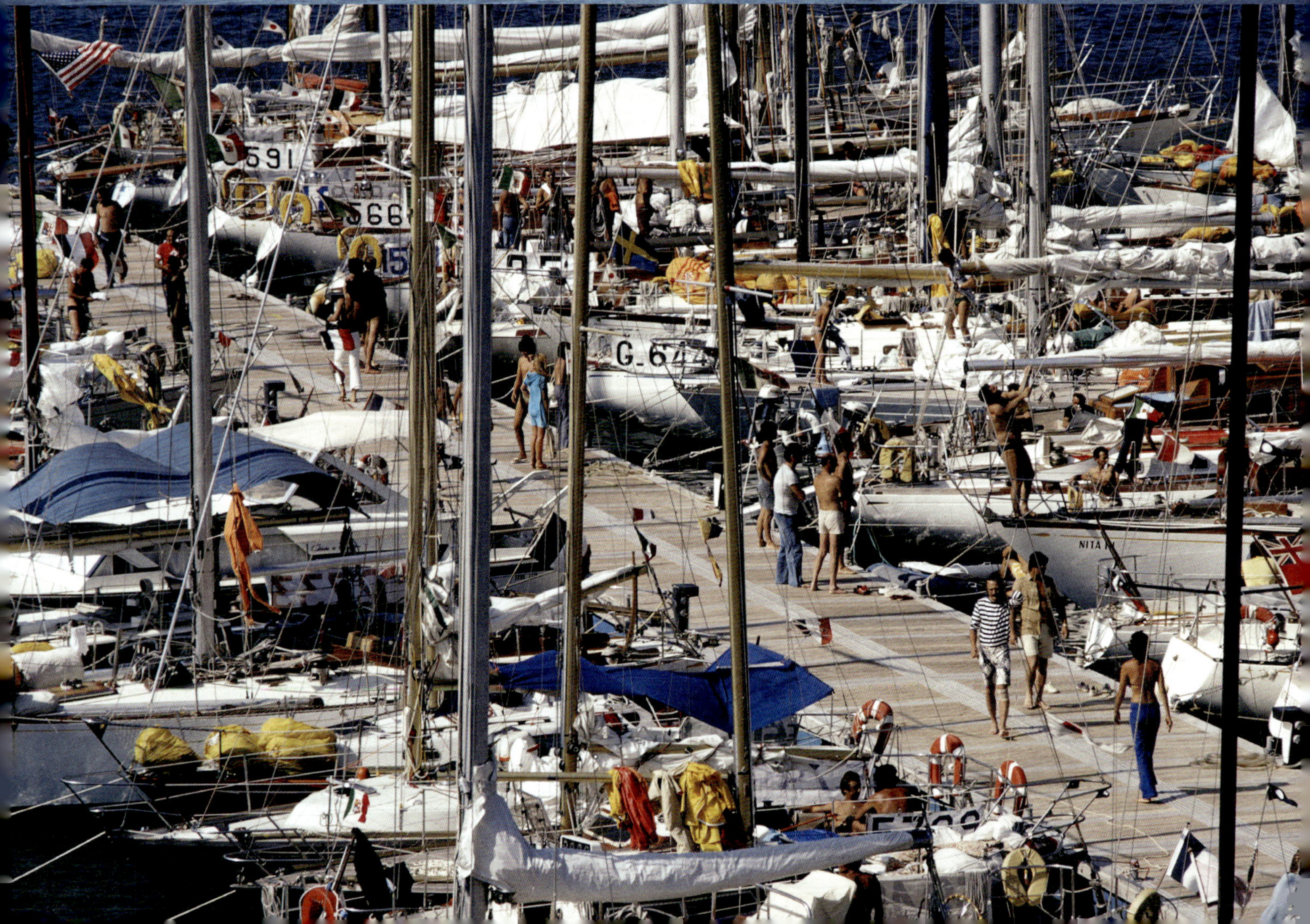

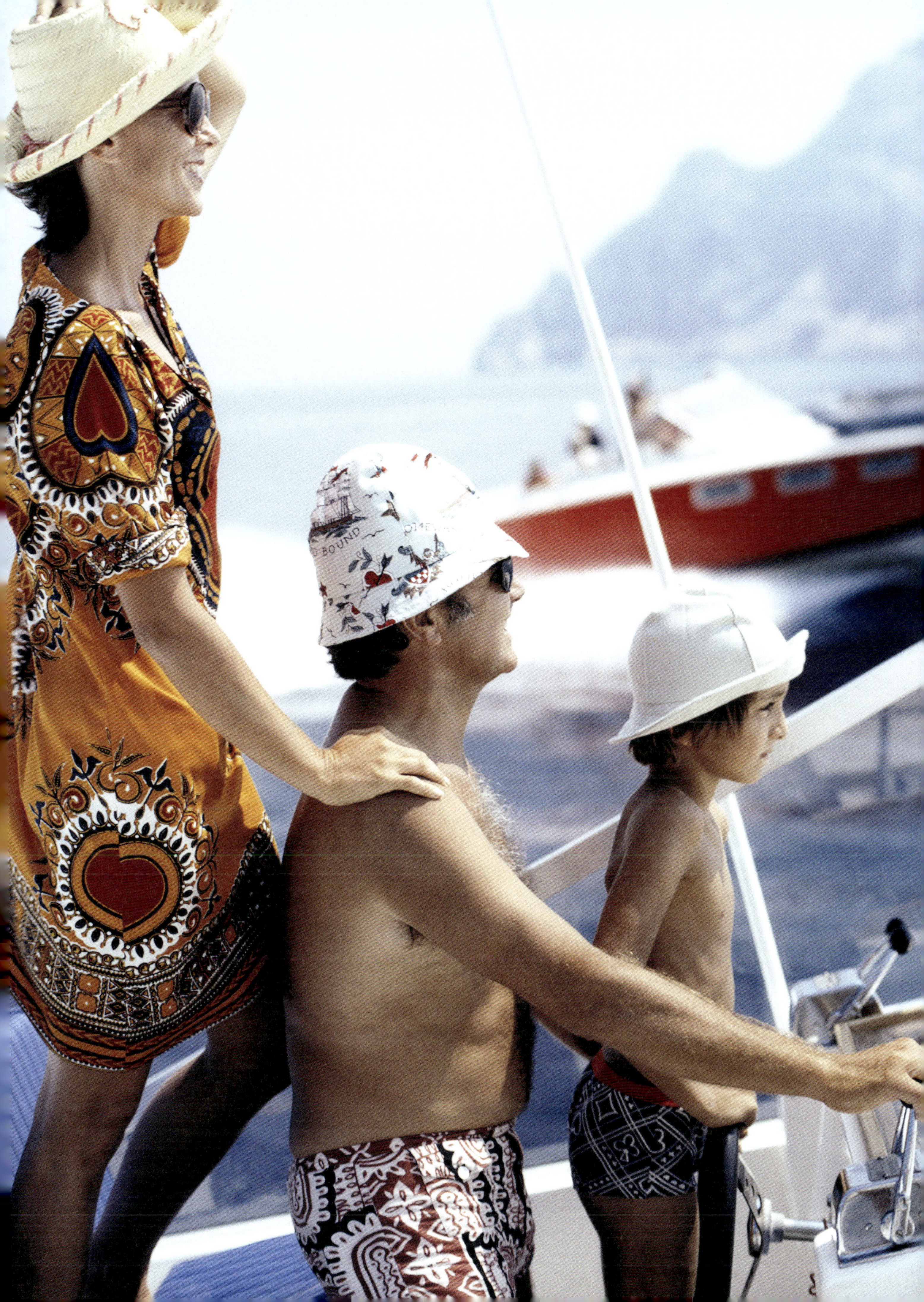

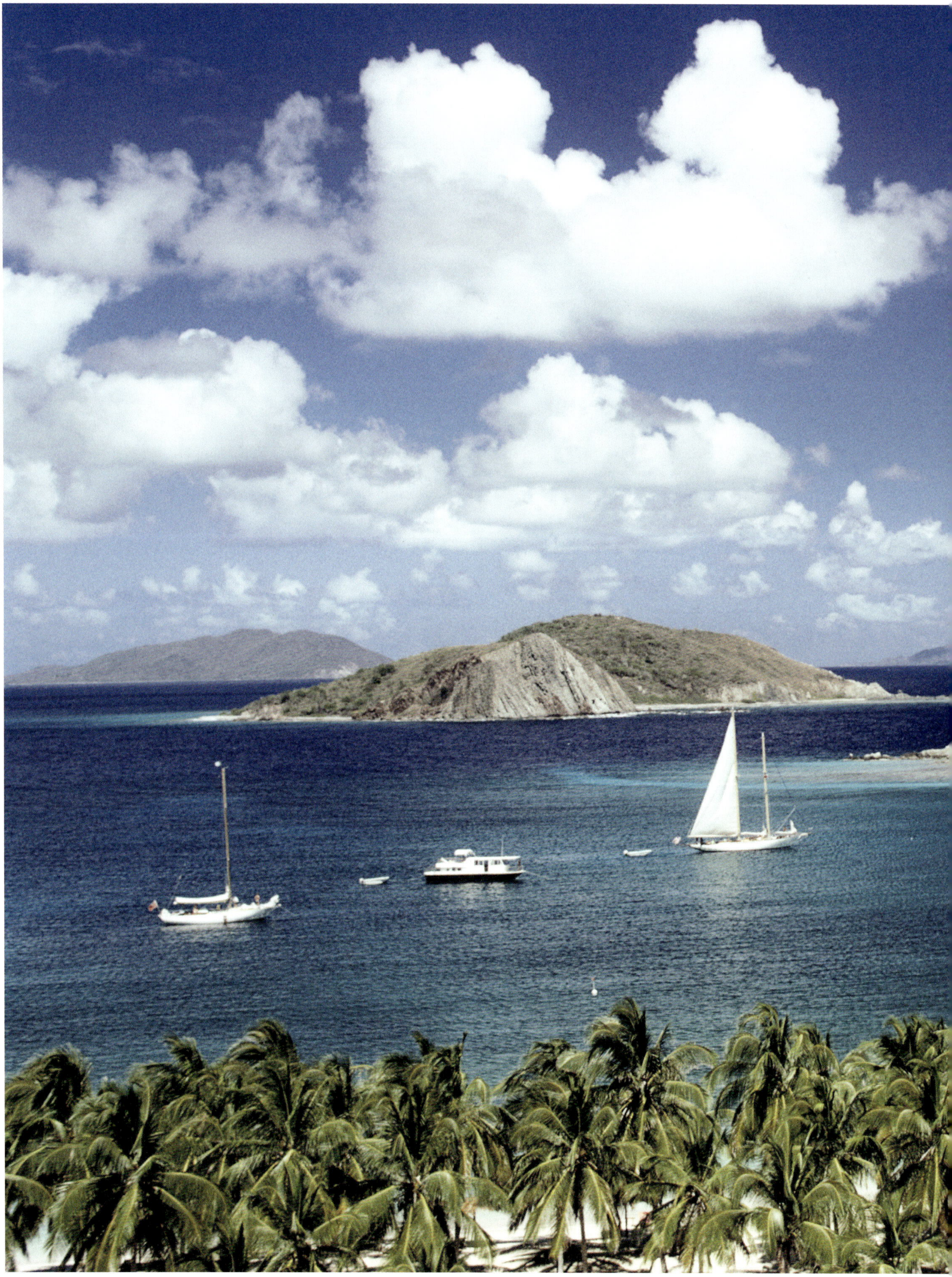

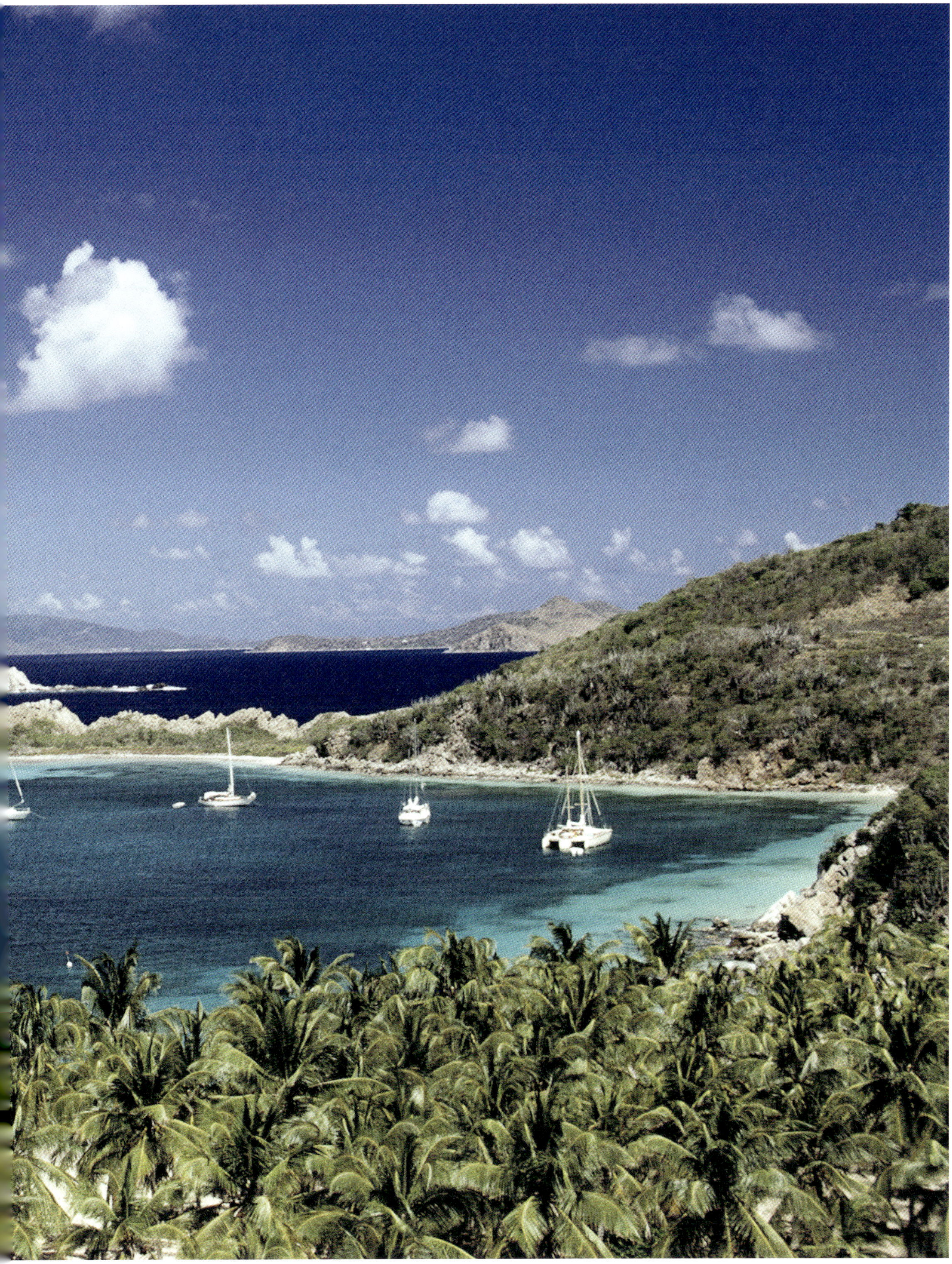

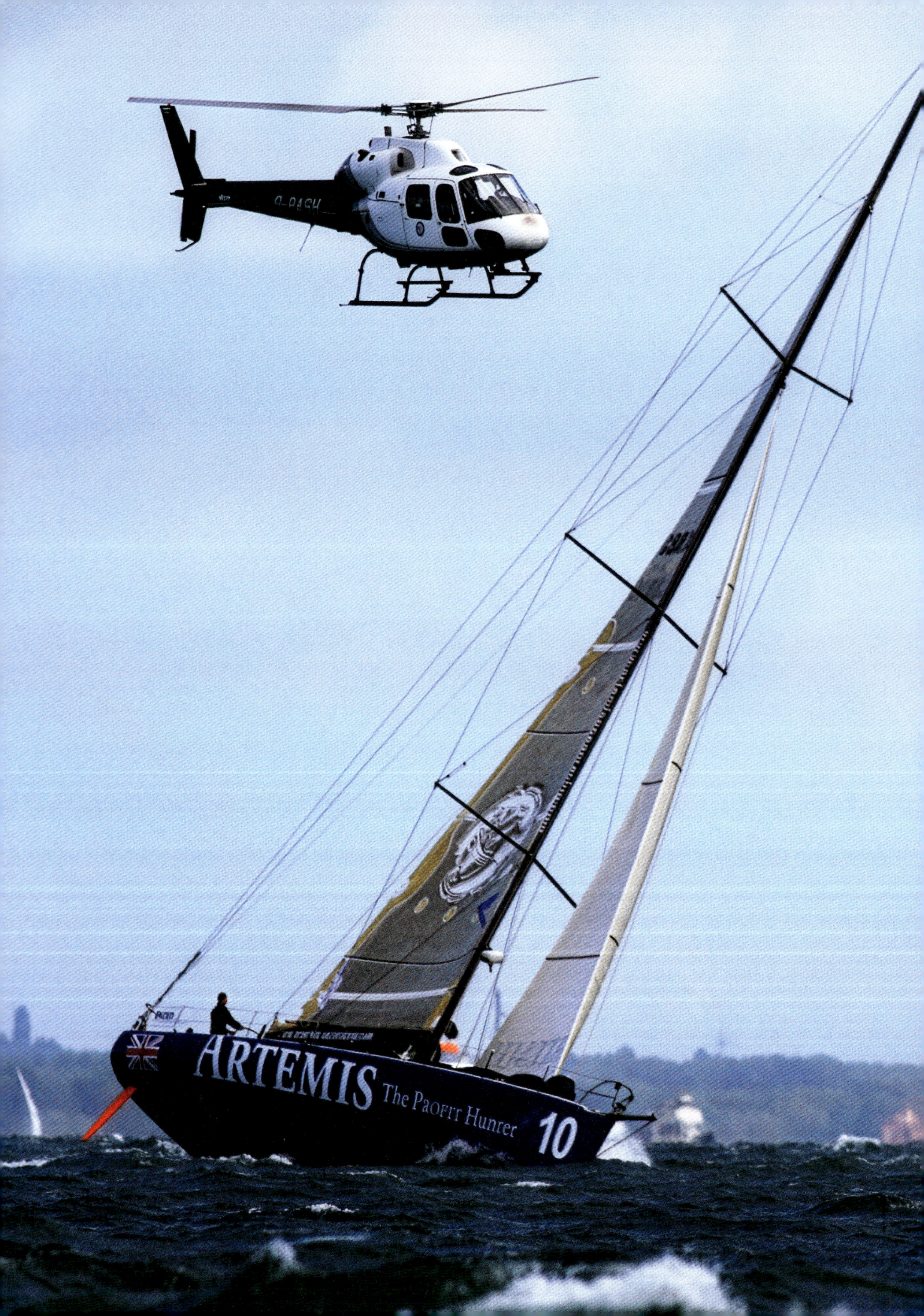
ARTEMIS
The Profit Hunter
10

YACHTS

SAILING ICONS

If you want to make fast friends with the owner of a yacht, simply ask them about their vessel. In the home or office of a sailor inevitably a handsome photograph or painting will be on display, and sometimes a full model will be a decorative centerpiece. For enthusiasts their yachts are hugely important parts of life, and they are rightly proud.

Naval architects work hard to create yachts that are sea-kindly and fast yet also able to carry a full crew and stores while remaining comfortable. Importantly, they also need to be pleasing to the eye, and indeed classic yachts seem to get more beautiful with age. Everyone takes notice when a traditional yacht built by Nathanel Greene Herreshoff, Charles Nicholson, William Fife or Johan Anker passes by. The best perspective from which to appreciate a yacht is on board. Every position is interesting. At the helm you feel the power of the boat working through the waves. On the leeward side you get a sense of the boat's speed as the spray and the water passes by. The thing that distinguishes the bow? Quiet and calm.

Yachts are places where special relationships are forged. After a long passage or an exhilarating race, a crew has a deep bond based on struggle, perhaps victory and certainly shared experience. Sky overhead, sails filled with breeze, hands on the wheel, feet on the deck, the hull moving through the water. There's the wind on your face and the sound of the water in your ears. It's no accident that sailor's wave at each other as they pass by. Even if they have never sailed on the same boat, everyone is a member of the community of the sea.

Opposite: *Sailing the Rolex Fastnet Race through the Solent, August 2007.*

J Class: In 1907 a conference was held in London, England to develop an international system of categorization for yachts. Until then every country used different criteria, making it difficult to score races in a fair way, but the conference created an international system of yacht-classes based on waterline length, width, sail area, displacement and other factors. The largest type reached 23 meters—the "J Class"—ten of which were built for America's Cup racing in the 1930s (six American and four British). This class of vessel is highly prestigious, and some classics remain in action today: in 1989, for instance, American yachtswoman Elizabeth Meyer relaunched the 1934 America's Cup challenger, "Endeavour," after an extensive five-year renovation, in turn inspiring others to build new or restore older J Class sloops. Three classics have been restored ("Velsheda," "Shamrock V," and "Endeavour"), and between 2004 and 2017 six new ones were built: "Ranger," "Hanuman," "Lionheart," "Rainbow," "Topaz," and "Svea."

A GREAT DAY FOR SAILING

As I came up on deck the crew was preparing "Endeavour" for a day of sailing off the coast of Maine. The warm sun was burning off the fog bank as a southwesterly breeze filled in, and just before the giant, 2000-pound mainsail was hoisted I was asked the best question a sailor can hear: "Would you like to take the helm?" I was ecstatic to be at the wheel of this magnificent yacht, with its mast towering 172 feet into the sky and a boardwalk-shaped boom over 60 feet in length. We released the mooring, and as the sails filled the 256,000-pound boat heeled over and gained speed. Soon we were sailing at 14 knots. The boat was a joy to steer, and I stayed at the wheel for three hours that felt like mere minutes.

International 12 Meter Class: The 12 Meter Class was another category created at the 1907 conference in London (there were a dozen classifications in total). The class of boat was instantly popular and was raced in the Olympic Games the very next summer at the Clyde Corinthian Yacht Club. The enthusiasm for the Universal Rule was strong, and the hope was that yachts would be able to race on a level basis: in other words, the first boat to cross the finish line would win. The J Class era came to an end with the Great Depression and World War II, but for the 12 Meter Class this represented an opportunity. In 1956 New York Yacht Club commodore Harry Sears was inspired to revive the America's Cup races, but he recognized that the cost of campaigning a J Class was simply too high. So he traveled to London to propose to the commodore of the Royal Yacht Squadron that 12 Meter vessels be used for the America's Cup. The British agreed to the concept and issued a challenge for the Cup. Once Sears had received a favorable ruling on his proposal from the State of New York, the 12 Meter became the yacht of choice for the Cup match in 1958.

The class has had an illustrious history ever since. President Eisenhower watched the America's Cup from a naval vessel that year. In 1962 President John F. Kennedy attended the first two days of racing in Newport, Rhode Island. President Richard Nixon went sailing on the 12 Meter "Intrepid "in 1970. President Ronald Reagan honored the victorious crew of "Australia II" at the White House in 1983, and Dennis Conner and his crew in 1987. President Bill Clinton visited the American crews in Auckland in 2000 and President Barack Obama honored Larry Ellison, Russell Coutts and the crew of "BMW Oracle Racing" at the White House in 2010. In all, 180 of the Twelves were built between 1907 and 1987.

The 1987 America's Cup was the last year there for the 12 Meter Class. But robust fleets continue to race in New England and Scandinavia, and the creators of the Universal Rule would surely be proud to see their designs still on the water a century later.

SAILING A 12 METER

When I was 12 my family took a vacation to Newport, Rhode Island during the America's Cup of 1962. I was awed by the sight of the big boats, their masts towering into the clouds, and impressed by the immaculate matching uniforms of the crew. It was that day I decided to one day sail a 12 Meter.

My dream came true 14 years later when Ted Turner asked me to be his tactician for the 1977 America's Cup. During the fall of 1976 I traveled to Marblehead, Massachusetts for the first of many training days on "Courageous," and I was surprised by two things in particular. The first was the immense size of the mainsail. The second was the strength of the wind that blew across the deck. But within a few days I became comfortable sailing on "Courageous," and the summer was especially magical as we ended up defending the America's Cup against the challenger from Australia. Having sailed 12 Meters almost every summer since 1977, I'm still inspired when the sails are hoisted.

TP 52 Class: Designed in compliance with a "box rule," a system in which yachts are allowed to be different weights and shapes so long as they fit inside a box of specified dimensions, the TP 52-foot class made its racing debut with a win at the 2003 Transpacific Race (TP stands for Transpacific). These vessels now compete around the world, perhaps most prominently in the races known as the "Super Series." The crews are all highly skilled professionals, but often captained by amateur sailor/owners: in 2010, for instance, King Harald of Norway won the Gotland Rund on his TP52 "Fram XVI."

TP 52s appear in many races worldwide, offshore and in-shore alike, and have won the Transpacific, Chicago to Mackinac and Sydney to Hobart Races. The 2008 Disney documentary "Morning Light" follows a team of high school-aged sailors as they race to Hawaii on a TP52.

International Star Class: Designed by Francis Sweisguth, this 22'9" two-person category got off to a slow start in 1922—perhaps because he originally named the first vessel "The Bug." But a friend suggested to Sweisguth that he should consider a different name, and renamed "The Star" the category became a legendary success story. Selected as an Olympic Class for the 1932 Games in Los Angeles, the vessels had a long run in the Olympics right through to 2012, and many top sailors have won Star World Championships, including Paul Elvstrom, Lowell North, Dennis Conner, Tom Blackaller, Mark Reynolds, Torben Grael, Robert Scheidt, Buddy Melges, and Durward Knowles. John F. Kennedy raced Stars, winning a Nantucket Star Class Championship in 1936, and in 2025 the 66-year-old American Paul Cayard sailed one to a win in the World Championship against a 101-boat fleet off Croatia.

Opposite: *The 2015 Louis Vuitton America's Cup World Series, held in Göthenburg, Sweden.*

Following pages: *SoftBank Team Japan at the Louis Vuitton America's Cup World Series, held in Oman in February 2016.*

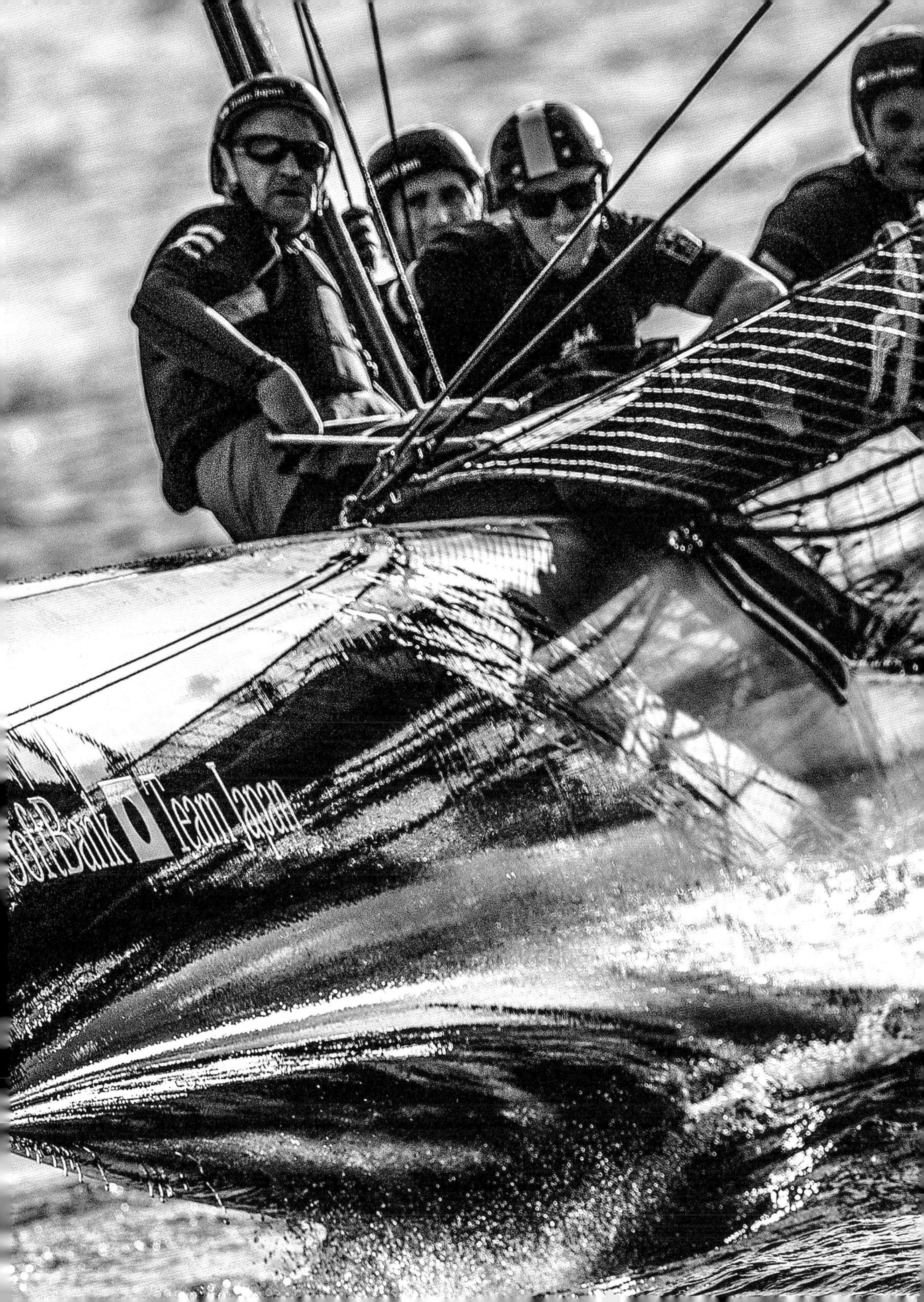

Team Japan

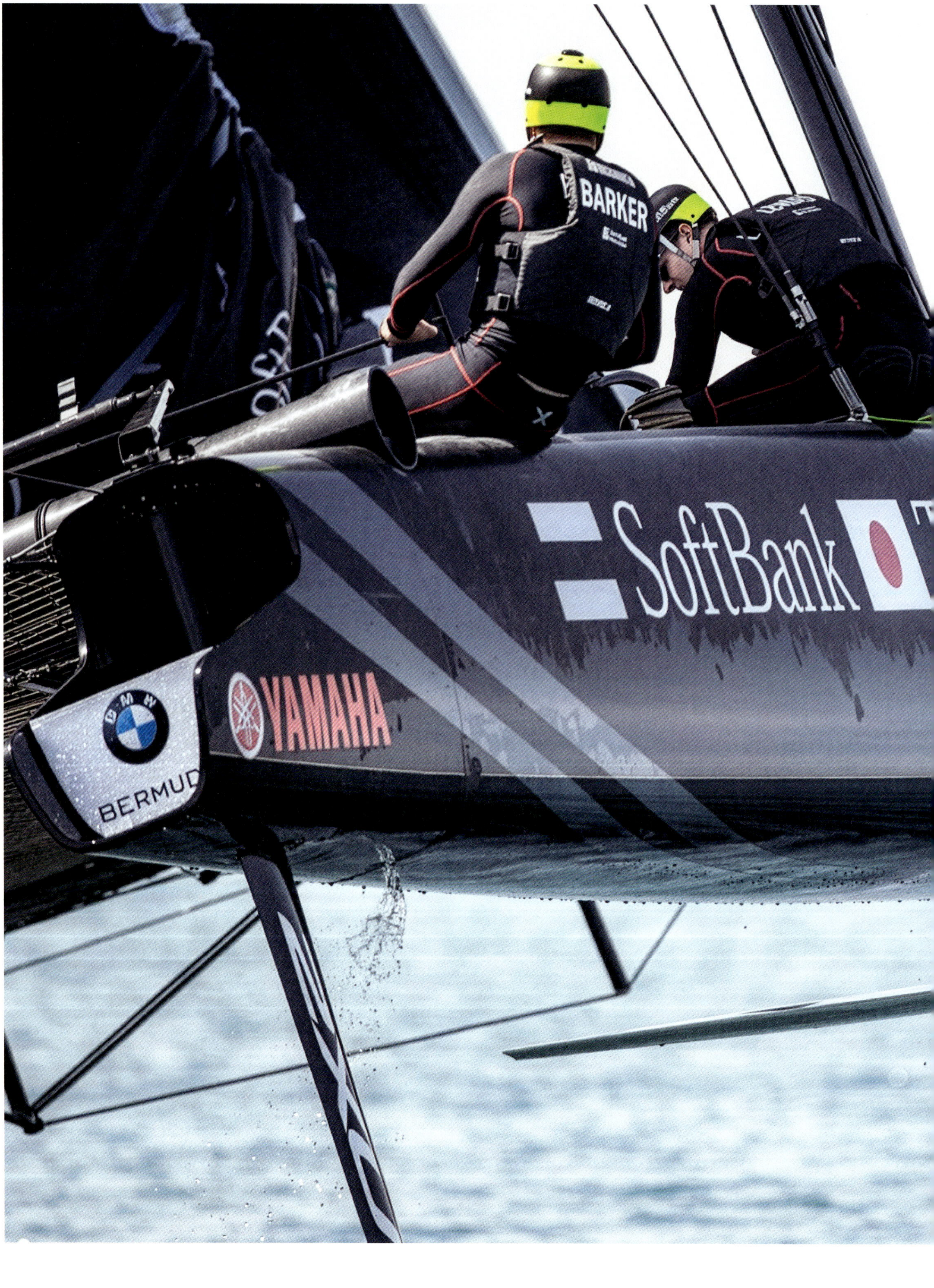

BARKER
SoftBank
YAMAHA
BERMUD

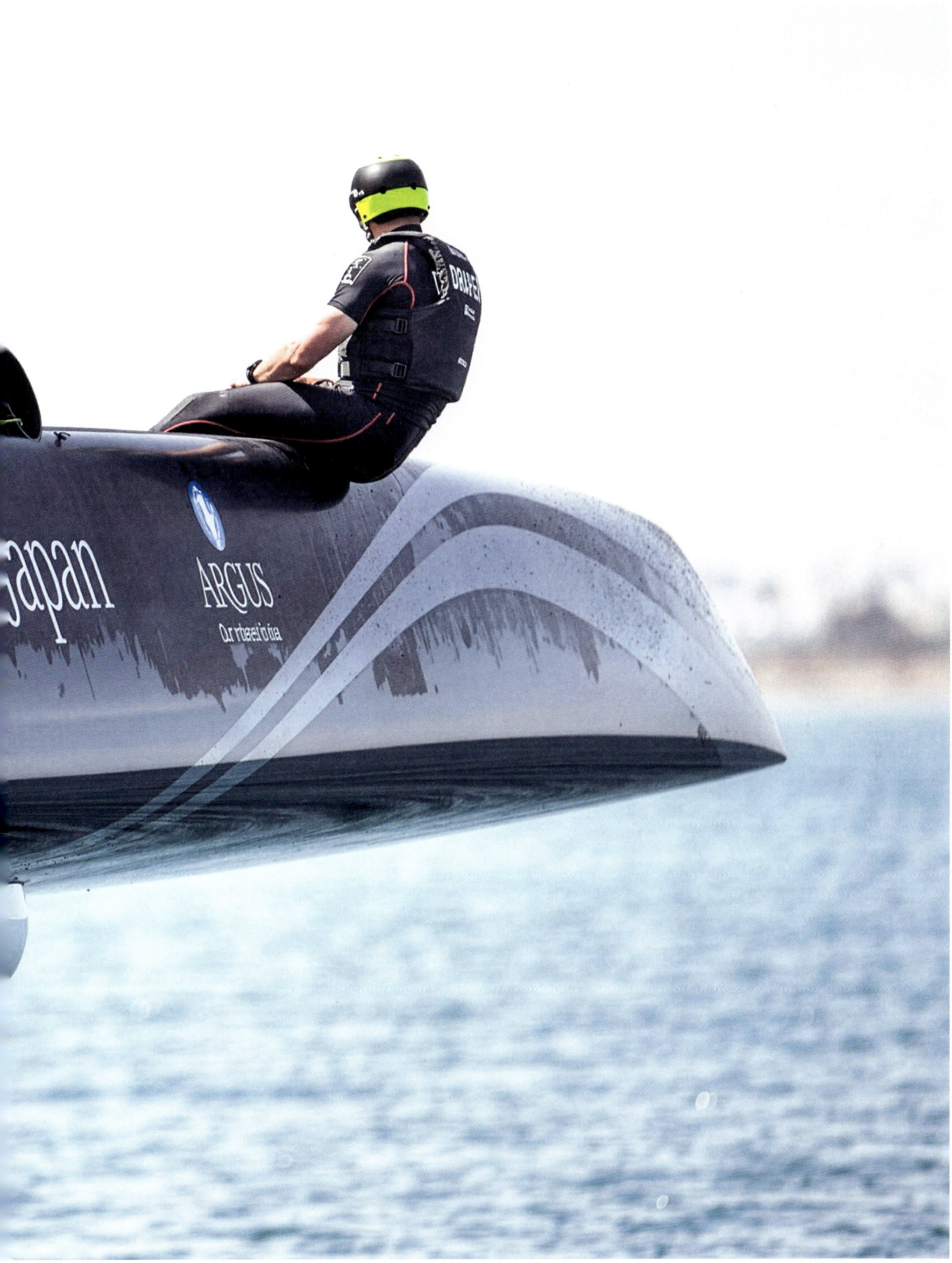
ARGUS

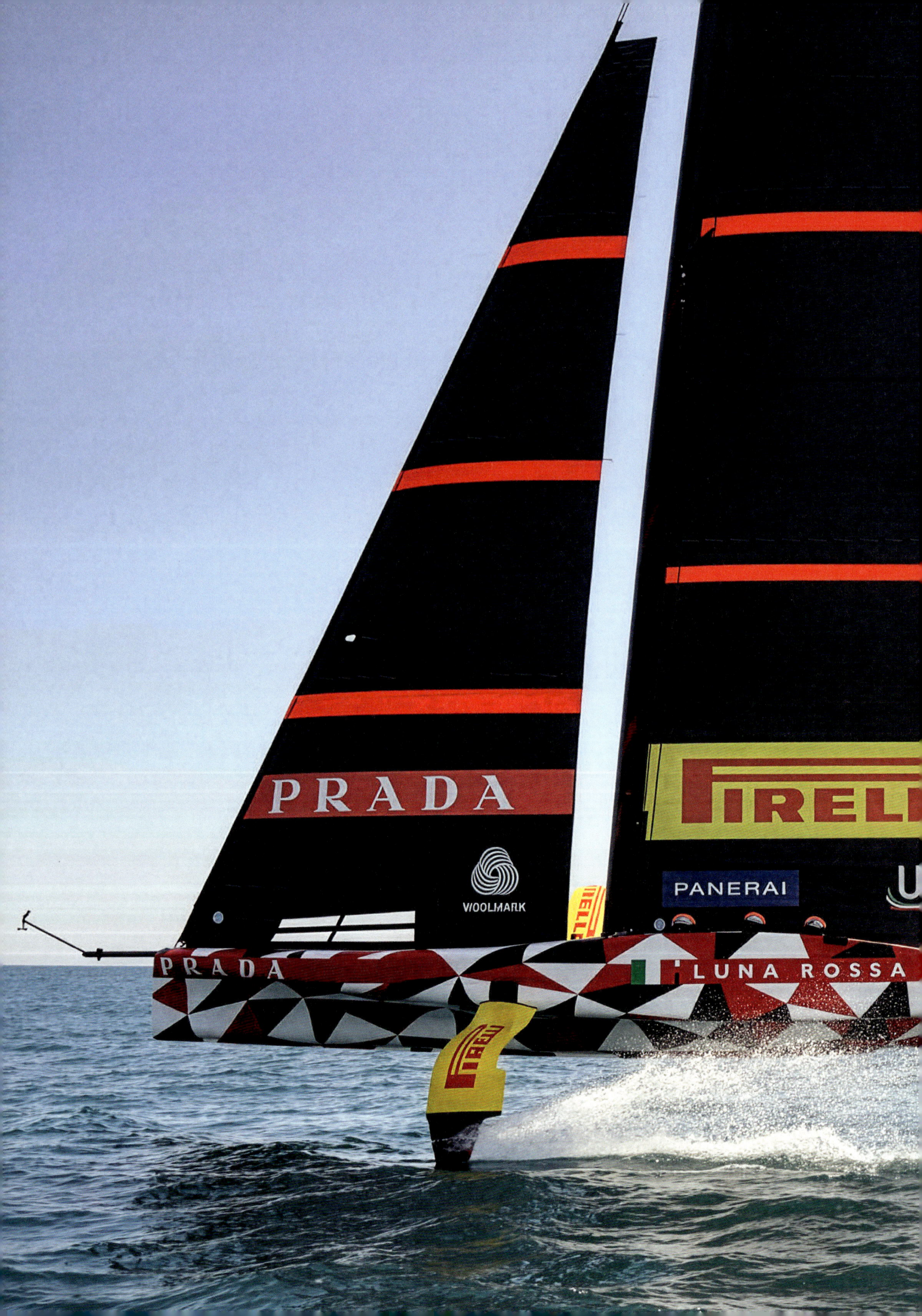
PRADA
WOOLMARK
PANERAI
PRADA
LUNA ROSSA

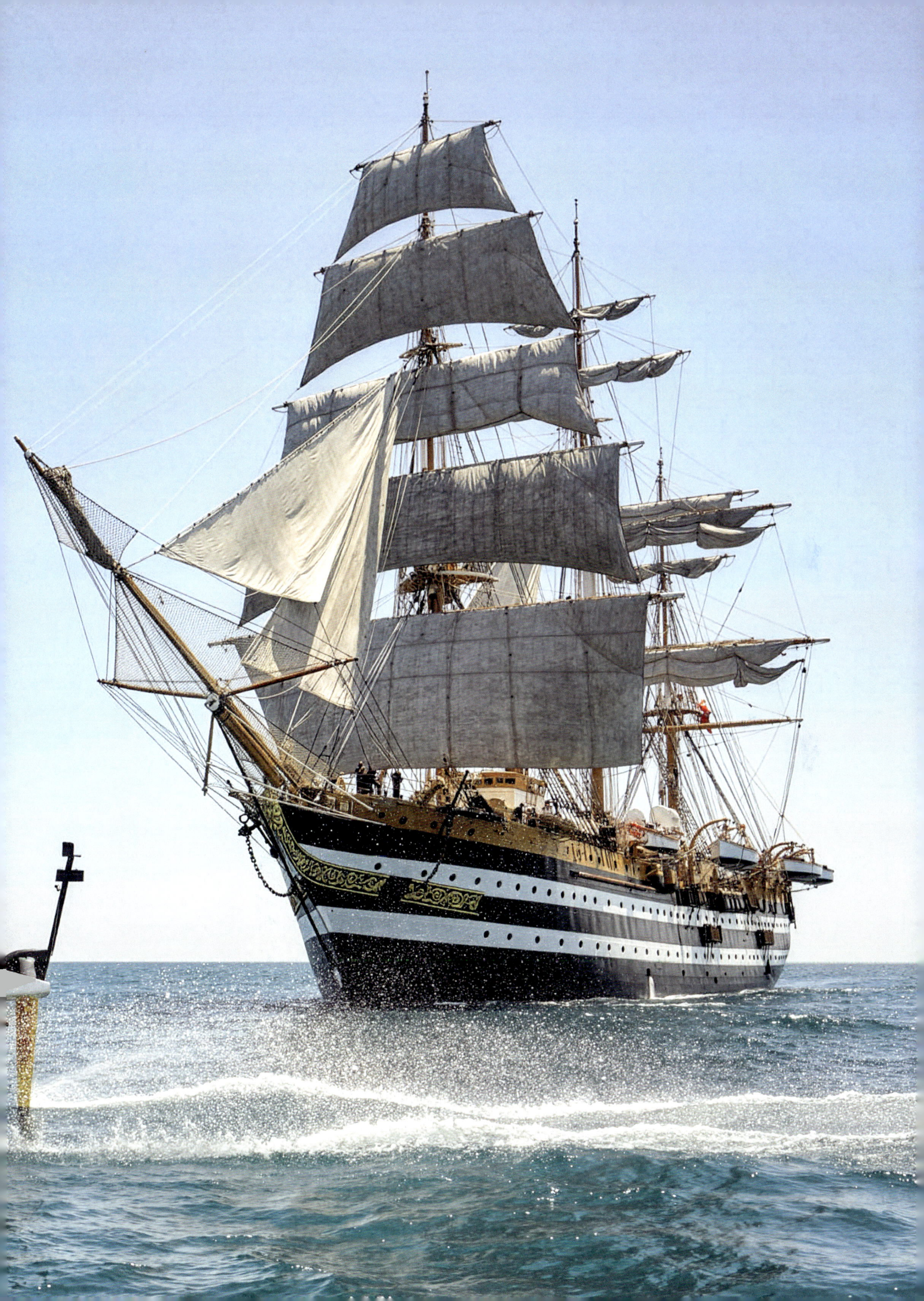

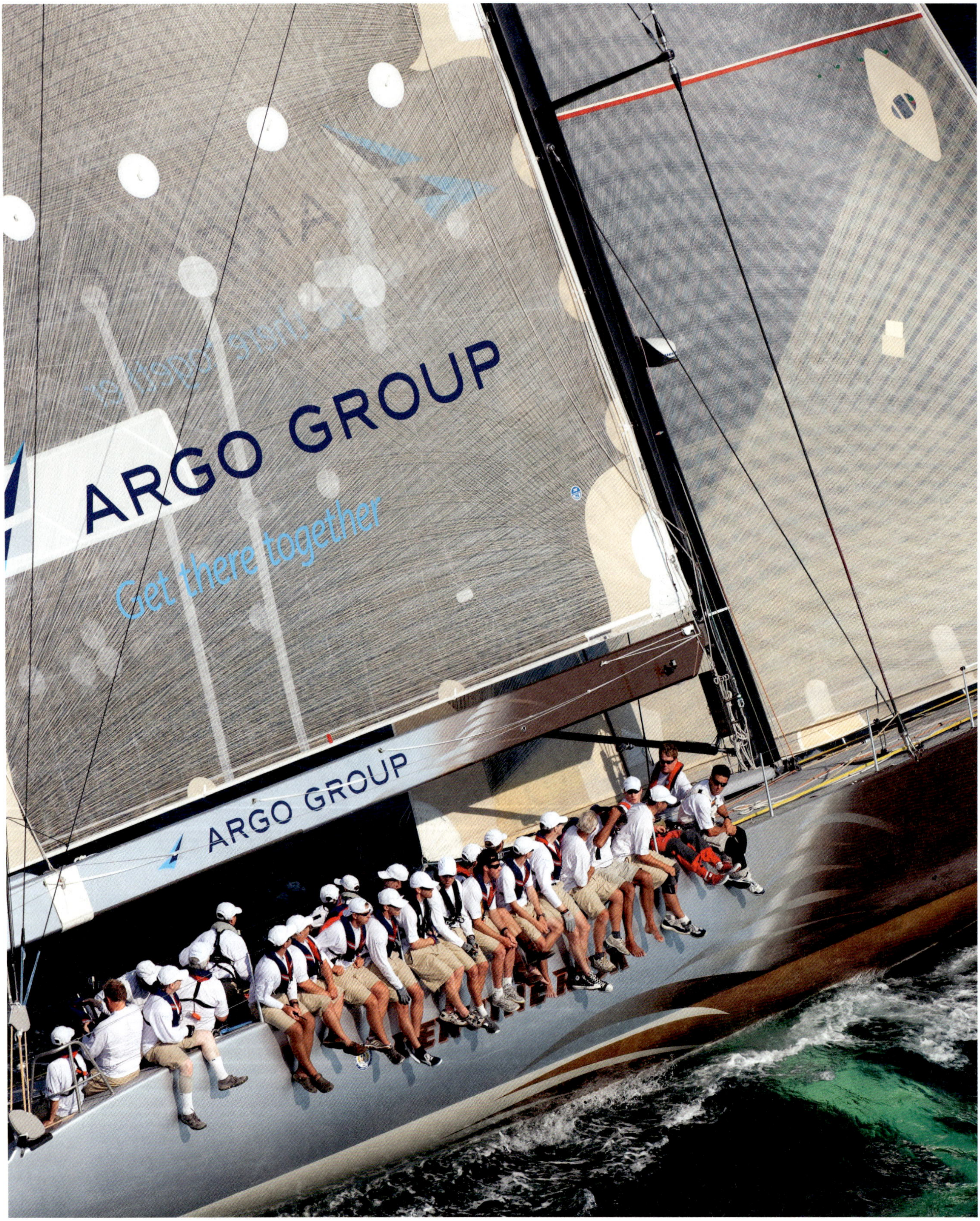

Previous pages: *An encounter in the gulf of Cagliari in May 2023 between the navy training ship "Amerigo Vespucci" and "Luna Rossa," the boat that will represent Italy at the next edition of the America's Cup. The prototype circled the older vessel several times with its sails unfurled as a sign of greeting.*

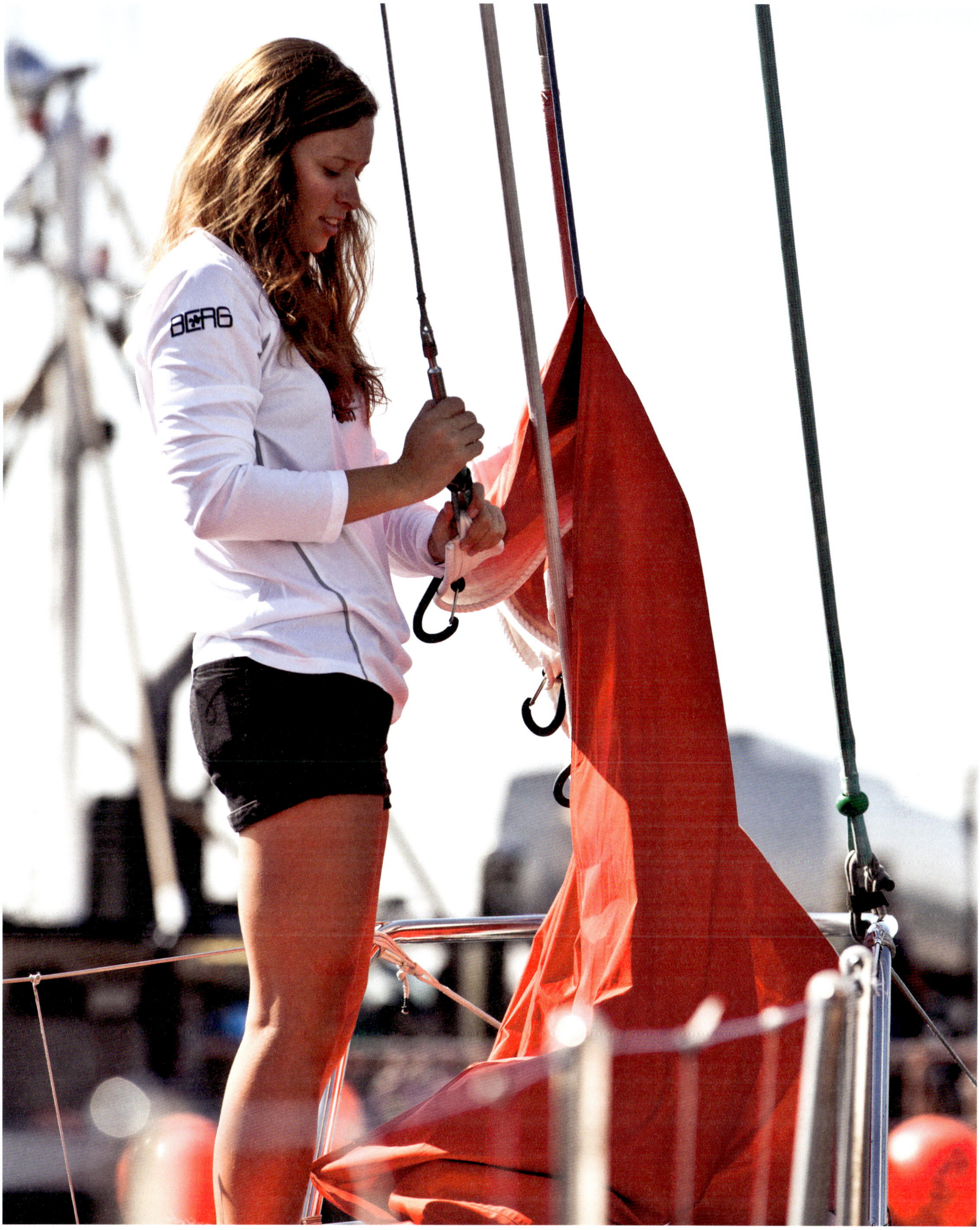

Opposite: *Aerial view of the crew hiking-out on "Genuine Risk" at the beginning of the Newport-Bermuda Race, June 2010.*

This page: *Checking sails ahead of the Newport-Bermuda Race, June 2010.*

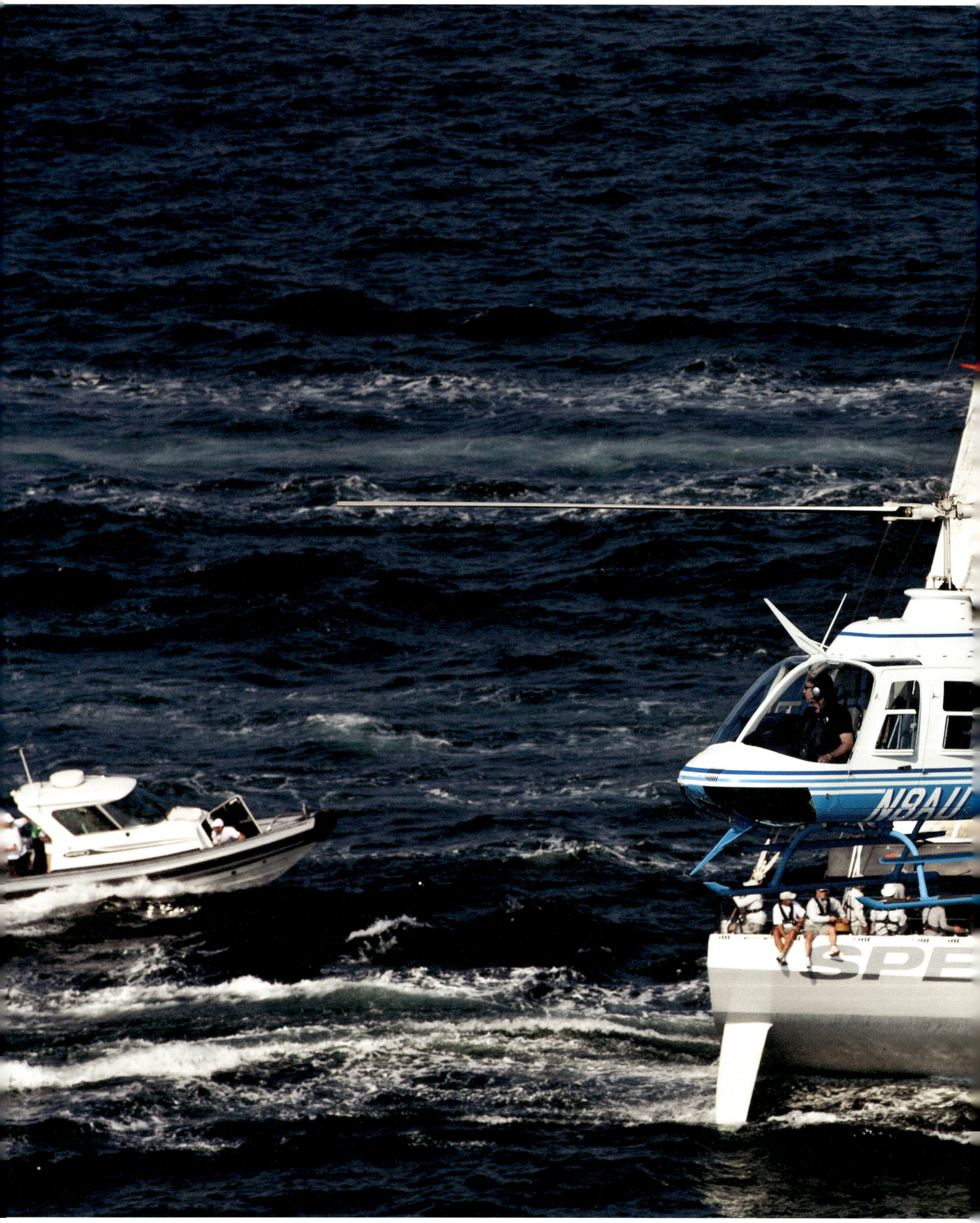

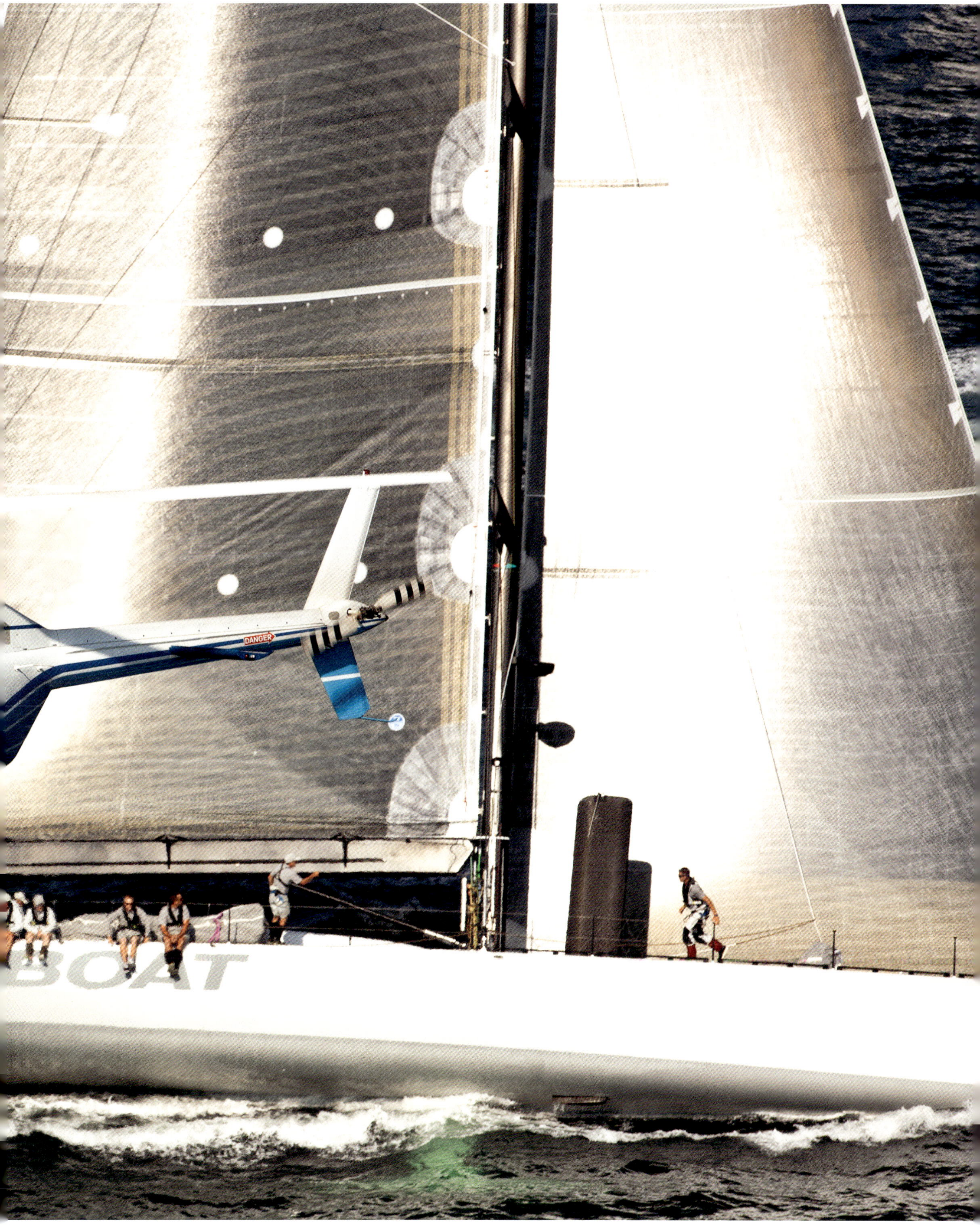
DANGER
BOAT

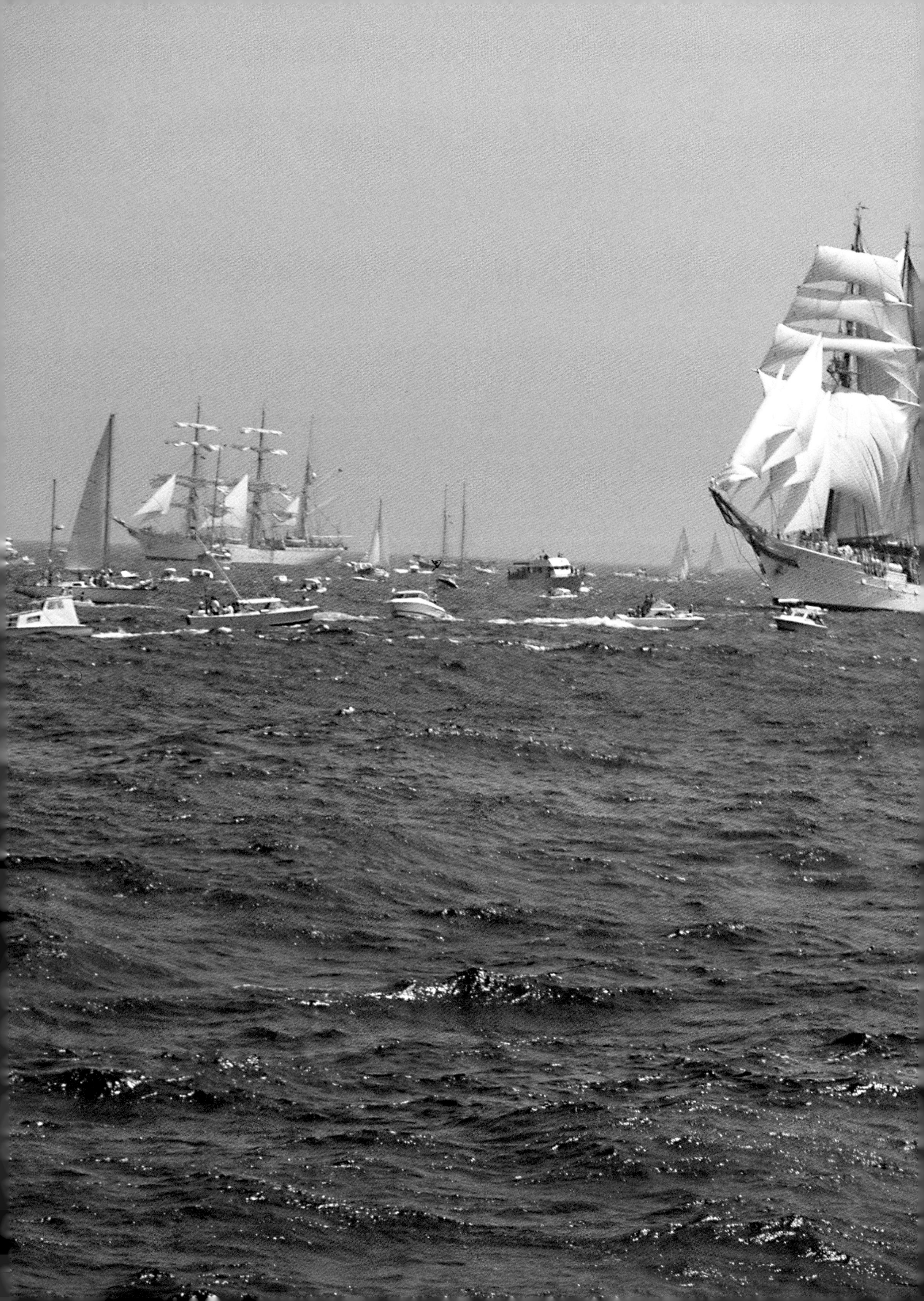

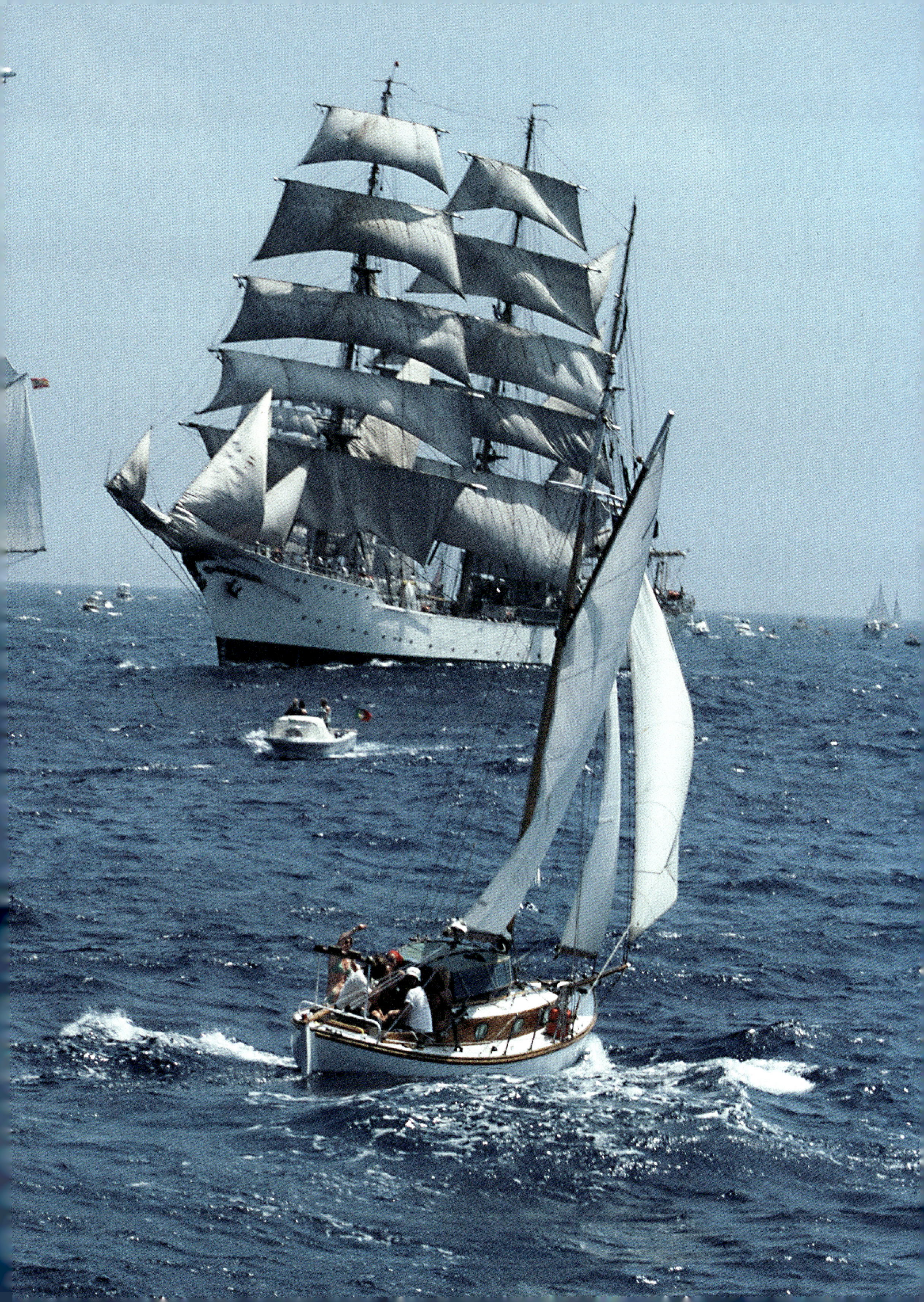

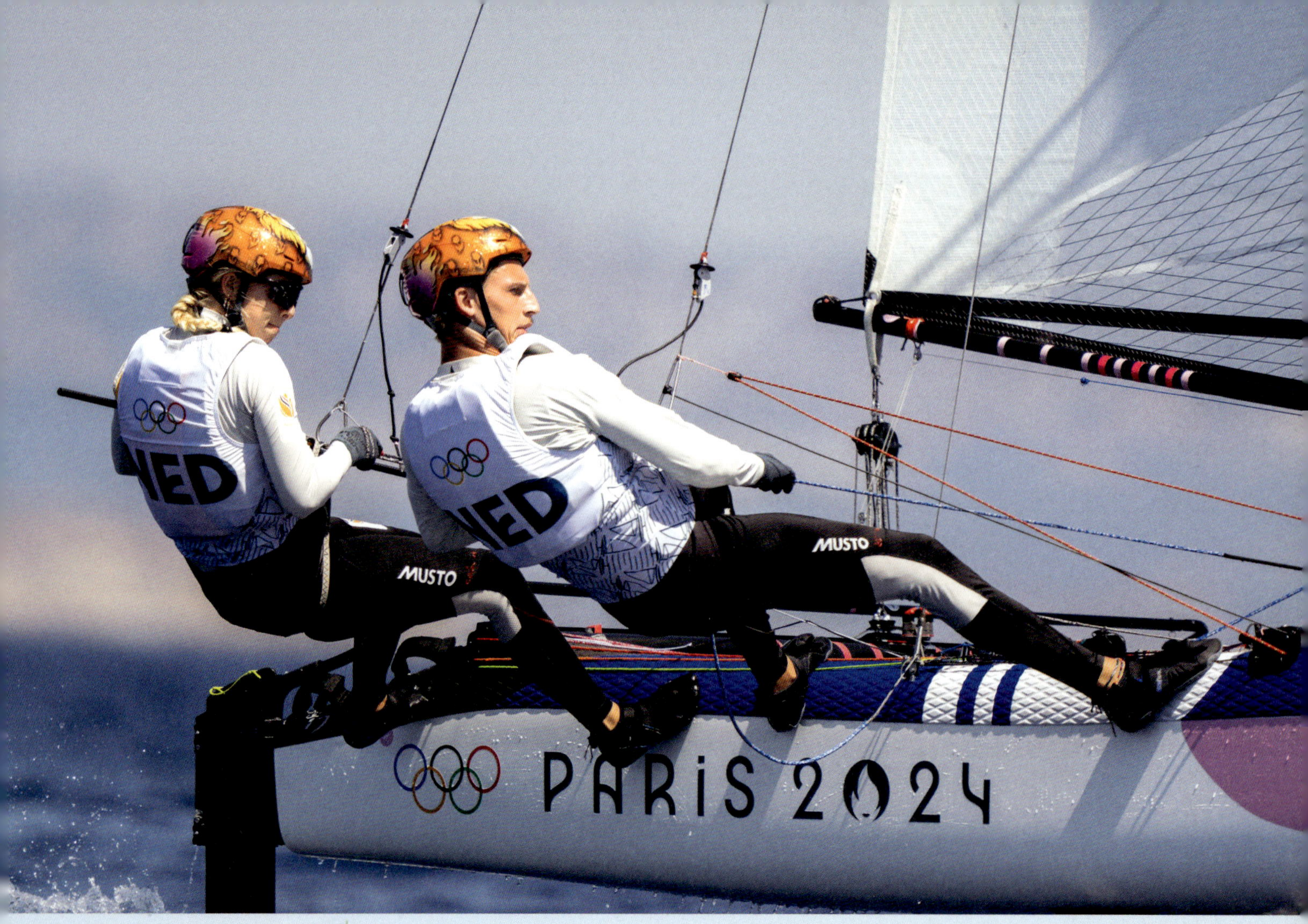
NED
NED
MUSTO
MUSTO
PARIS 2024

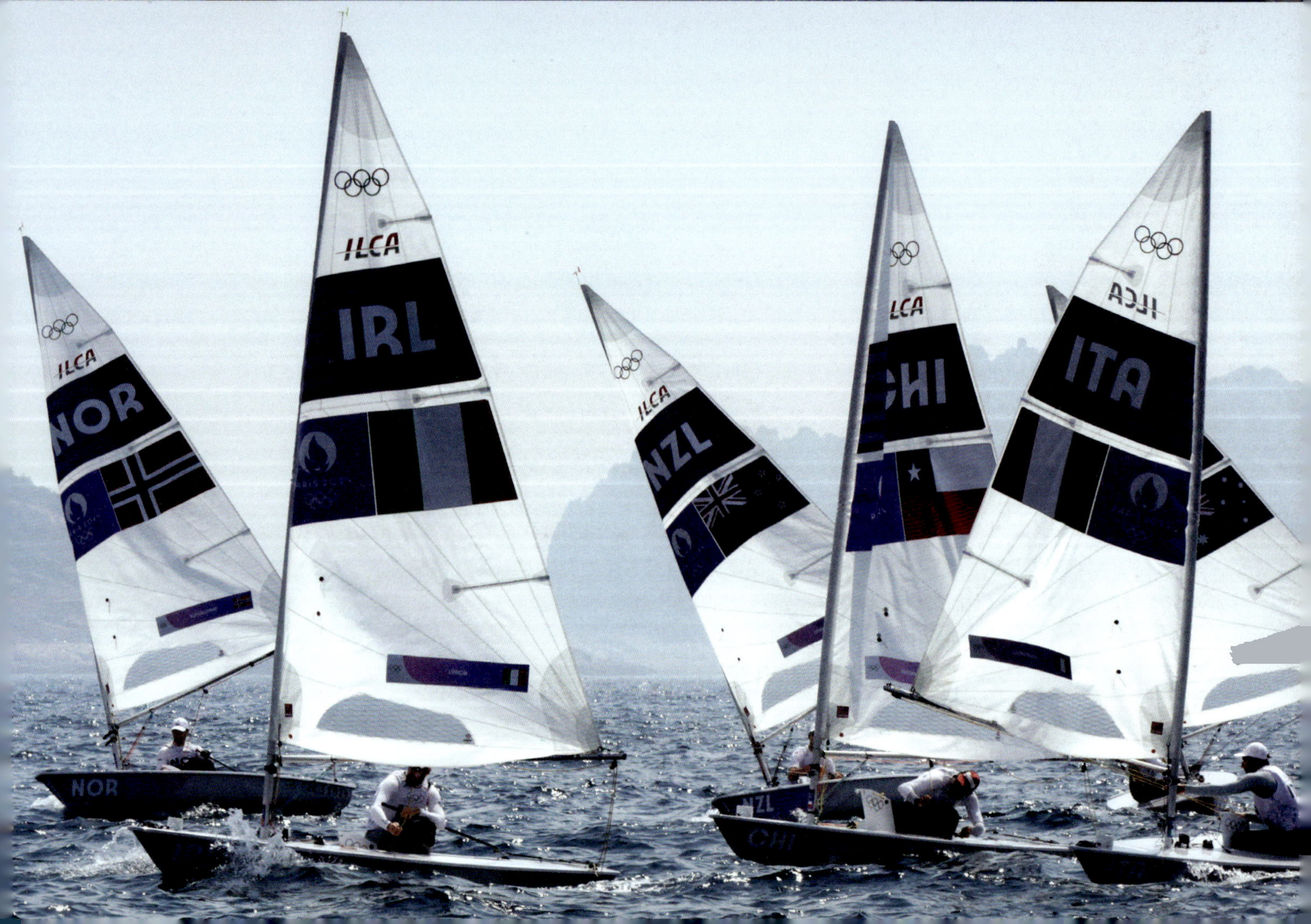
ILCA
IRL
ILCA
NOR
ILCA
NZL
ILCA
CHI
ILCA
ITA
NOR
NZL

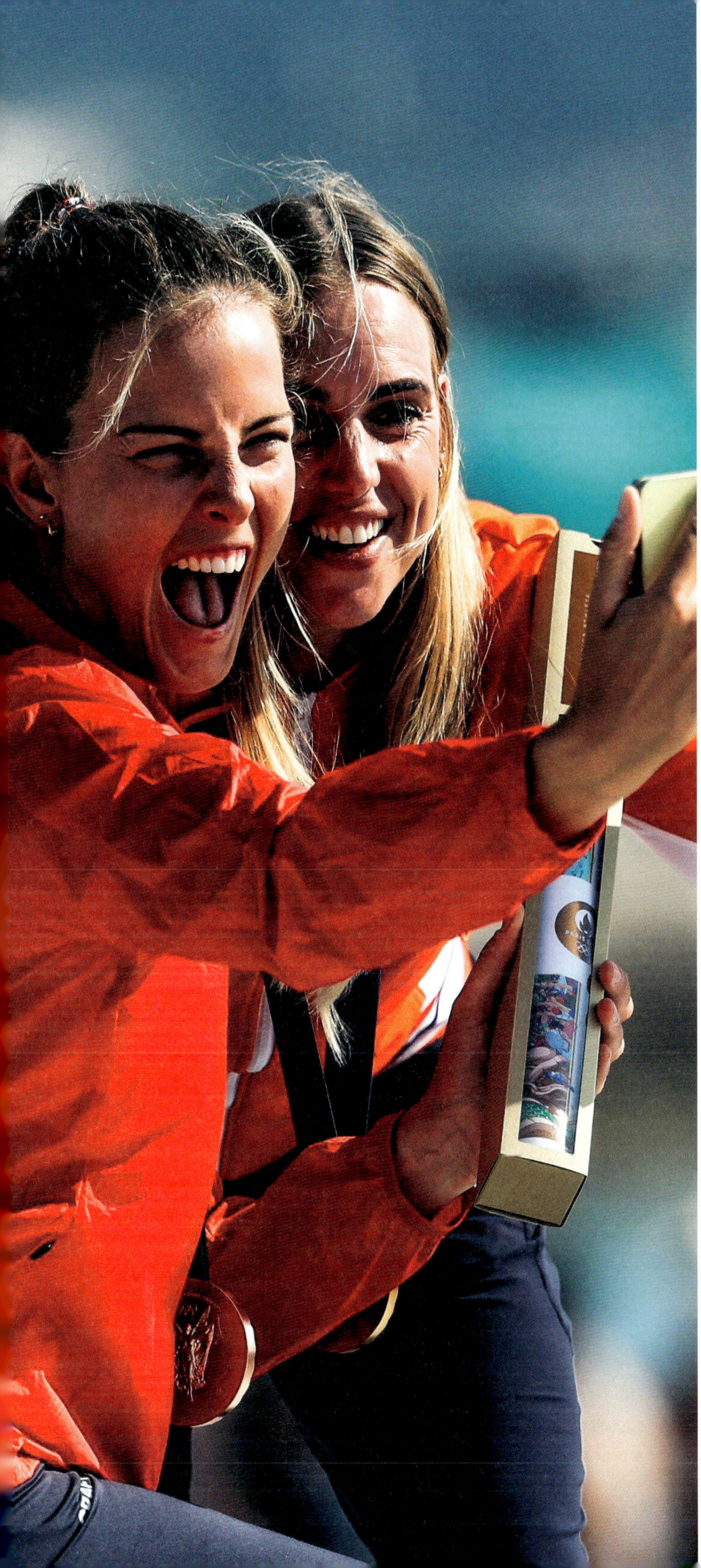

Pages 84/85: *A helicopter approaches "Speedboat" at the beginning of the Newport-Bermuda Race, June 2010.*

Previous pages: *Tall ships under full sail await the start of the Bermuda-Newport leg of the Tall Ships Race in Hamilton, Bermuda in June 1976. In the foreground is a group of Bermudans in a small boat out to see the start of the race. The tall ship on the right is Colombia's "Gloria," and on the left is the Spanish vessel "Juan Sebastian de Elcano."*

Opposite, top: *Sailors Laila van der Meer and Bjarne Bouwer in action during the Nacra 17 fleet races at the Olympic Games in Marseille, August 2024.*

Opposite, bottom: *The Men's Dinghy Medal Race at Marseille Marina on the 12th day of the 2024 Paris Olympic Games.*

This page: *Marit Bouwmeester of the Netherlands competing in the Women's Dinghy Medal Race at Marseille Marina on Day 11 of the 2024 Olympic Games.*

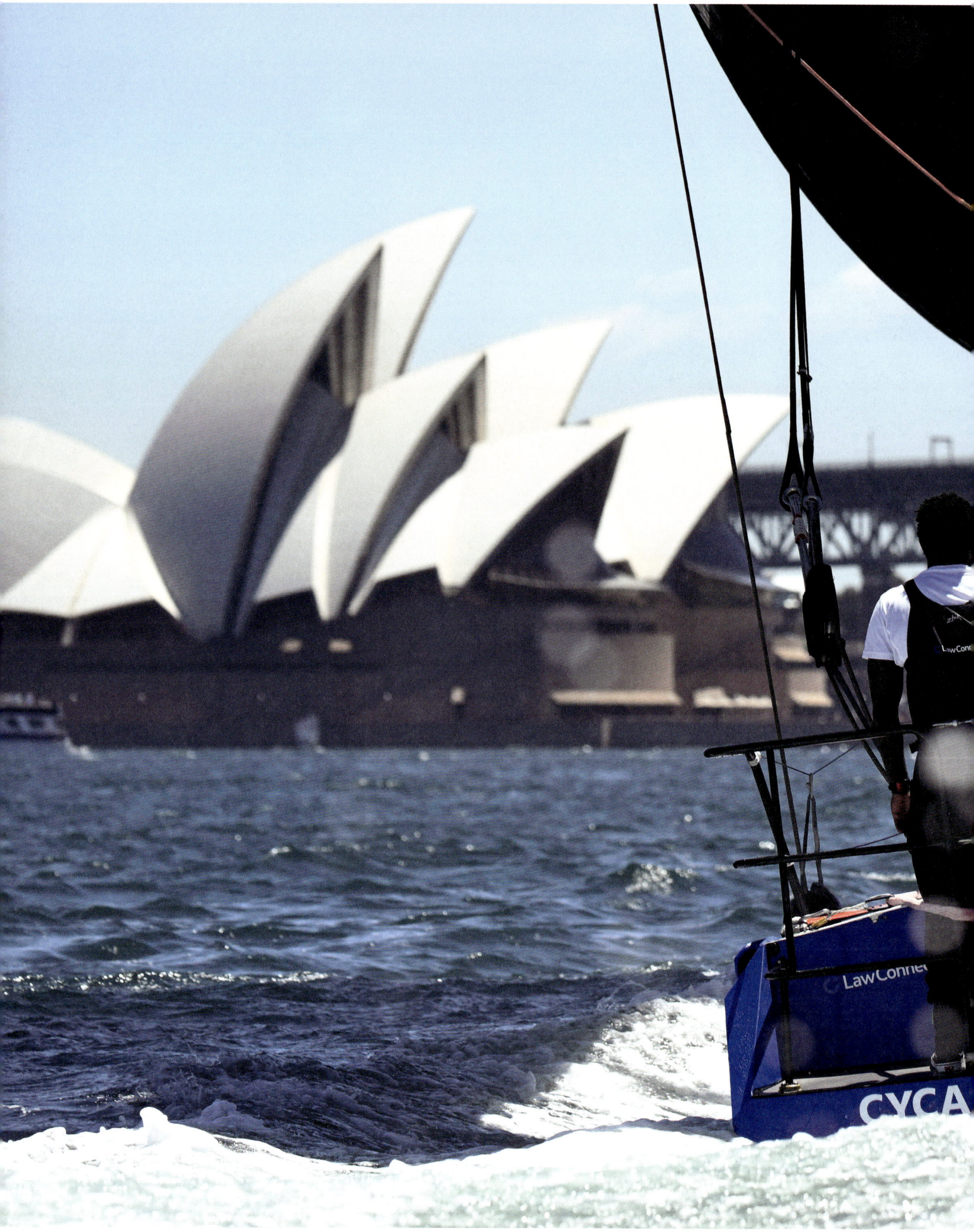
LawConne
CYCA

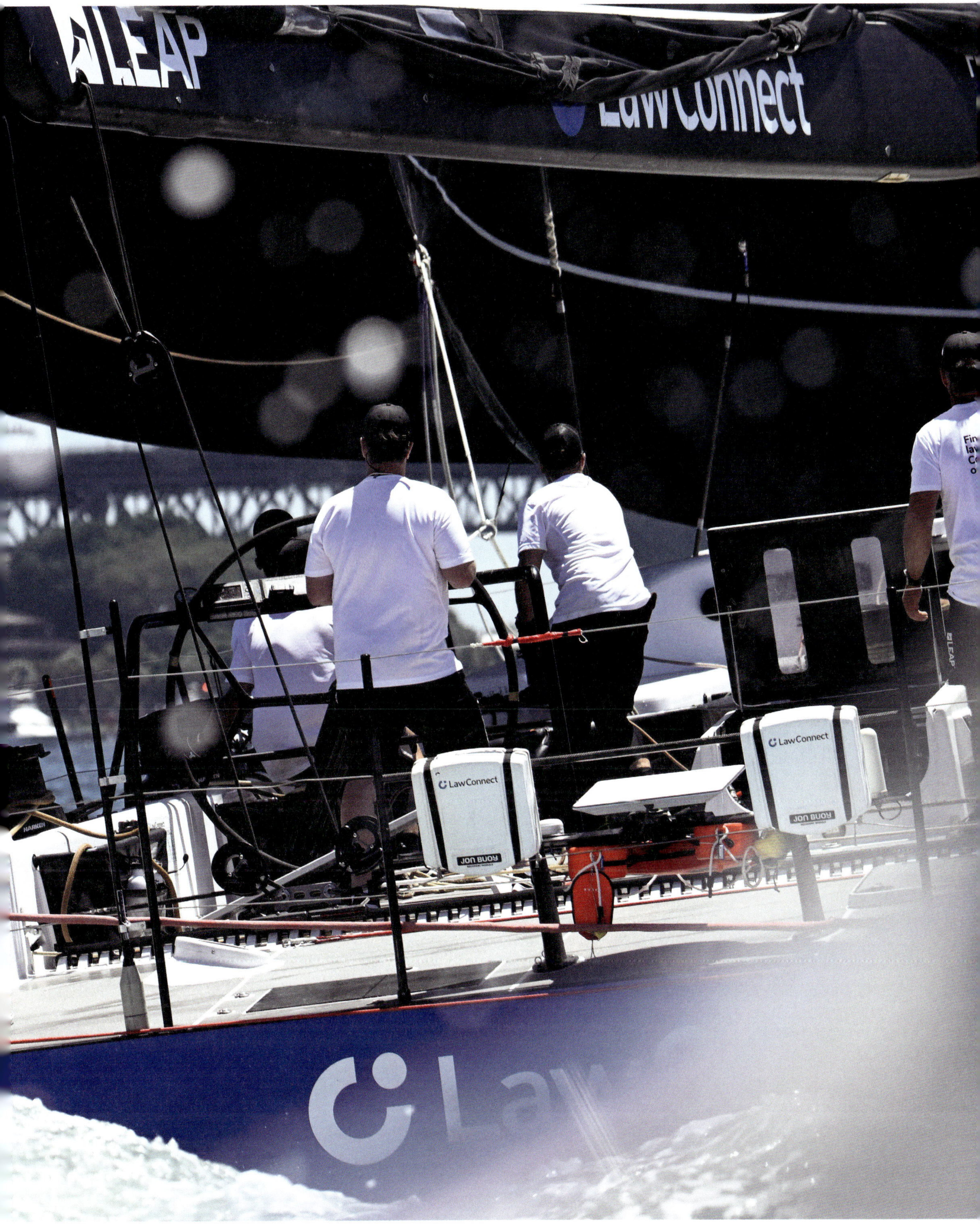
LEAP
LawConnect
LawConnect
JON BUOY
LawConnect
JON BUOY

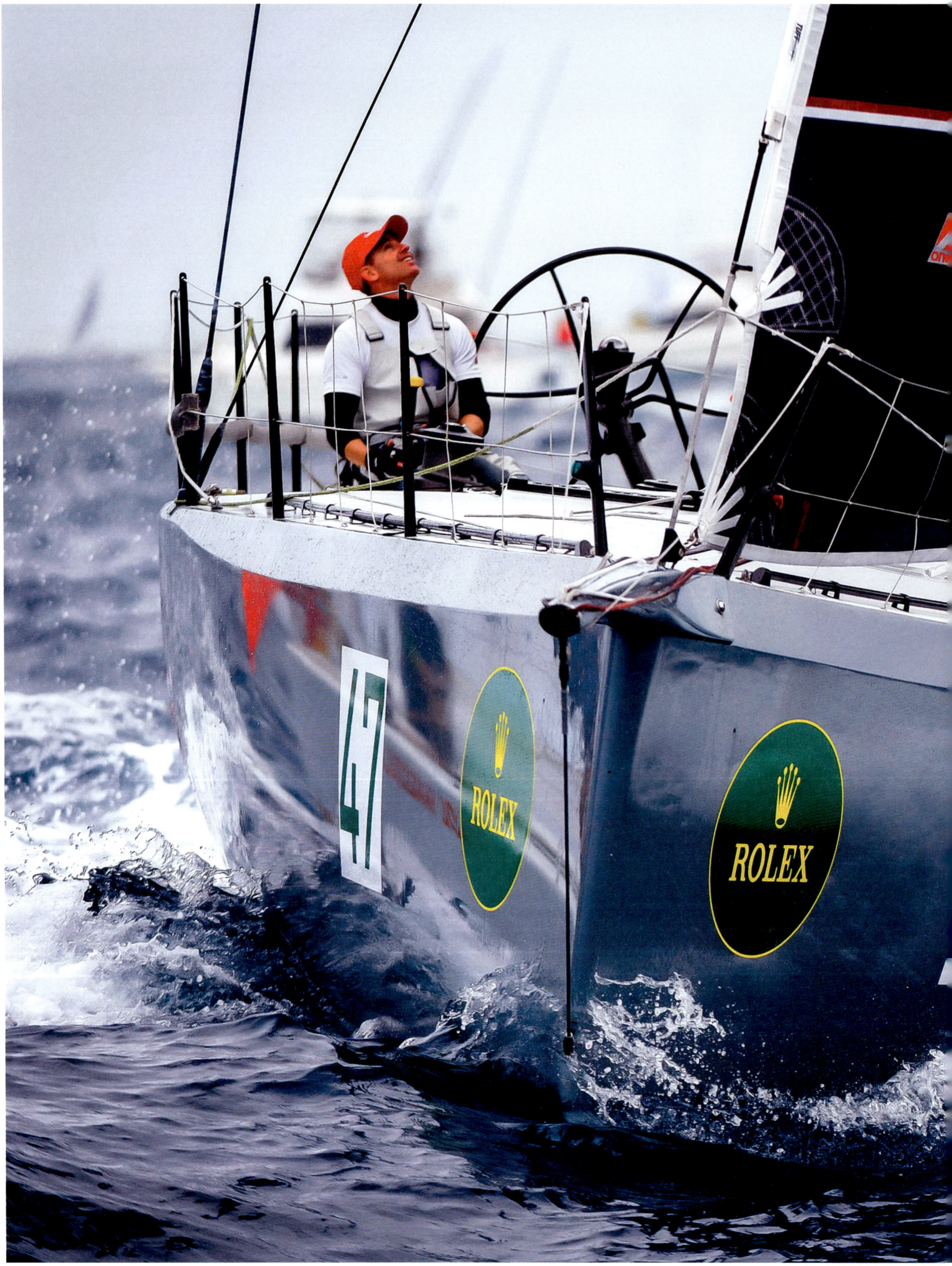
47
ROLEX
ROLEX

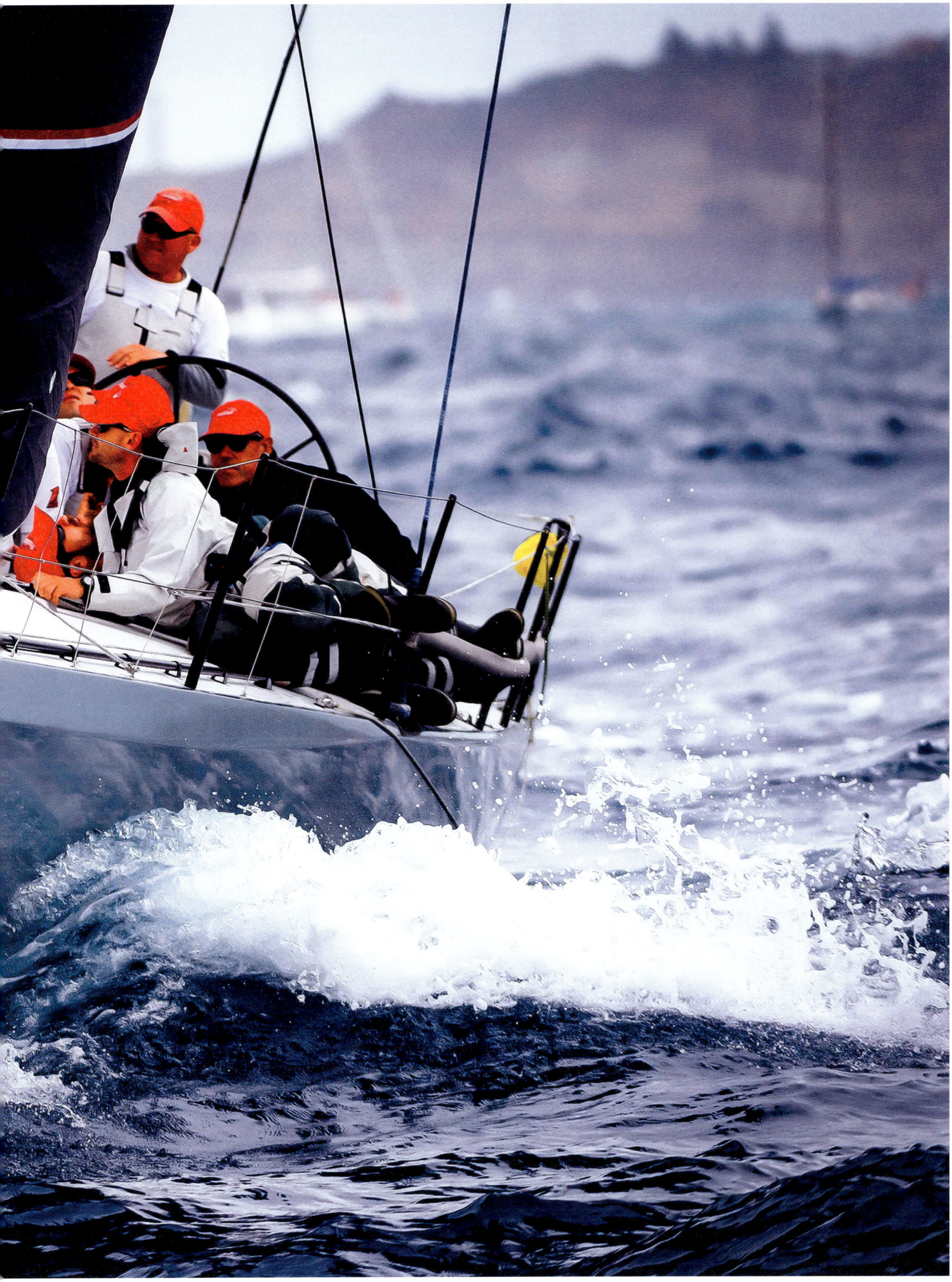

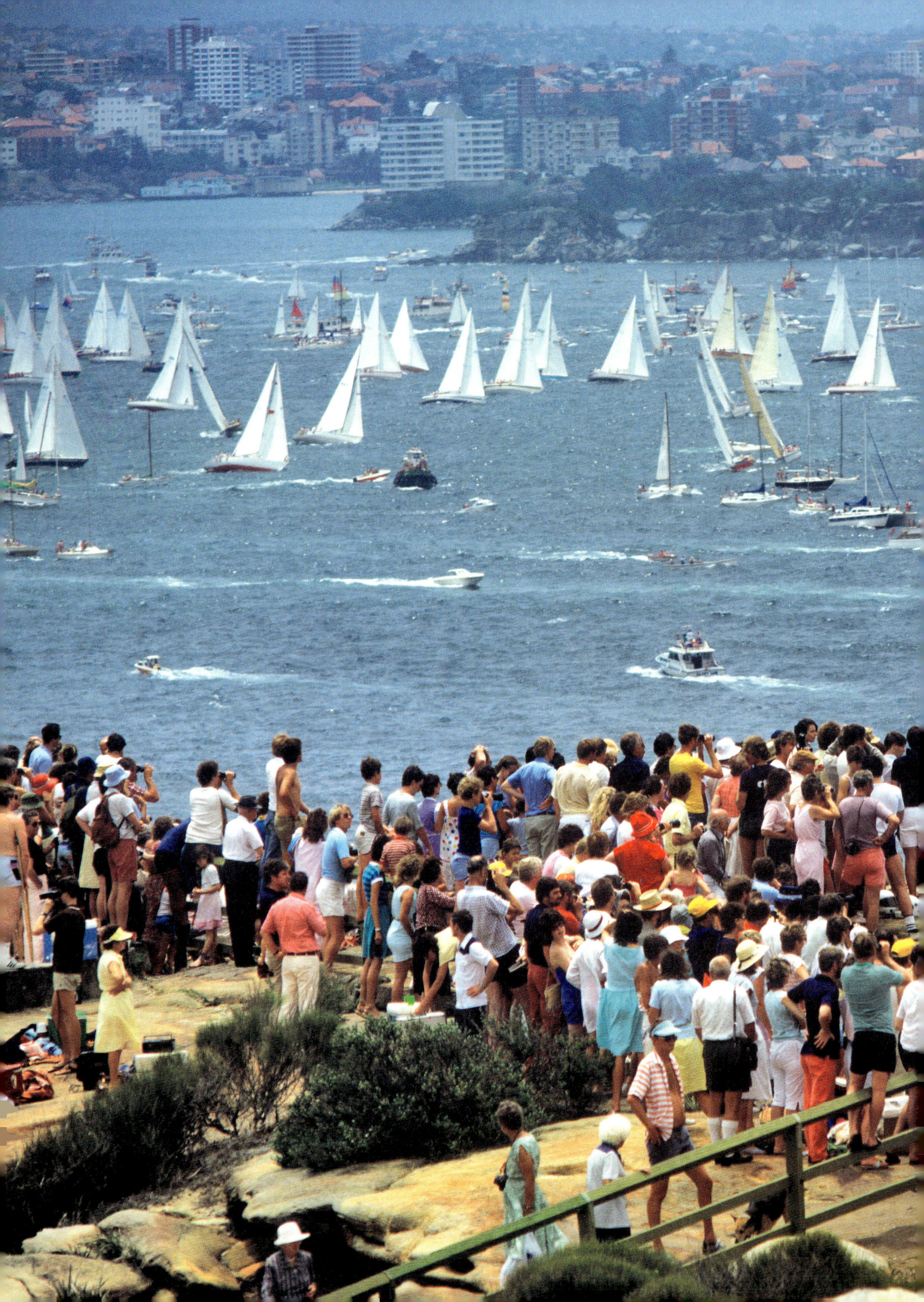

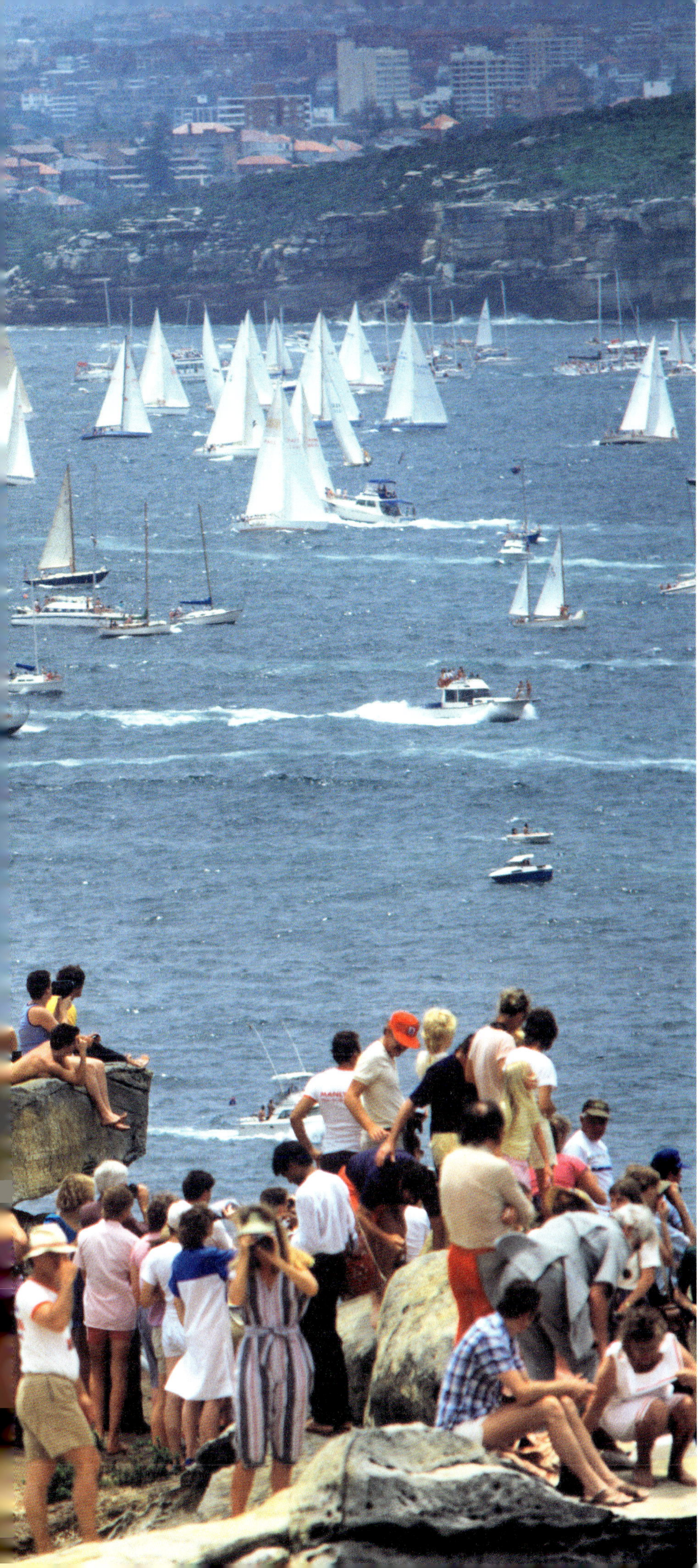

Pages 90/91: *The maxi yacht "LawConnect," skippered by Christian Beck, wins the Solas Big Boat Challenge in front of Sydney Opera House in December 2023.*

Previous pages:: *"Indian," owned and skippered by Craig Carter, heads out of Sydney Harbour into open ocean at the start of the 73rd Rolex Sydney Hobart Yacht Race in 2017.*

These pages: *Yachts passing the South Head at the start of the Sydney to Hobart Yacht Race in December 1984.*

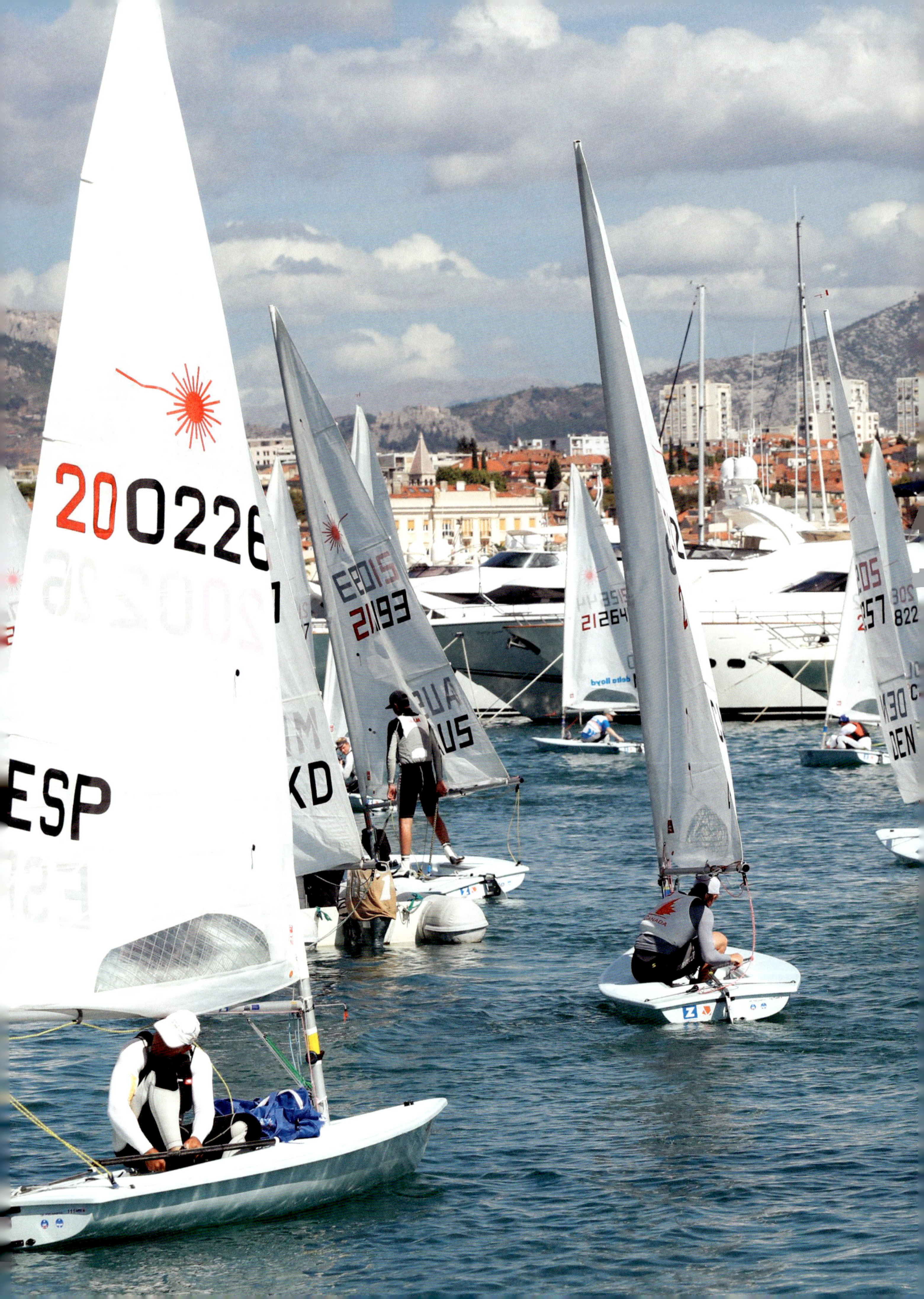

200226
ESP
21193
AUS
KD
21264
257
822
DEN

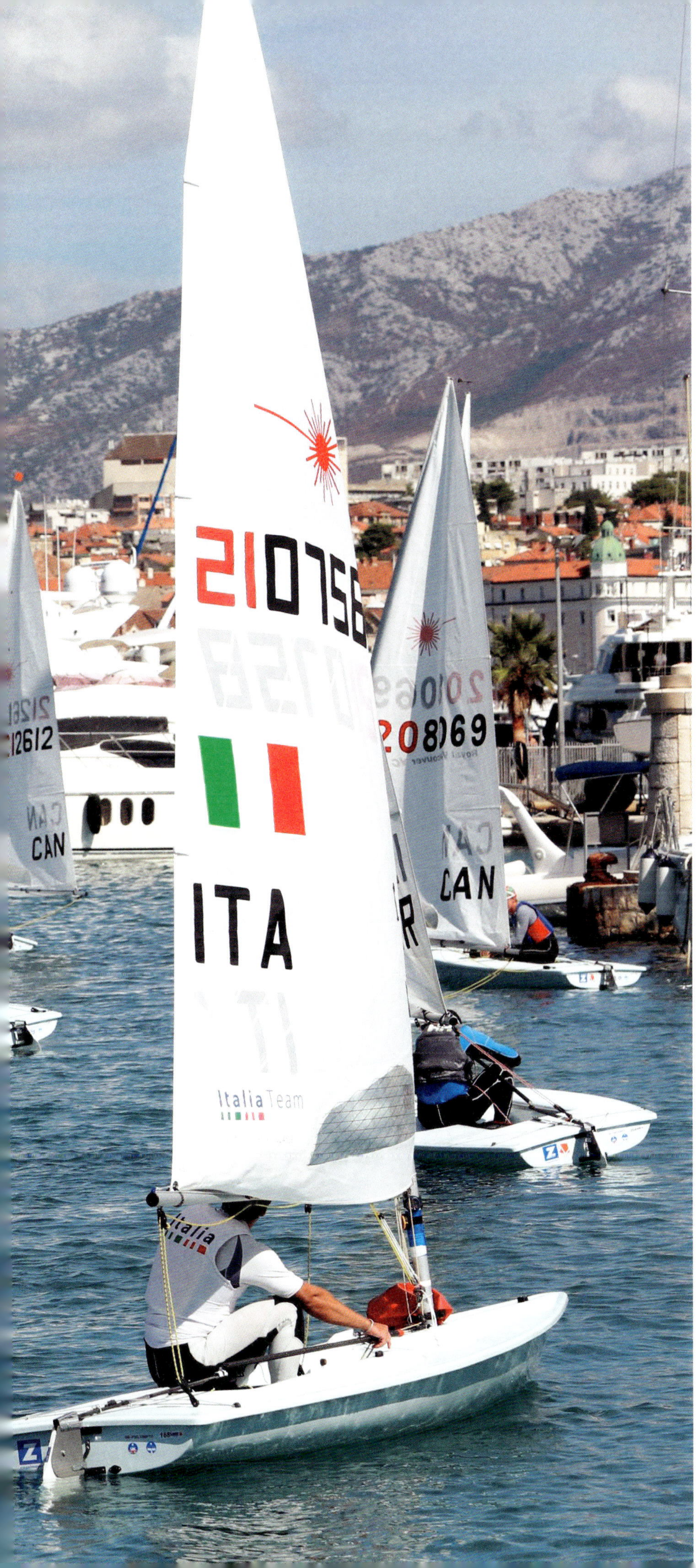

These pages: *The finals of the World Sailing Championships, Laser class, in Croatia in September 2017.*

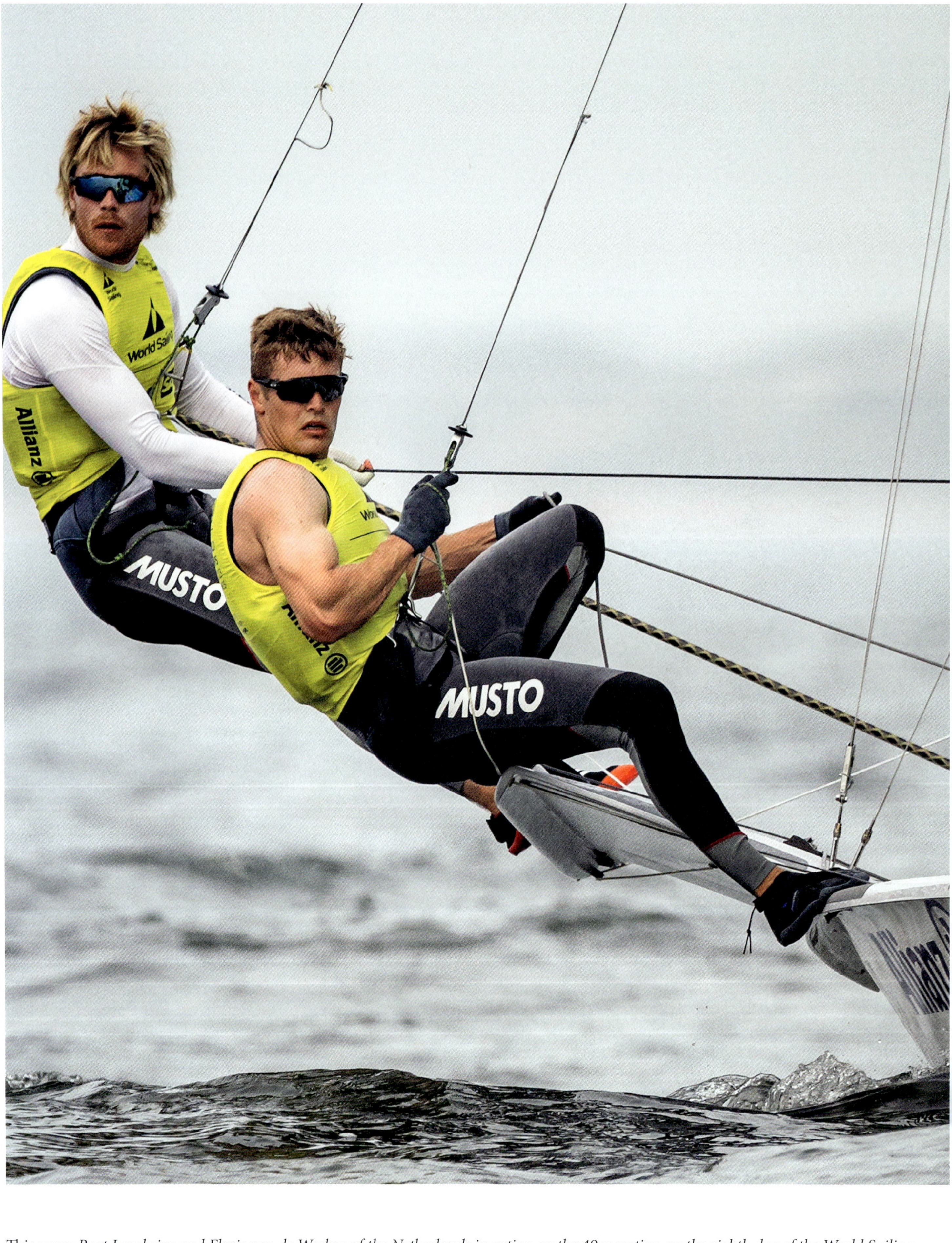

This page: *Bart Lambriex and Floris van de Werken of the Netherlands in action on the 49er section on the eighth day of the World Sailing Championships in Scheveningen, the Netherlands in August 2023.*

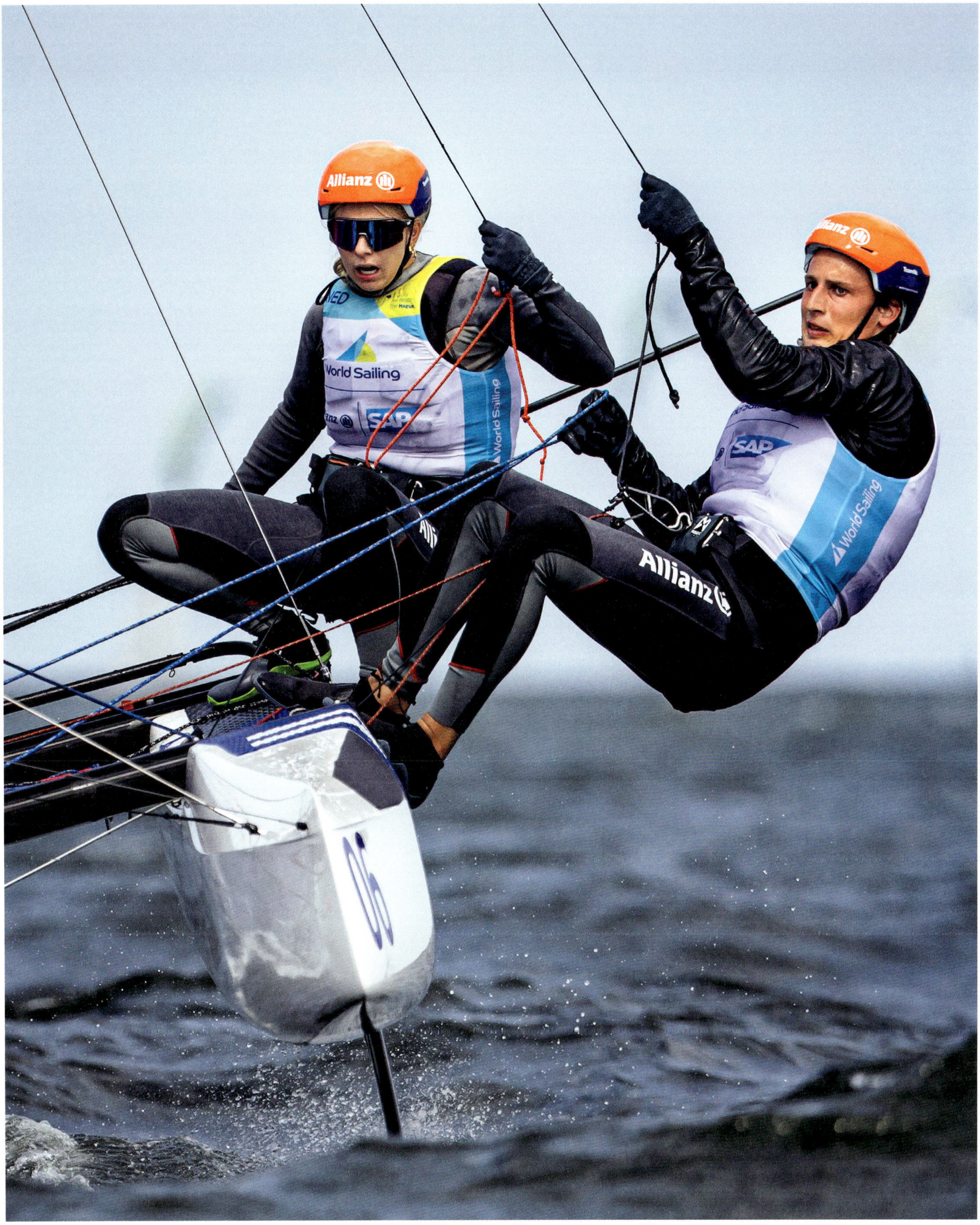

This page: *Laila van der Meer and Bjarne Bouwer of the Netherlands in action on the Nacra 17 section on the seventh day of the World Sailing Championships, Scheveningen August 2023.*

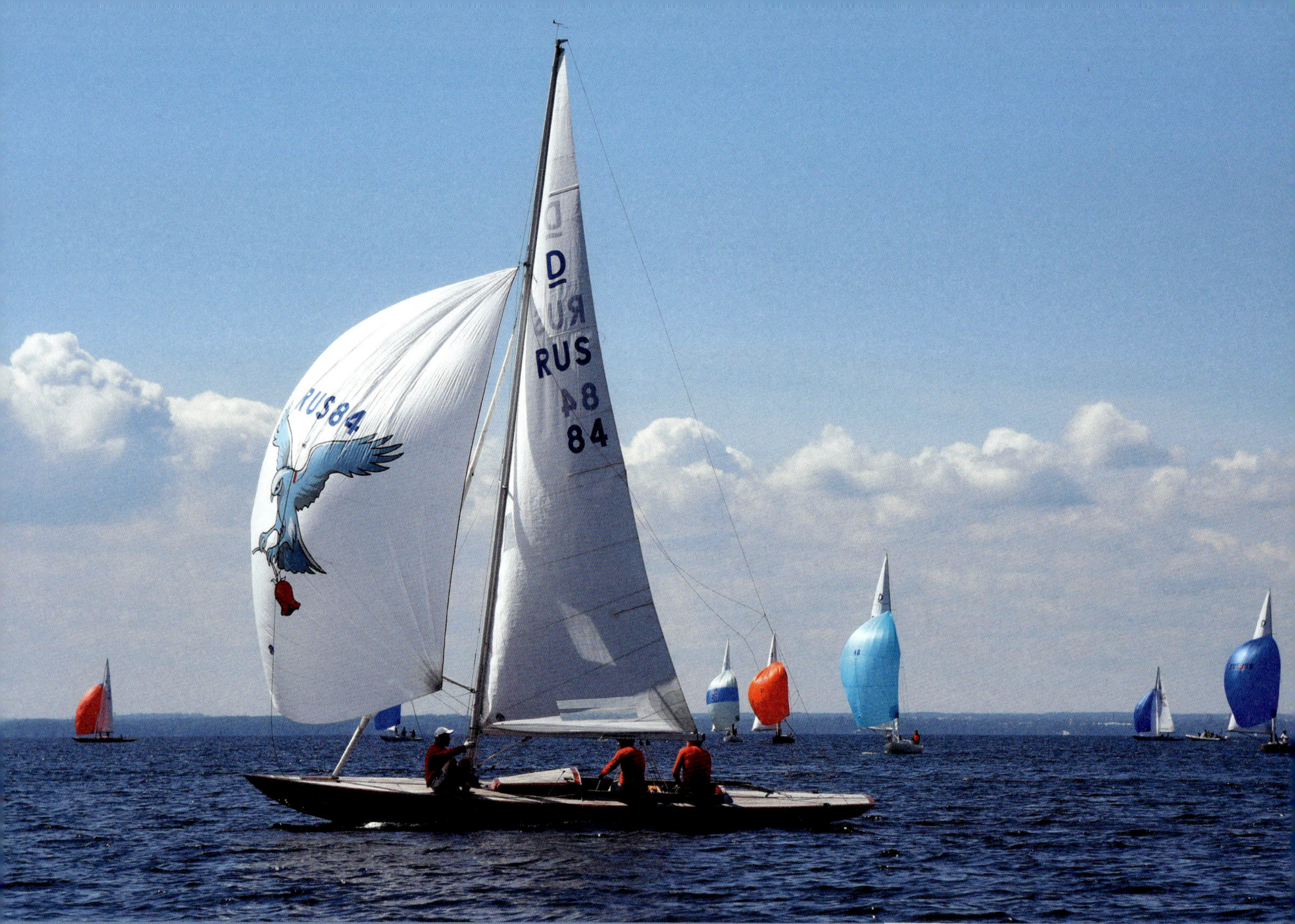
RUS84
D
RUS
48
84

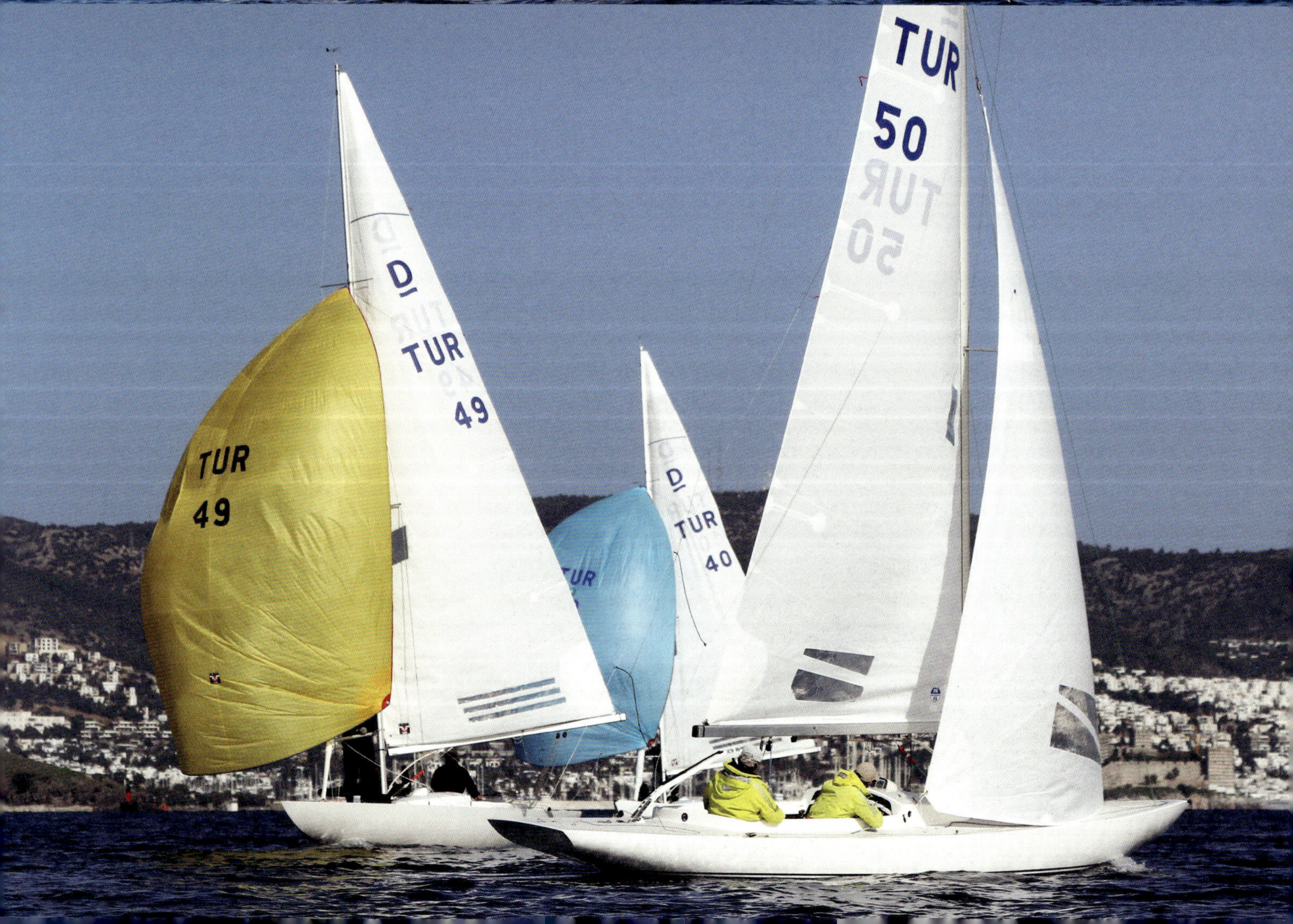
TUR
50
D
TUR
49
TUR
49
D
TUR
40

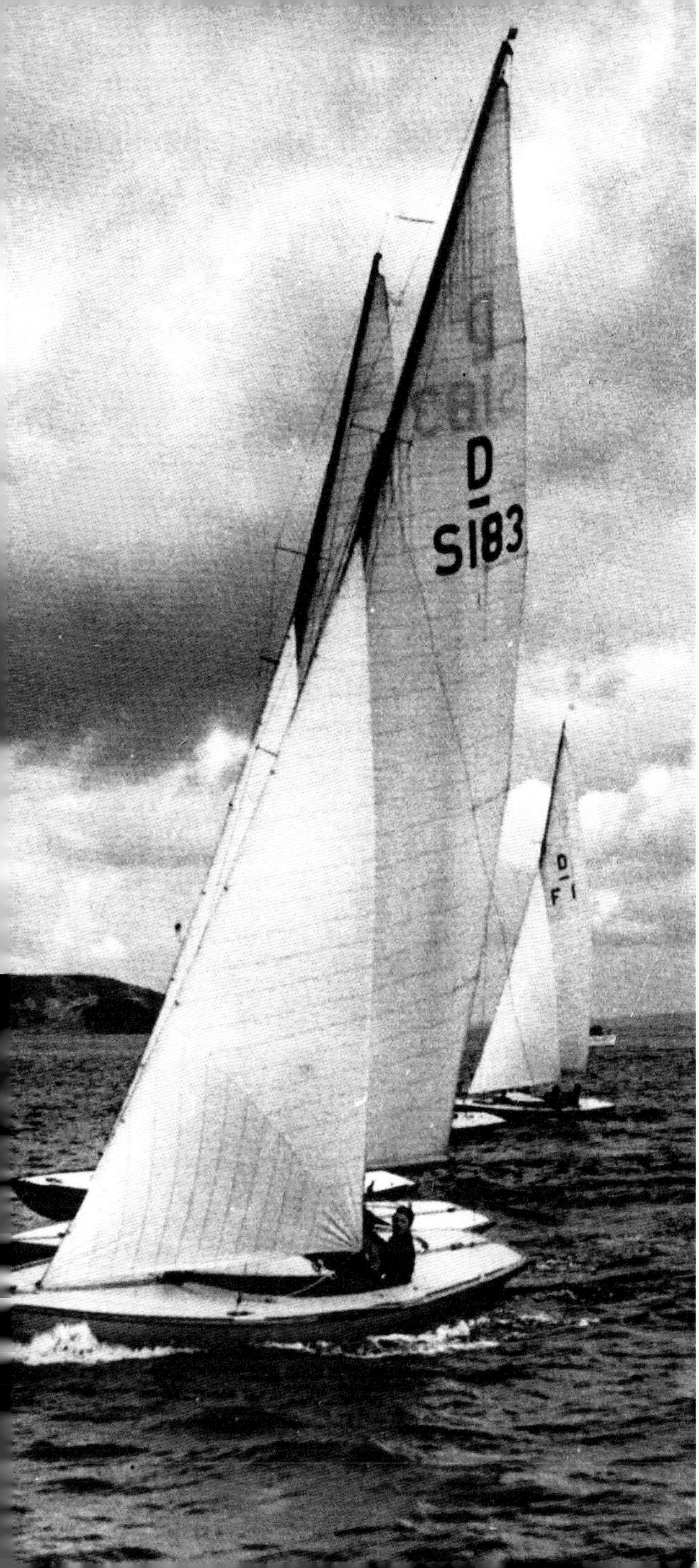

Opposite, top: *The Open Russian Sailing Championship in Saint Petersburg, Russia in July 2017.*

Opposite, bottom: *Dragon boats competing for the Dragon Cup in Bodrum, Turkey in August 2020, sailing very close to one other.*

This page: *Yachts at the start of the Dragon class race at the 1948 Olympics in Torbay, UK. L to R: "Slagnoken" (Sweden), "Allegro" (France), "Pamfsero" (Argentina), "Joy" (Holland) and "Ausonia" (Italy).*

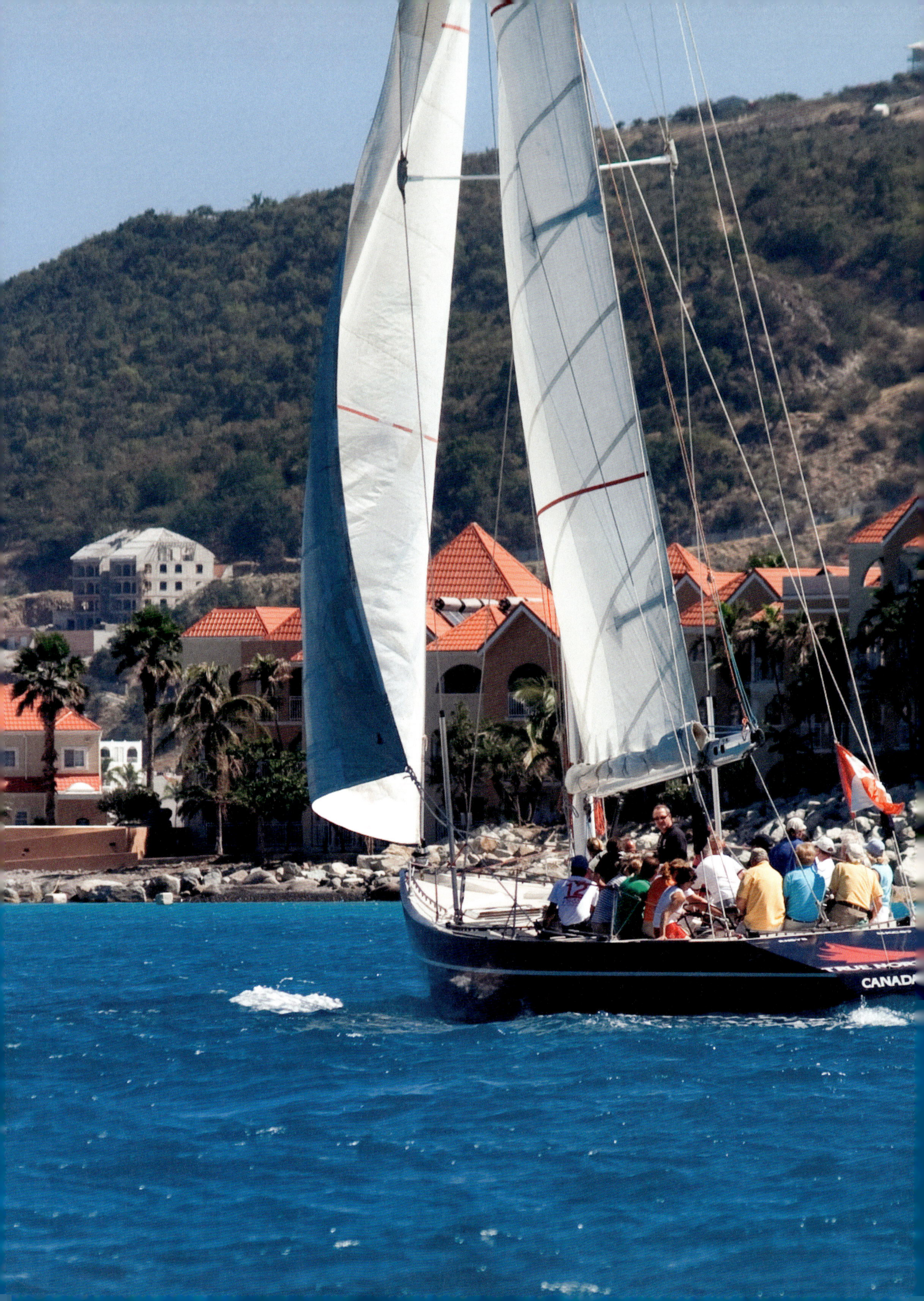

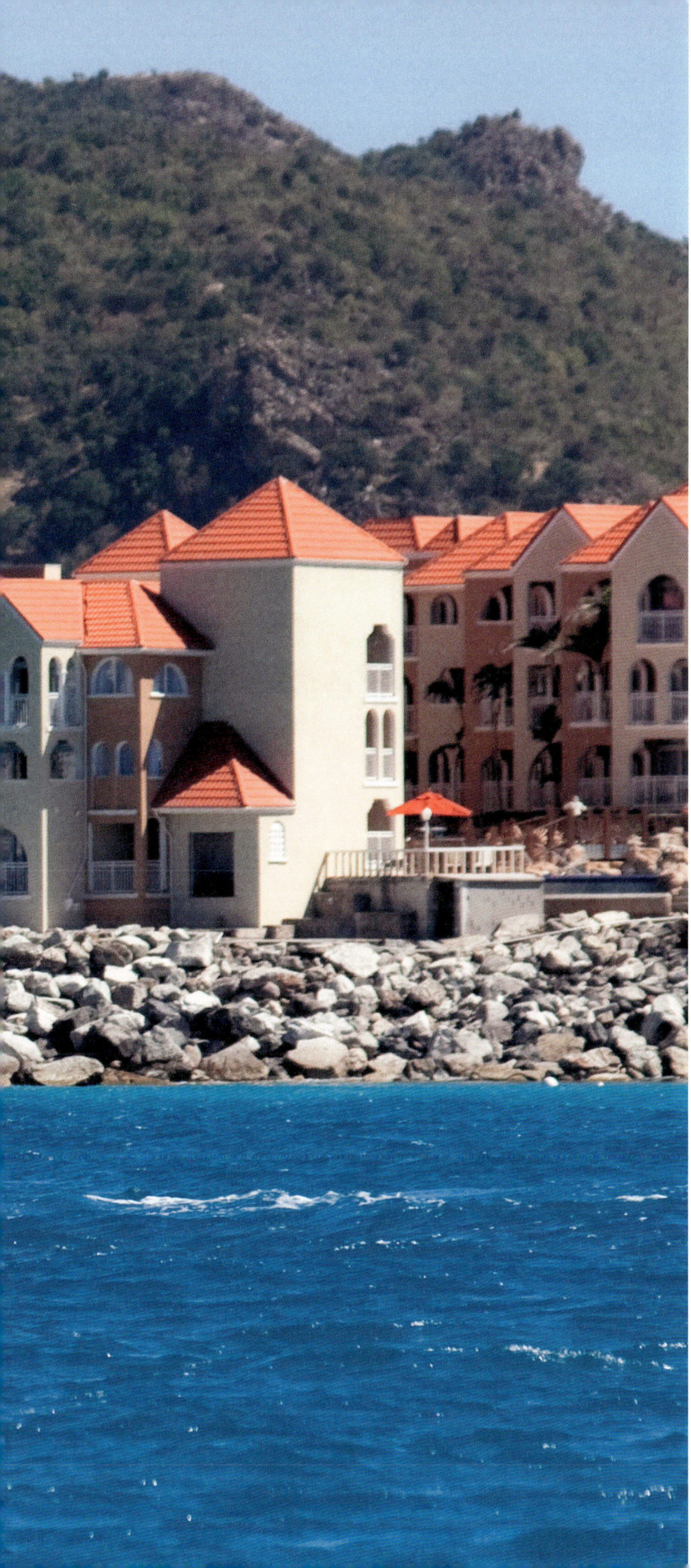

These pages: *The 12-meter yacht "True North," originally of Canada, sailing in Great Bay, Philipsburg, Sint Maarten.*

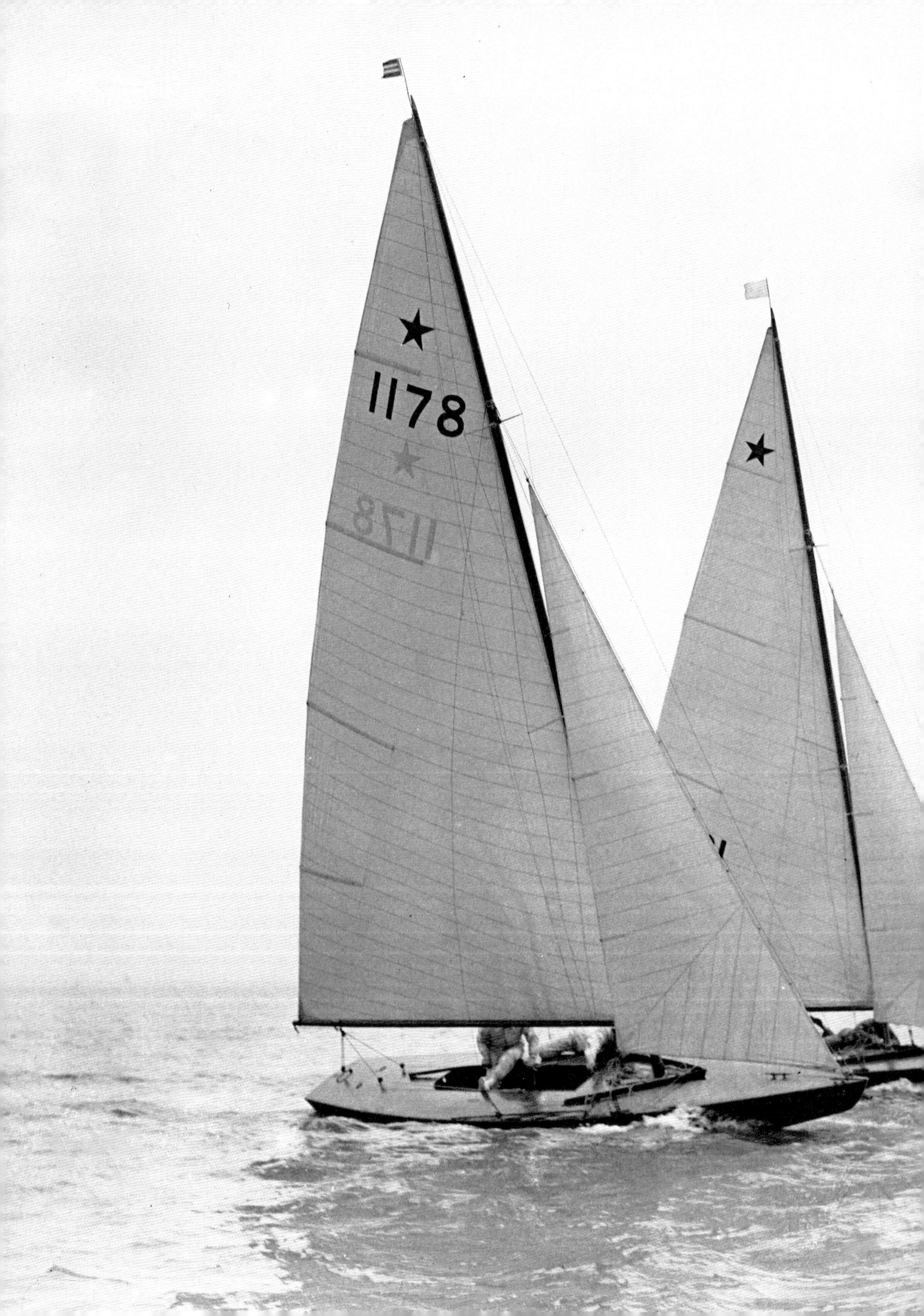
1178

These pages: *"Lady Betty" (1178), owned by Colin Ratsey, and another international Star Class Yacht rounding a buoy during trials for the Olympic Games at Burnham-on-Crouch, UK.*

Following pages: *Yachts competing in the very windy J Class Barcelona Regatta in 2024.*

Pages 108/109: *A crew sits on the edge of their slanted yacht during a regatta race in Marseille in June 2011.*

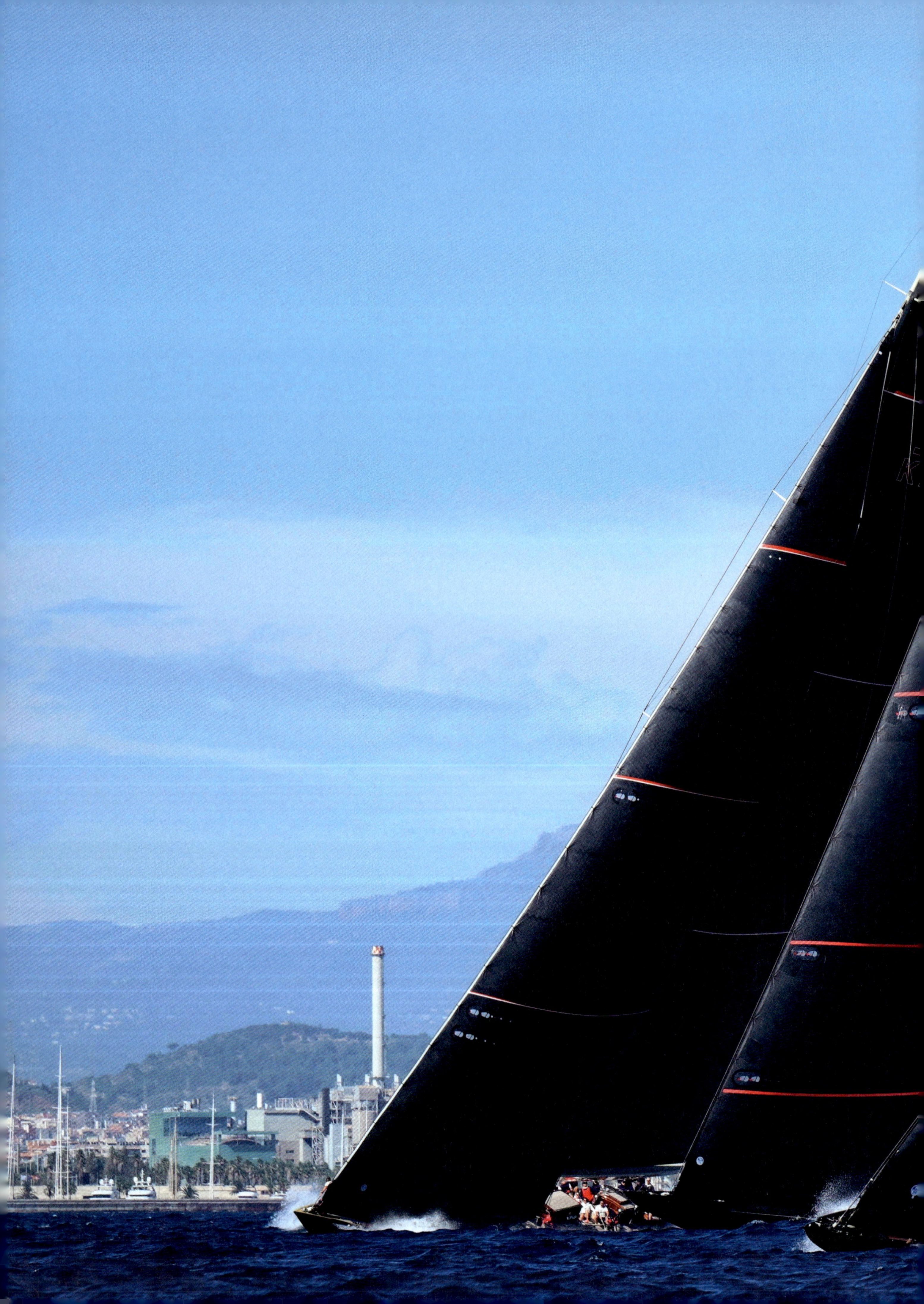

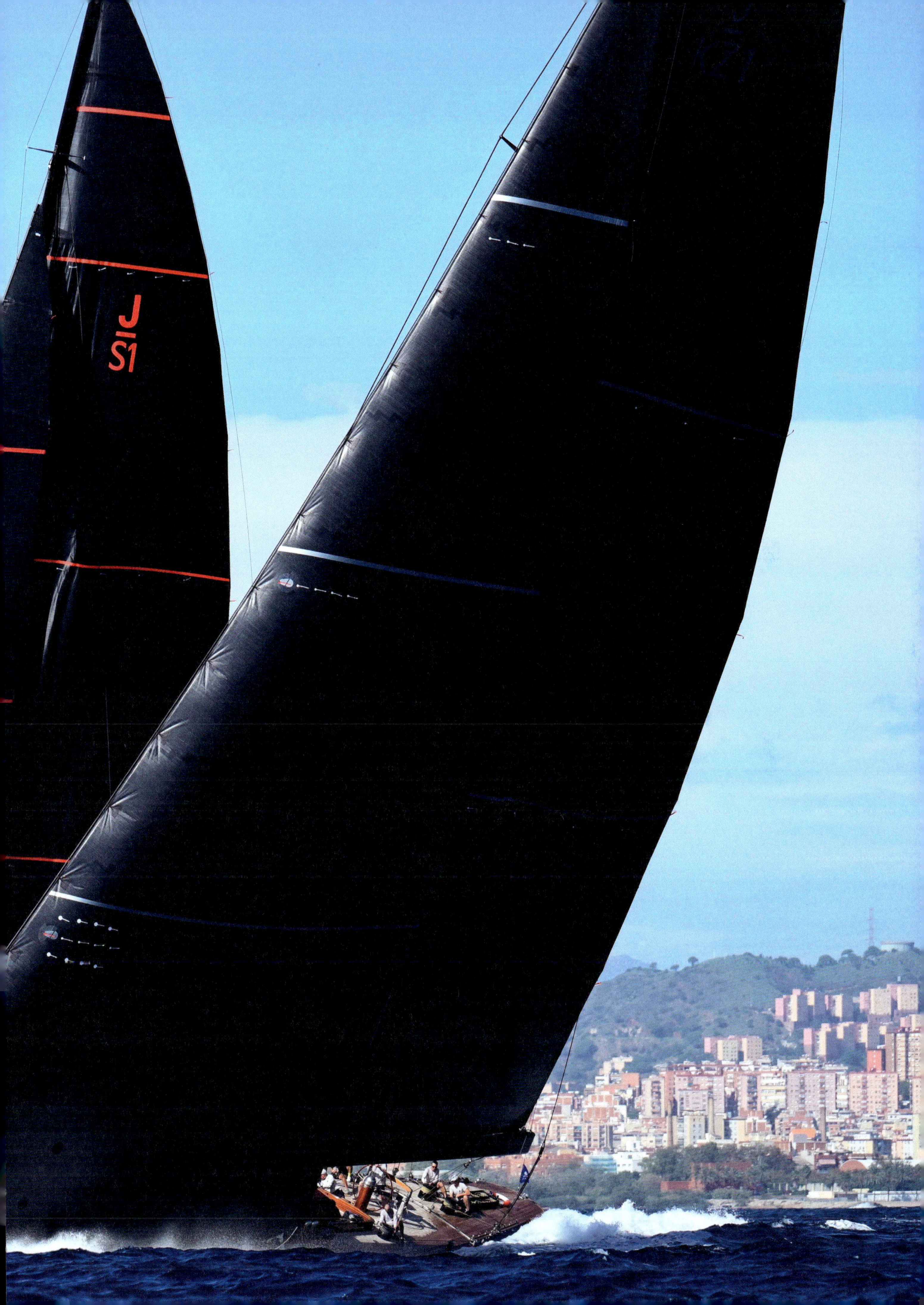
J
S1

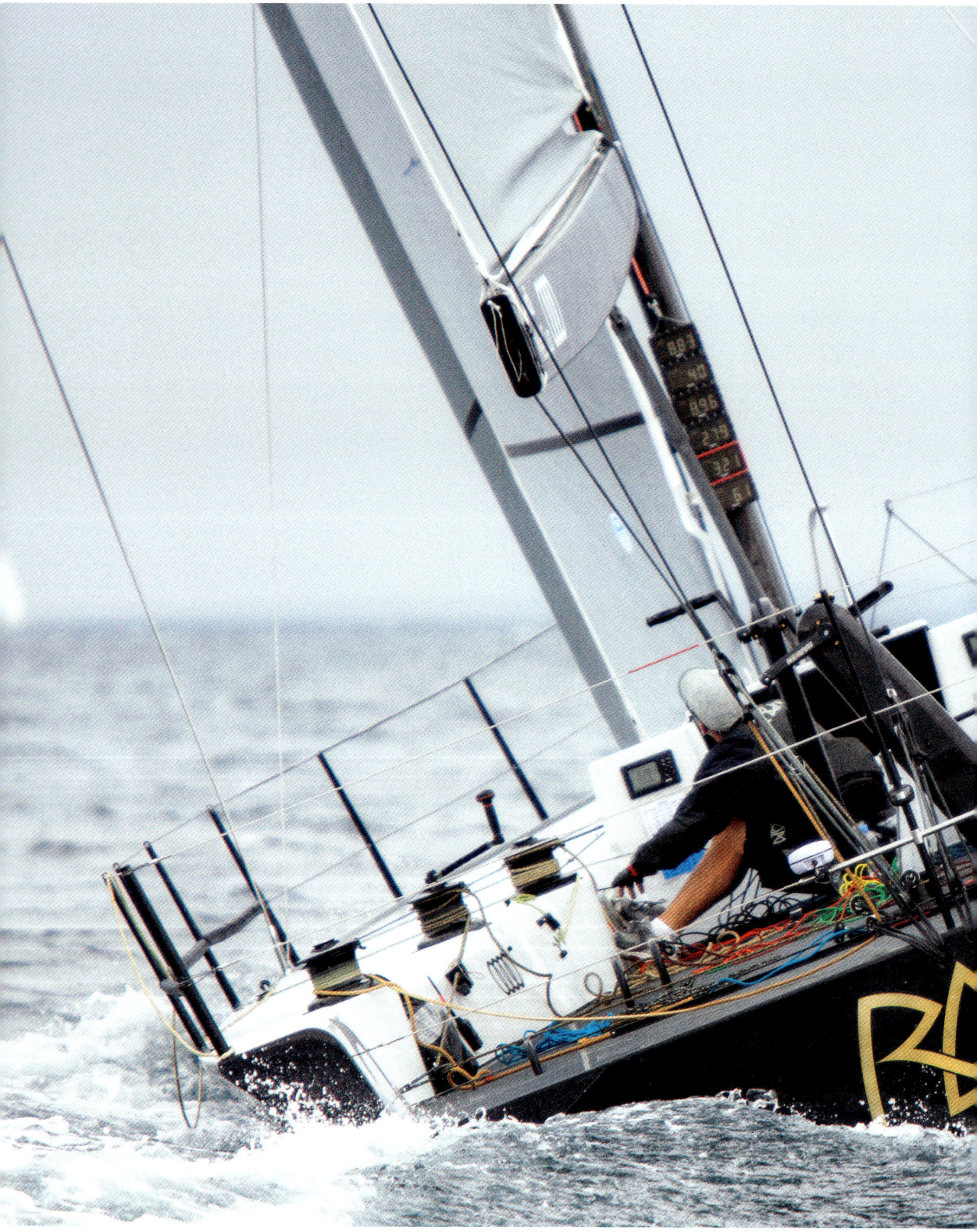

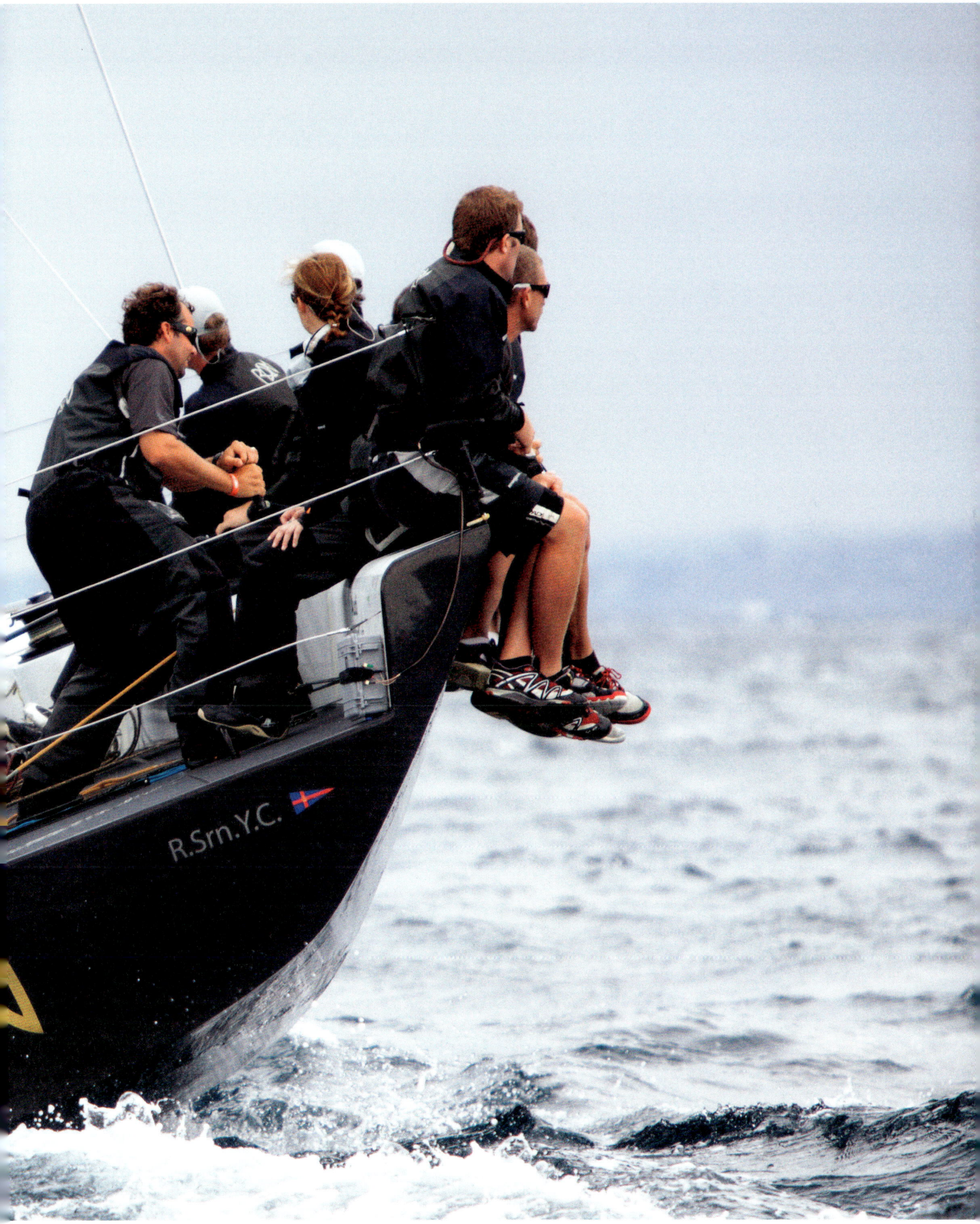
R.Srn.Y.C.

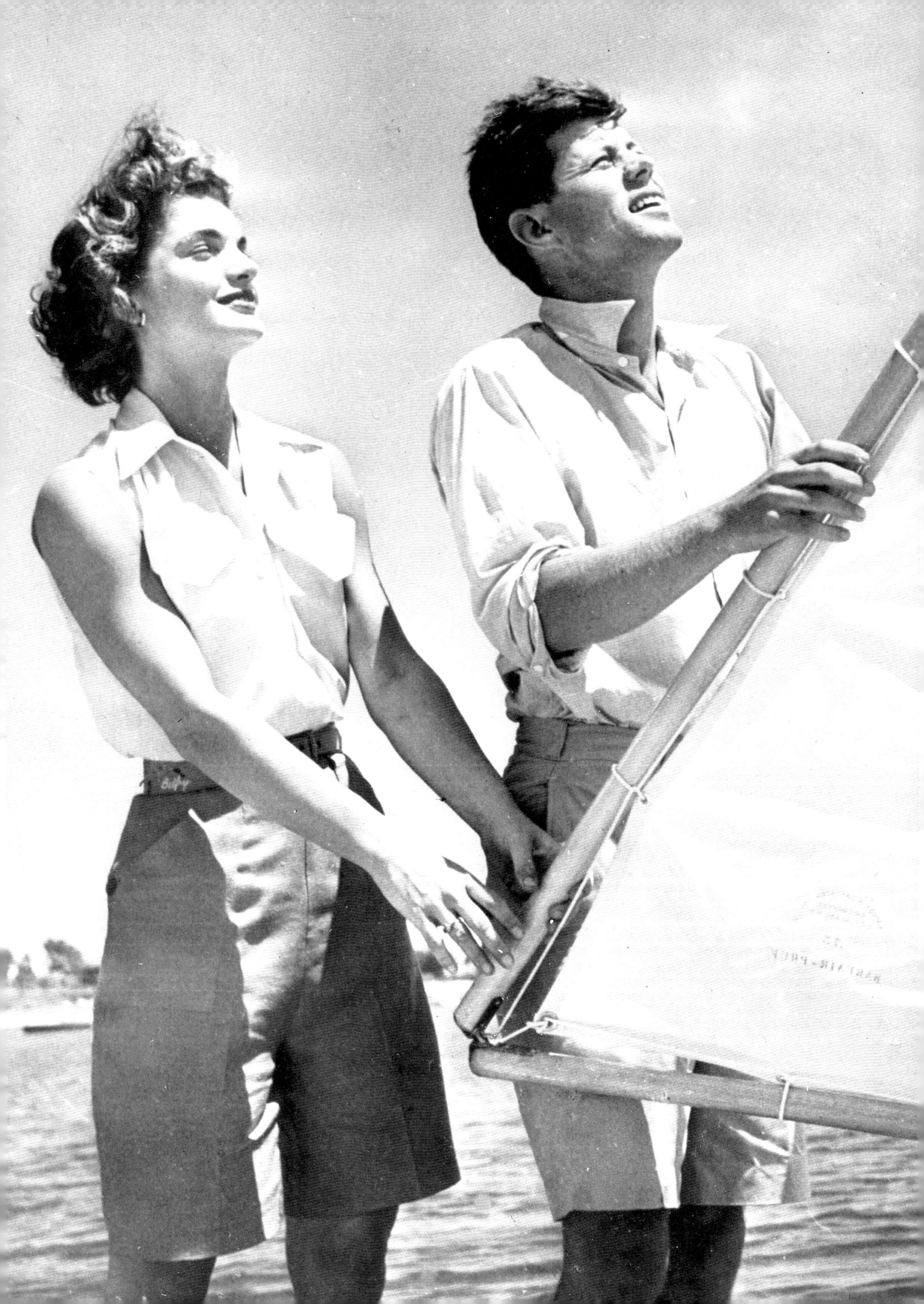

PEOPLE

CHARACTERS OF THE SAILING WORLD

Enjoyable, smooth sailing is the reward for hard work and preparation. The sport can seem easy once you're out on the water enjoying the fresh air—but getting all the pieces in place beforehand is a big task. The first problem is scheduling adequate time on the water. Then there's recruiting a crew and preparing the yacht for sailing. I sometimes joke that the most difficult task in winning the America's Cup is just getting the boat away from the dock with the correct sails on board, the latest weather information, sufficient drinking water for the crew, all the necessary tools and equipment for if something breaks, and most importantly the right attitude. The best sailors pay strict attention to details: big races are the equivalent of a space launch, and everything needs to be checked and re-checked.

Leadership and teamwork are key ingredients. The first step is to define and set a goal. Next each member of the team is assigned a specific task. As in the military, the ethos is to do your job and not let your teammates down. Of course, mistakes are inevitable, but the important thing is to learn from those errors and improve. Over my racing career I feel lucky to have met, sailed with or competed against many prominent people, and from each I was able to glean important lessons on how to do better in life. I always made a point of asking questions during quiet moments, and I appreciated each person's willingness to share their thoughts and suggestions.

Opposite: *John Kennedy with his fiancée Jaqueline Bouvier at the Kennedy's summer home in Hyannis Port, Massachusetts in June 1953.*

CELEBRITIES

Gianni Agnelli: Gianni Agnelli, the patriarch of Fiat Automobiles, arrived at the wharf in St. Tropez right on schedule to spend the afternoon sailing with the renowned symphony orchestra conductor Herbert von Karajan. Dressed in shorts, a French-style sailing shirt and a colorful scarf, Agnelli was thrilled to be on the water, and made his desire to steer obvious by sitting near the wheel. But with a full list of practice maneuvers scheduled, it was only some hours into the sail that von Karajan finally invited the Italian industrialist to the helm. "Make her sail fast," he said as he did so.

Jimmy Buffet: 1987 was an exciting time in Fremantle, Australia, with the sleepy seaport and fishing town coming alive thanks to the America's Cup yachts filling the harbor. The rich, the famous, the nearly rich and the not so famous: all were in town to watch the races and absorb the atmosphere, and there were plenty of side shows as well—one of which involved me! An enterprising sailor had acquired a fleet of small sailing craft, each just big enough for two adults, and when the famous singer Jimmy Buffet received an invitation to race one of the pocket yachts I was recruited to be his teammate. Competing against 20 of these nifty little craft, many of them sailed by notable international sailors, we quickly claimed the lead thanks to some favorable wind, and much to Buffet's delight we went on to win. He showed up at our ESPN television study the next day with a recording of a song he'd written that morning about the race, and we aired the tune at the start of our next show.

Errol Flynn, Humphrey Bogart, Lauren Bacall, Johnny Weissmuller: Errol Flynn owned a 74-foot ketch named "Sirocco" that he sometimes raced against fellow actor Humphrey Bogart, who sailed a 57-foot yawl named "Santana." Joining them on occasion was the Champion swimmer Johnny Weissmuller, famous for playing Tarzan in a series of films, who raced on a 58-foot schooner named "Allure." All these yachts were berthed in the harbor of Marina del Rey, California. Bogart's boat, which he owned for 12 years and often sailed alongside his wife Lauren Bacall, has been completely renovated, and is currently raced by Wendy Schmidt, wife of former Google CEO Eric Schmidt.

John Lennon: John Lennon became an active sailor when he was living in New York City, and in 1980 he accepted an invitation to sail to Bermuda on a 43-foot sloop named the "Megan Jaye." The crew of five left Newport, Rhode Island for the 600-mile sail with the weather looking fair, but 300 miles south of Newport ran into a violent storm. The wind blew over 50 knots and the waves were huge—yet when he arrived in Bermuda Lennon described his time steering the boat as "thrilling," telling writer Christian Winthrop that once he'd overcome his initial fear, he passed his time at the helm singing sea shanties. Lennon was shot in New York six months later, on December 8, 1980.

John F. Kennedy and family: John Kennedy spent summers sailing at his family's compound in Hyannis Port, a small waterfront town about 60 miles south of Boston. Kennedy and his brothers were all good racing sailors; in fact, John and his older brother Patrick represented Harvard University in the annual McMillan Cup yacht race. When war broke out in 1941, America's Cup sailor Sherman Hoyt was asked by the navy to train young officers to command patrol torpedo boats, and among the racing sailors Hoyt recruited to skipper the boats was John Kennedy, captain of PT 109.

Princess Anne, the Princess Royal: All the proof we need that Princess Anne is a true sailing aficionado is supplied by a speech she gave at a black-tie dinner at London's Hilton Hotel in 2008. The evening was a fundraiser for the British Olympic Sailing Team, and as hostess it fell to the princess to introduce the team. Standing at a microphone with no podium or notes, she brought each of the 18 sailors on stage and delivered a short biography and list of their sailing accomplishments, making clear her knowledge of each and every competitor who would travel to Beijing for the Olympics a month later.

Franklin Roosevelt: President Franklin D. Roosevelt was elected during a challenging time, inheriting the devastating Great Depression and then being called upon to lead the nation during World War II. Perhaps during those times, he sometimes longed for the calmer days of his youth, much of which he spent sailing. He was a long-time member of the New York Yacht Club, and prior to serving as Governor of the State of New York he was the Assistant Secretary of the United States Navy. Among his many achievements, however, there was at least one disappointment. During his tenure at the navy, the U.S. Naval Academy owned the schooner "America," which Roosevelt believed should be restored (it had been allowed to fall into disrepair). But during the winter of 1942 a severe snowstorm caused the vessel's poorly-constructed Annapolis storage facility to collapse, and the boat was never rebuilt.

SAILORS

Paul Elvstrom: The secret to the great Danish sailor Paul Elvstrom's racing success? He quite simply practiced longer and worked harder than his competitors. Elvstrom used a hiking bench to get in shape for sailing, spending hours working out on the contraption, and his physical strength gave him the mental confidence he needed to win four Olympic gold medals in four different Games. But he didn't stop there. At the age of 56 he teamed up with his 22-year-old daughter Trine to race a Tornado catamaran in the 1984 Olympics. It was unheard of for a man of his age to race at the Games, but the father and daughter team nevertheless finished 4th out of 20 countries, within touching-distance of a bronze medal. As well as being a fearsome competitor, however, Elvstrom was also a great role-model, and lived by the following maxim: "You haven't won the race if in winning the race you've lost the respect of your competitors."

Susan Henn: The America's Cup had only just been created when Scottish couple Lt. William Henn and his wife Susan Matilda Cunningham-Graham-Henn launched their 102-foot steel-hulled yacht "Galatea" in 1886. They were a colorful couple, becoming famous in part for the racoon and sailor-suit-clad monkey that Susan kept on board. But she was also a formidable yachtswoman, taking over as captain when her husband was unable to compete in the America's Cup. Susan was inducted into the event's hall of fame in 2025.

Edith Hope Goddard Iselin: Hope Iselin raced with her husband Charles Oliver Iselin in the 1899 and 1901 America's Cups aboard the defender, "Columbia." She was an engaged member of the crew, and also served as the timer, photographer and even occasional peacemaker, a role which she said required "coolness, a good sense of humor, and a fund of funny stories."

Prince Philip, Duke of Edinburgh: Prince Philip, best known as the husband of Queen Elizabeth II, was also a passionate sailor. He raced aboard a series of yachts during nearly 70 years' worth of Cowes Week regattas, and was there hosted by Sir Owen Aisher and his son Sir Robin Aisher. (Sir Robin won a medal himself at the 1968 Olympic Games.) In 2001, at the America's Cup Jubilee celebrating the 150th year of the event, Prince Philip was the keynote speaker at a gathering of 5000 sailors on the Isle of Wight, and received a standing ovation for his thoughtful remarks.

Herbert von Karajan: The famous Austrian conductor Herbert von Karajan brought the same level of seriousness to yachting that he did to music. But he also had a sly sense of humor that surfaced at surprising moments. Having picked up a member of his sailing crew at the airport in Nice, he proceeded to scare the poor passenger out of his wits by speeding through the hilly countryside. At one point von Karajan stopped the sportscar and remarked, "The trick of a good driver is how many flies you can kill with the side windows in the summer." With that, sped off once more at the same breakneck pace.

On another occasion, von Karajan met a few of his crew at the private jet terminal in Zurich for a flight to Palma de Majorca. One of them looked surprised when von Karajan hopped into the co-pilot's seat, and sensing the man's anxiety von Karajan leaned back and reassured him with the following promise: "Don't worry my friend, I will land this plane just like a butterfly with sore feet."

Sir Thomas Lipton: Sir Thomas Lipton is best known today as the founder of the famous tea company, but he was also an enthusiastic sailor who challenged for the America's Cup five times between 1899 and 1930, always on green yachts named "Shamrock" in honor of his Irish heritage. Though Sir Thomas' vessels never won and he didn't in fact race himself, instead watching from his larger escort vessel "Erin," he became a popular celebrity nevertheless and was eventually inducted into the America's Cup Hall of Fame.

Ted Turner: Ted Turner's achievements were many and varied. Over the course of his life he owned at least six television networks, most notably the Cable News Network (CNN), a professional baseball team, a professional basketball team, a movie studio and 25 properties that totaled 2.1 million acres. But he was also a keen and very accomplished sailor. On the first day of practice for the America's Cup trials of 1977, Turner was sitting on a hill looking out over Marblehead Harbor. His 12 Meter, "Courageous," was tied up below at a floating dock. Turner turned to the crewmember sitting beside him and asked, "Did you ever think you would get to sail on a boat like this?" The surprised crew answered in the negative. "Neither did I," Turner said. "Isn't this the greatest thing you've ever done?"

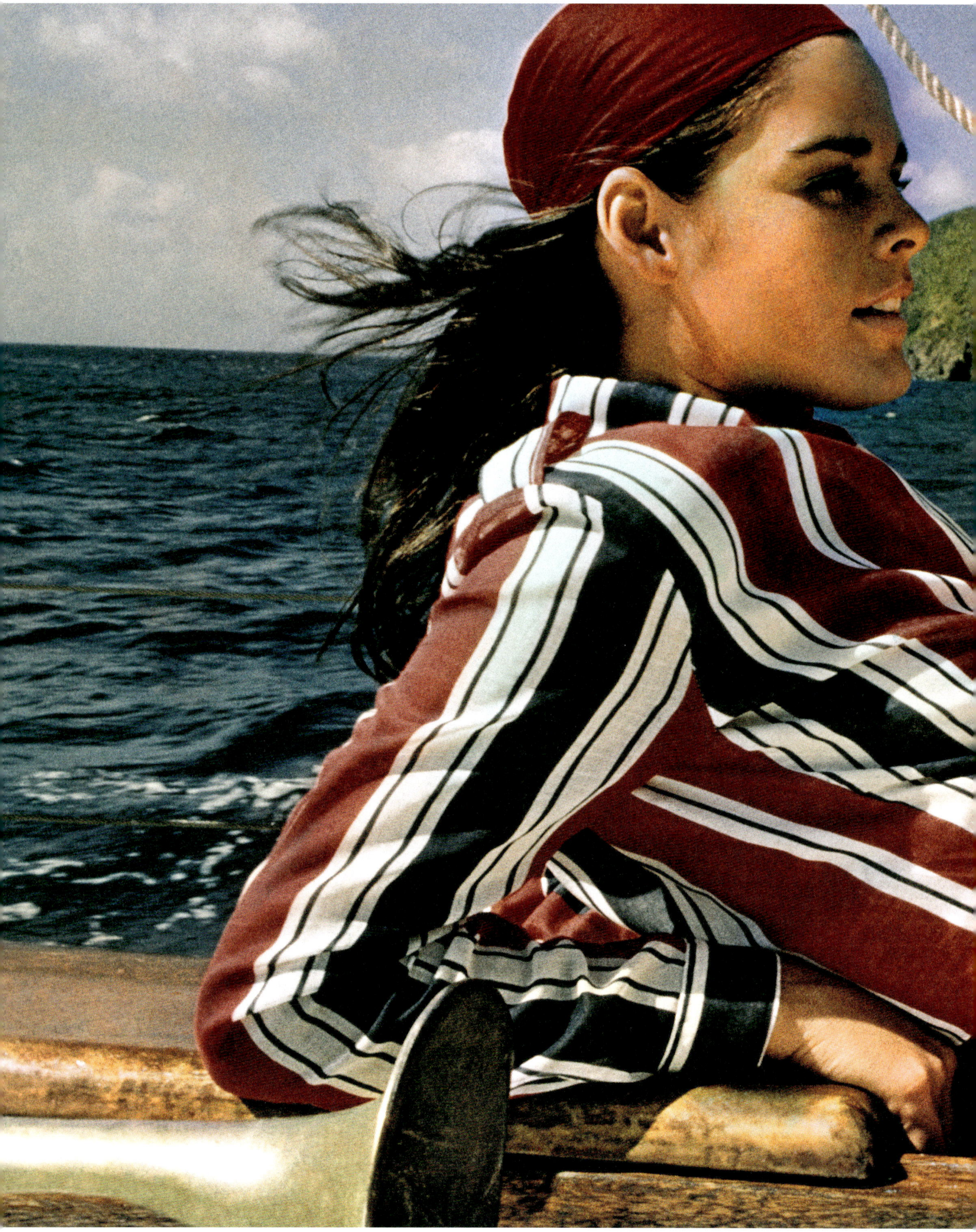

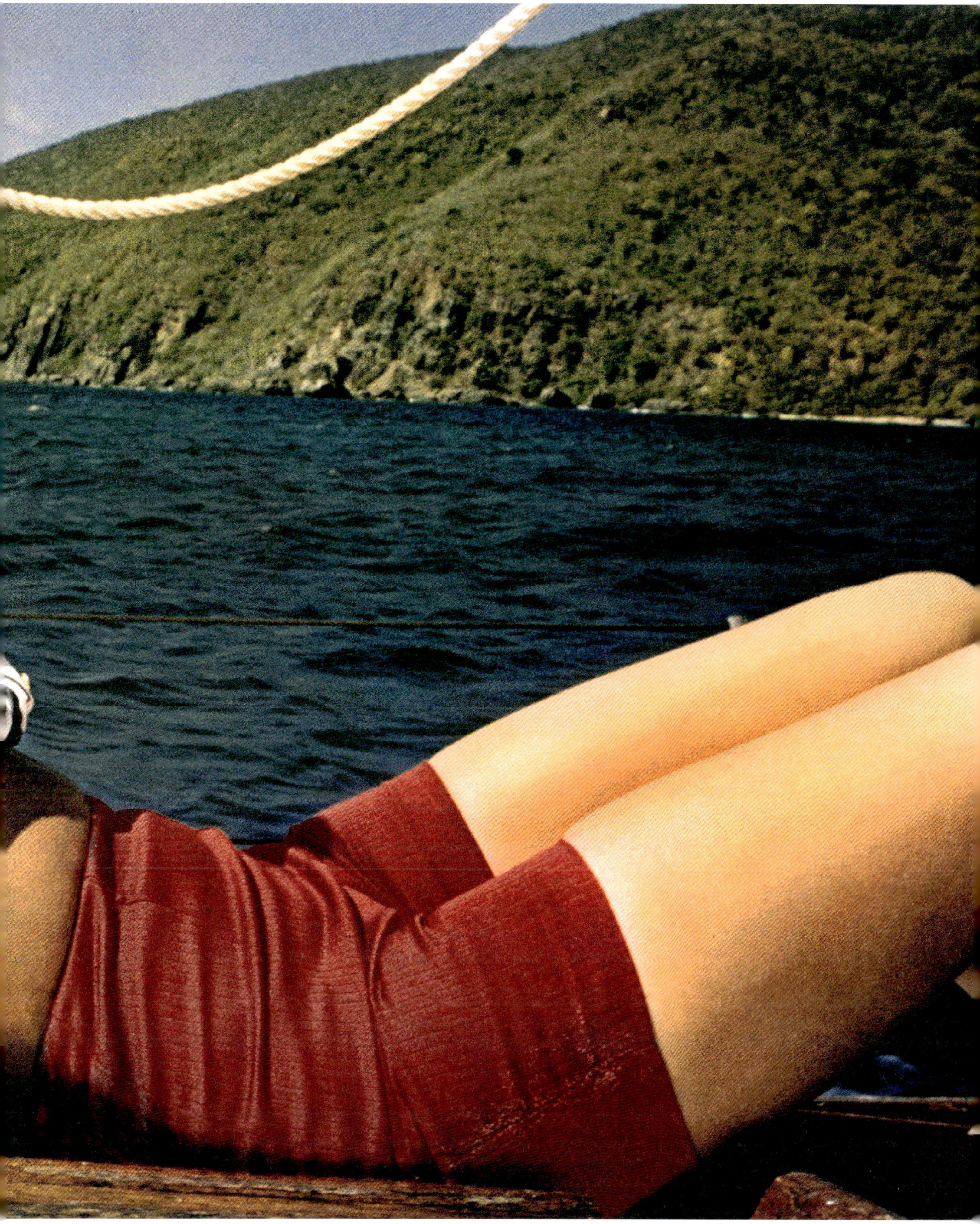

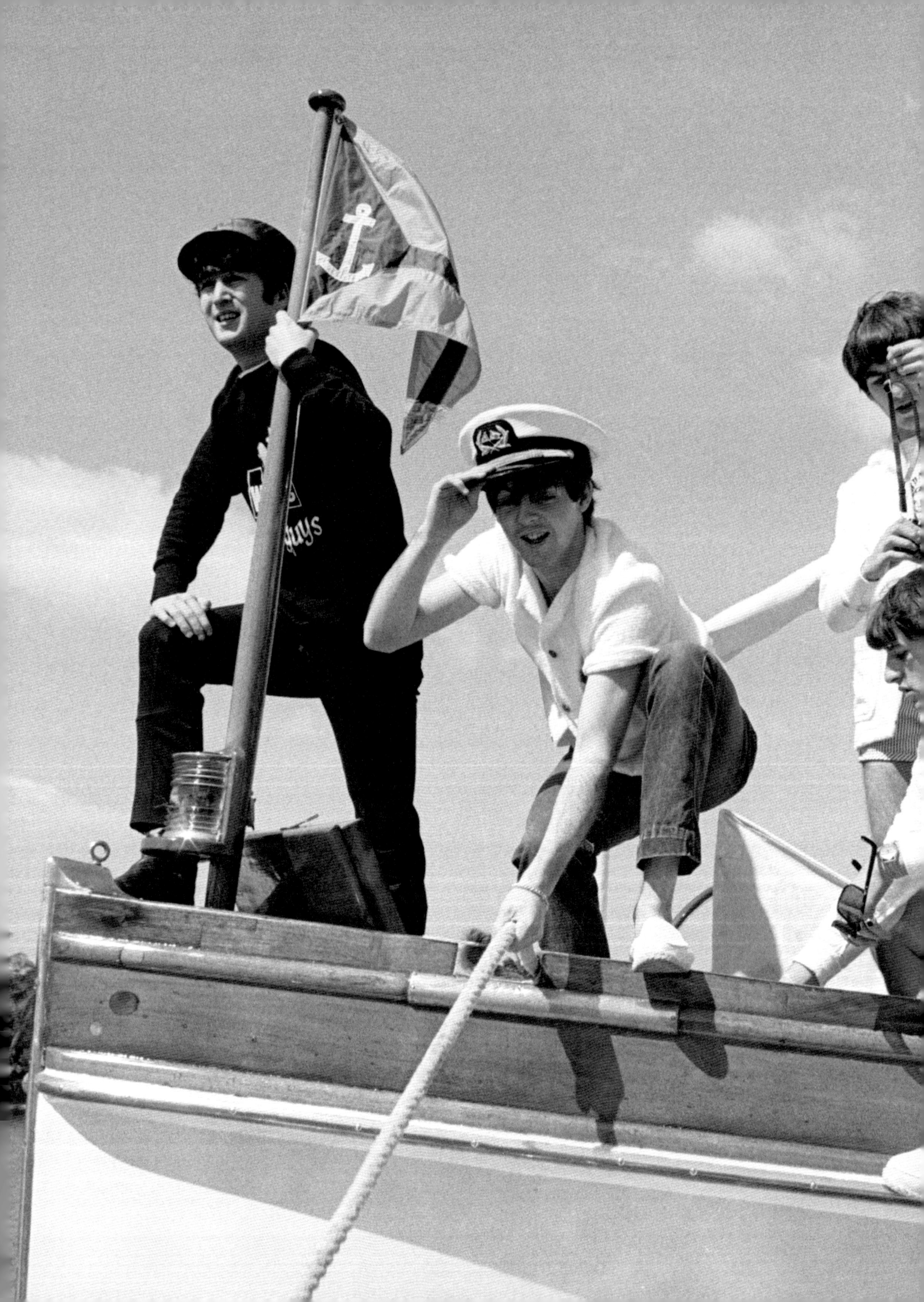

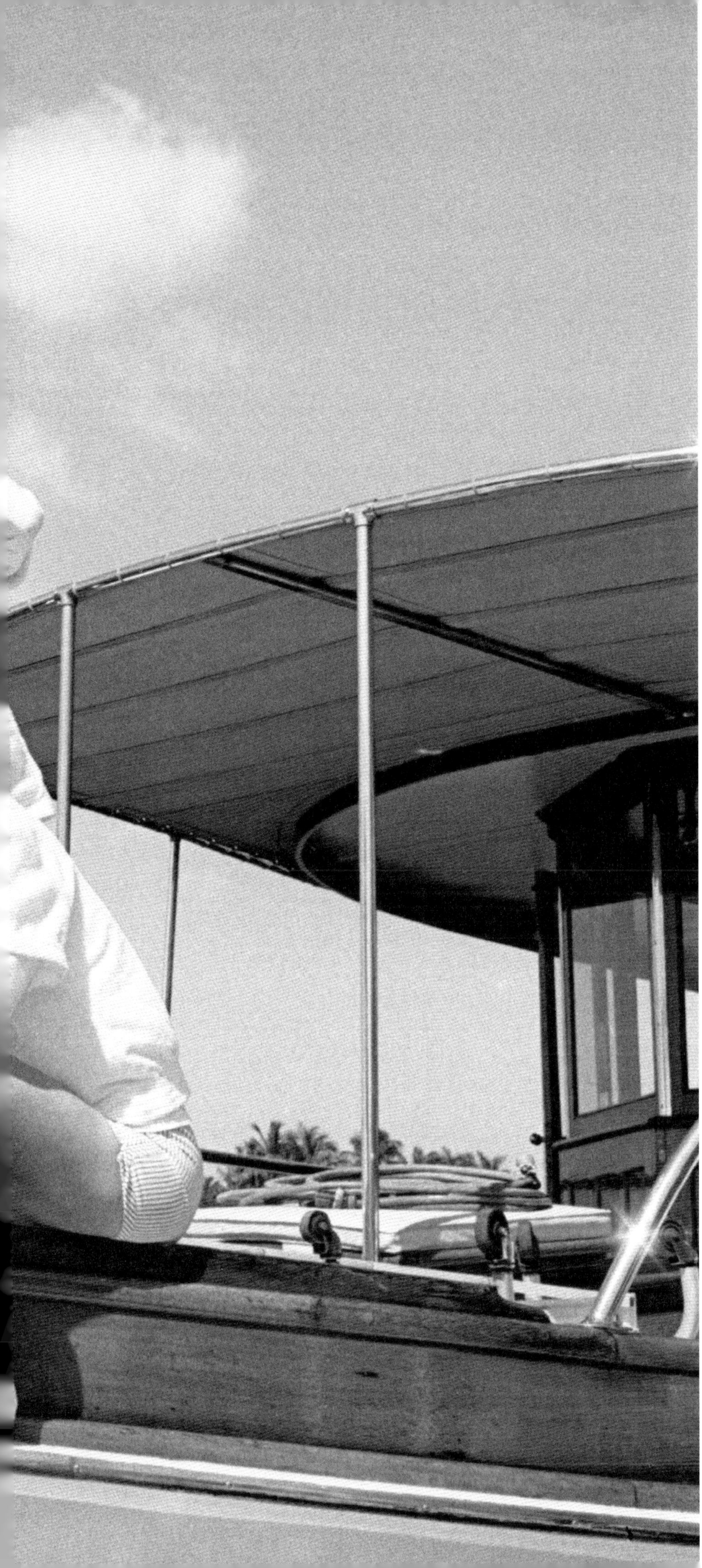

Previous pages: *Ali MacGraw reclining on a sailboat in a striped shirt and long shorts (both by Koret of California) and a scarf by Christa in April 1967.*

These pages: *The Beatles on the bow of a boat in Miami Beach, 1964.*

Page 120: *Gary Cooper, c. 1939.*

Page 121: *Actor Errol Flynn and his wife, actress Lili Damita on their ketch "Sirocco" in April 1938.*

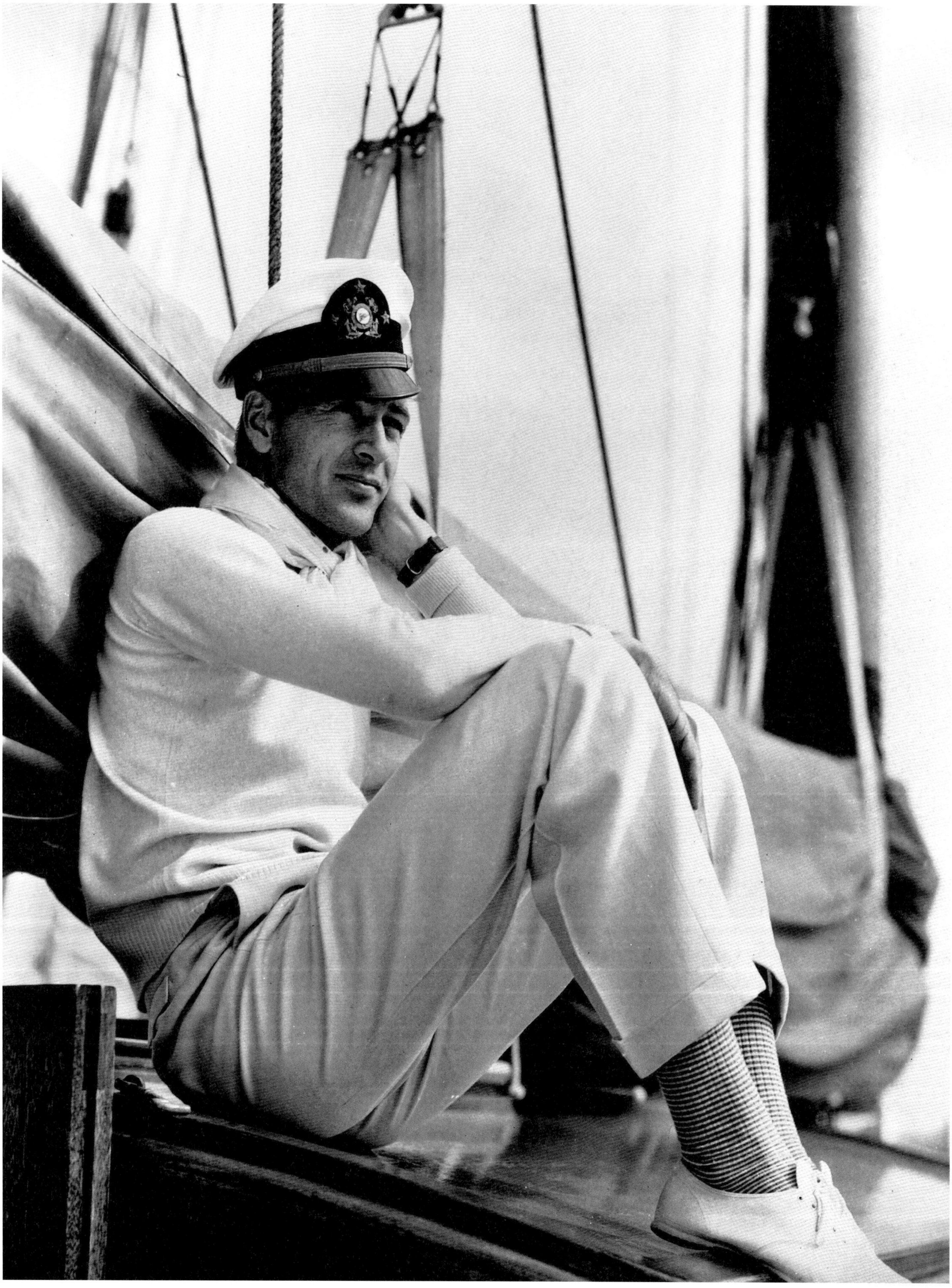

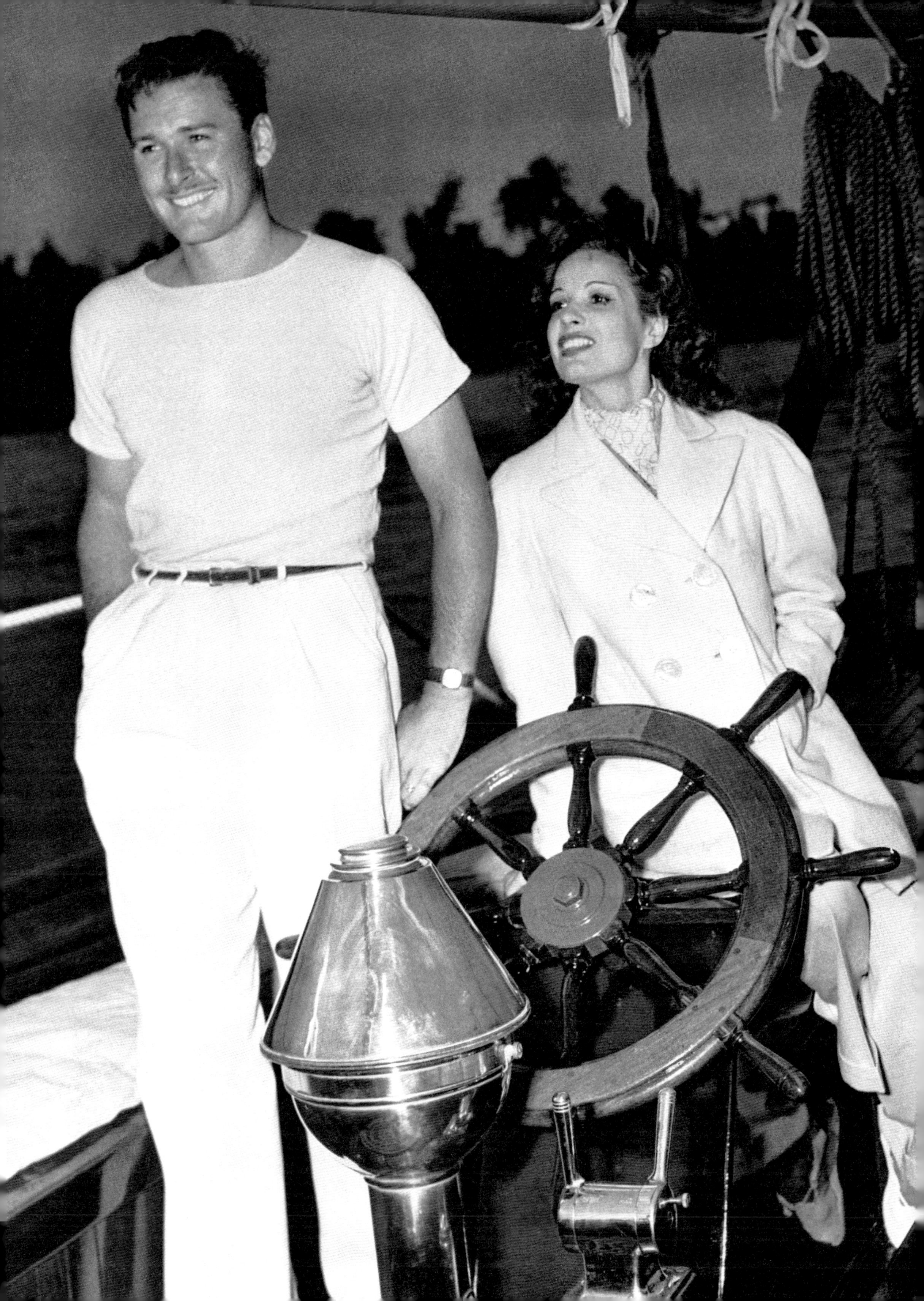

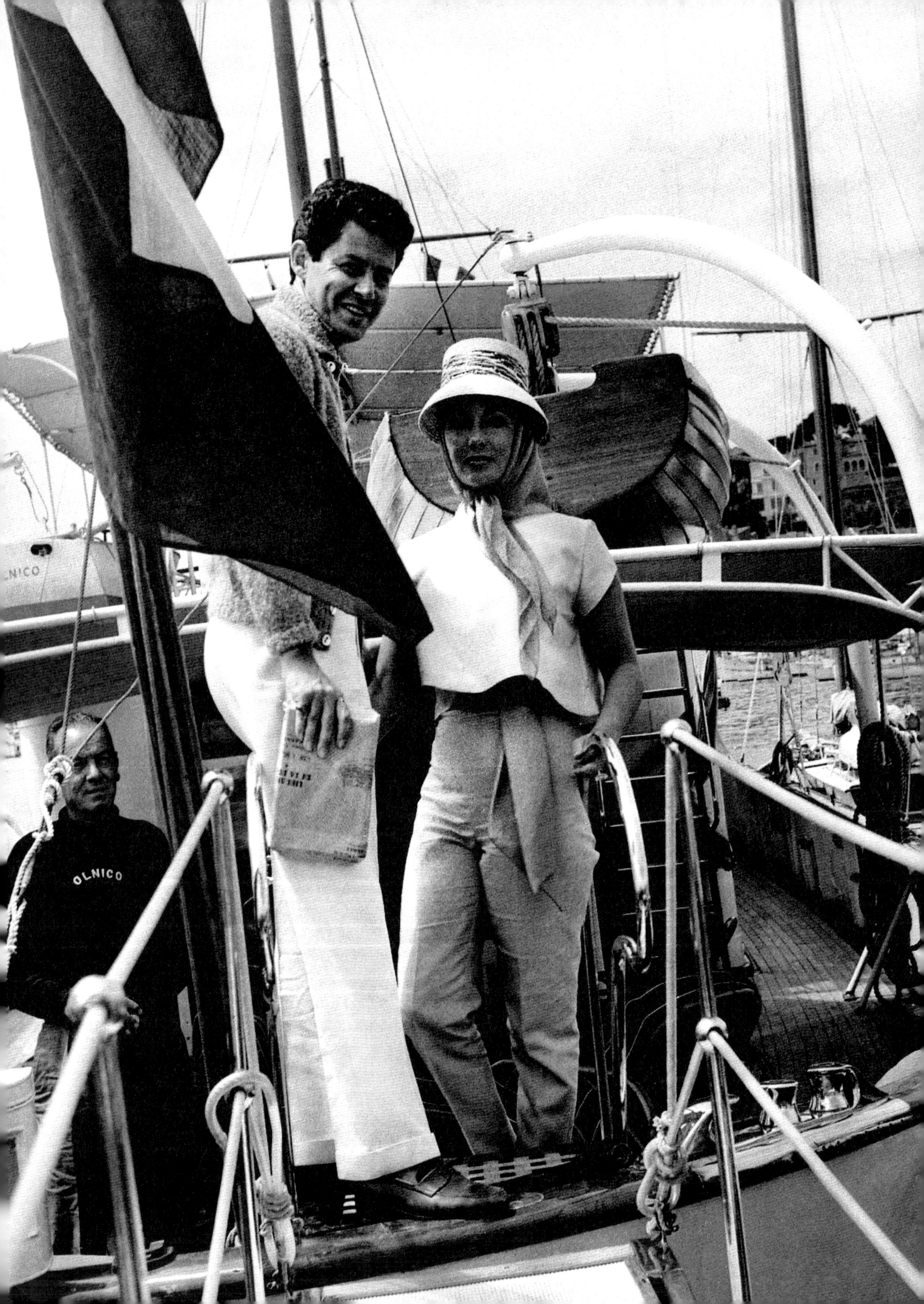
OLNICO

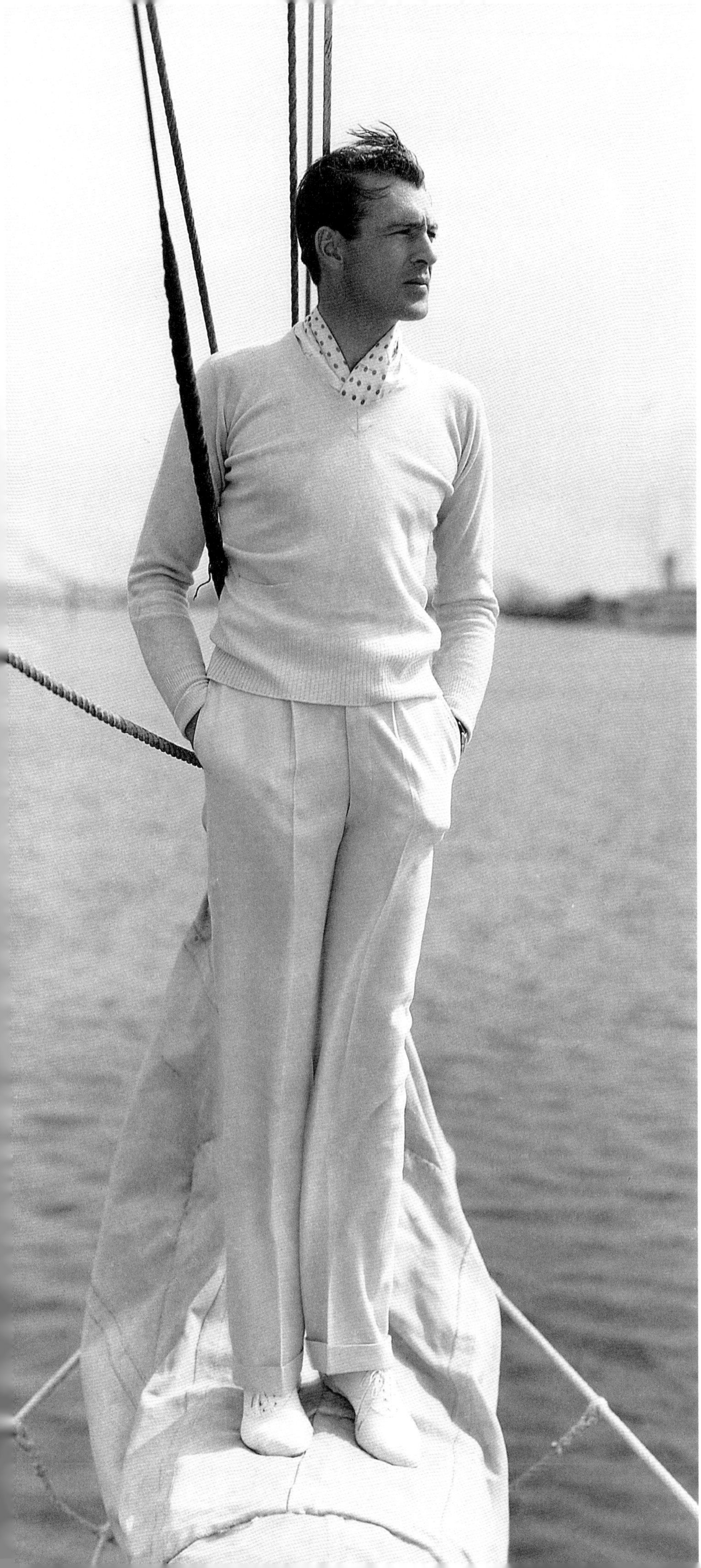

Opposite: *Newlyweds Eddie Fisher and Elizabeth Taylor board their luxury yacht "Olinico" in France before setting sail for Italy during their honeymoon cruise of the Mediterranean in 1959.*

This page: *Publicity portrait of Gary Cooper standing on the prow of a sailboat, c. 1939.*

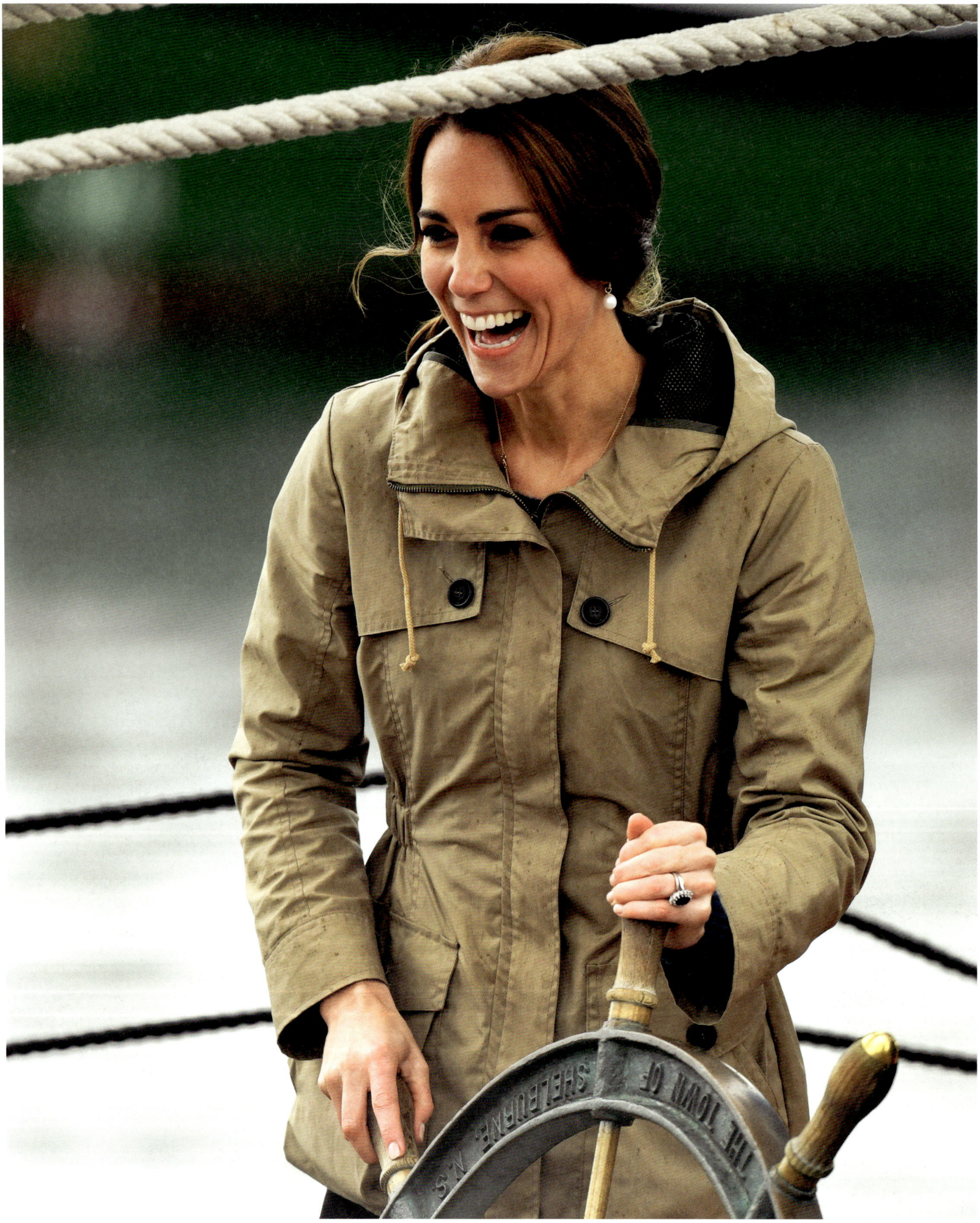

This page: *Catherine, Duchess of Cambridge steers the tall ship "Pacific Grace" on the final day of the Royal Tour of Canada in 2016.*

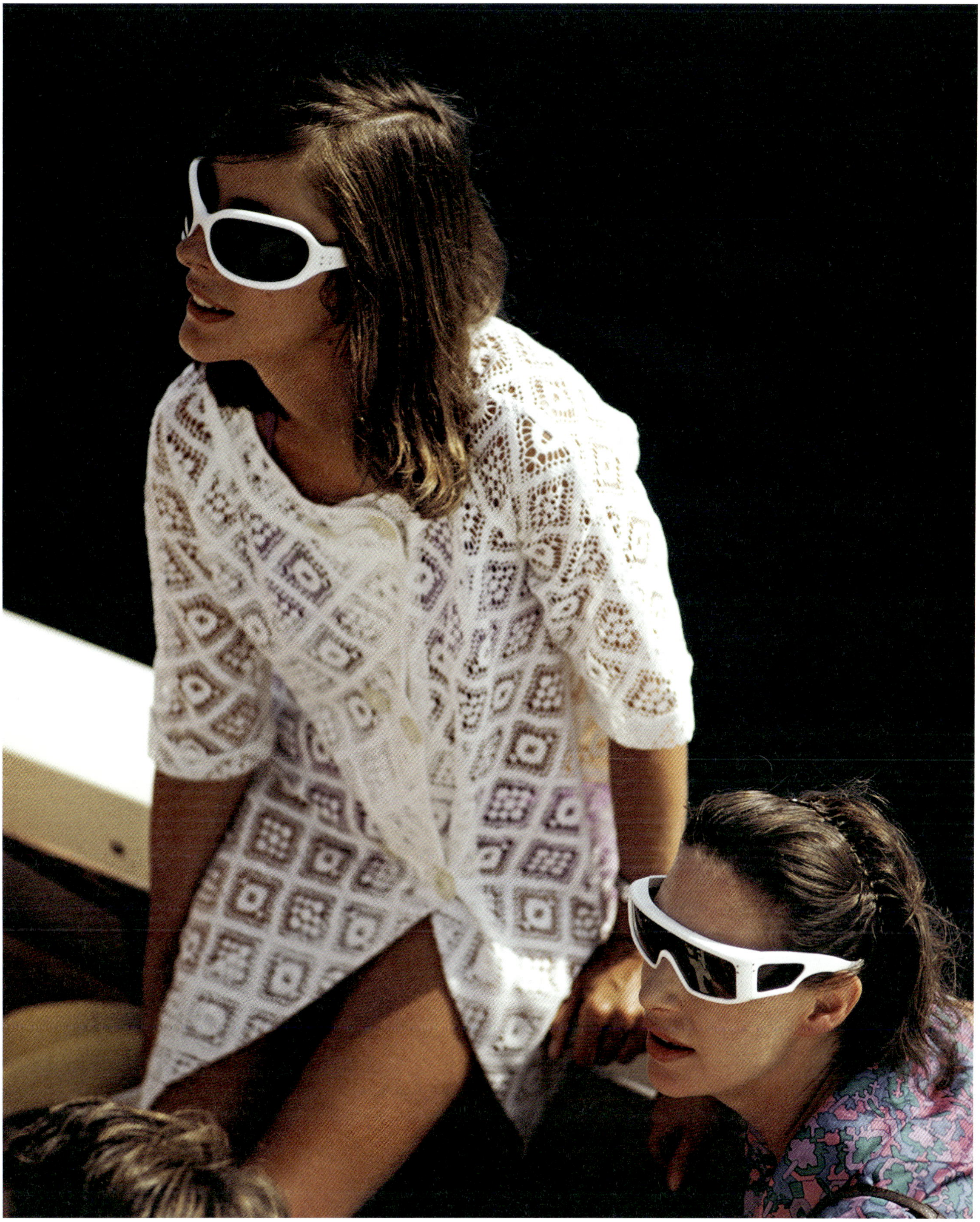

This page: *Princess Margaret, Countess of Snowdon (right) wearing futuristic sunglasses on the Aga Khan's yacht in Costa Smeralda, Sardinia in August 1967.*

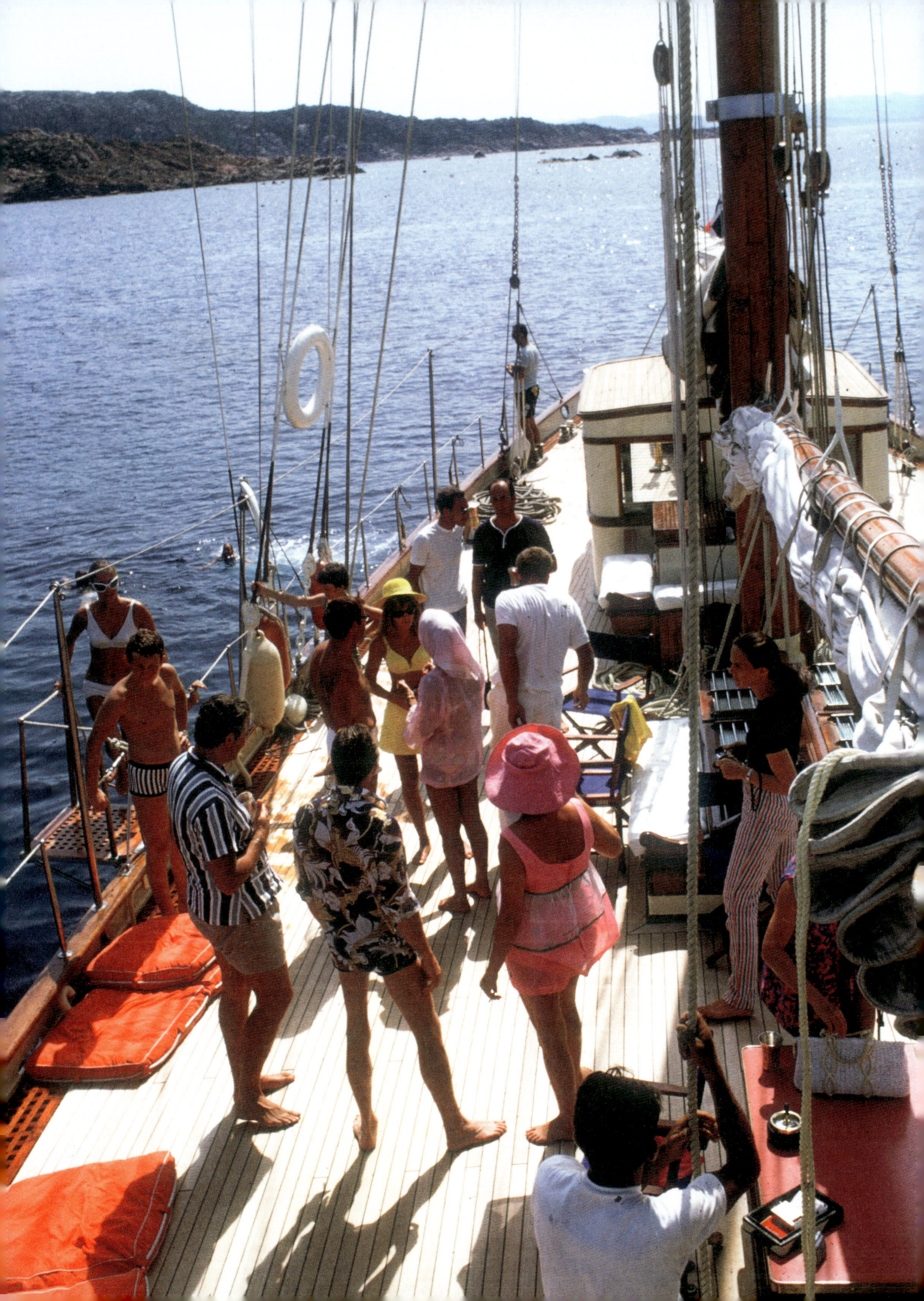

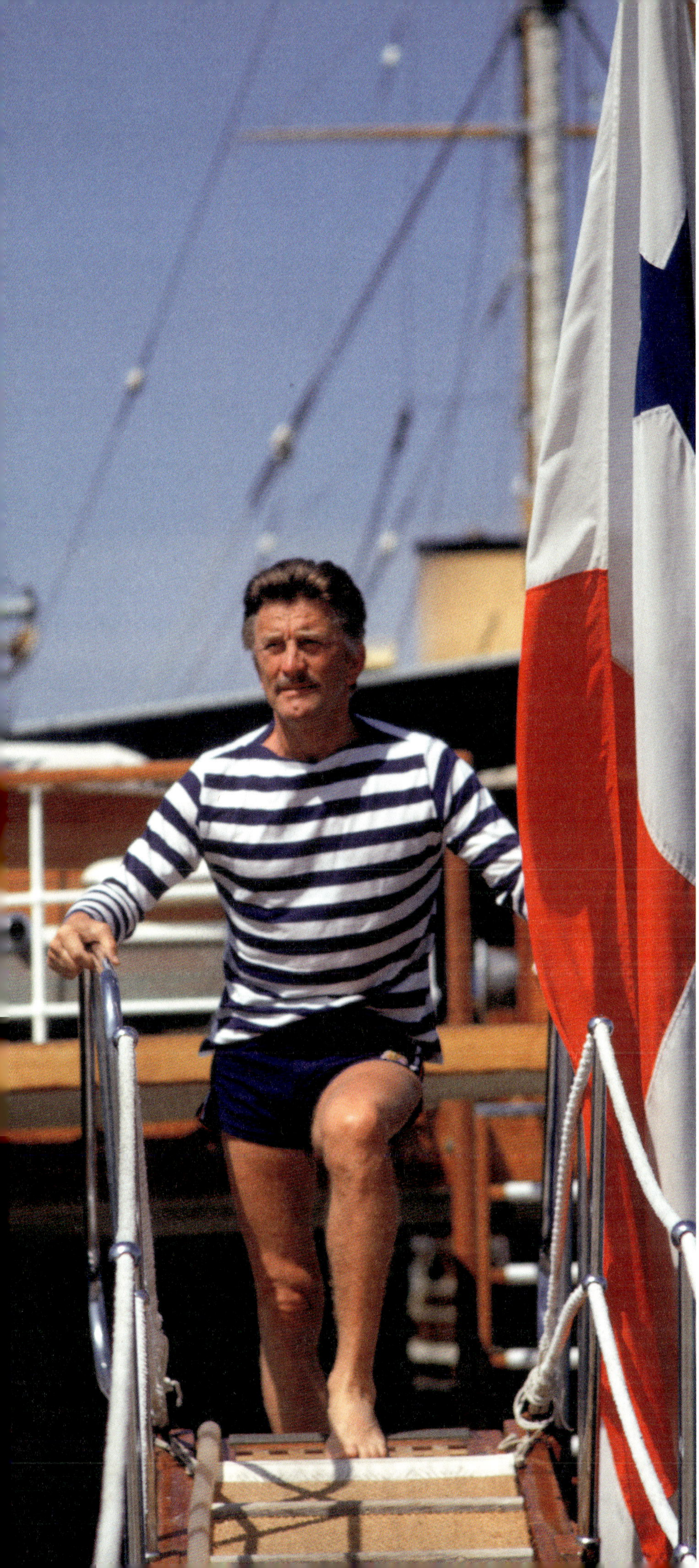

Opposite: *Holidaymakers on the deck of a luxury yacht off Costa Smeralda in August 1967, amongst them the Aga Khan and Peter Sellers.*

This page: *Kirk Douglas on holiday in Costa Smeralda, Sardinia in August 1967.*

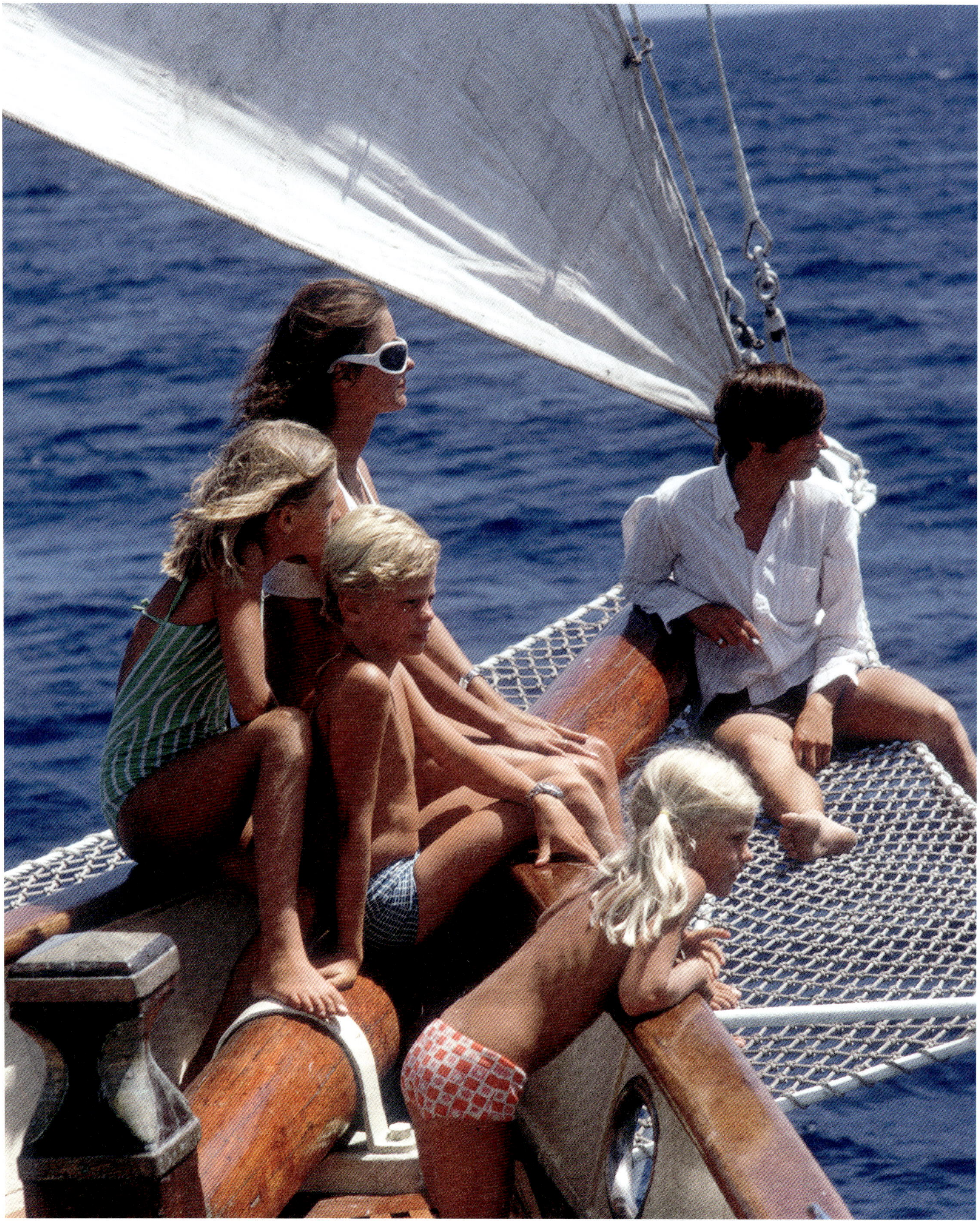

This page: *Members of the Guinness family sailing off Costa Smeralda, Sardinia in August 1967.*

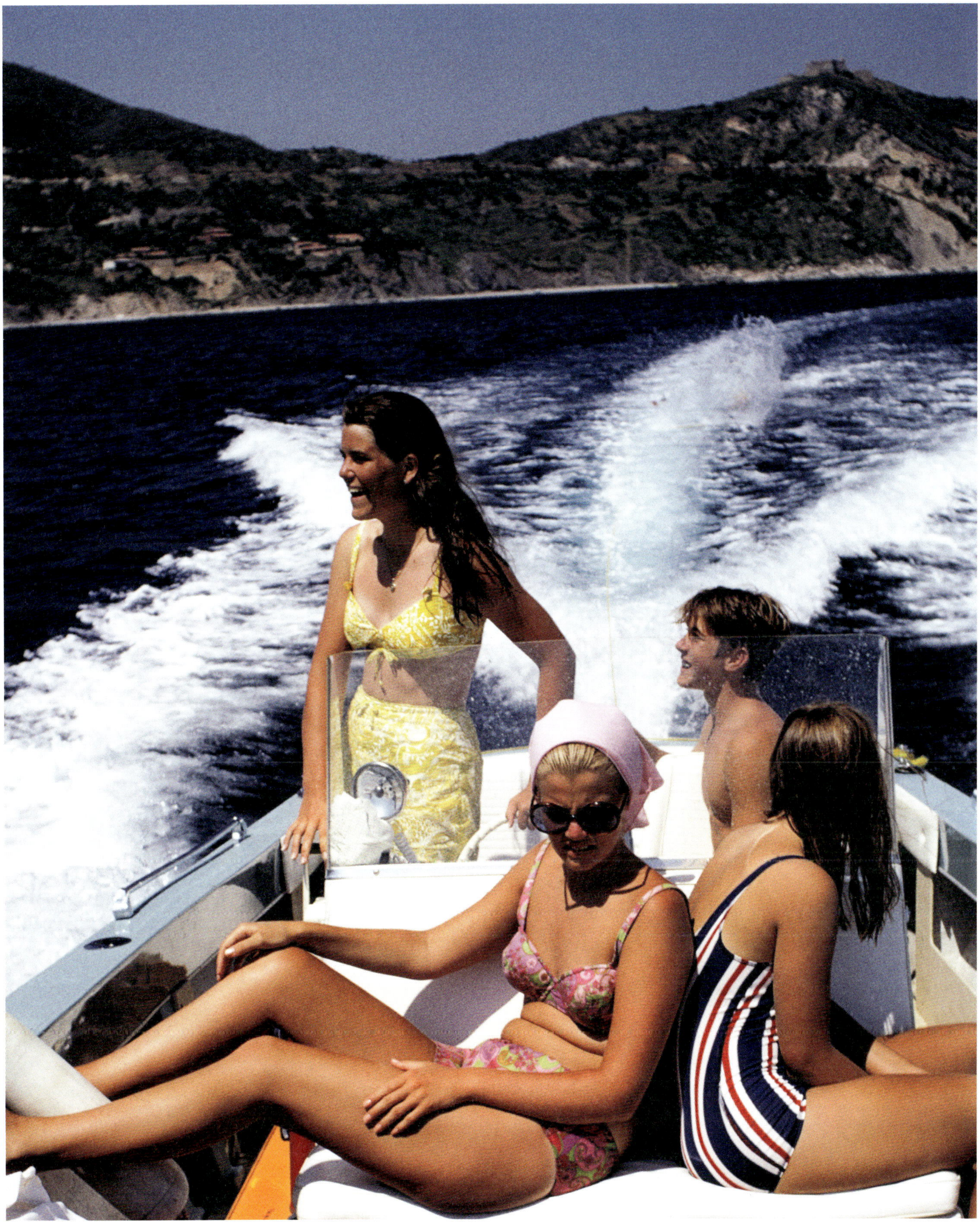

This page: *The Pucci family take a motorboat trip off the Italian coast in August 1969.*

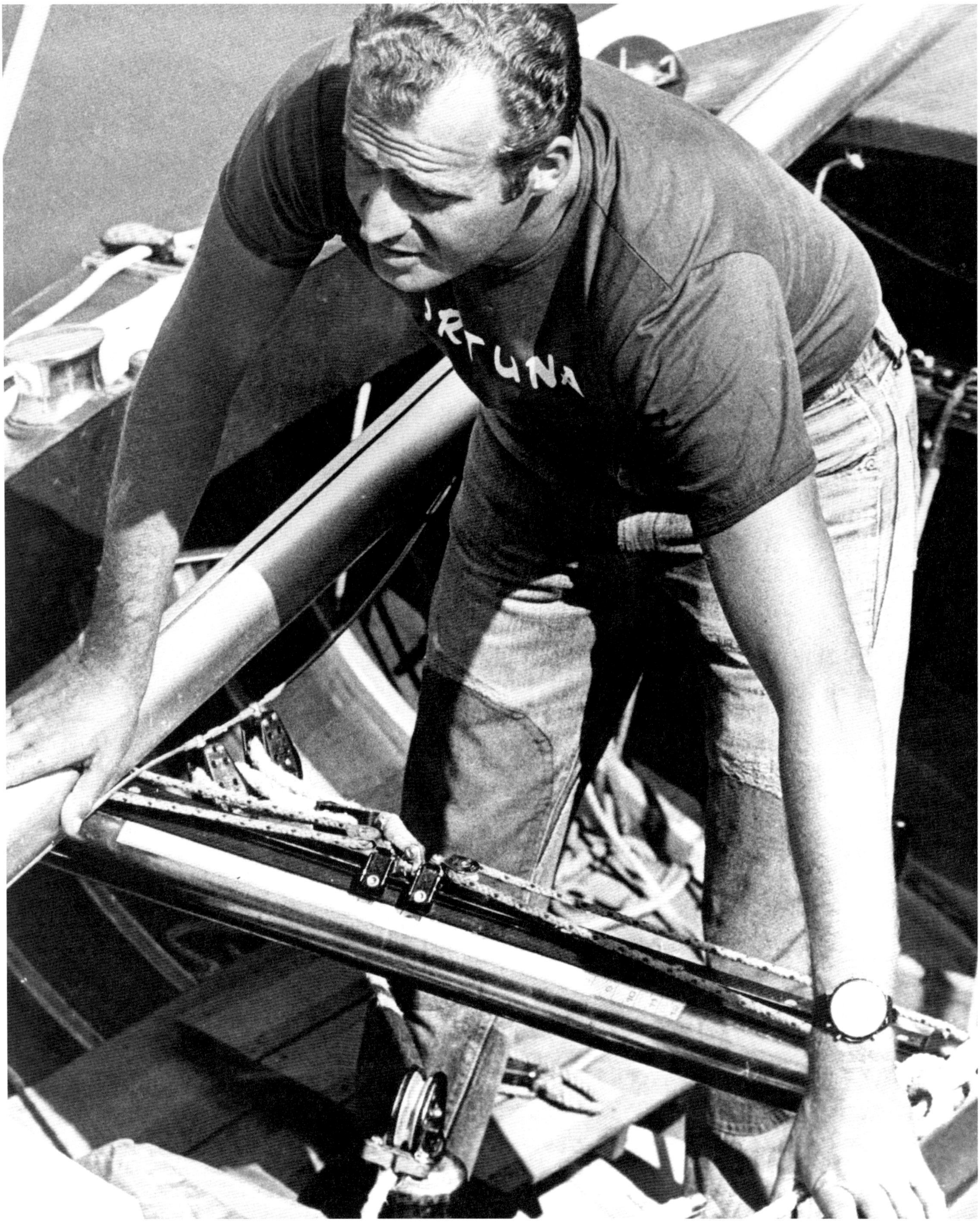

This page: *Juan Carlos, Prince of Spain on his yacht "Fortuna" ahead of a race at Arenys de Mar, Catalonia in August 1973.*

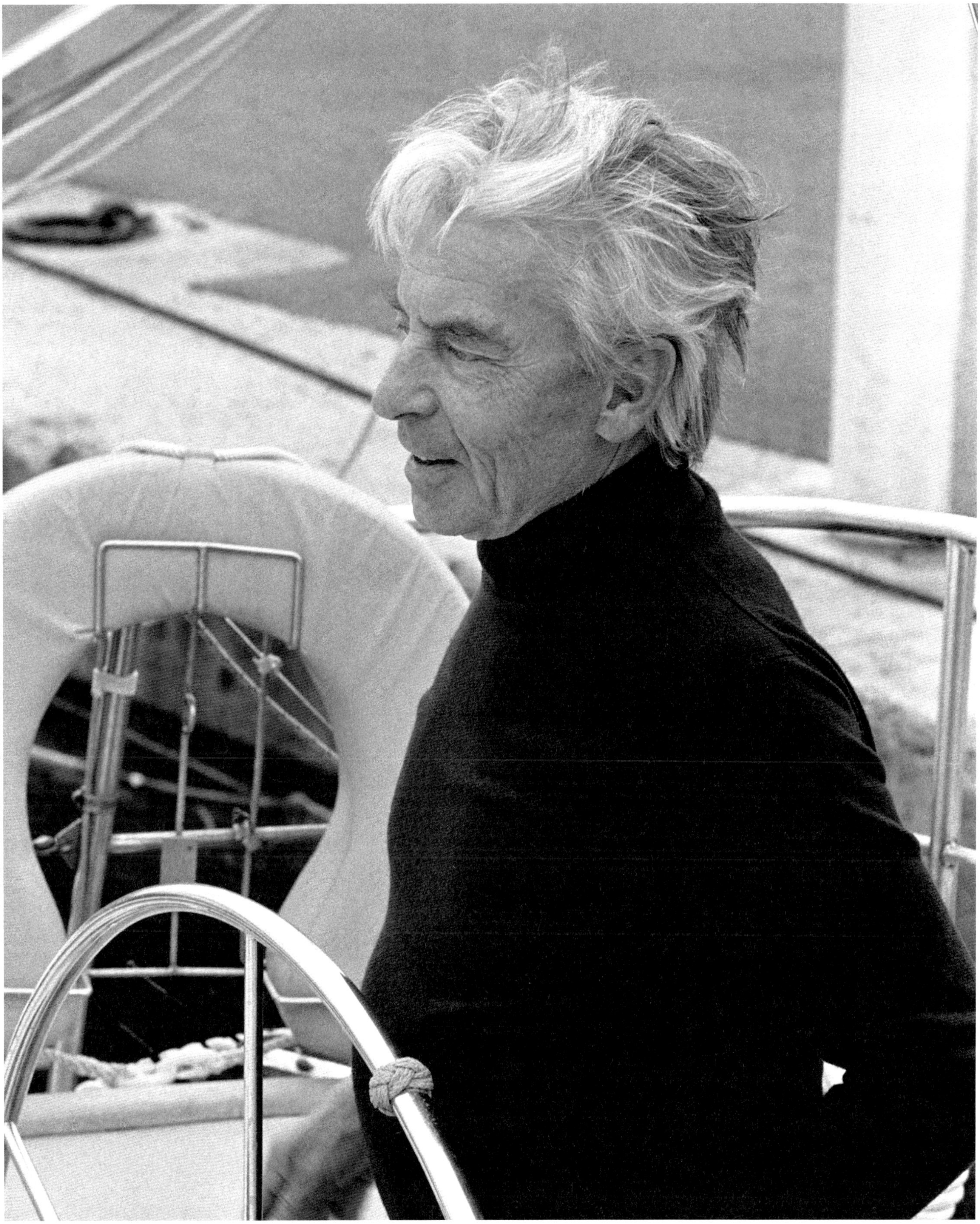

This page: *Conductor Herbert von Karajan at the helm of his yacht "Hélisara" in June 1978.*

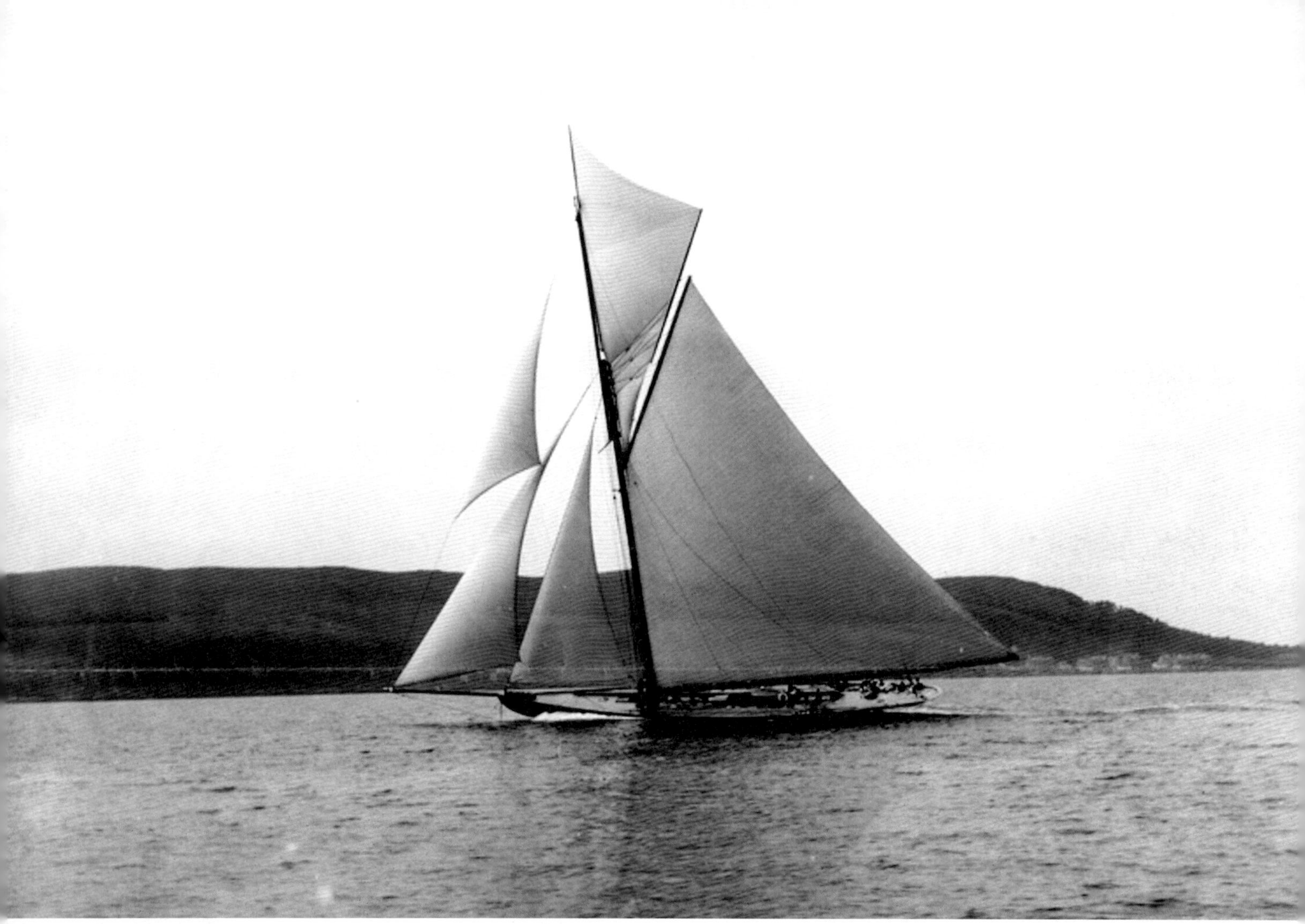

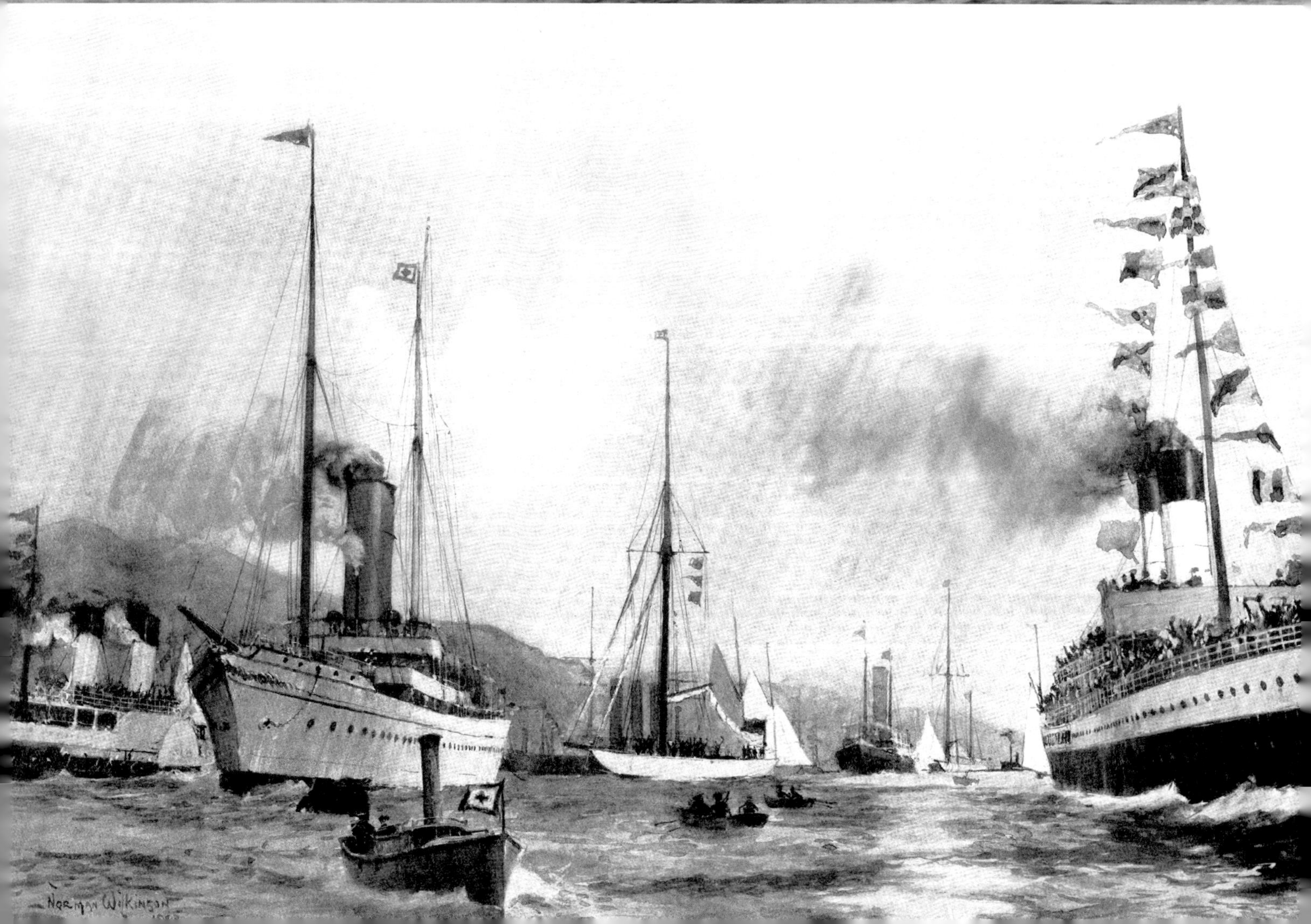
NORMAN WILKINSON

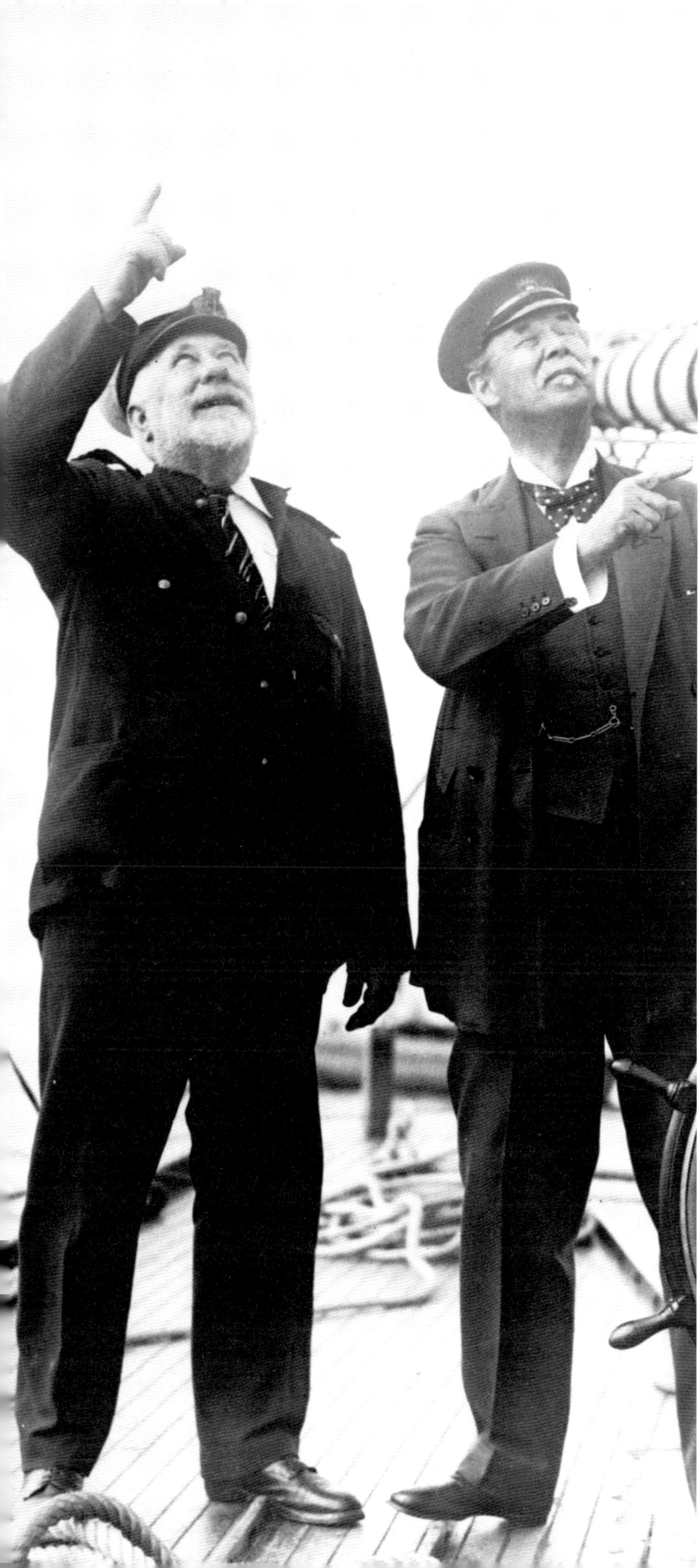

Opposite, top: *Sir Thomas Lipton's "Shamrock I" sailing off the Scottish coast in 1901. The yacht was designed for the America's Cup competition.*

Opposite, bottom: *The new America's Cup challenger, Sir Thomas Lipton's "Shamrock III," leaves Gourock Bay for Sandy Hook, accompanied by a flotilla of attendant craft and his other yacht, "Shamrock I," in May 1903.*

This page: *Sir Thomas Lipton and Captain W. Manning on the "Shamrock" in 1923. Lipton had inspected it at City Island, New York. He challenged for the America's Cup in 1923 for a match in 1925, but the New York Yacht Club waited until 1930 to host the match. It was Lipton's fifth and final challenge which were all unsuccessful.*

Following pages: *Conductor Herbert Von Karajan with his wife Eliette aboard their yacht "Hélisara" in the bay of Saint Tropez in July 1967.*

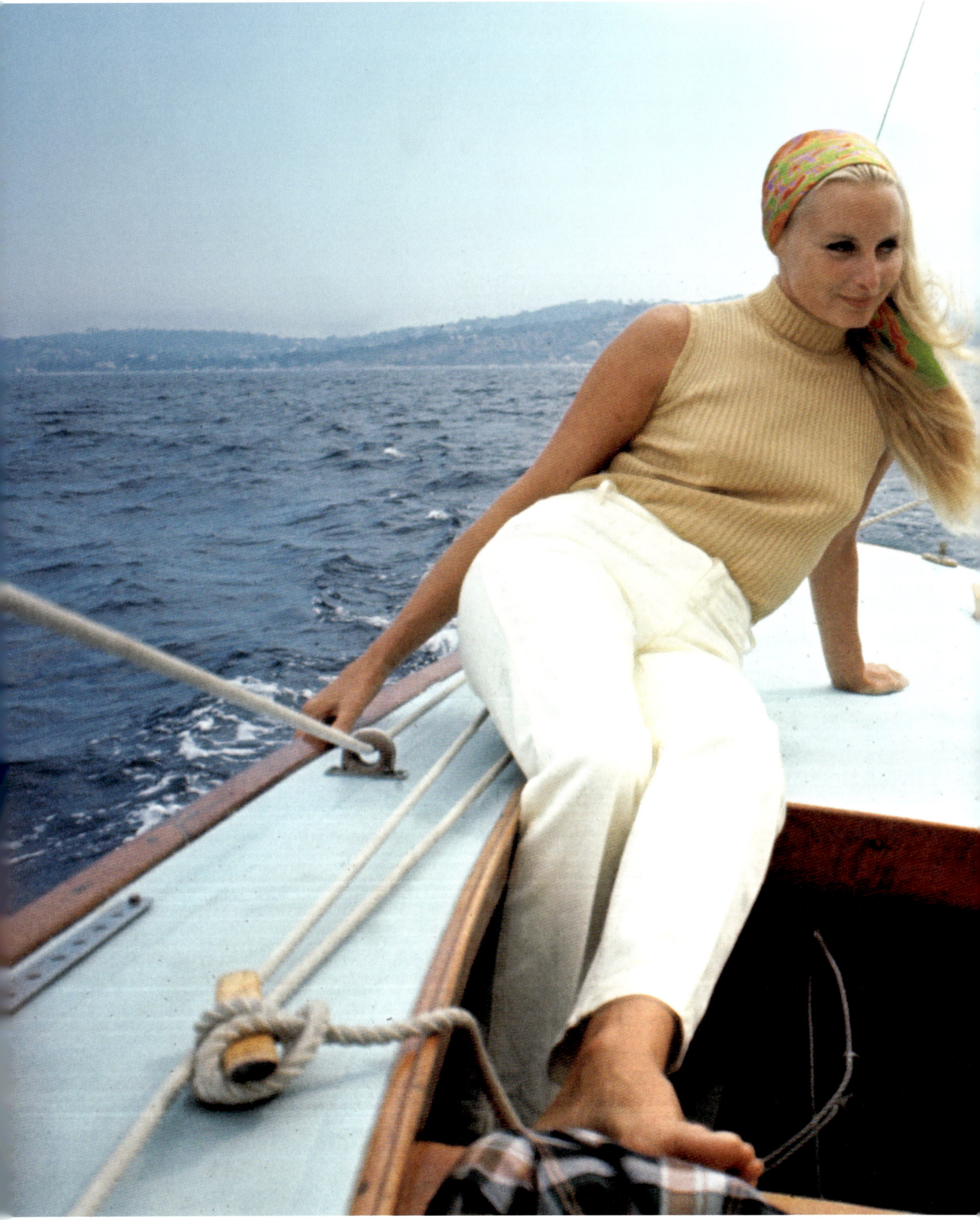

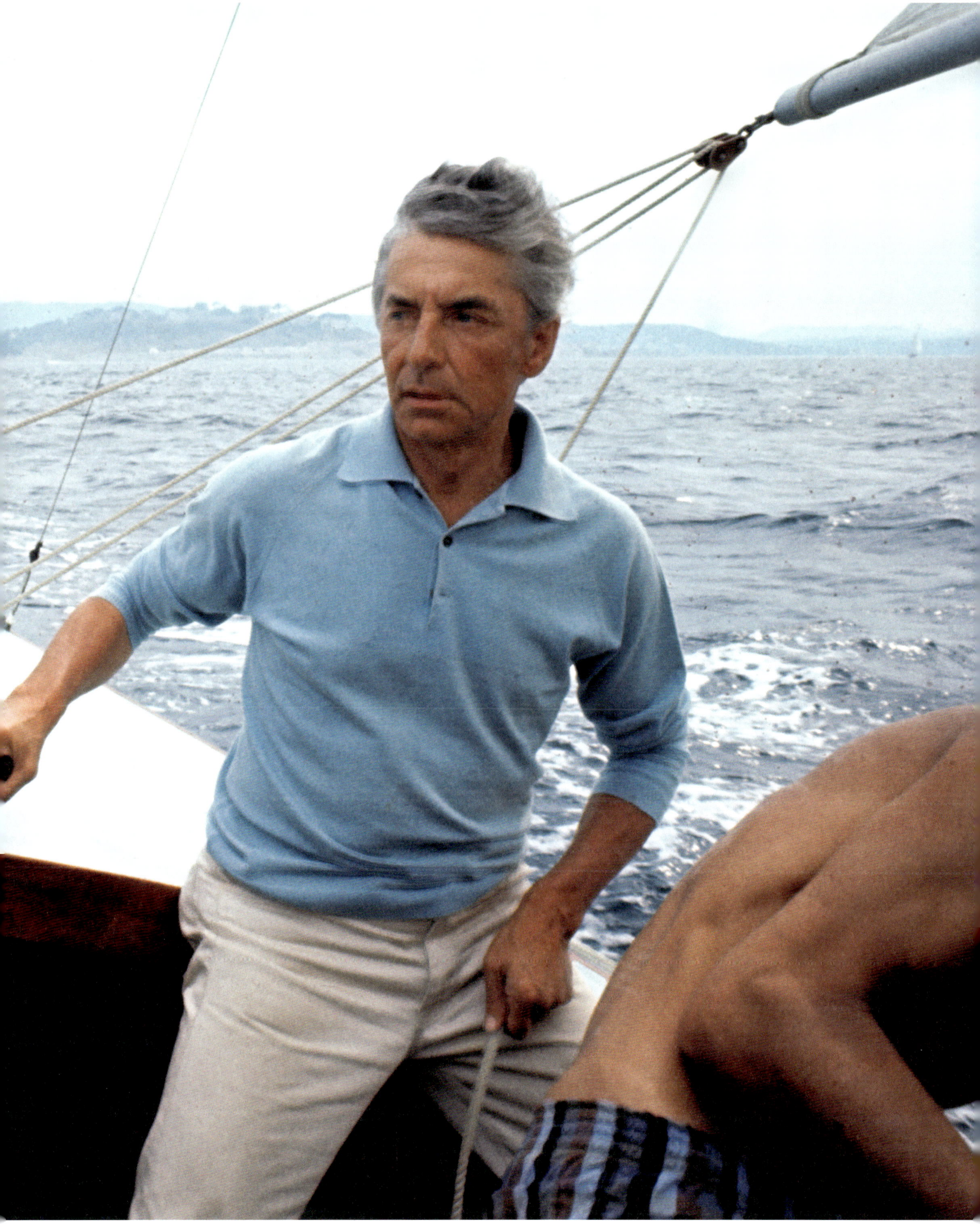

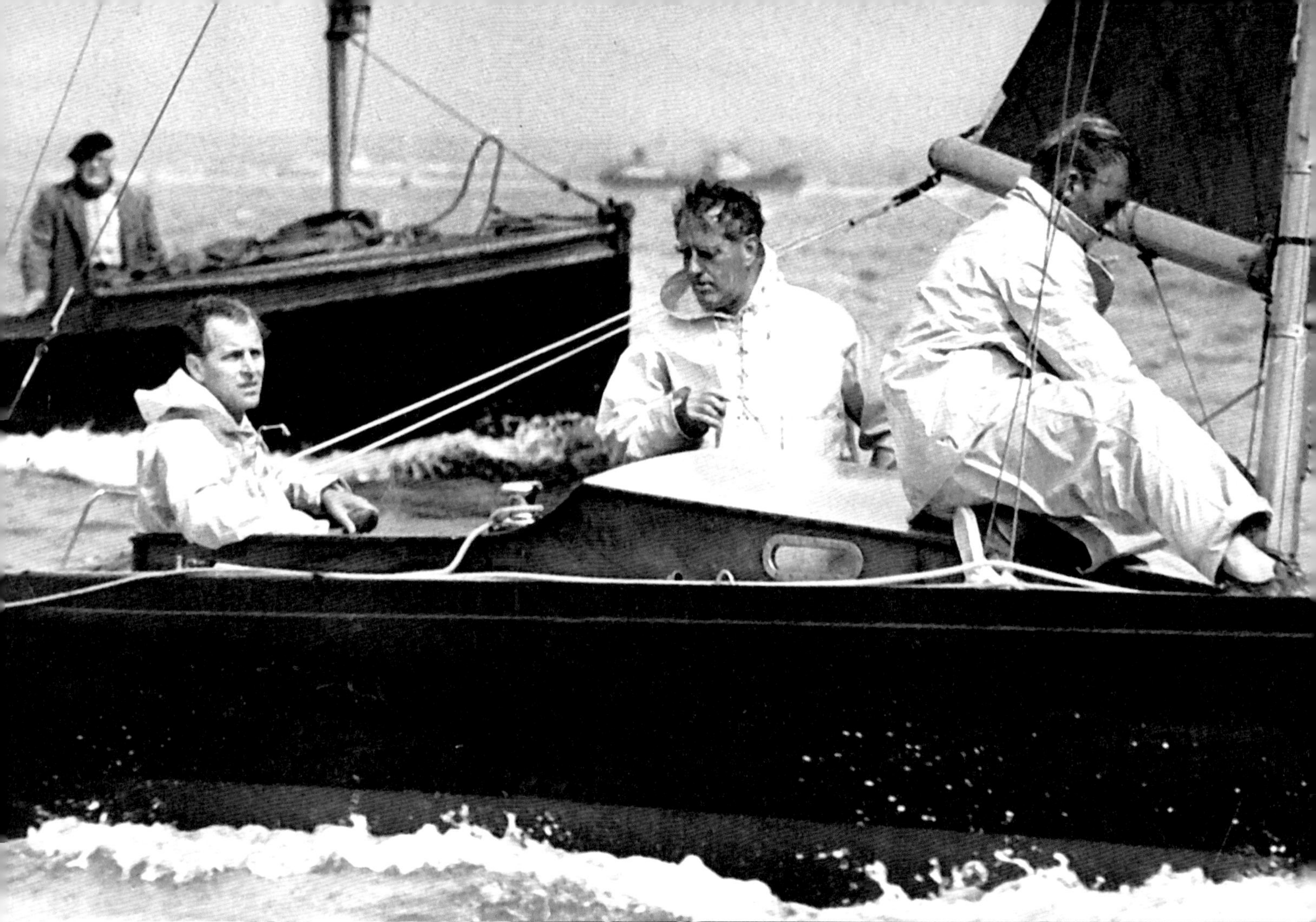

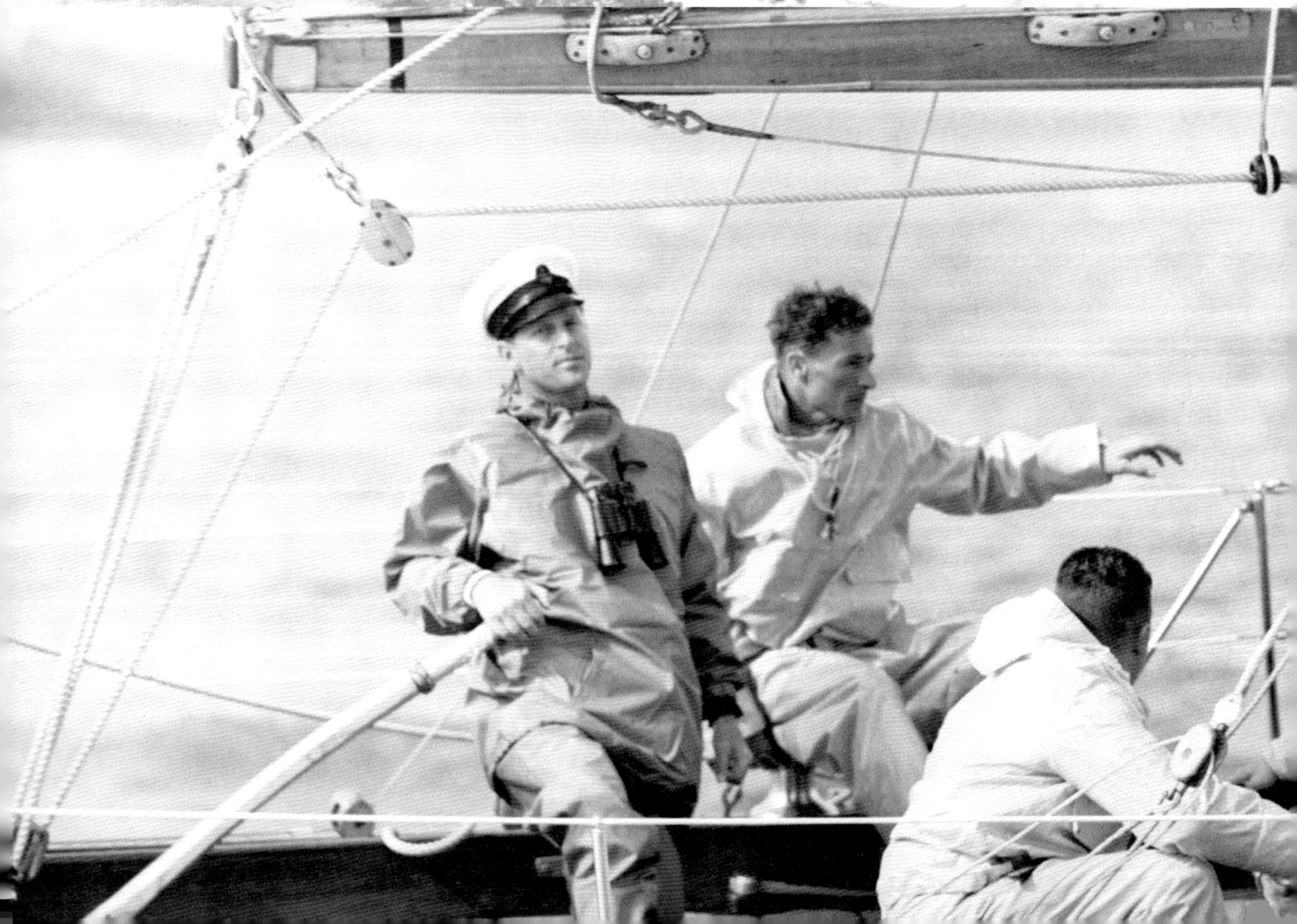

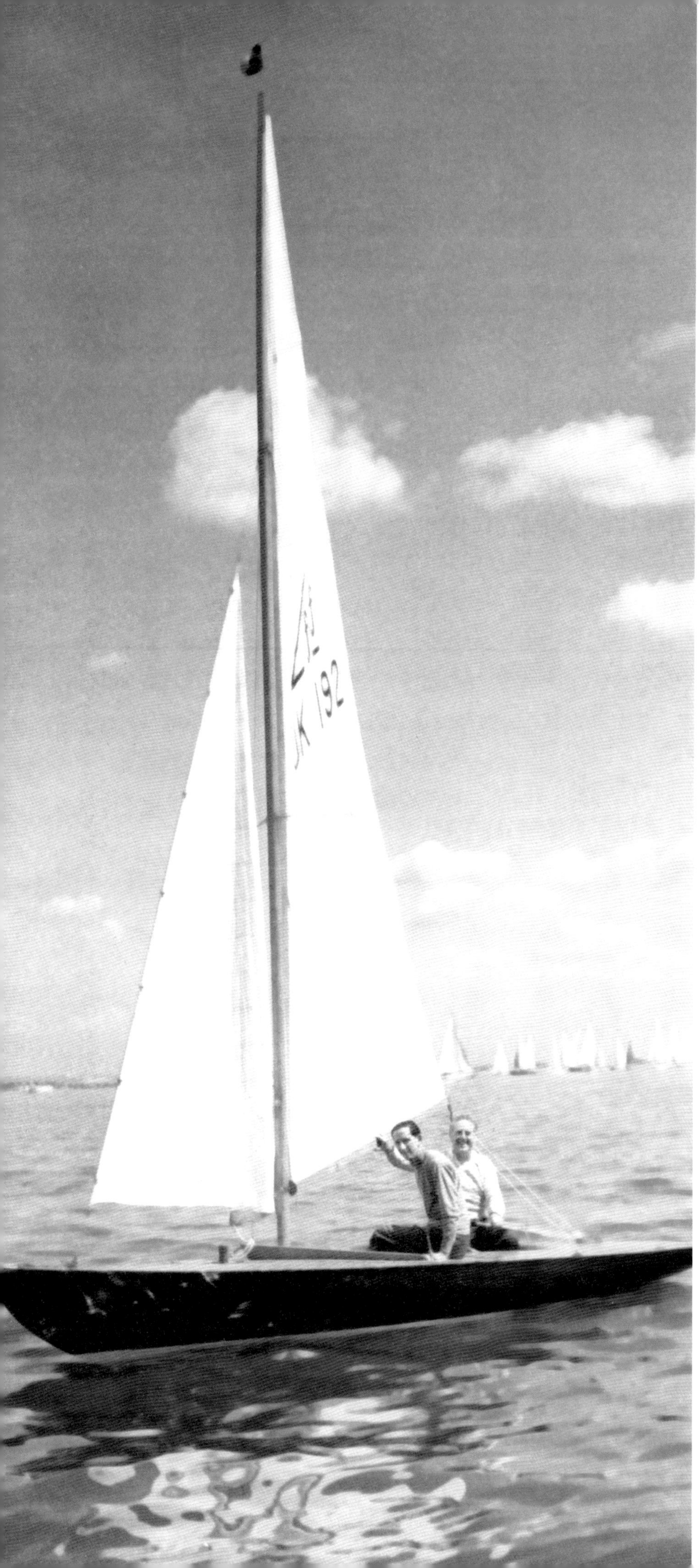

Opposite, top: *All-round sportsman the Duke of Edinburgh at the helm of the yacht "Bluebottle," competing in a race at Cowes Regatta. The burly Uffa Fox stands in the cockpit.*

Opposite, bottom: *Prince Philip (left) and sailor Uffa Fox on the ocean racing yacht "Bloodhound" during Cowes Week off the Isle of Wight in August 1962.*

This page: *The Duke of Edinburgh's yacht "Coweslip" anchored while awaiting a wind or change of tide during the Royal London Yacht Club Regatta during Cowes Week in 1953. The Duke arrived too late to take part in the racing, and it was Uffa Fox who took the craft out for the Flying Fifteen race.*

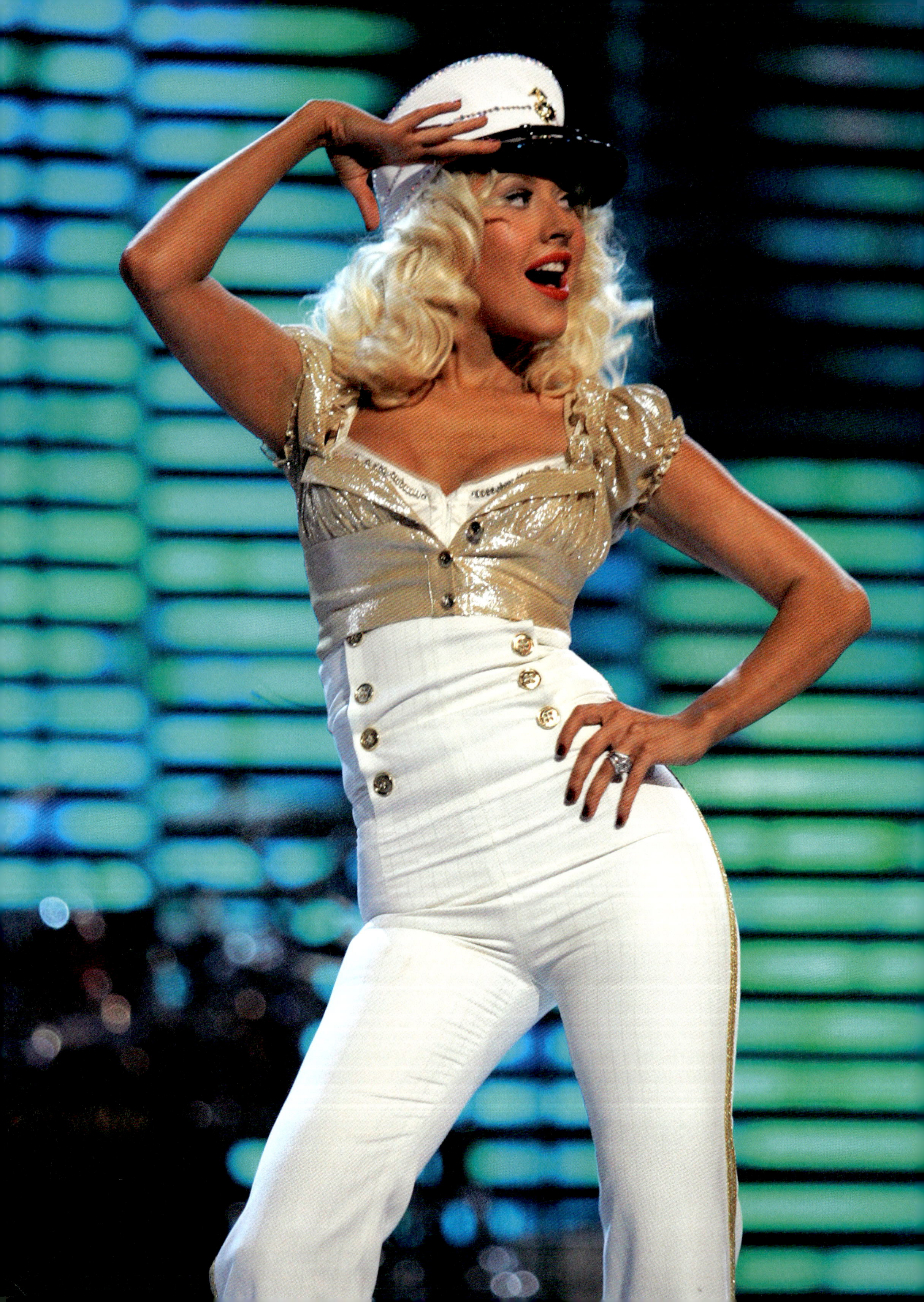

FASHION

FROM GLAMOUR TO GEAR

If you want to see how standards of dress have fallen, just watch a movie from the 1930s to the 1960s that includes a scene on an aircraft. People dressed formally and well for a flight, whereas now for the most part passengers wear clothes that are as casual as possible. Yachting attire has changed too, of course. But it's done so to a far lesser degree, because in sailing there's still the feeling that time-honored traditions and styles should be respected.

There are also a lot of practical concerns when thinking about how to dress on a boat. You can be enjoying a warm day with a soft breeze one moment and the next be struggling through a cold, fierce gale with powerful waves. So sailors must be prepared for all weather conditions. Historically, crews on ships and racing yachts wore uniforms with bell-bottom shaped trouser legs so boots and shoes could be removed easily. A sailor's "kit" also included heavy cotton and wool tops for warmth. But the problem with these garments was that they absorbed water and didn't dry easily. Early forms of foul weather gear usually consisted of "oil skins" (the oil was usually some kind of grease or lanolin to deflect spray and water), but these were uncomfortable to wear and often leaked. As a result of all this the smells down deck below could be very ripe after several days at sea. But the fact was—and often still is—that for a professional sailor things like comfort and pleasant odors aren't the top priorities.

Opposite: *Singer Christina Aguilera performs at Condé Nast Media Group's Third Annual Fashion Rocks Concert at Radio City Music Hall, in New York City in September 2006.*

The attire of yacht-owners and their guests, on the other hand, was generally impeccable and stylish, featuring yachting blazers, ties, captain's hats, and white cotton duct pants made of heavy-duty fabric. Women generally wore long dresses, and often large hats. Nothing could prevent the weather taking its toll on even the highest-quality garments, of course, but the owner's party (known as the afterguard) likely had multiple outfits for each day of sailing.

Clothing for yacht racing has improved over recent years. "Breathable" fabrics have made foul weather gear more comfortable and effective at keeping the sailor dry. Taped seams over stitched areas keeps water out. Jackets are longer in the back to prevent them from riding up. Secure closures around the neck keep warmth in and water out. Sleeves have an inner cuff to keep water from leaking in. High collars and hoods keep the bright sun and water off the neck. Reflector tape on the sleeves and hood help to locate a person requiring rescue from the water. Fleece-lined pockets help keep hands warm when it's cold.

At parties, awards ceremonies, social events and clubs in the yachting world proper clothing is mandatory. Gentlemen will always wear a jacket and tie, and yacht club crests on blazers indicate that you belong. Sailors often also sport pins signifying race victories, special honors or for charitable giving. Scarves, ties, hats, shirts, jackets and sweaters are often emblazoned with the sail number or name of a yacht. An active sailor's closet is filled with clothing with logos, names and numbers embroidered on them.

A sailor's posture on a boat or around the docks says a lot about them. The best helmsmen stand when they steer, both hands resting lightly on the wheel, or lean forward as if urging their yacht to sail a little faster. When a tactician folds his arms across his chest this is a confident pose and indicates the race is going well. If the hands slide down the hip, however, it indicates concern and tension. Both hands on the back of the head signal frustration.

Following pages: GQ, *May 1975: two male models stand on a sailboat wearing (left) a Pebble Beach of California cardigan and V-neck with raw silk trousers by Barry, and (right) a cardigan by International Apparel Inc, a T-shirt by Giovanni De Moura and slacks by Lee Cooper for Barney Sampson. The female model wears Stephen Burrows.*

Page 144: *A young man hoists a sail while the woman leans against the boom aboard a sailboat, c. 1935. He wears a captain's hat while she wears a sailor's cap, and both hold cigarettes.*

Page 145: *Susanna Wassaman sailing during trial runs in Newport harbor in July 1974.*

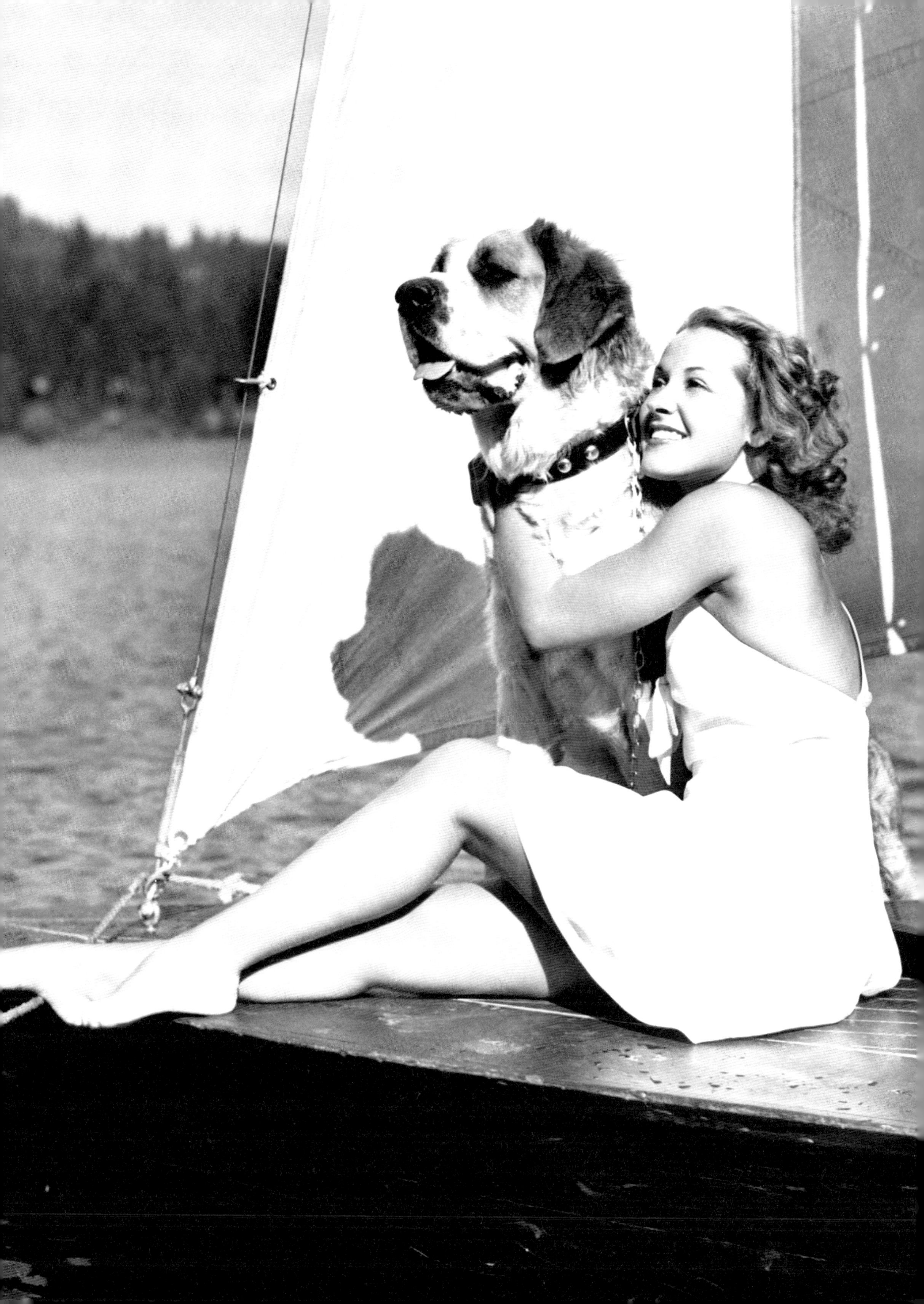

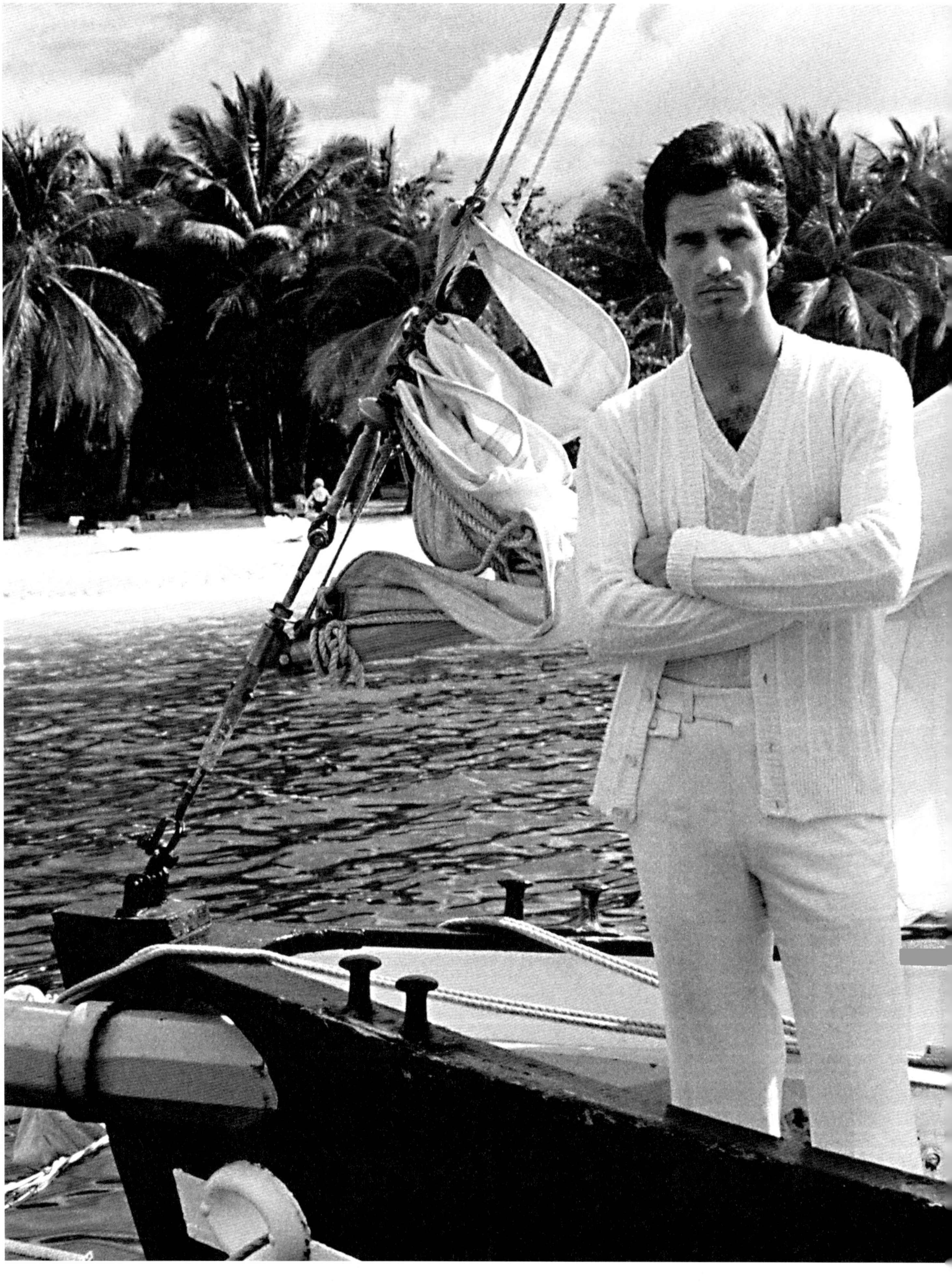

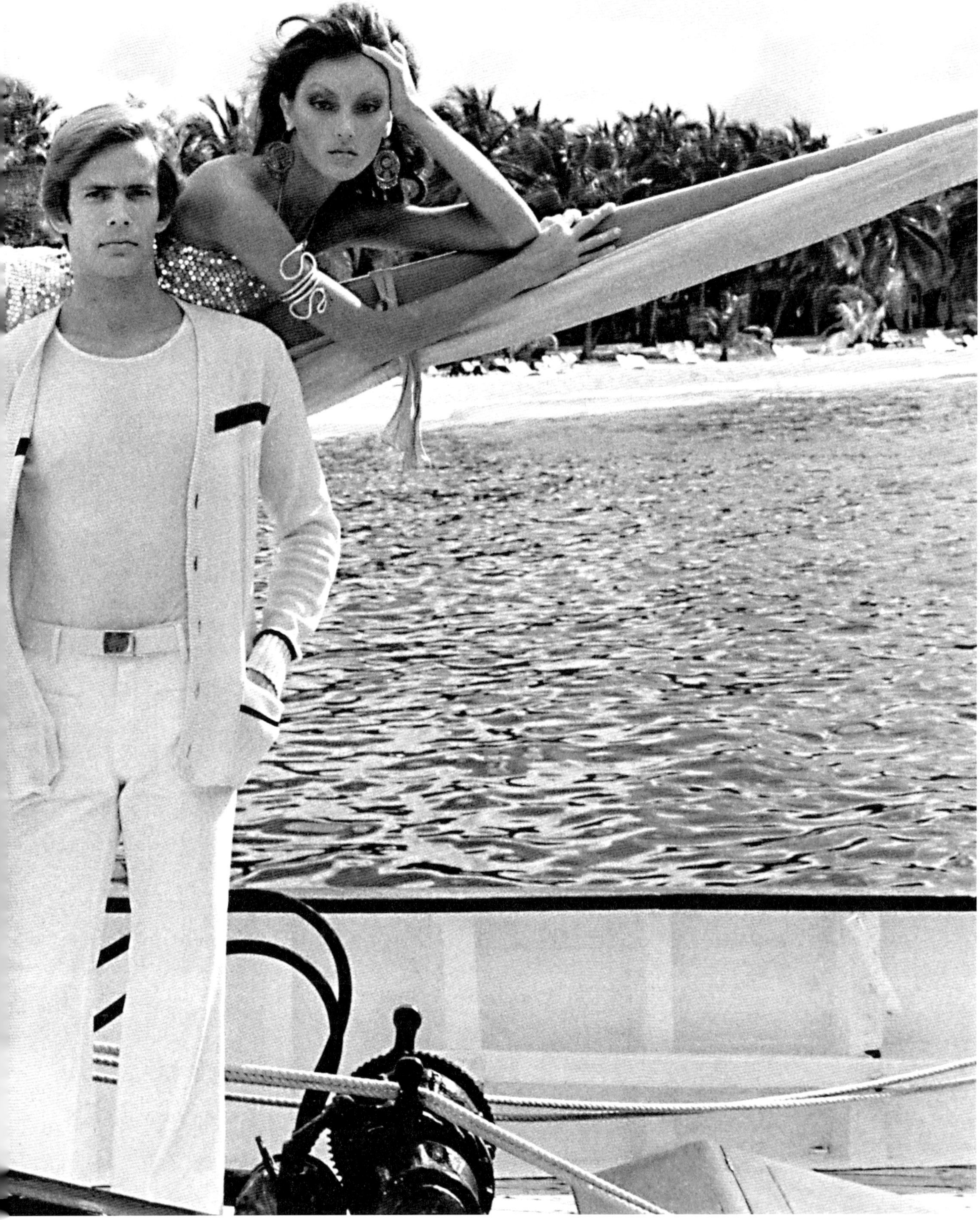

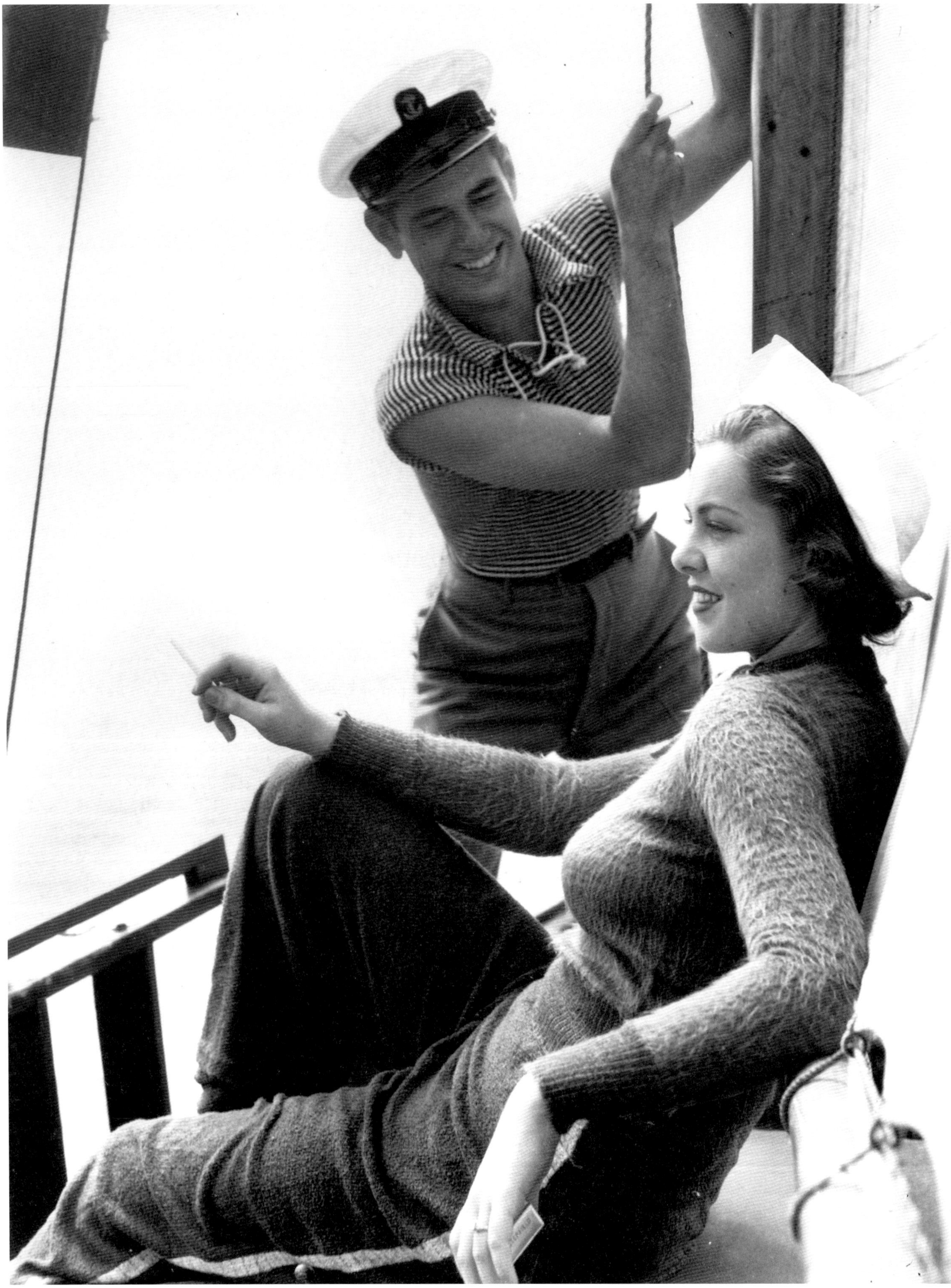

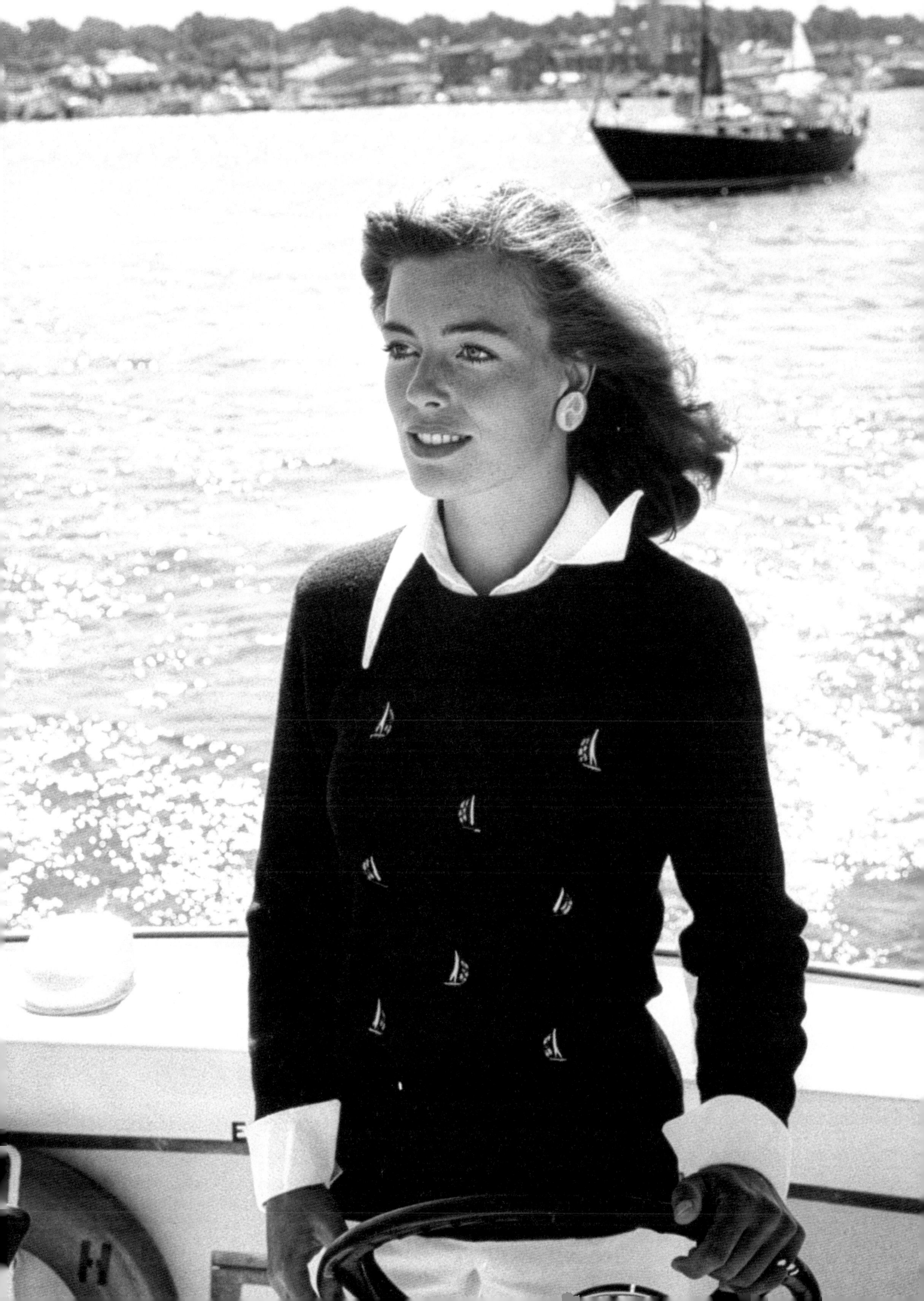

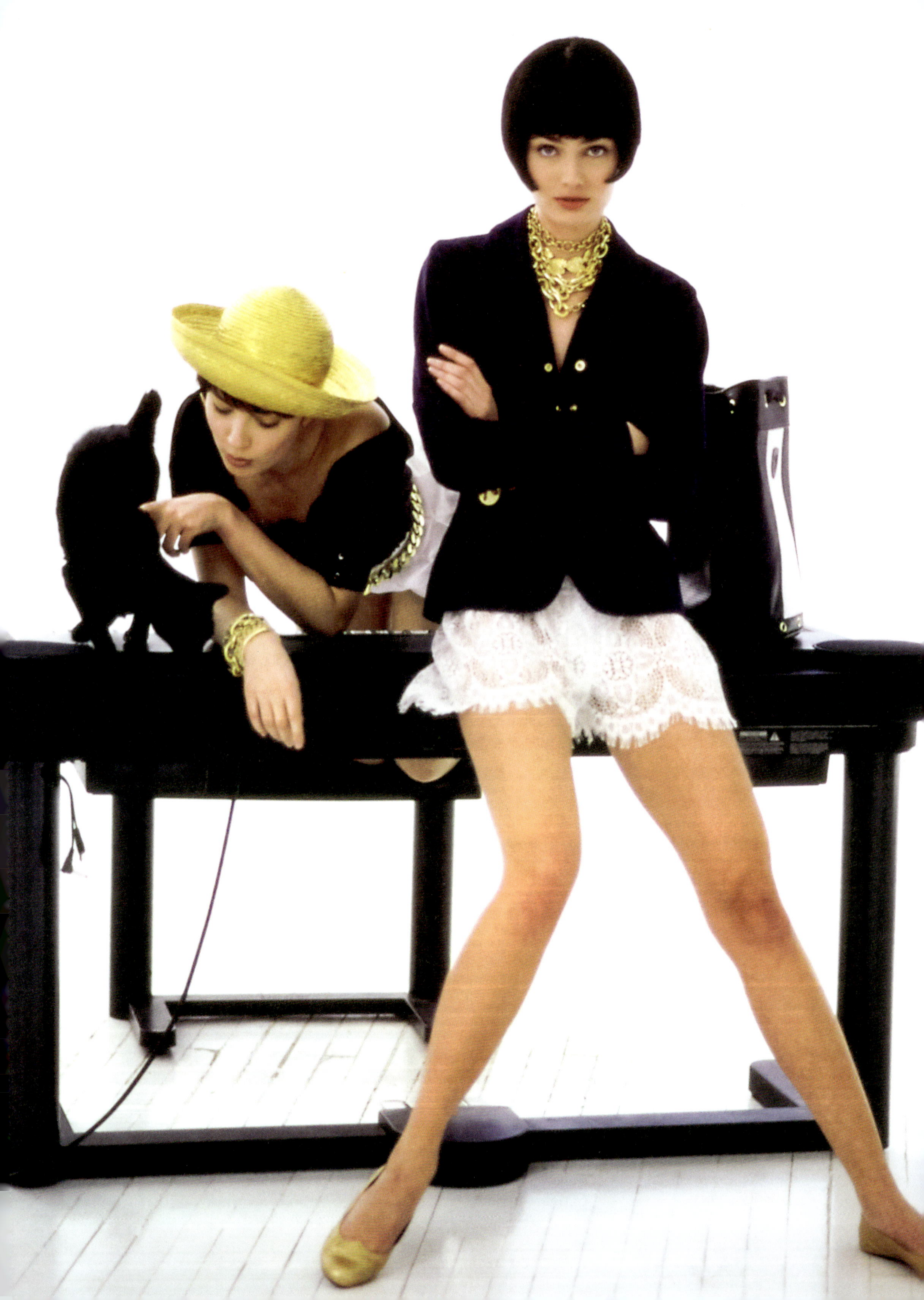

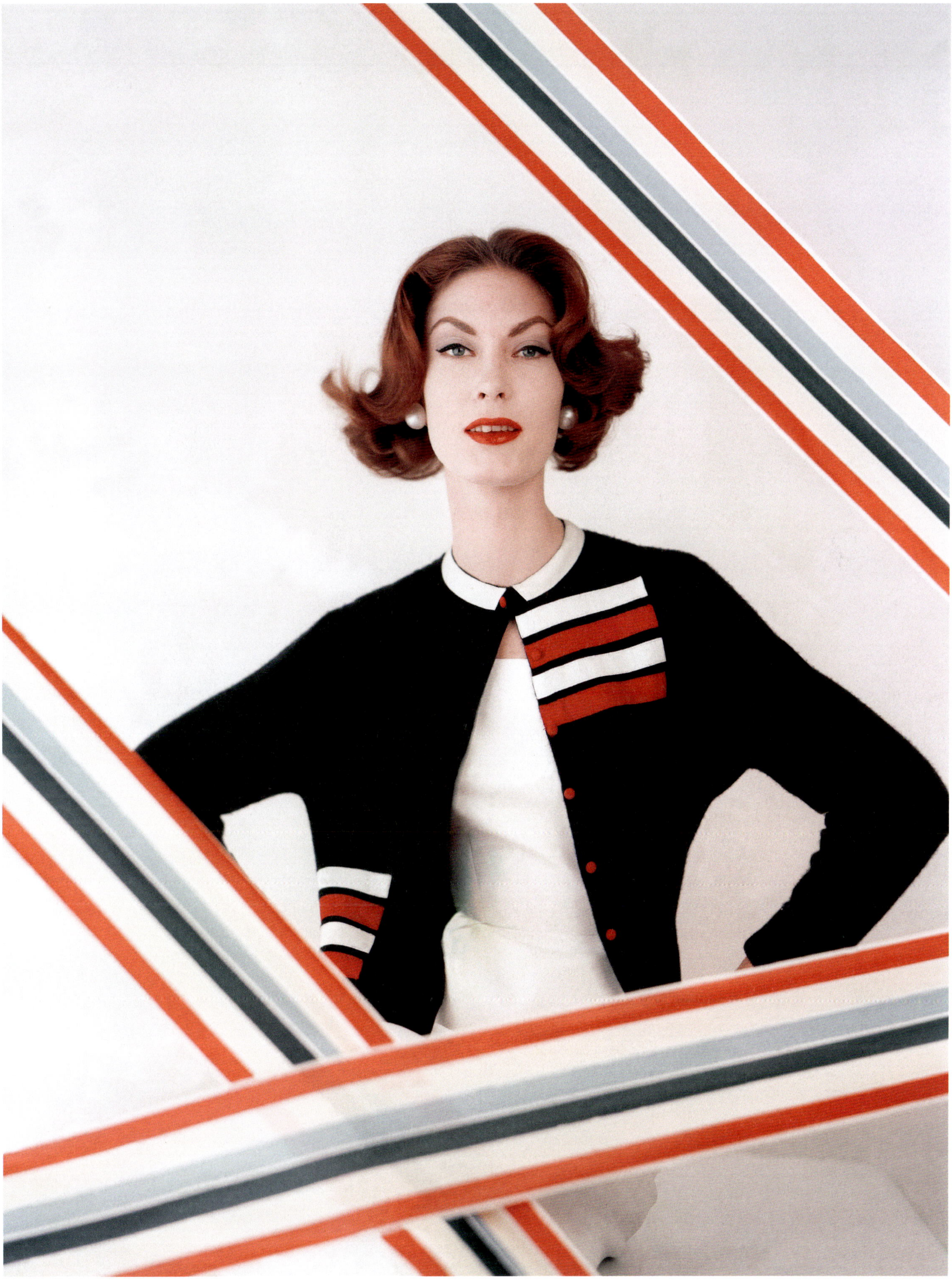

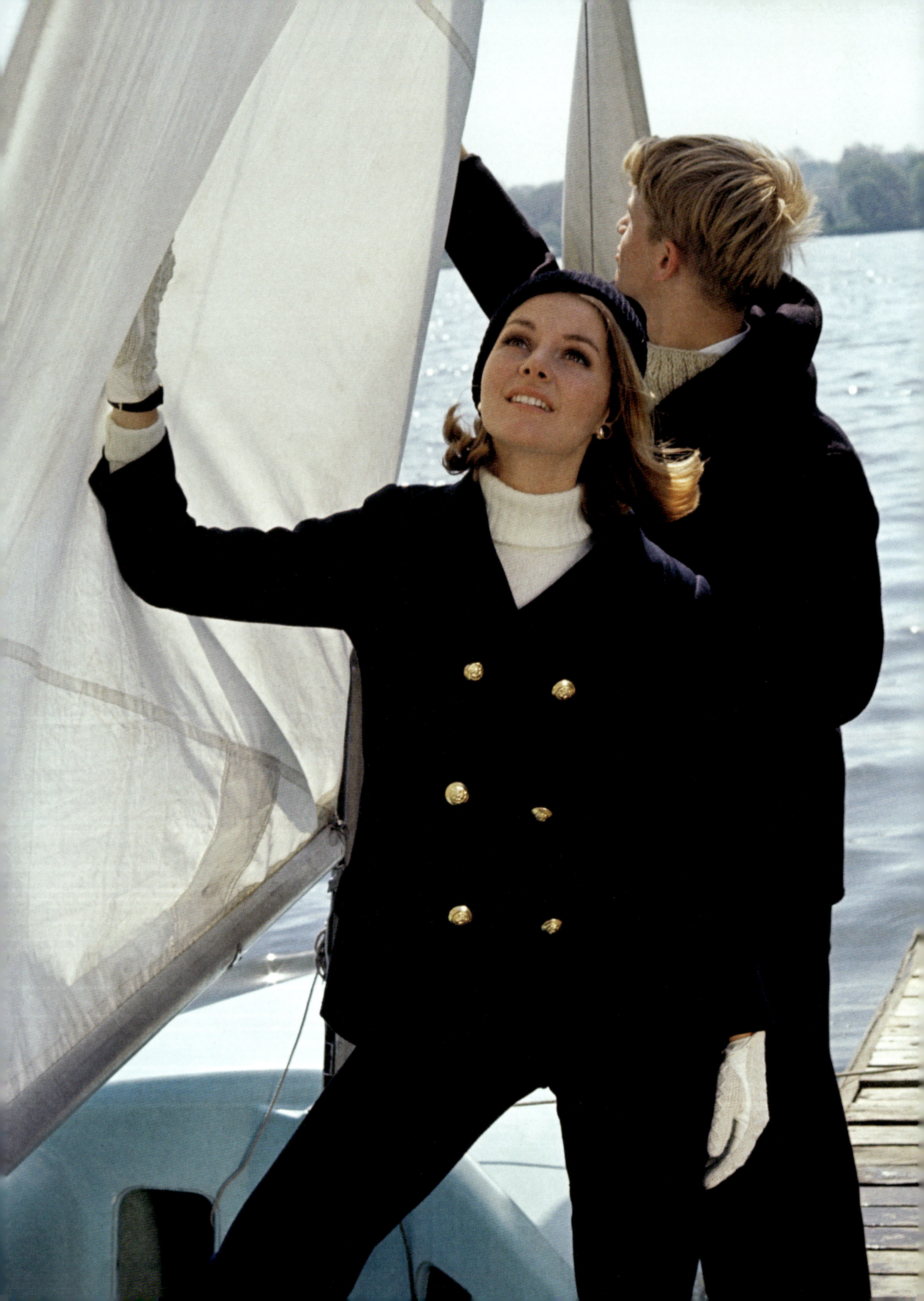

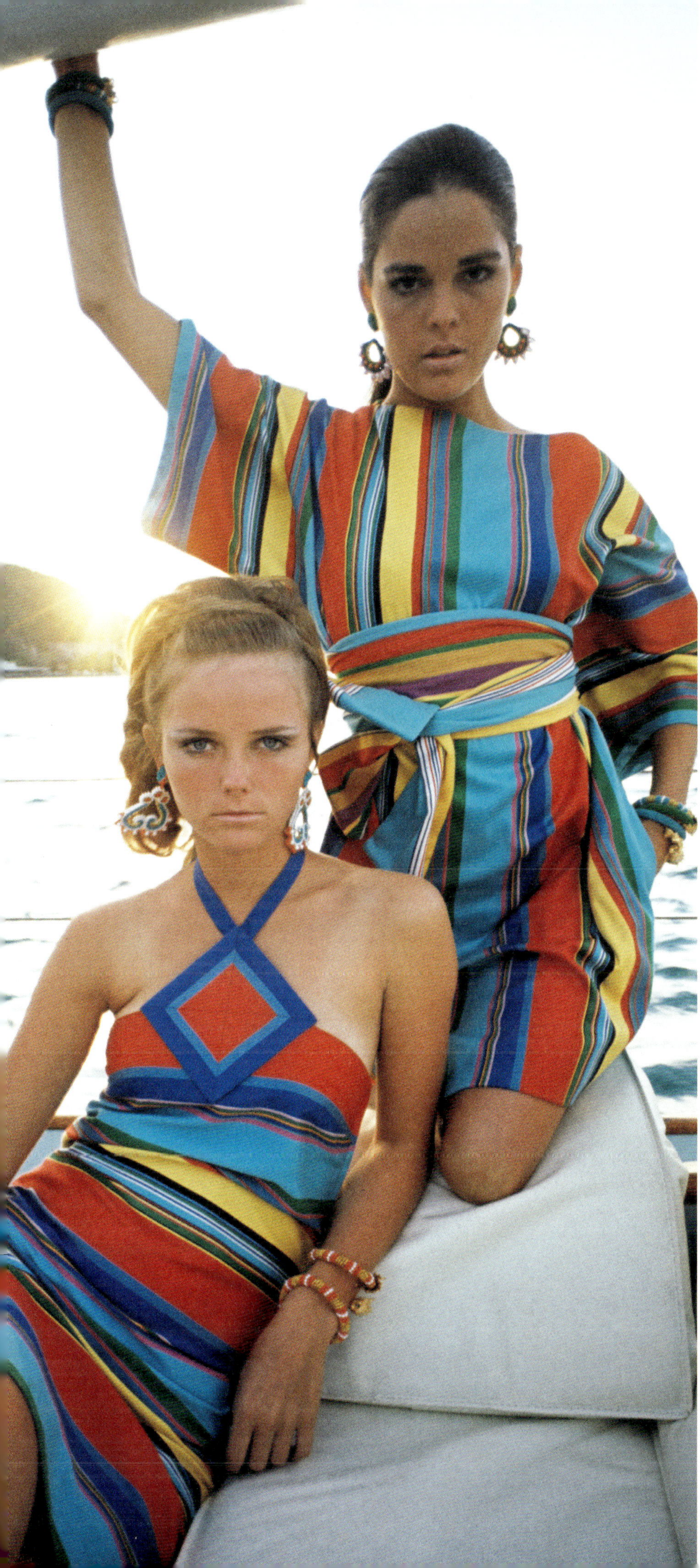

Page 146: Vogue, *May 1990: model Paulina Porizkova with an unidentified model and black cat, leaning against a synthesizer. She wears a navy cotton twill riding jacket by Randolph Duke, white lace shorts by Thea Anema, gold chain necklaces by Jay Feinberg, a hammered gold heart necklace by Erwin Pearl, and flat gold slippers by Sam and Libby. On the second model: a Black taffeta peasant top by Tarlazzi II, a straw hat by Kokin, and gold chain bracelets and belt by Erwin Pearl. Hairpieces were supplied by Theresa's Wigs, makeup was by Sonia Kashuk, and the shoot was styled by Michael Tammaro for Bumble+Bumble.*

Page 147: *A model wearing a Vera Stewart sweater of navy-blue cashmere with red and white grosgrain sailing signals down the front in May 1957.*

Opposite Page: *Katherine Ellis on a sailboat, wearing a navy blue pea jacket with brass buttons and matching pants by Claret. Her friend David Felsen is in the background* (Glamour, *1965).*

This Page: *Ali MacGraw and Cheryl Tiegs on a sailboat, modelling matching striped dresses from Mam'selle Boutique* (Glamour, *1967).*

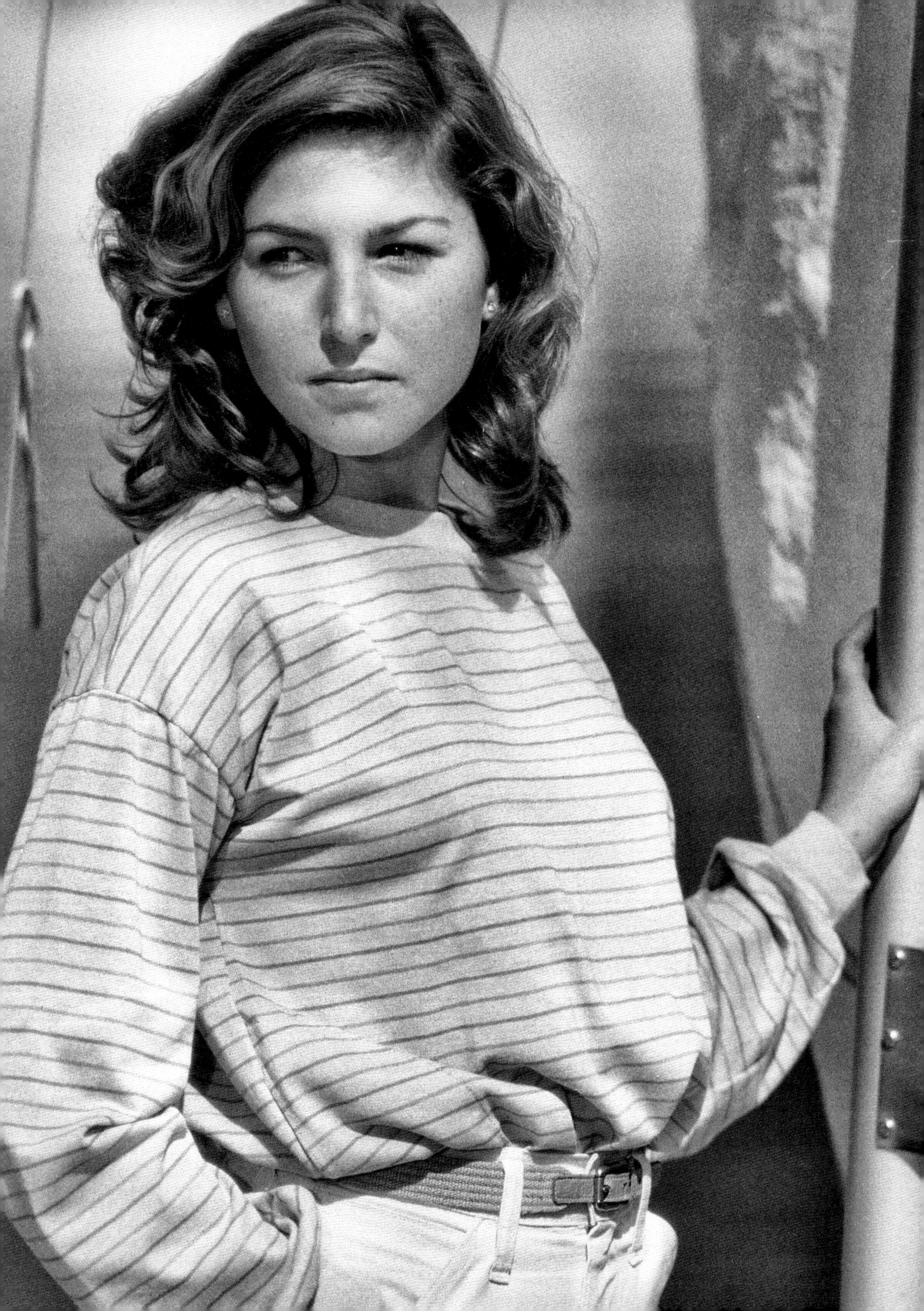

FILM

THE OCEAN AS STAGE

Human courage and ingenuity, the wild forces of nature, powerful technology: in sailing all these come together in a way that's unique and uniquely compelling. It's no wonder, then, that cinema regularly takes to sea, and has done since almost the beginning of the medium. On film, the sailboat often becomes a microcosm in which human life is condensed, where people vie for power amongst themselves or struggle for survival against the elements with spectacular seascapes as the backdrop. As a subject for cinema, sailing comes charged with associations of freedom, deadly risk and isolation, but also of community, selflessness and achievement against the odds.

The following examples illustrate the draw of the sea for filmmakers, and the different kinds of stories they have used it to tell: tales of loners attempting to survive in isolation, of teams falling apart or coming together to achieve greatness, of people falling in or out of love, of historic events or wild fantasy.

All is Lost—Robert Redford (Chandor, 2013): Academy Award-winning actor and director Robert Redford is the only cast-member in this unique film about a sailor desperately trying to keep his 39-foot sailboat from sinking. It's a story of struggle against the odds that relies almost entirely on Redford's performance to hold our attention Three different Cal 39s were used in the production.

High Society—Bing Crosby, Grace Kelly, Frank Sinatra (Walters, 1956): The action of this musical romantic comedy unfolds in Newport, Rhode Island at a time when many mansions are being sold because property taxes have gotten too high. Dexter (Bing Crosby) gives his wife Tracy (Grace Kelly) a model of their former sailboat, appropriately named "True Love," in an attempt to remind her of their good times sailing.

Mister Roberts—Jack Lemmon, Henry Fonda and James Cagney (Ford, LeRoy, Logan 1955): This John Ford-directed picture takes place on a US navy cargo vessel. A war film with real emotion, it was nominated for three Academy Awards, and Jack Lemmon won for Best Supporting Actor.

Wind—Matthew Modine, Jennifer Grey and Cliff Robertson (Ballard, 1992): This film is full of sailing action, human drama and comedy, and although it failed to light the box office on fire for sailors it's become a must-see. It portrays an attempt to defend the America's Cup in Newport, Rhode Island, and was inspired by the loss of the Cup to Australia in 1983.

Mutiny on the Bounty—Marlon Brando, Richard Harris (Milestone, 1962): This is a heavily fictionalized account of a famous real-life mutiny that took place in 1789, starring Marlon Brando as Fletcher Christian, Richard Harris as a veteran seaman, and Trevor Howard as Captain William Bligh. MGM built a full-size sailing ship for the production, which at the time was the most expensive film ever made, and the vessel went on to be used in movies including *Treasure Island* (1989) and *Pirates of the Caribbean: Dead Man's Chest* (2006).

What even this short survey makes abundantly clear: ships and the sea open up an endless range of storytelling opportunities for filmmakers, allowing human nature, relations and ethics to be explored in dramatic and exciting ways. But on top of all that there's the sheer style involved. From naval uniforms to pirate garb to sophisticated yachting attire, and from racing yachts to battleships, sailing offers to cinema a rich history of style, design and technology that's perennially fascinating to viewers—even (or perhaps especially) those who've never spent time at sea themselves.

Previous page, opposite: *16-year-old Tatum O'Neal, daughter of Ryan O'Neal, pictured holding on to the mast of a boat during the filming of* Circle Of Two *(Dassin, 1981) in Toronto in 1979.*

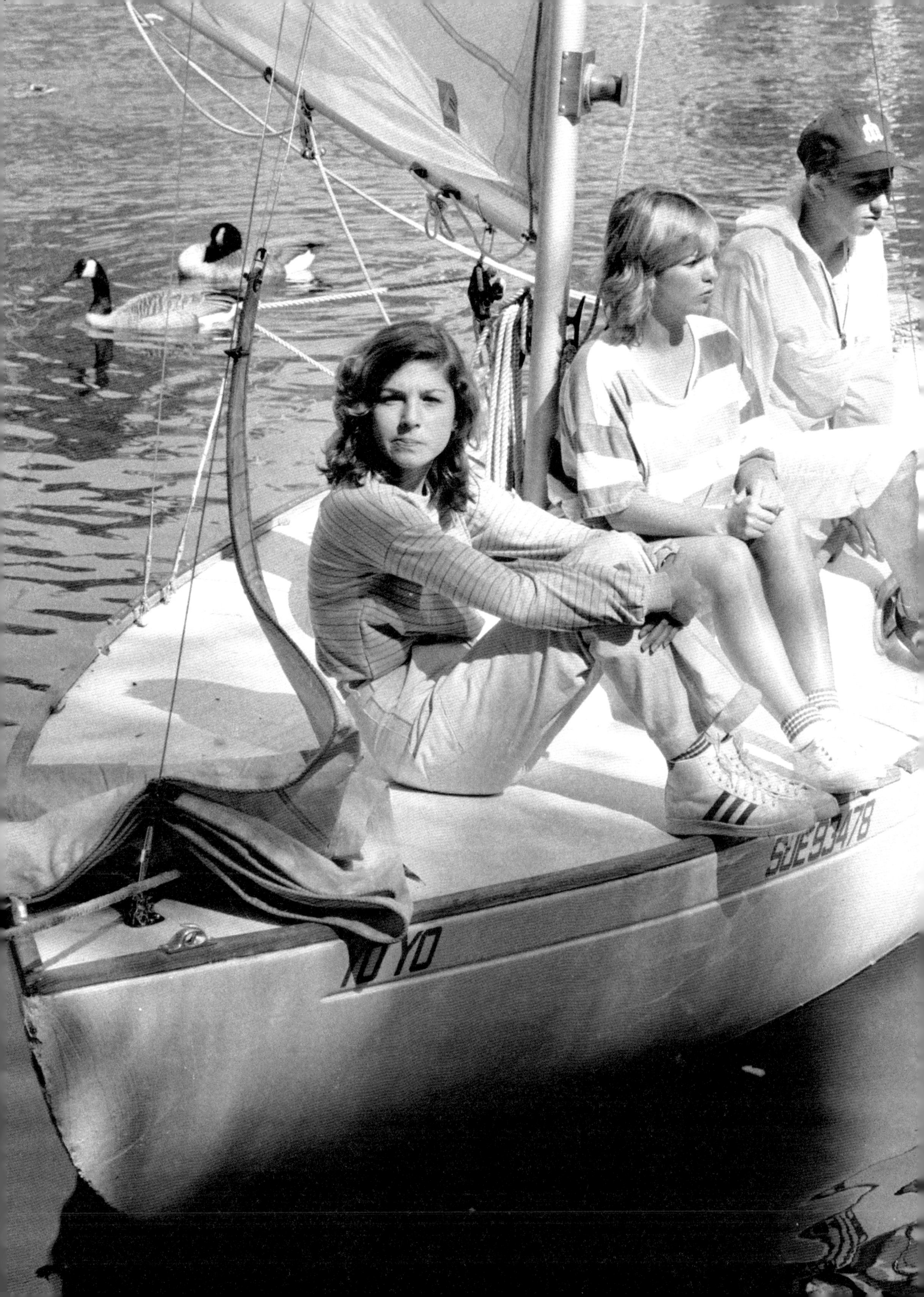
SUE 93478
YO YO

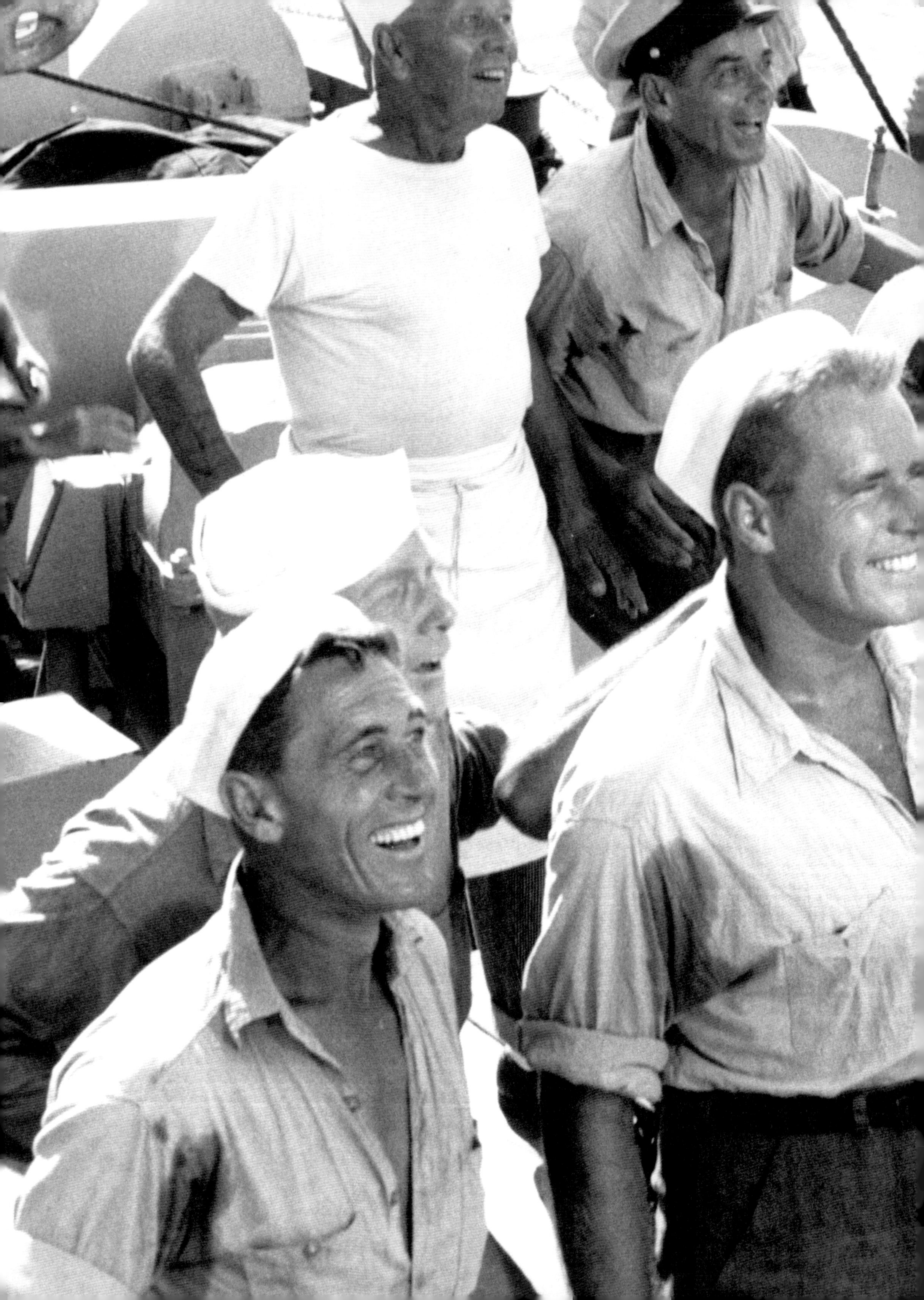

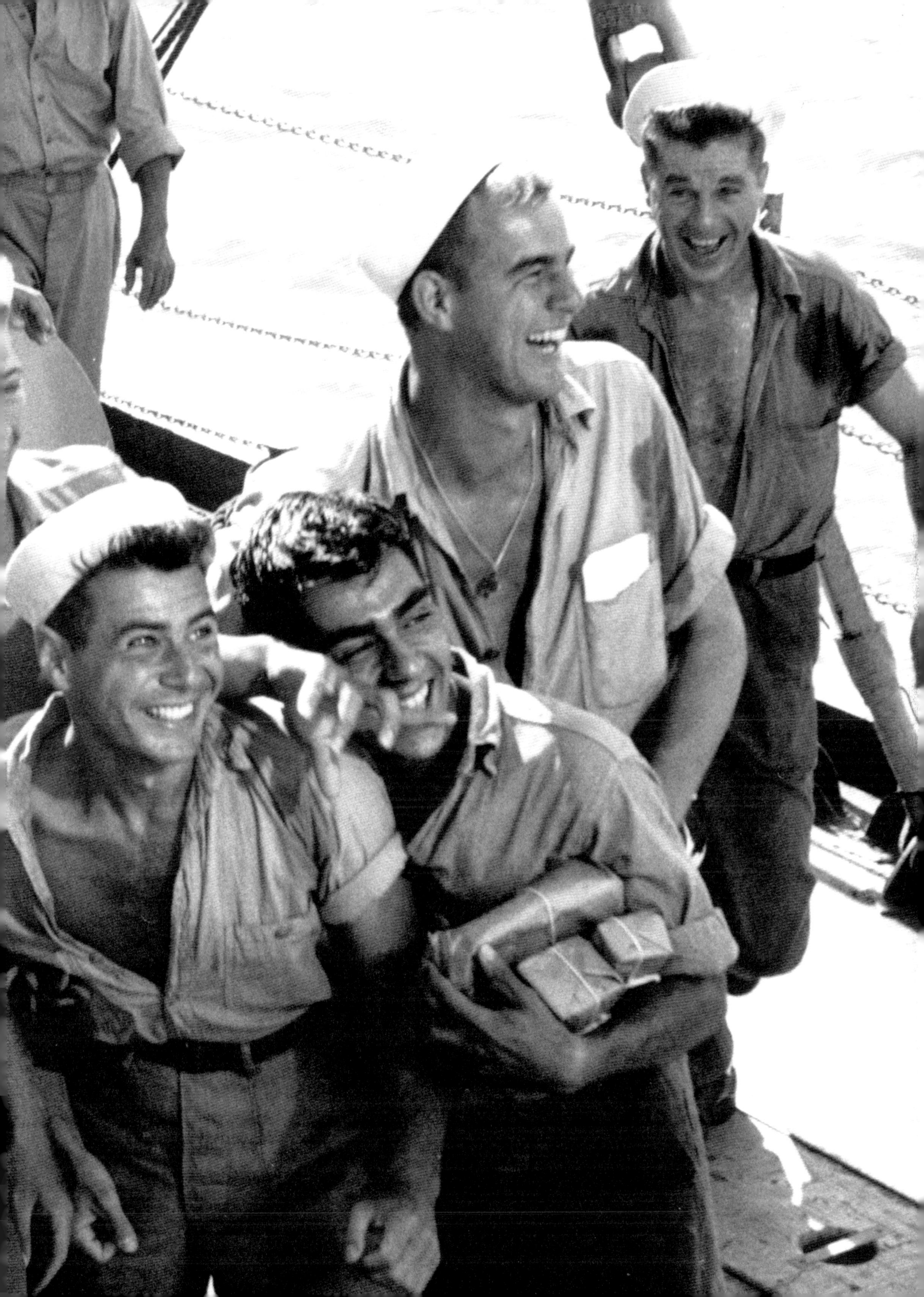

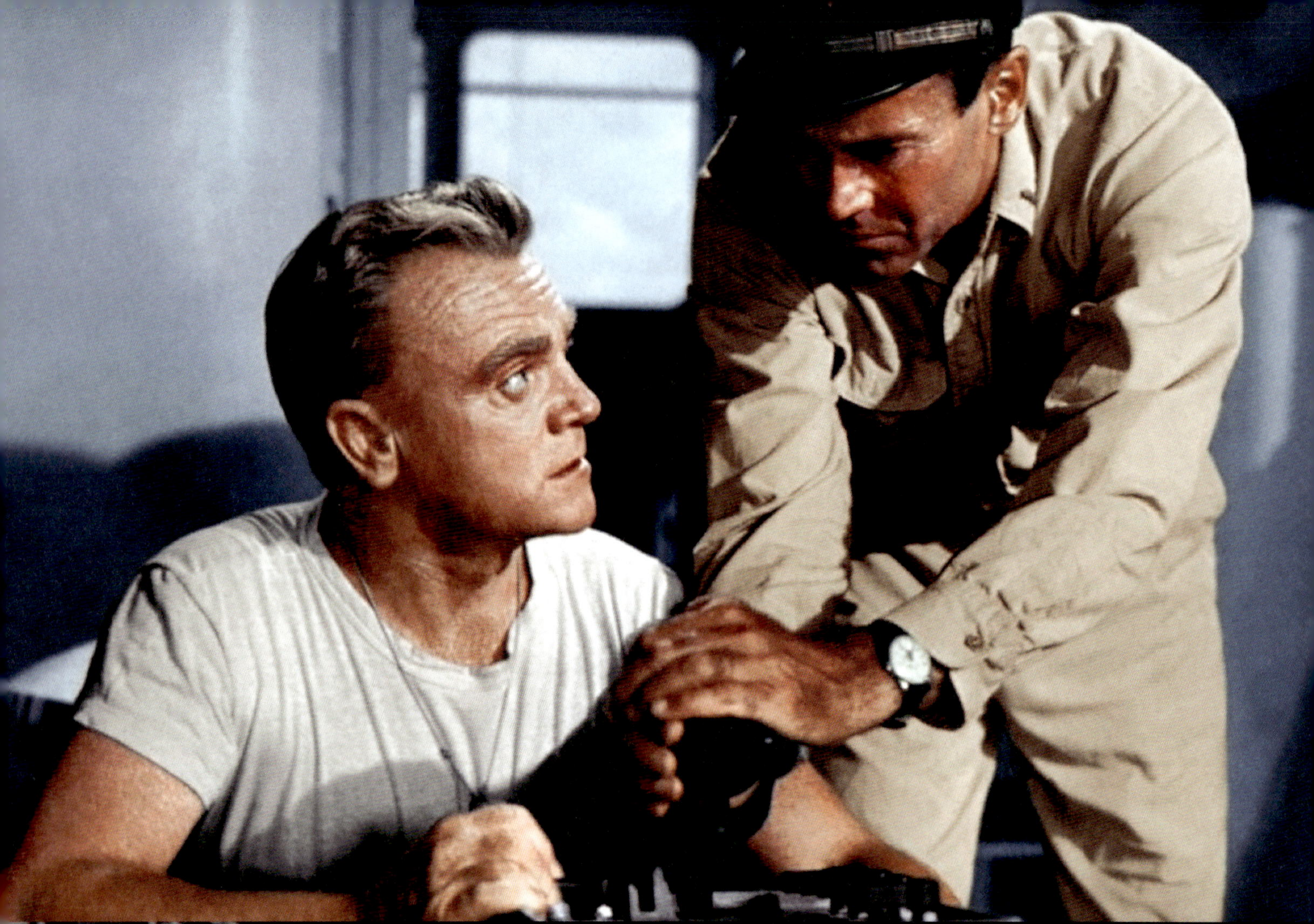

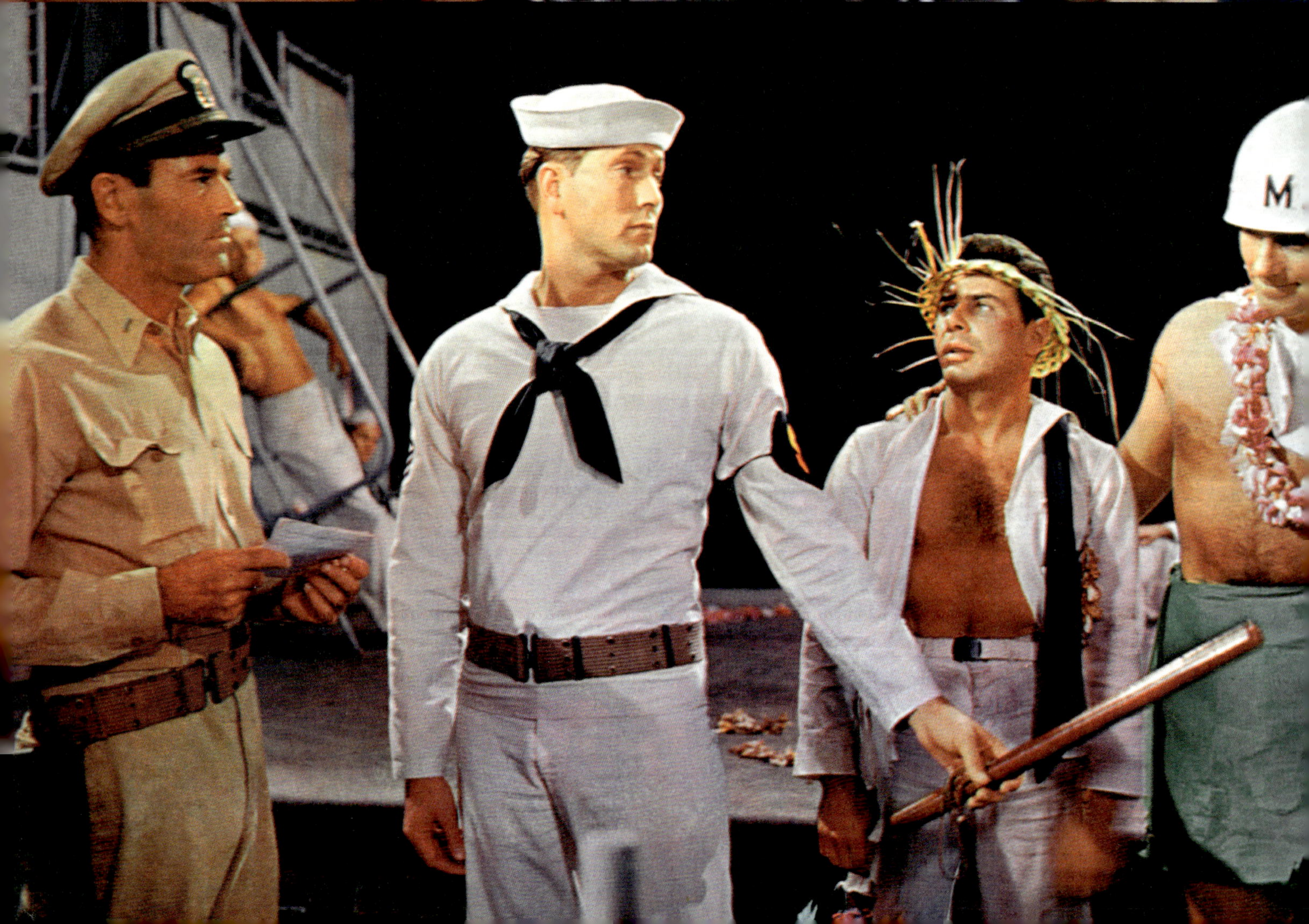
M

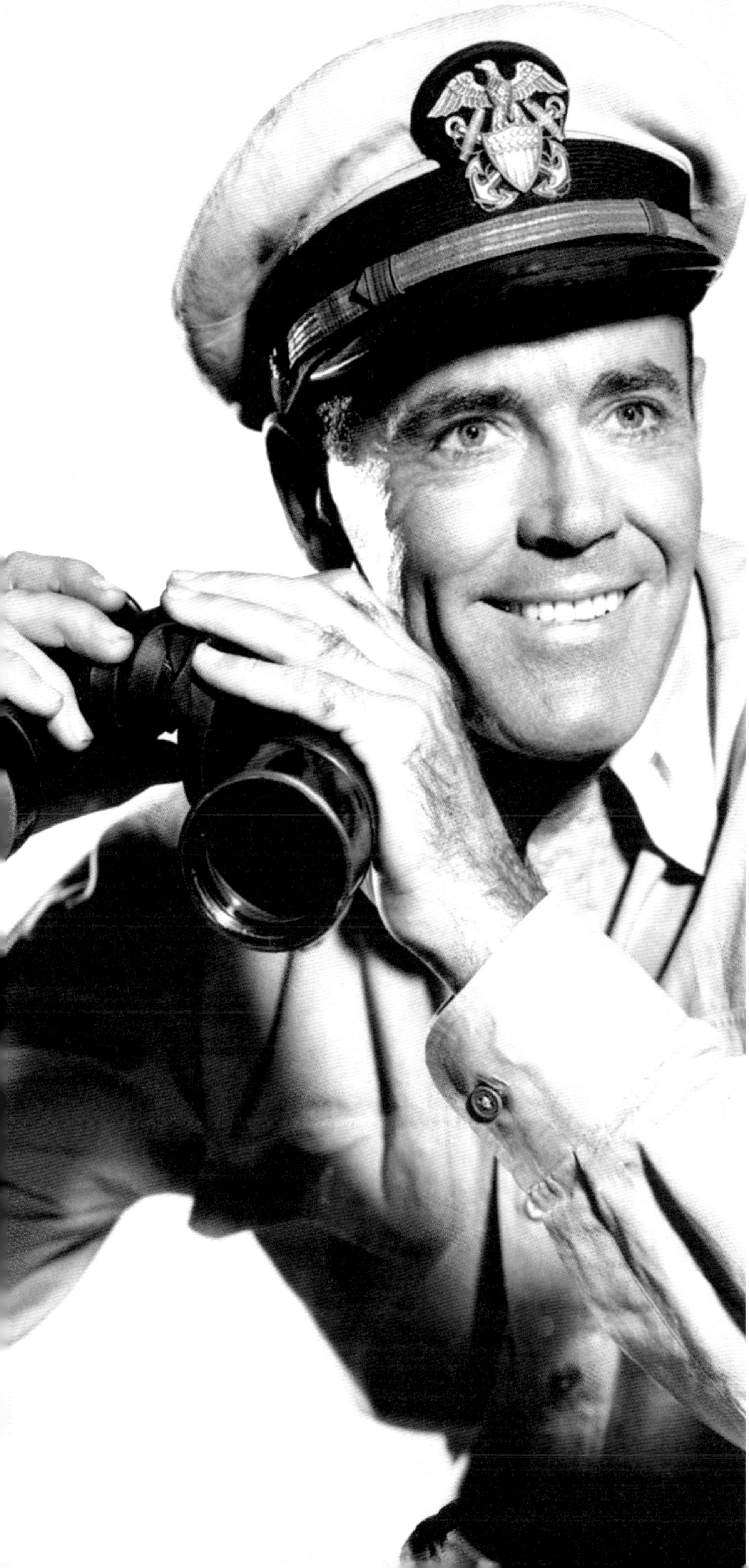

Previous pages: *'Crew' members of the USS Reluctant during the filming of* Mister Roberts *(1955), directed by John Ford and Mervyn LeRoy.*

Opposite top & bottom: *Scenes from* Mister Roberts *(Ford, LeRoy, Logan 1955).*

Pages 158 & 159: *Promotional materials for* All Is Lost *(2013), starring Robert Redford and directed by J. C. Chandor.*

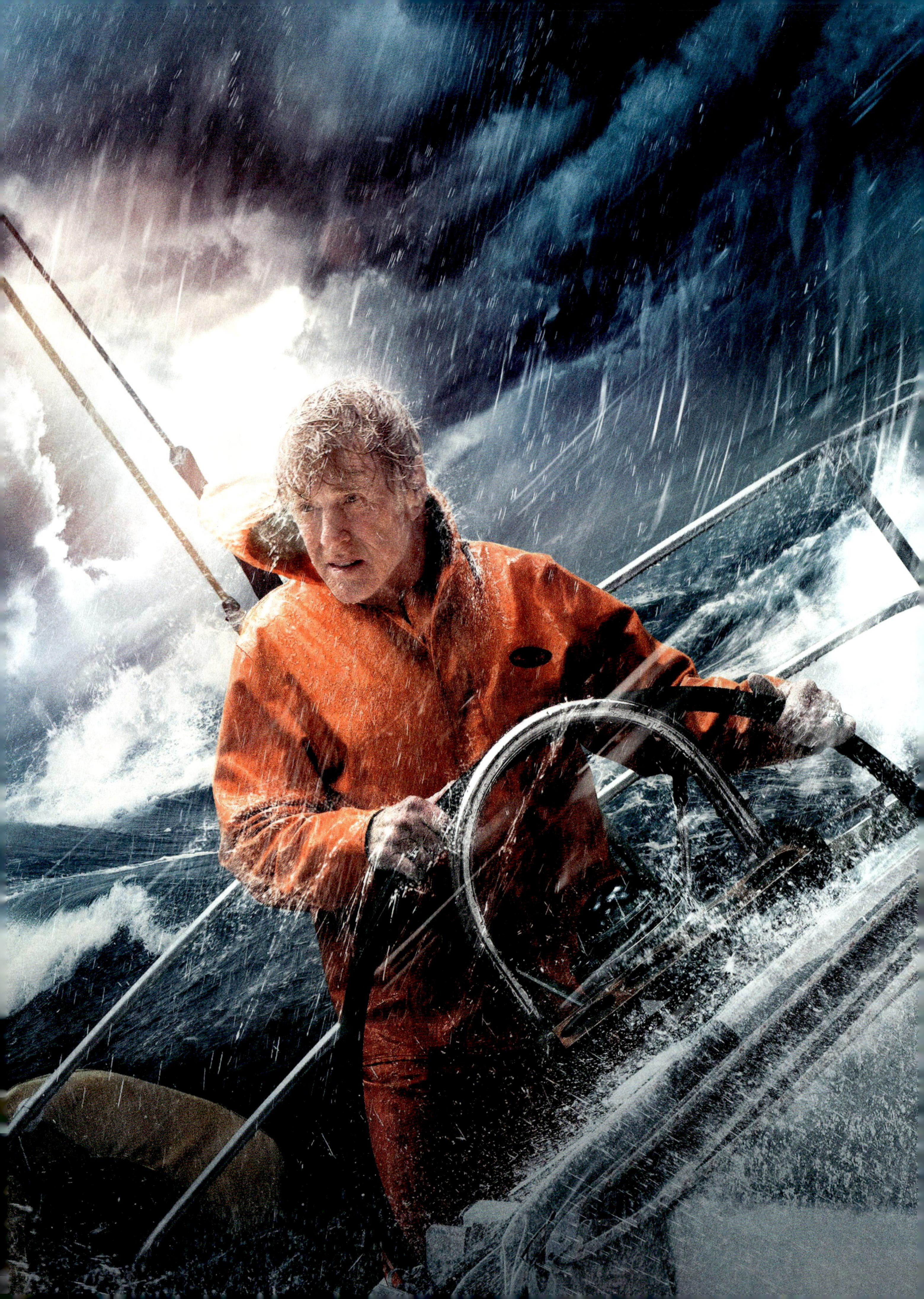

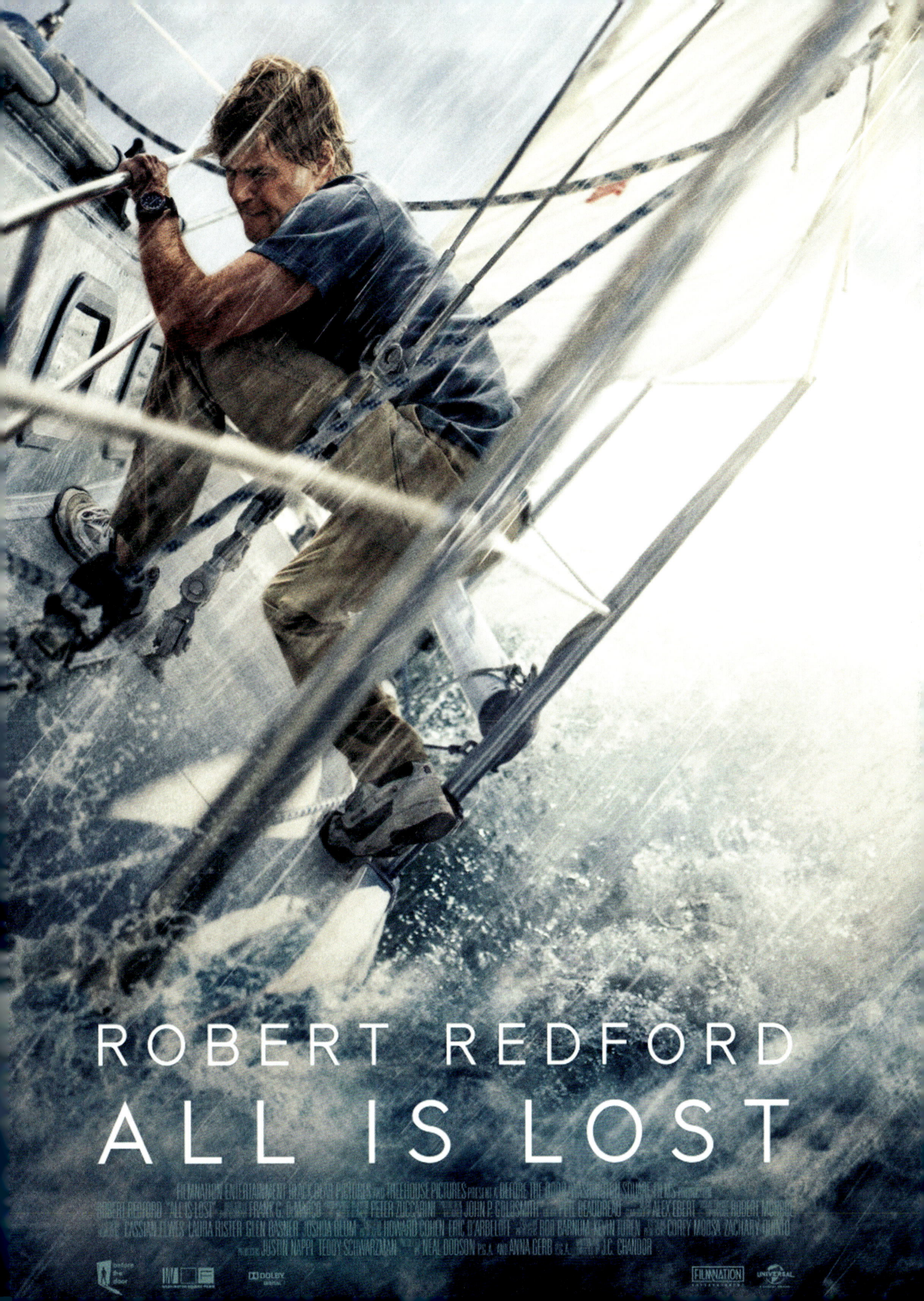
ROBERT REDFORD
ALL IS LOST
JUSTIN NAPPI TEDDY SCHWARZMAN
NEAL DODSON p.g.a. ANNA GERB p.g.a.
J.C. CHANDOR
DOLBY
FILMNATION
UNIVERSAL

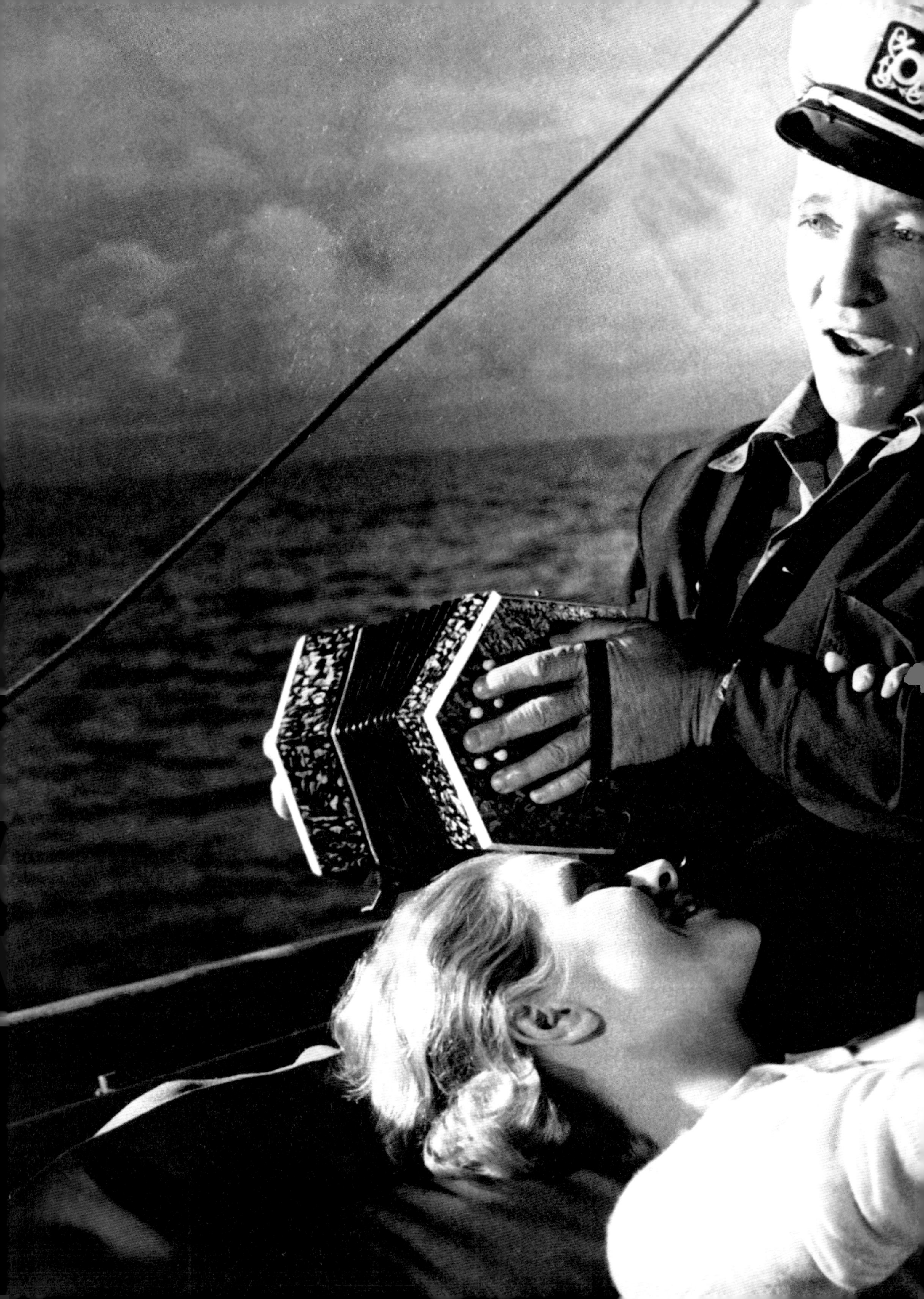

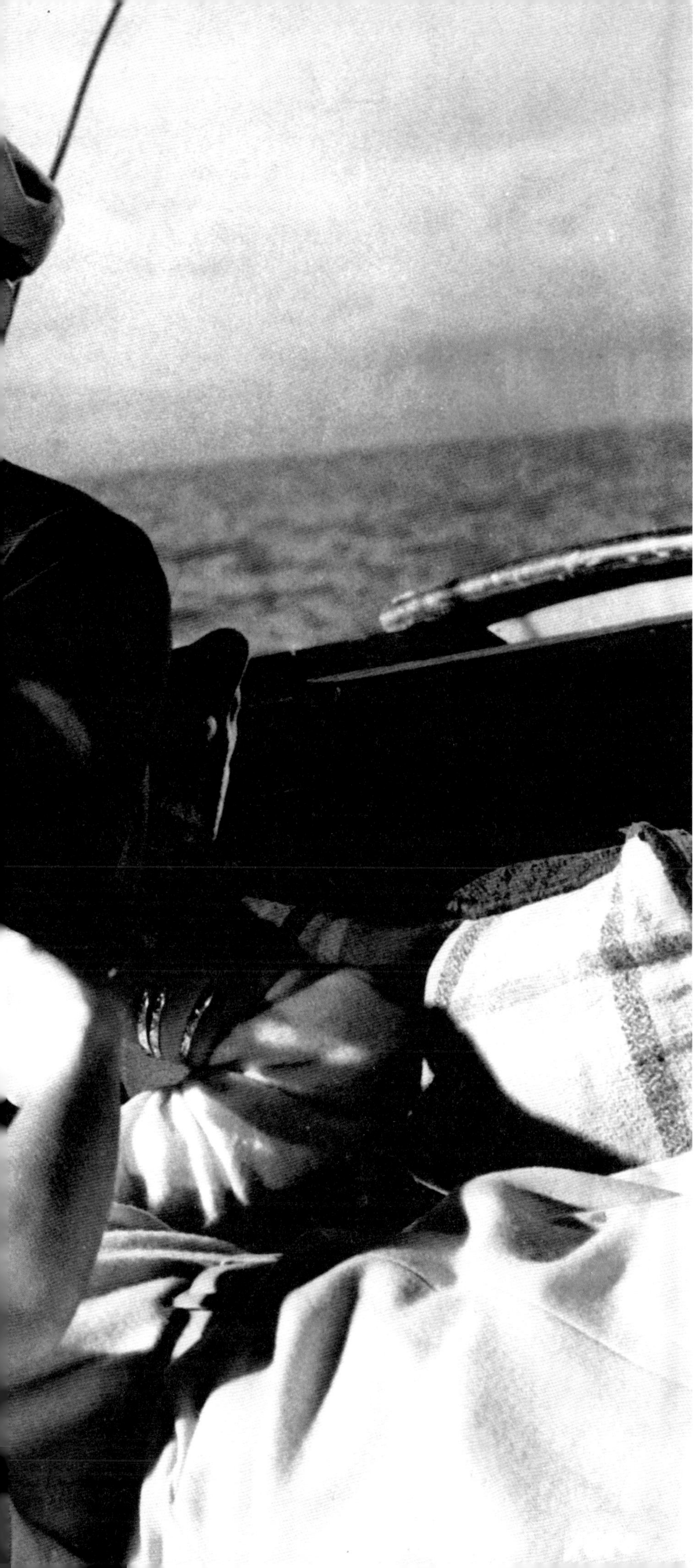

These pages & pages 162/163: *Scenes from* High Society *(Walters, 1956).*

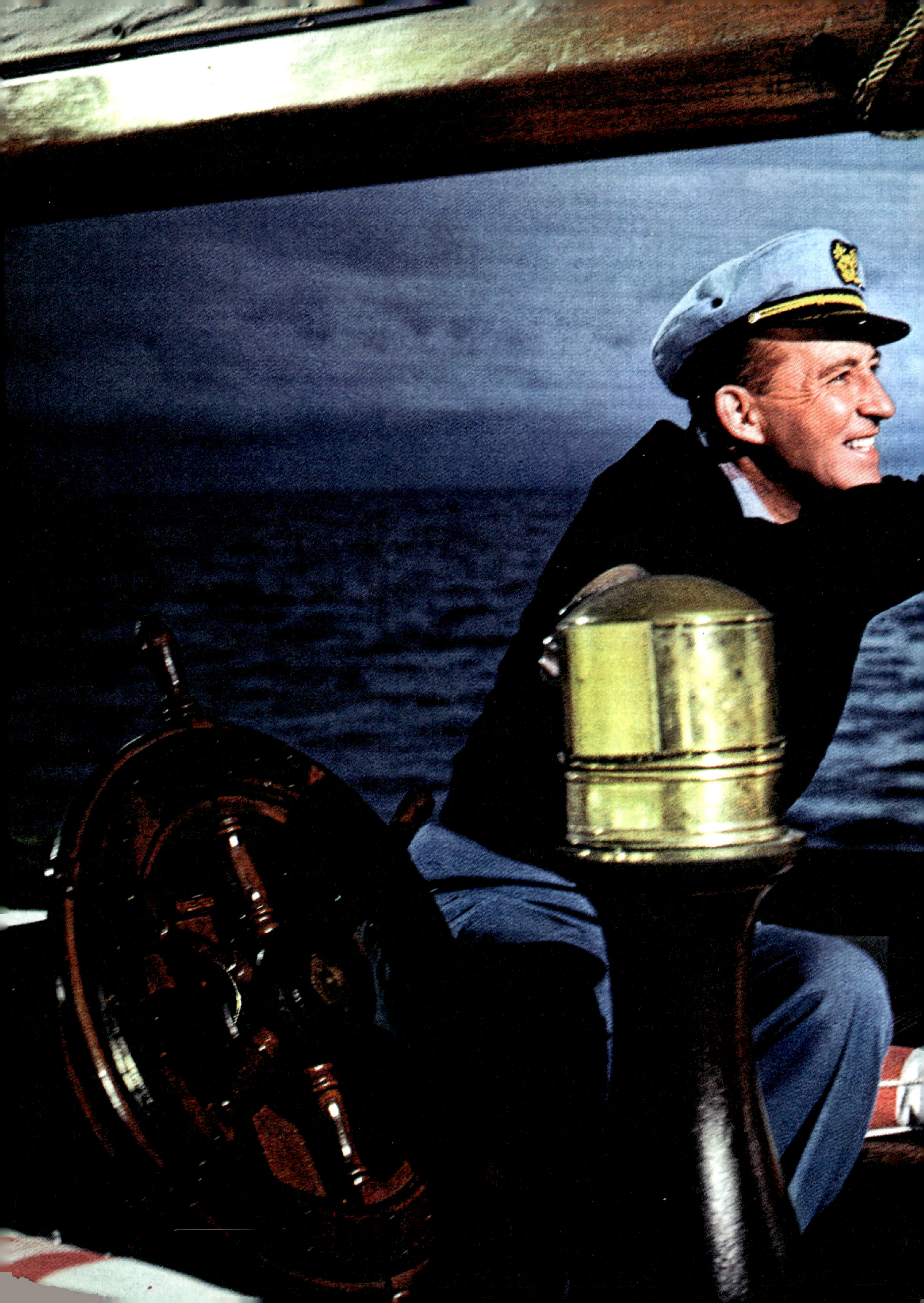

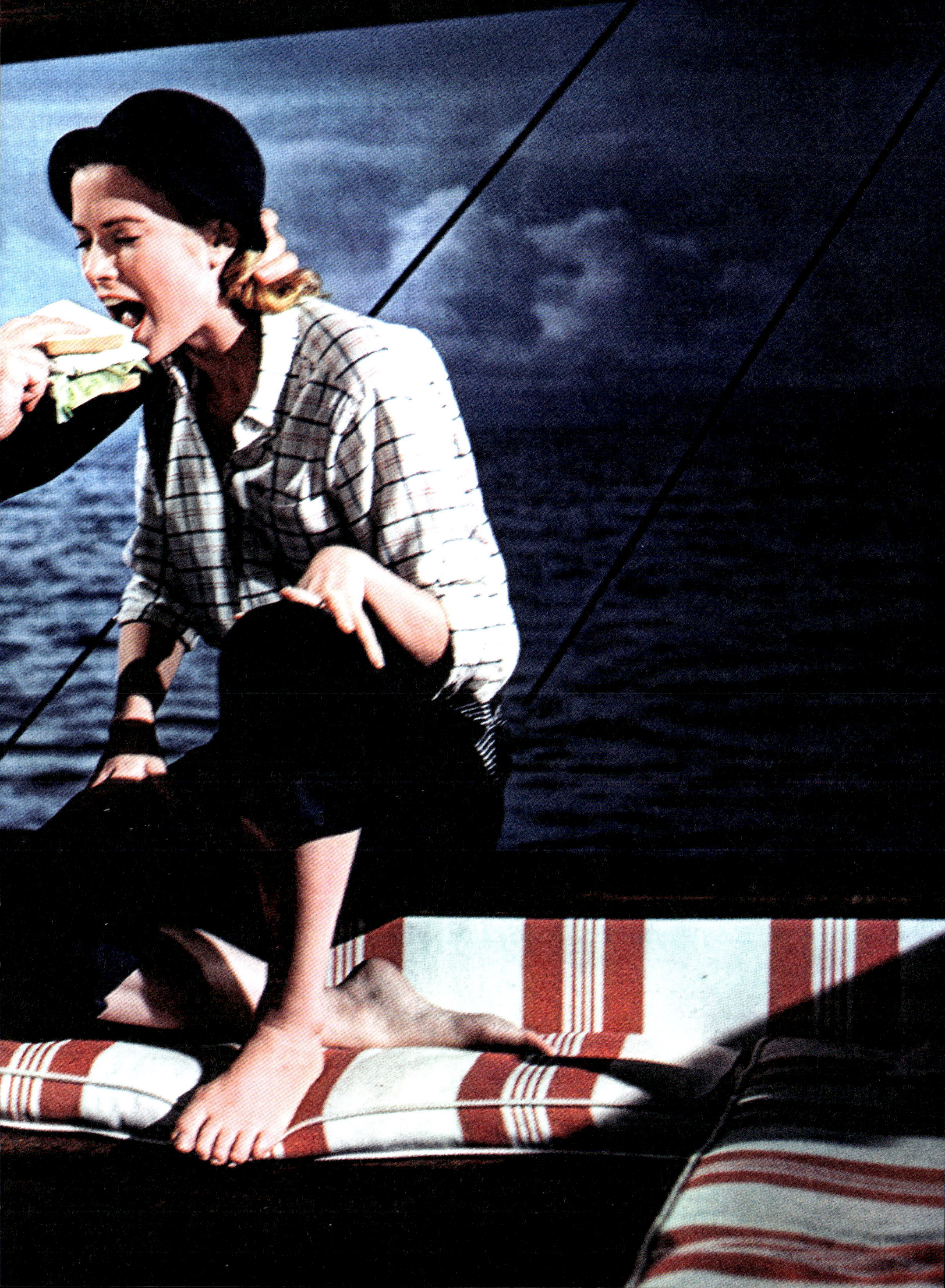

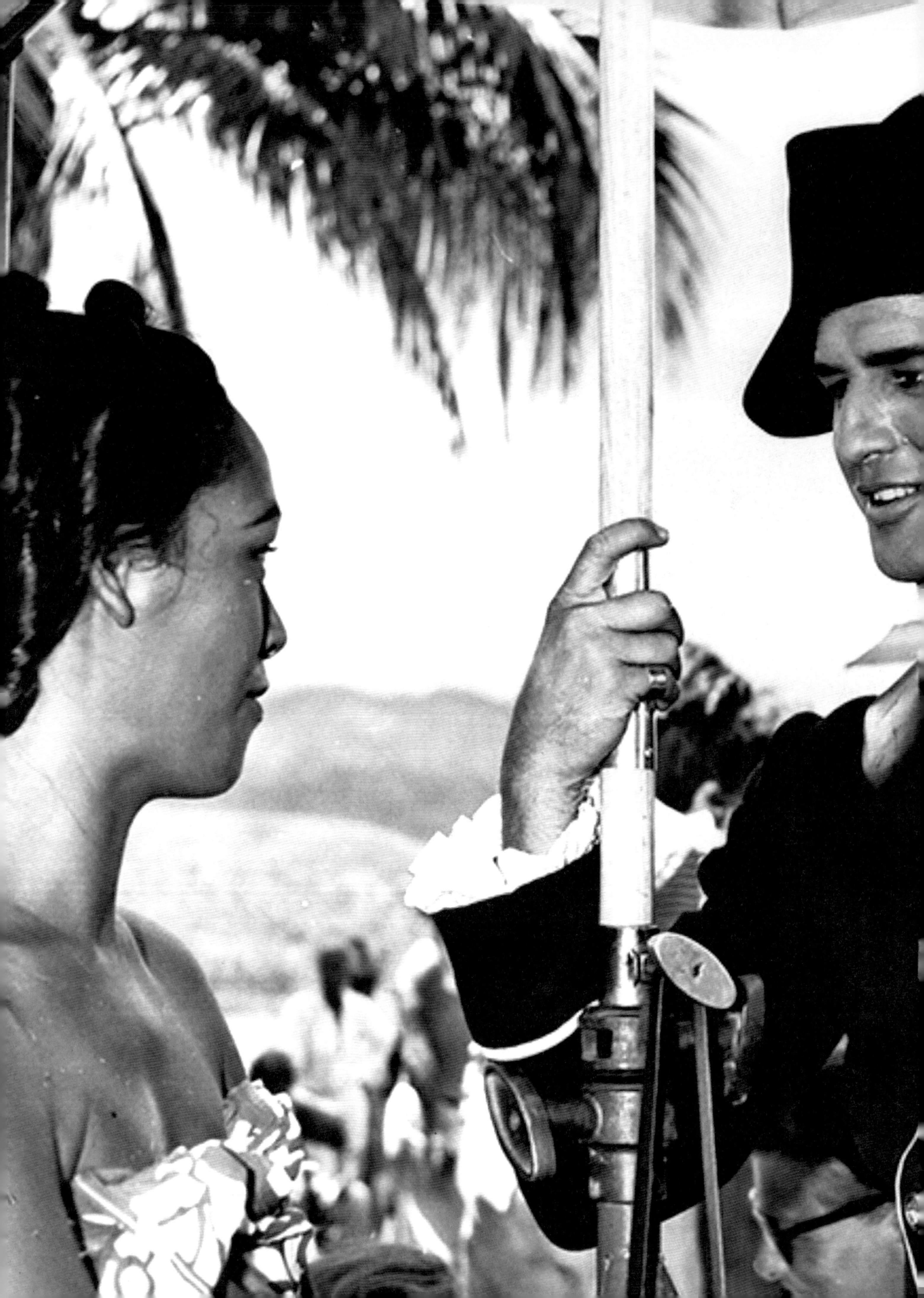

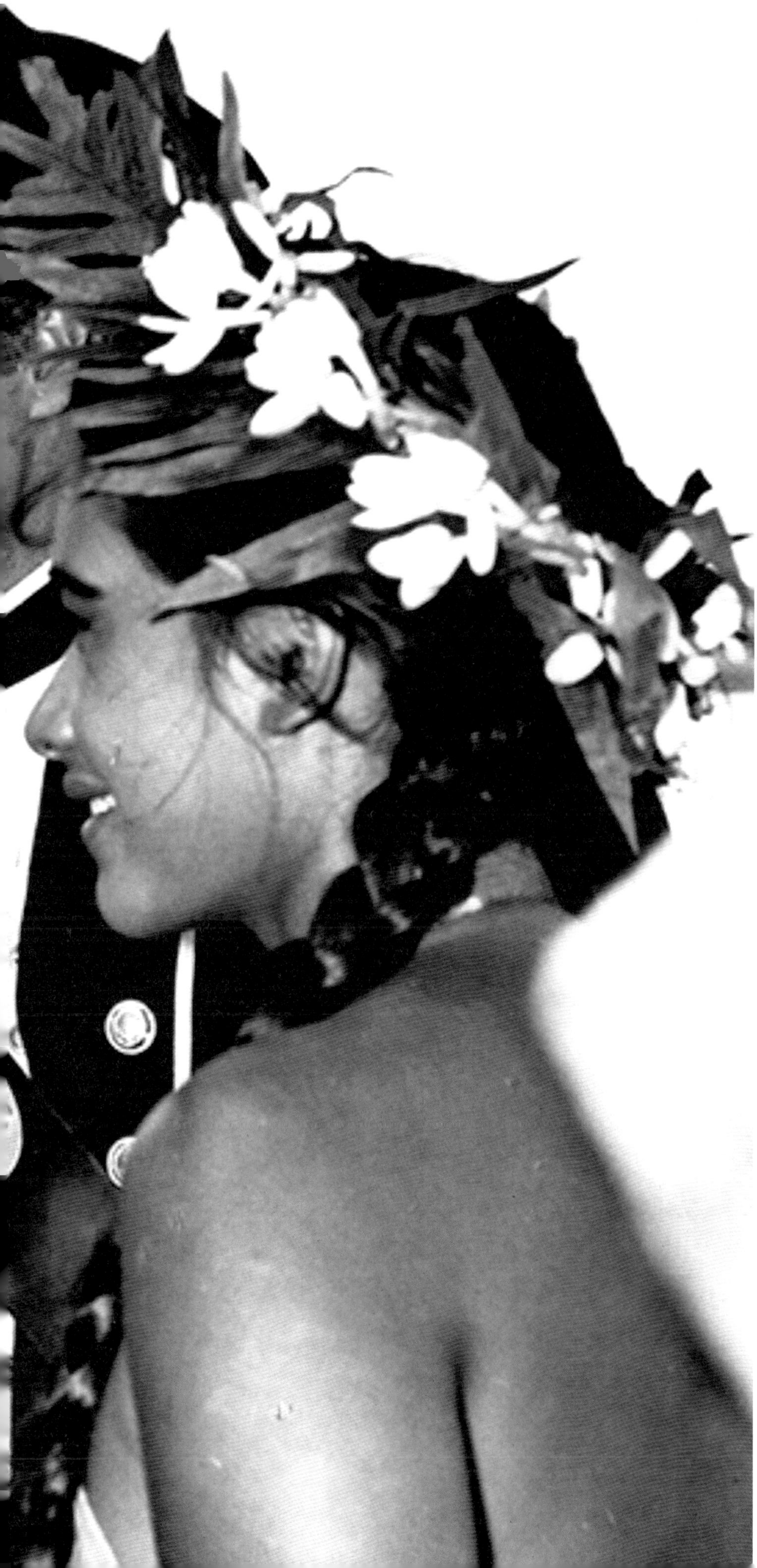

These pages & pages 166/167: *Scenes from* Mutiny On the Bounty *(Milestone, 1962), starring Marlon Brando.*

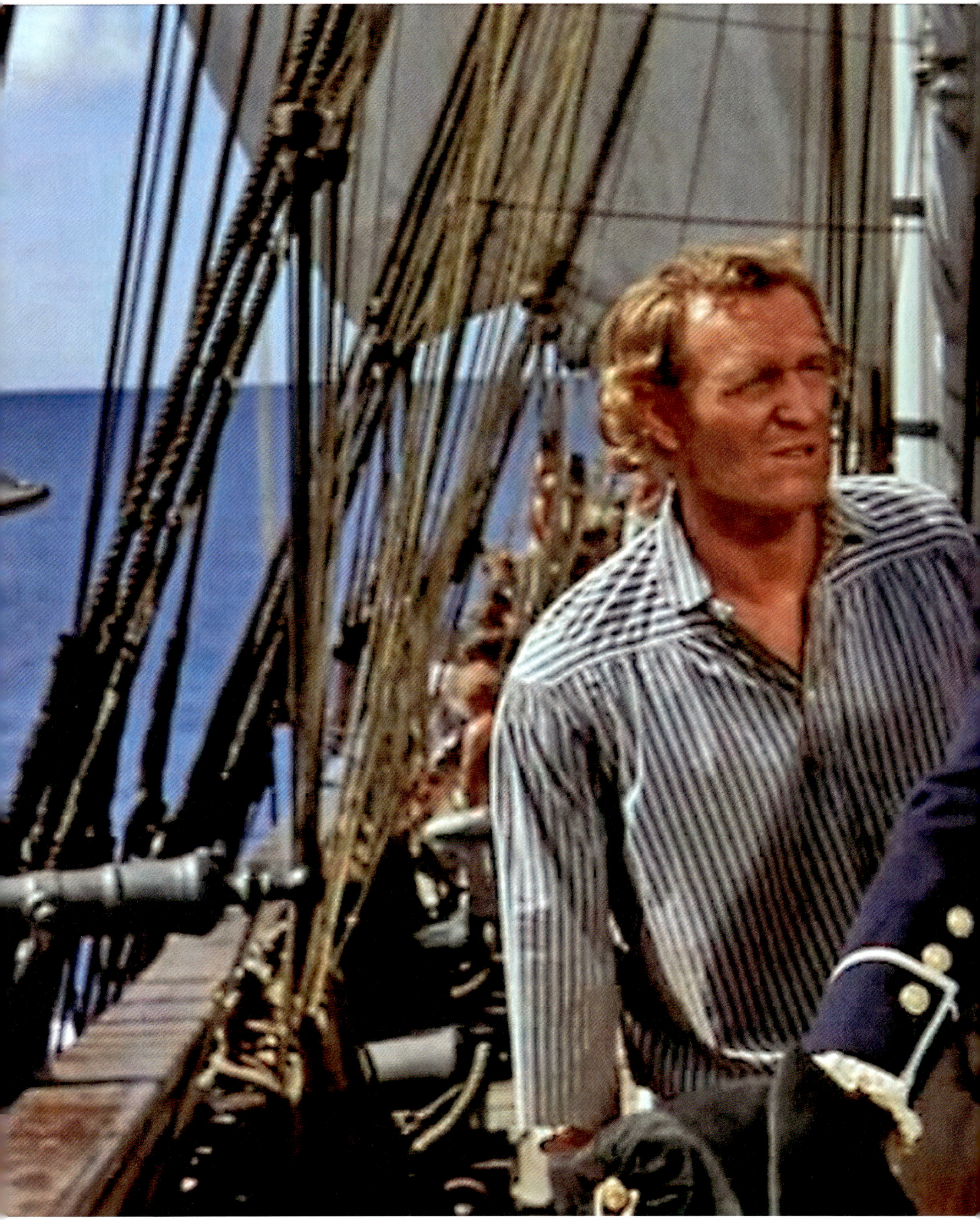

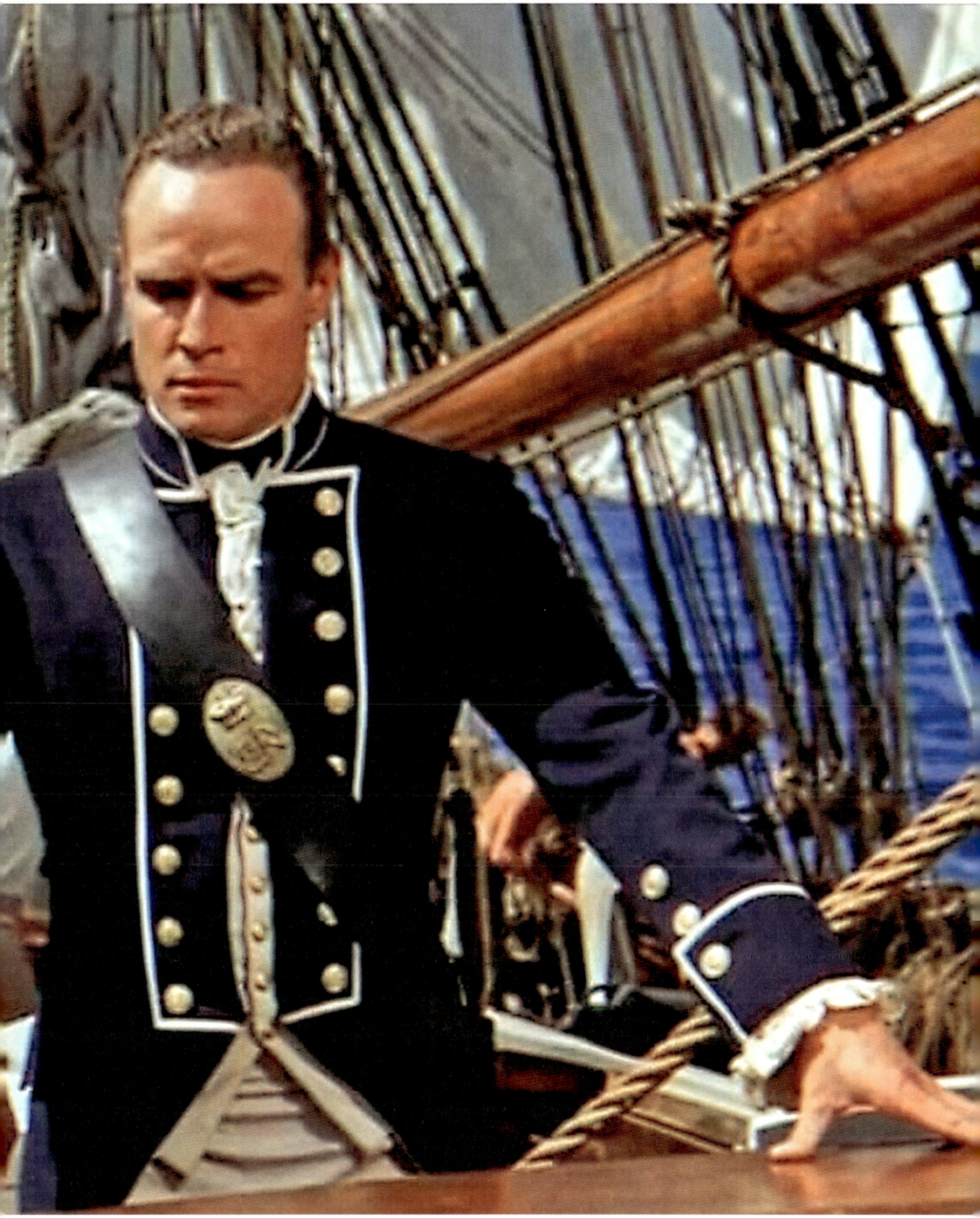

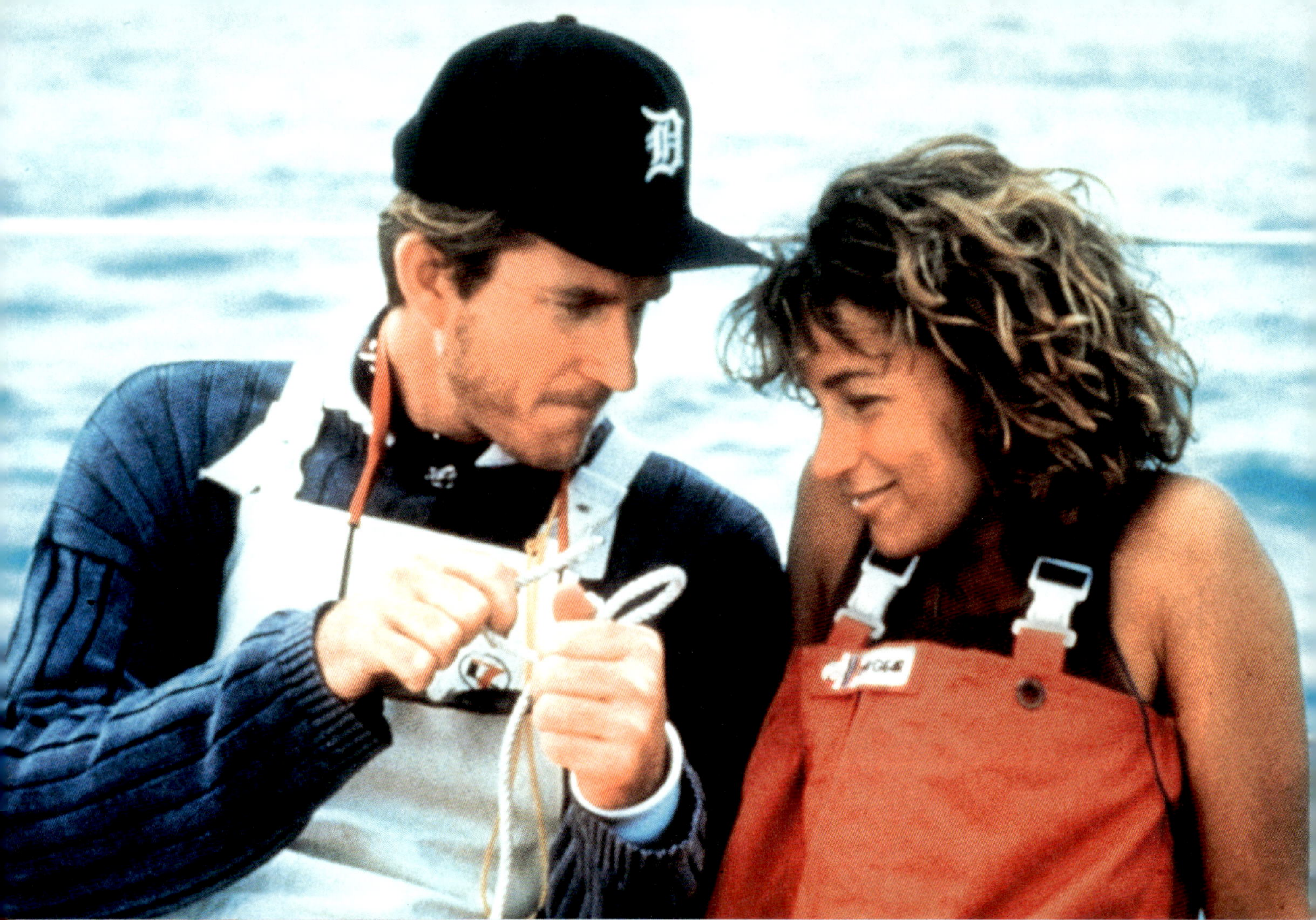

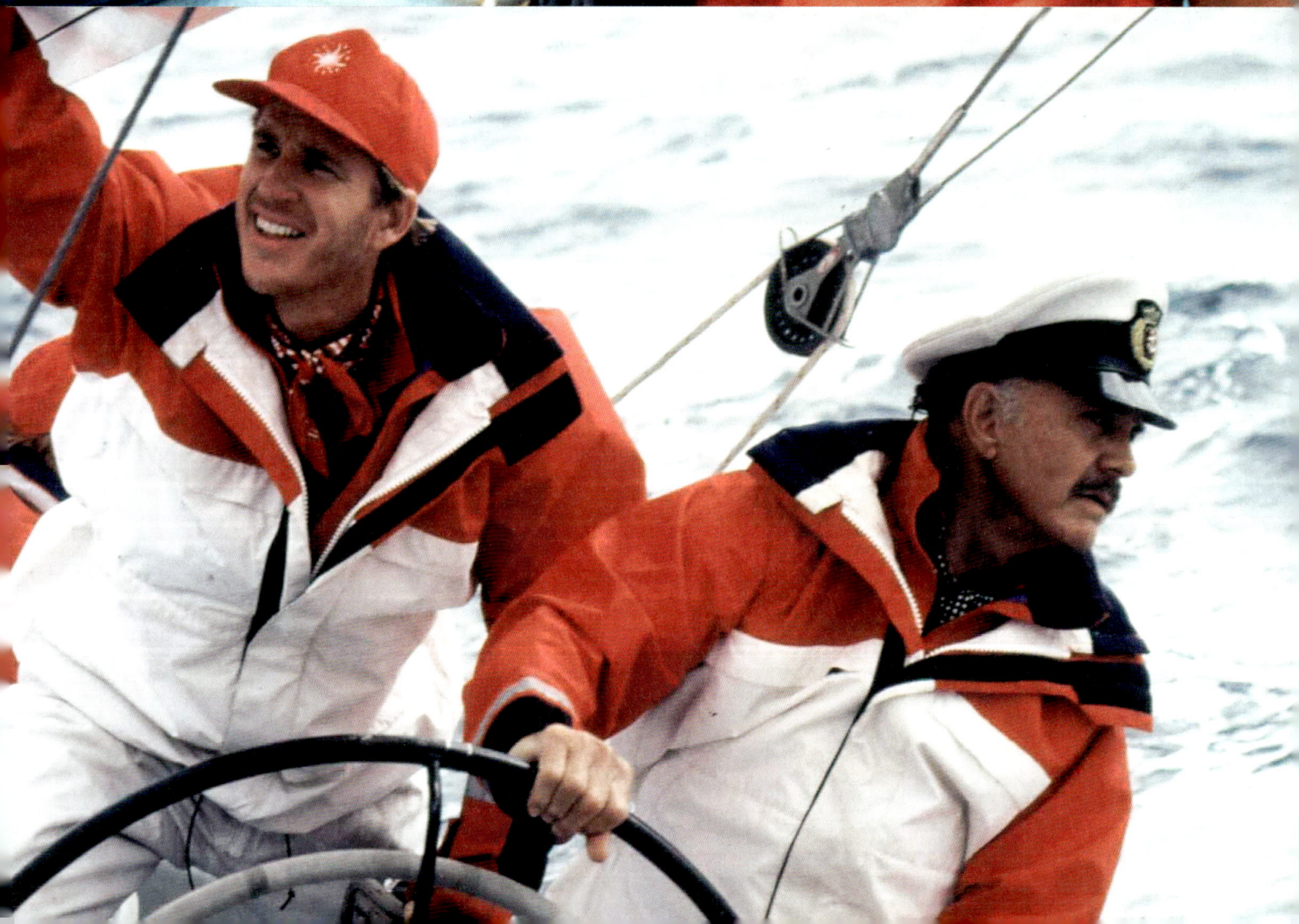

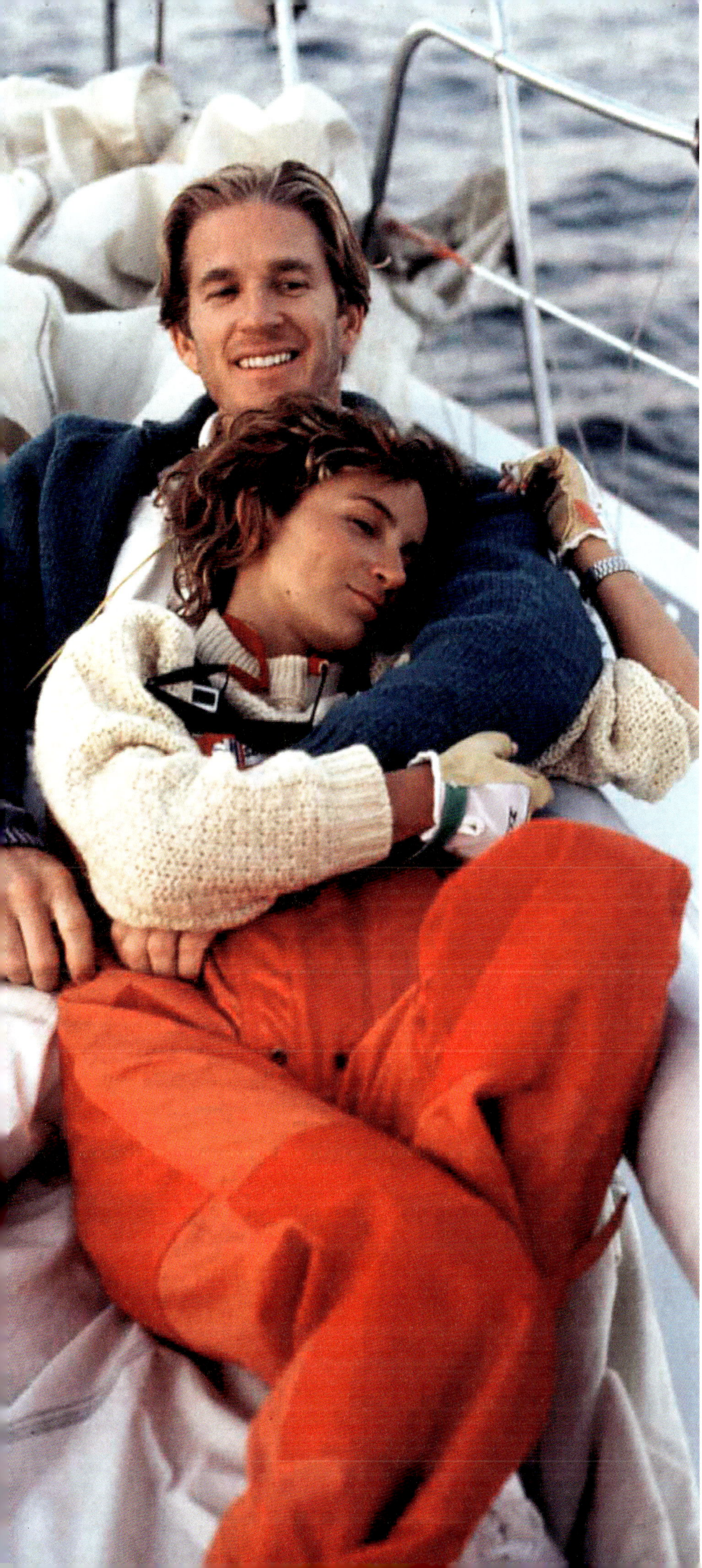

Pages 168 top & bottom, page 169: *Stills from* Wind *(Ballard, 1992), featuring Matthew Modine and Jennifer Grey.*

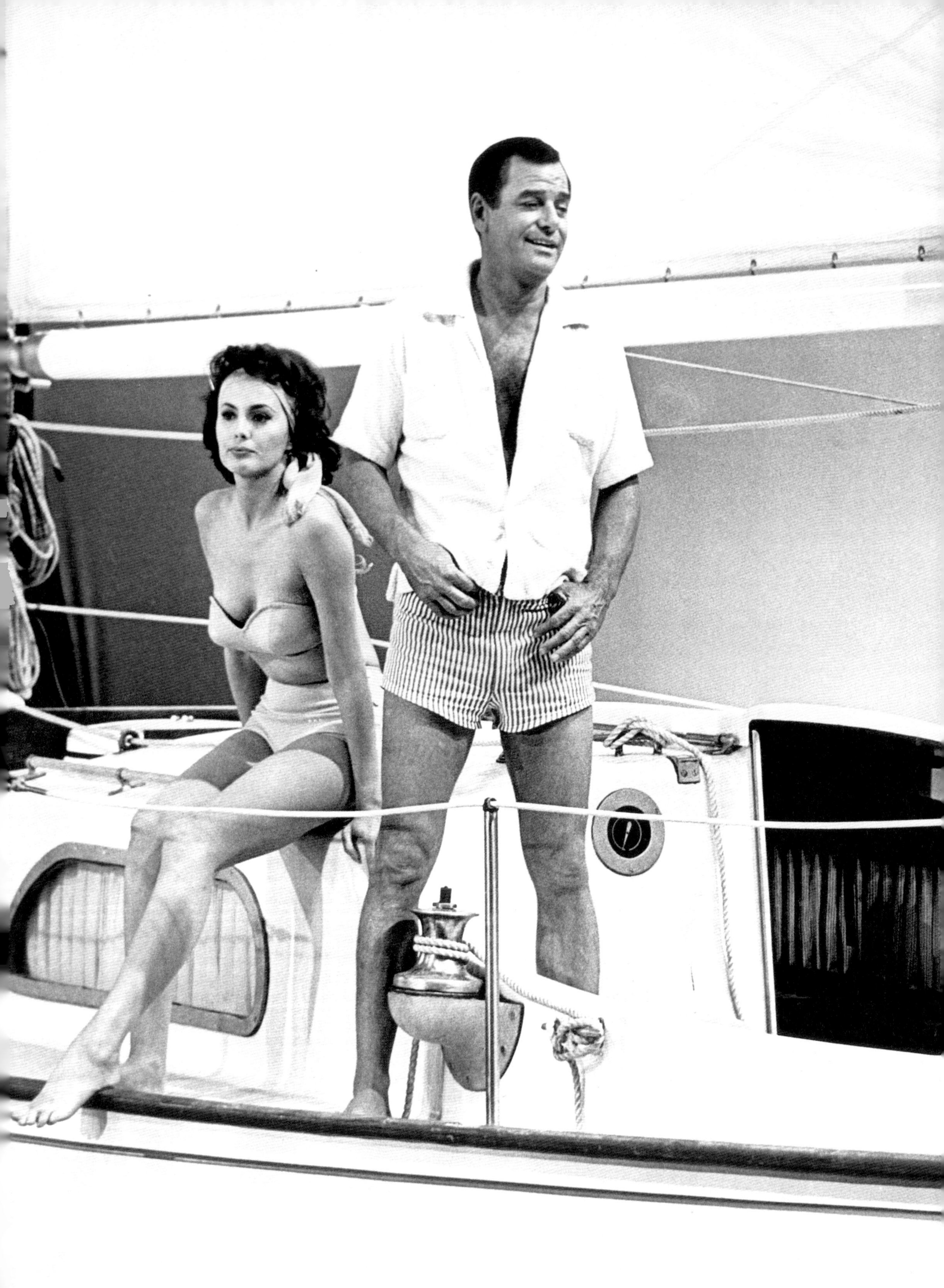

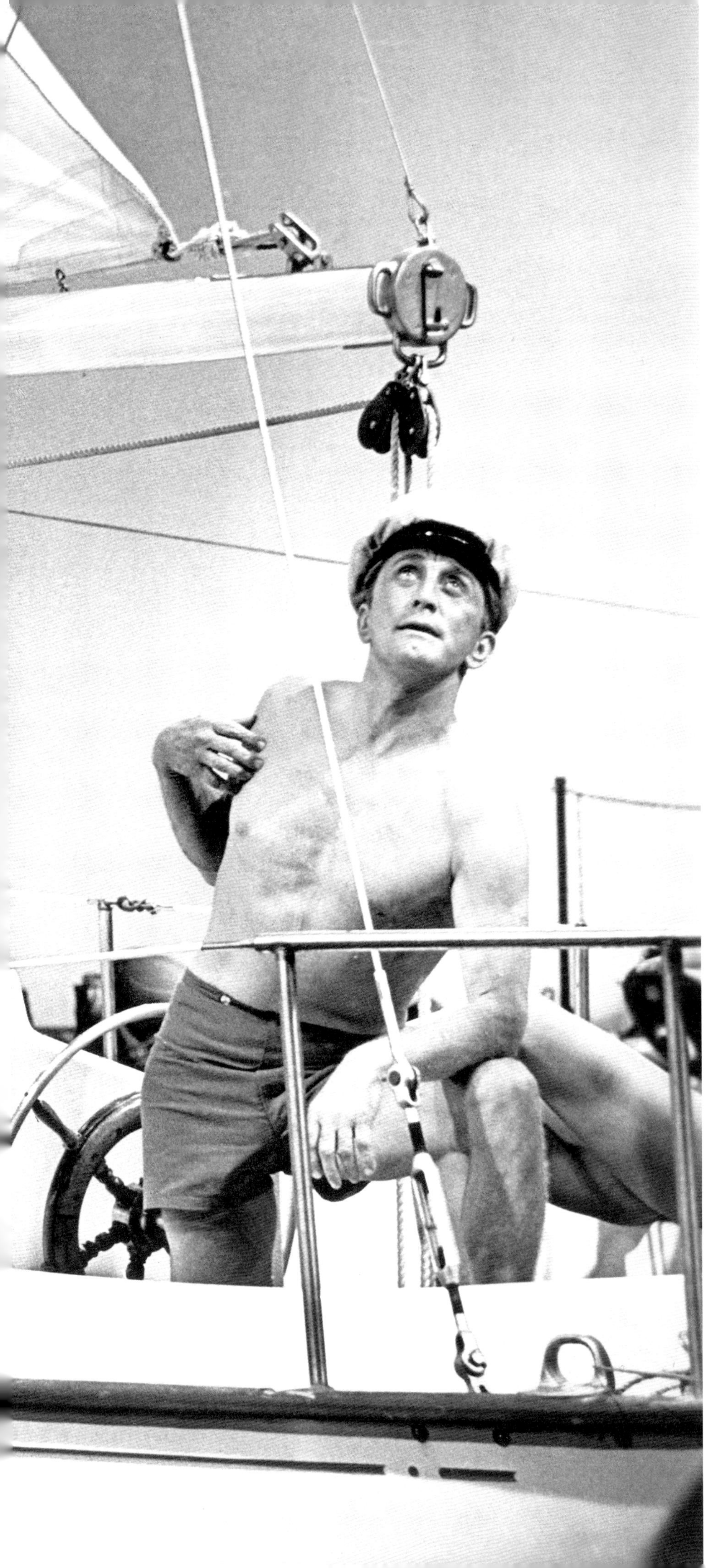

These pages: *Gig Young and Kirk Douglas on the set of* For Love or Money *(Gordon, 1963).*

IMAGE CREDITS

Cover: Getty Images/Slim Aarons
Backcover: mauritius images/Edward Roth/Alamy

p. 2 Getty Images/Slim Aarons; p. 5 Getty Images/Slim Aarons; p. 6 AFP PHOTO/William WEST; p. 11 Getty Images/Chadwick Hall/Condé Nast Collection; pp. 12/13 Getty Images/Henri Bureau/Sygma; pp. 14/15 Getty Images/Chris von Wangenheim/Condé Nast Collection; p. 16 Getty Images/Chris von Wangenheim/Condé Nast Collection; p. 17 Getty Images/Bob Stone/Condé Nast Collection; pp. 18/19 mauritius images/Christophe Launay, Cavan Images/Alamy; p. 20 bottom & top, 21 mauritius images/Sjoberg/imageBROKER; p. 22 Getty Images/Nextrecord Archives/Archive Photos; p. 23 Getty Images/G. Howard Hilder/Condé Nast Collection; pp. 24/25 Getty Images/Maurice Ambler/Picture Post; p. 26 Getty Images/Slim Aarons; pp. 32/33 Getty Images/Slim Aarons; p. 37 Getty Images/Slim Aarons/Hulton Archive; pp. 38/39 Getty Images/Slim Aarons; p. 40 bottom mauritius images/Chromorange/Jürgen Feuerer; p. 40 top mauritius images/Cody Duncan/Alamy; p. 41 Getty Images/Slim Aarons; p. 42 Getty Images/Slim Aarons; p. 43 Getty Images/Slim Aarons; pp. 44/45 Getty Images/Slim Aarons; p. 46 top & bottom Getty Images/Slim Aarons; p. 47 Getty Images/Slim Aarons; p. 49 Getty Images/Slim Aarons; pp. 50/51 Getty Images/Slim Aarons; p. 52 top & bottom Getty Images/Slim Aarons, p. 53 Getty Images/Slim Aarons; p. 54 Getty Images/Slim Aarons; p. 55 Getty Images/Slim Aarons; 56 top shutterstock/Alexandre F. Fagundes; 56 bottom Getty Images/Slim Aarons; p. 57 Getty Images/Slim Aarons; pp. 58/59 Getty Images/Buyenlarge/Archive Photos; p. 60 top & bottom Getty Images Slim Aarons; p. 61 Getty Images/Pictorial Parade/Staff/Archive Photos; p. 62 Getty Images/Slim Aarons; p. 67 Getty Images/Slim Aarons; p. 68 top & bottom Getty Images/Slim Aarons; p. 69 Getty Images/Slim Aarons; pp. 70/71 Getty Images/Slim Aarons; p. 72 mauritius images/Chris Ison, PA Images/Alamy; pp. 77, 78/79 IMAGO/Americas Cup; pp. 80/81 IMAGO/ZUMA Press Wire; p. 82 IMAGO/Bluegreen; p. 83 mauritius images/Bluegreen Pictures; pp. 84/85 mauritius images/Bluegreen Pictures/Onne van der Wal; pp. 86/87 Getty Images/Bettmann; p. 88 top mauritius images/ANP/Alam; p. 88 bottom mauritius images/Patrick Aventurier, PA Images/Alamy; p. 89 mauritius images/BSR AGENCY/Alamy; pp. 90/91 IMAGO/Action Plus; pp. 92/93 mauritius images/Hugh Peterswald/Alamy; pp. 94/95 mauritius images/Manfred Gottschalk/Alamy; pp. 96/97 IMAGO/ Pixsell; p. 98 mauritius images/ANP/Alamy; p. 99 mauritius images/ANP/Alamy; p. 100 top mauritius images/ZUMA Press/Alamy ;p. 100 bottom IMAGO/Dreamstime; p. 101 mauritius images/SuperStock/Wide World Photos/Sydney Morning Herald; pp. 102/103 mauritius images/Jim Kidd/Alamy; pp. 104/105 mauritius images/TopFoto; pp. 106/107 mauritius images/Louis Kruk/Alamy; pp. 108/109 mauritius images/Christophe Launay/Aurora Photos, Cavan Images/Alamy; p. 110 mauritius images/TopFoto; pp. 116/117 Getty Images/Condé Nast Collection; pp. 118/119 Getty Images/Bettmann; p. 120 mauritius images/Cinema-Legacy-Collection/The Hollywood Archive; p. 121 Getty Images/Bettmann; p. 122 Getty Images/Bettmann; p. 123 Getty Images/Bettmann; p. 124 Getty Images; p. 125 Getty Images/Slim Aarons; p. 126 Getty Images/Slim Aarons; p. 127 Getty Images/Slim Aarons; p. 128 Getty Images/Slim Aarons; p. 129 Getty Images/Slim Aarons; p. 130 Getty Images/Hulton Archive; p. 131 Getty Images/Sygma; p. 132 top mauritius images/Piemags/AN24/Alamy; p. 132 bottom mauritius images/TopFoto; p. 133 mauritius images/TopFoto/Central News; pp. 134/135 Getty Images/Paris Match Archive; p. 136 top mauritius images/Superstock/Sydney Morning Herald; p. 136 bottom Getty Images/Hulton Royals Collection; p. 137 mauritius images/Superstock/Reuterphoto/Sydney Morning Herald; p. 138 Getty Images; p. 141 mauritius images/Old Visuals; pp. 142/143 Getty Images/Condé Nast Collection Editorial; p. 144 Getty Images/Hulton Archive Archive Photos; p. 145 Getty Images/The Chronicle Collection; p. 146 Getty Images/Condé Nast Collection Editorial; p. 147 Getty Images/Karen Radkai/Condé Nast Collection; p. 148 Getty Images/Condé Nast Collection; p. 149 Getty Images/Lionel Kazan/Condè Nast Collection; p. 150 Getty Images/Derek Hudson/Hulton Archive; p. 153 Getty Images/Derek Hudson; pp. 154/155 Getty Images/Slim Aarons; p. 156 top mauritius images/Collection Christophel/Warner Bros. Pictures; p. 156 bottom mauritius images/Collection Christophel/Warner Bros. Pictures; p. 157 mauritius images/Collection Christophel/Warner Bros. Pictures; p. 158 mauritius images/Landmark Media, LANDMARK MEDIA/Alamy; p. 159 mauritius images/Moviestore Collection, Moviestore Collection Ltd/Alamy; pp. 160/161 mauritius images/Collection Christophel/MGM/Sol C. Siegel Productions; pp. 162/163, 164/165 & 166/167 mauritius images/Pictorial Press, Pictorial Press Ltd/Alamy; p. 168 top mauritius images/Collection Christophel/American Zoetrope; p. 168 bottom mauritius images/IFA Film, United Archives GmbH/Alamy; p. 169 mauritius images/IFA Film, United Archives GmbH/Alamy; pp. 170/171 Getty Images/Slim Aarons; pp. 174/175 mauritius images/AA World Travel Library, AA World Travel Library/Alamy

Opposite: *Hungarian-born film actress Eva Gabor on a boating day-trip in Jamaica, c. 1955.*

Following pages; A sunset throws an orange glow over a yacht sailing in front of Sydney Harbour Bridge, seen from Bradley's Head in Sydney Harbour National Park.

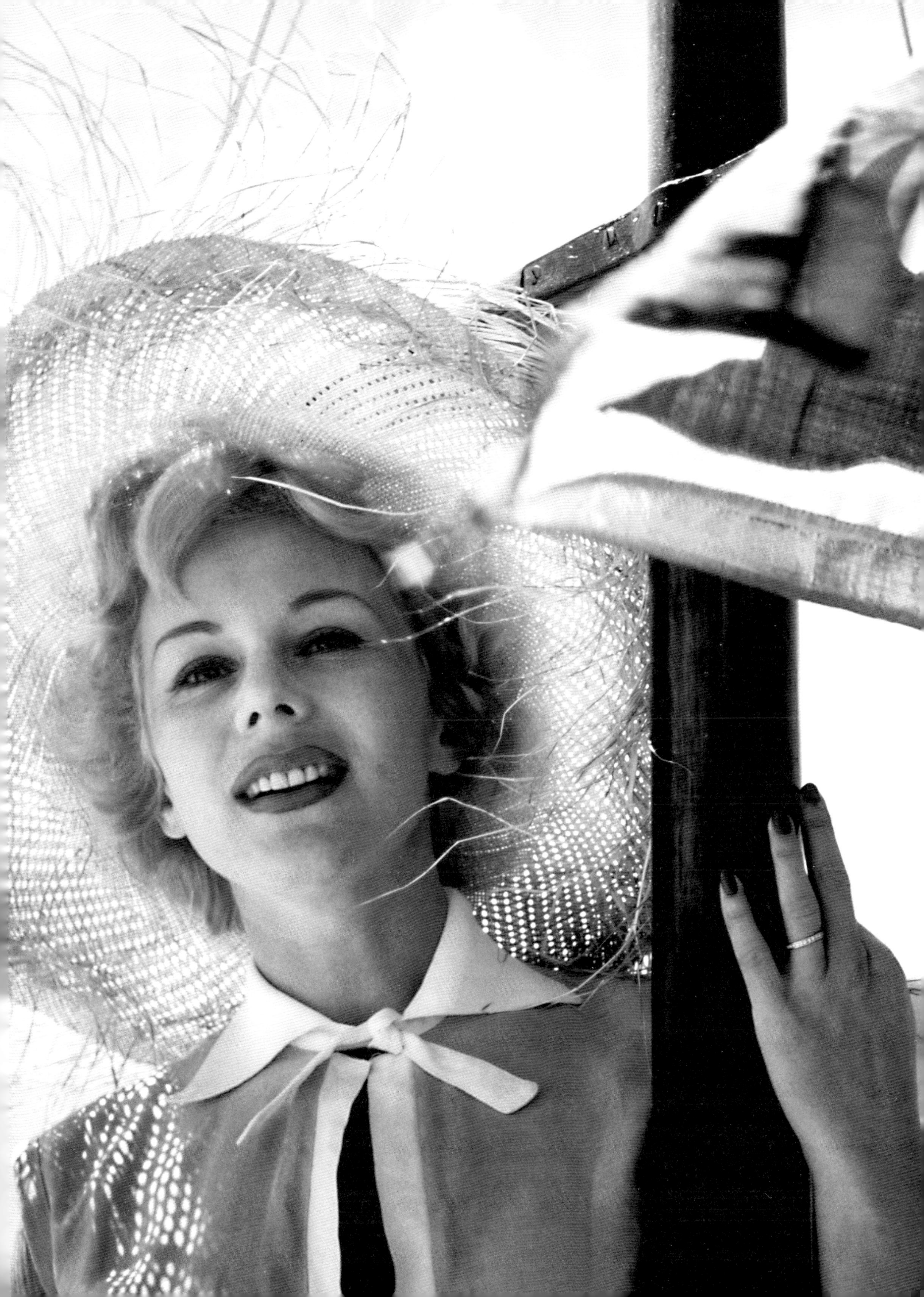

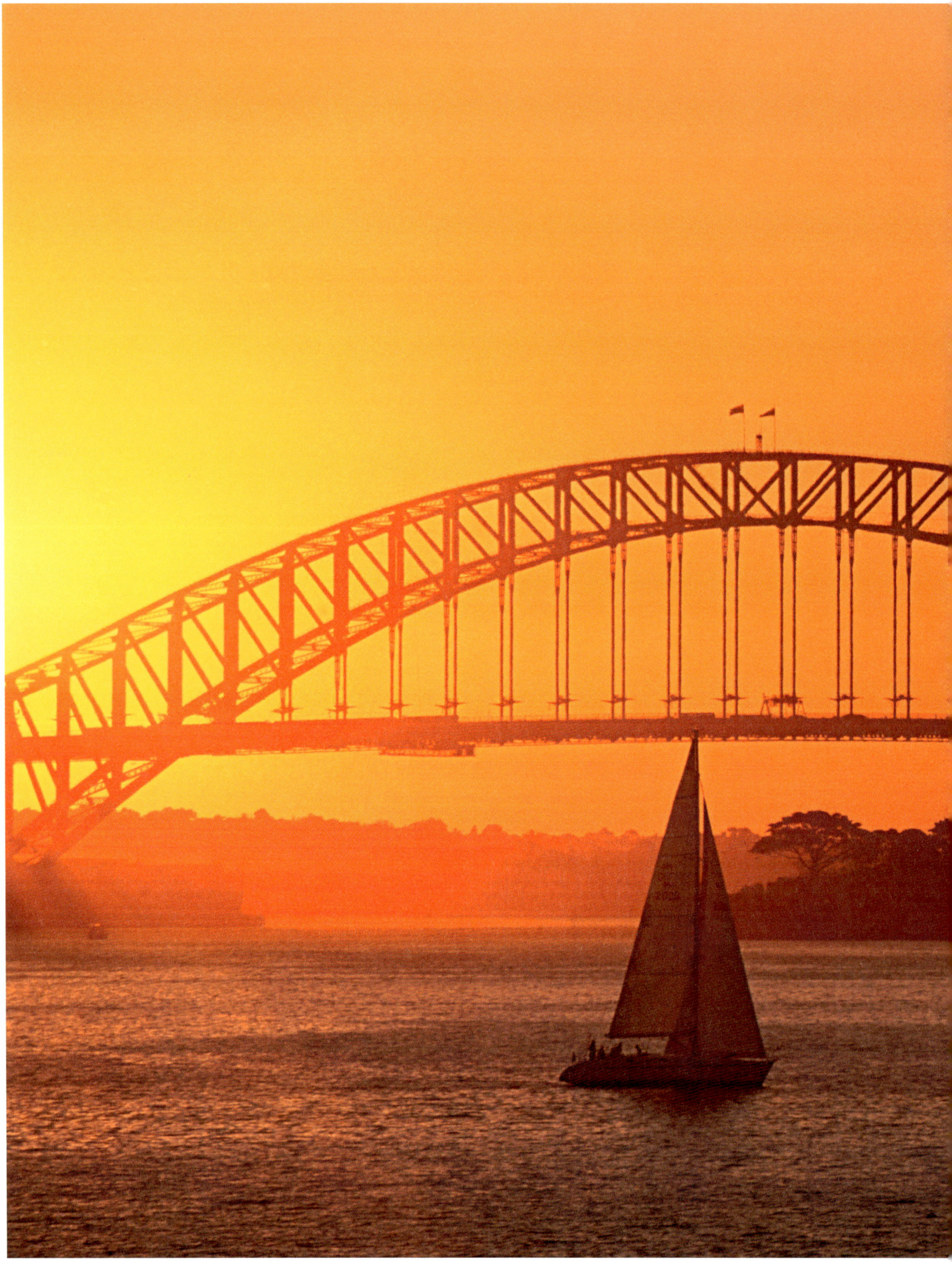

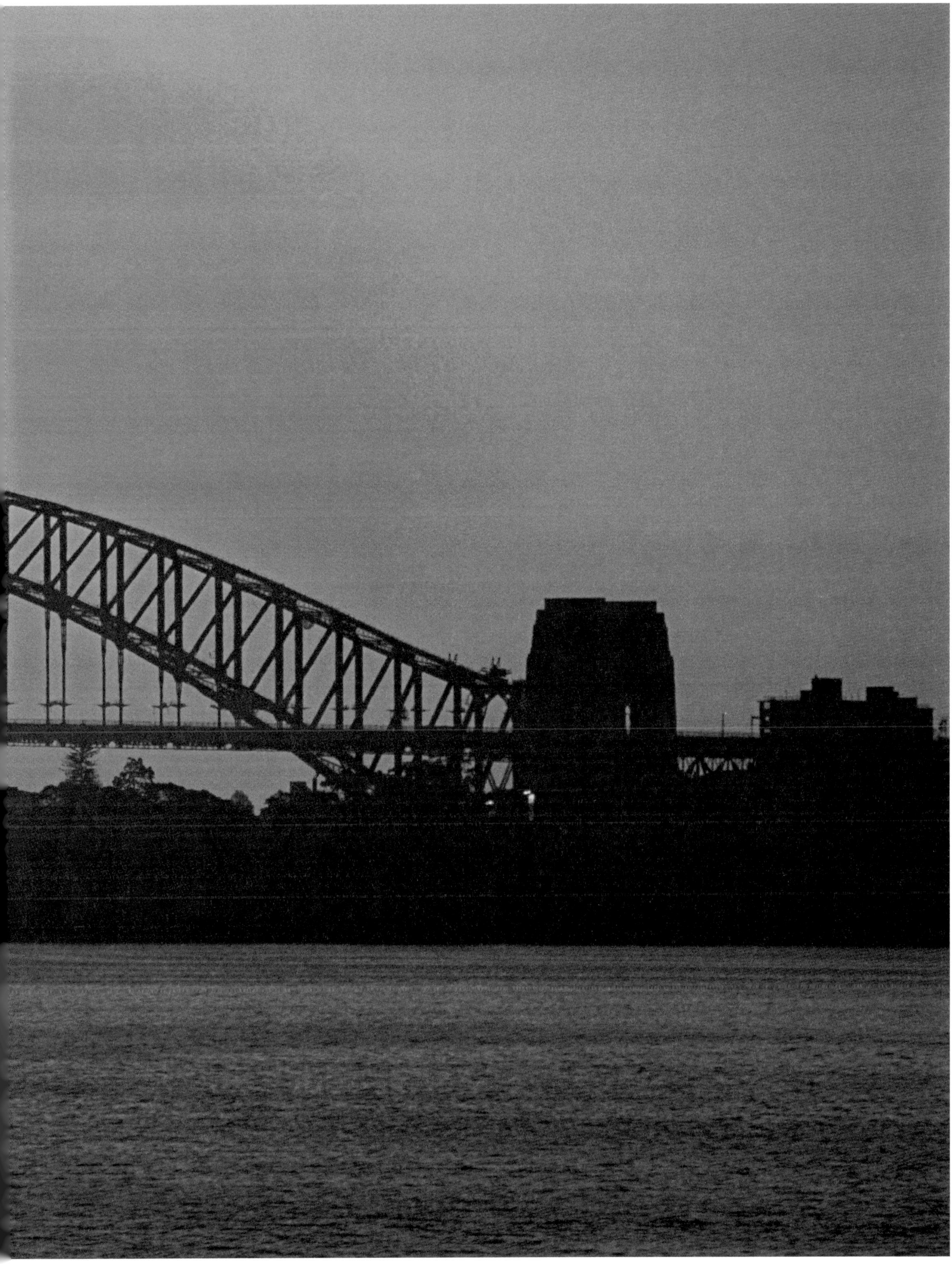

IMPRINT

THE STYLISH LIFE SAILING
This book was conceived, edited, and designed by teNeues.

Text & Preface by Gary Jobson
Copyediting by Abe Davies
Editorial Management by Stephanie Rebel, gestalten
Design & Layout by Marcus Taeschner
Picture Editing by Heide Christiansen
Production by Sandra Jansen-Dorn, gestalten
Color Separation by Jens Grundei

Printed by Schleunungdruck GmbH,
Marktheidenfeld, Germany
Produced in Europe

MIX
Paper | Supporting responsible forestry
FSC® C105039
FSC www.fsc.org

Published by gestalten, Berlin 2026
ISBN 978-3-96171-789-7

1st printing, 2026

For more information and to order books, please visit
www.teneues.com and www.gestalten.com

Die Gestalten Verlag GmbH & Co. KG
Mariannenstrasse 9–10
10999 Berlin, Germany
hello@gestalten.com

Krefeld Office
Uerdinger Str. 265 / Villa Pattberg
47800 Krefeld, Germany
verlag@teneues.com

teNeues Press Department
press@gestalten.com

Bibliographic information published by the Deutsche Nationalbibliothek. The Deutsche Nationalbibliothek lists this publication in the Deutsche Nationalbibliografie; detailed bibliographic data is available online at www.dnb.de

https://instagram.com/teneuespublishing

www.teneues.com